CONTENTS

Plan Your Trip

JERRY SHARP/SHUTTERSTOCK

Powell-Hyde cable car line (p30)

The Guide

Toolkit

Storybook

BENJAMIN HEATH FOR LONELY PLANET

Cable car, Chinatown (p116)

SAN FRANCISCO

THE JOURNEY BEGINS HERE

Life in this boomtown is like a cable-car ride, with 175 years of heady climbs and surprisingly giddy downhill slides. The little city that launched free speech, gay and trans rights, the internet, organic cuisine, fortune cookies and AI is onto its next big dream. Adventure is a given and San Francisco welcomes all. So hop on board, grab a creaky, leather cable-car strap, and hang on: you're right on time for San Francisco's next mind-expanding, world-changing peak moment.

Alison Bing

Bluesky @alisonbing.bsky.social

Alison has survived booms, busts, live-action robot wars and performance-art potlucks to tell only-in-San-Francisco stories for global media outlets.

Alison wrote Plan Your Trip; The Presidio, Marina & Fisherman's Wharf; Chinatown & North Beach; Japantown, Fillmore & Pacific Heights; The Mission, Dogpatch & Potrero; Golden Gate Park & the Avenues; Toolkit; History of San Francisco in 15 Places; and Meet the San Franciscans.

My favourite experience is downstairs at City Lights (p130), where a 1930s cult sign says: 'I am the door.' It's true. San Francisco is the threshold between fact and fiction, past and future. I'm honored to hold that door open for you.

lonely planet

San Francisco

Chinatown & North Beach p116

The Presidio, Marina & Fisherman's Wharf, p54

Nob Hill & Russian Hill p140

Japantown, Fillmore & Pacific Heights p152

Downtown, Civic Center, & SoMa, p82

Golden Gate Park & the Avenues p222

The Haight & Hayes Valley p206

The Castro p192

The Mission, Dogpatch & Potrero p166

Alison Bing, Dylan Lalanne-Perkins, Margot Seeto

LUCIUS RUEEDI/SHUTTERSTOCK

Sentinel Building (p135)

WHO GOES WHERE

Our writers and experts choose the places which, for them, define San Francisco.

SHEILA FITZGERALD/SHUTTERSTOCK

I used to work at the massive **Ferry Plaza Farmers Market** (p101), but going now as a patron still feels exciting each time. The bursting bounty of fresh produce and more from the diverse farmers, restaurateurs and entrepreneurs reminds me how lucky us San Franciscans are.

Margot Seeto

Instagram @beyondmeato

Margot is a third-generation San Franciscan, freelance food and travel writer – and the dumpling columnist for SFGATE. She wrote the Downtown, Civic Center & SoMa; Nob Hill & Russian Hill; and Day Trips chapters.

NITO/SHUTTERSTOCK

While much of the city is famous for its calf-burning climbs, **The Wiggle** (p217) is a blissfully flat bike route through the Haight. I love coasting the neighborhood along this zigzagging path, dodging inclines on my way to Golden Gate Park.

Dylan Lalanne-Perkins

linkedin.com/in/dylanlalanneperkins

Born and raised in San Francisco, Dylan is a writer in love with his hometown. Dylan wrote The Castro and The Haight & Hayes Valley chapters, and Trans History in the Tenderloin.

OFF THE WALL ART

Art explodes from frames and jumps off pedestals in San Francisco, where murals wrap around entire buildings, immersive shows envelop you with sound and vision, and interactive art installations make you part of the art. SF arts venues engage your senses, and invite you to make your own mark on the local art scene.

Wraparound Murals

Murals line Mission streets, including **Calle 24** (p176), **Clarion Alley** (p180; pictured) and **Balmy Alley** (p180) – don't miss the multistory *Maestrapeace* on the **Women's Building** (p180) and Agana's **Brava Theater** (p173) mega-mural.

Immersive Art

SF museums shows are portals to other worlds, from the Agnes Martin room at **SFMOMA** (p86; pictured) to the basement blockbuster shows at **de Young** (p224) and the video installations at the **Asian Art Museum** (p108).

Interactive Installations

You complete the art at participatory shows at **Edge on the Square** (p118), **ICASF**'s artist-run makerspace, and David Ireland's 'social sculpture' at **500 Capp St** (p181).

FROM LEFT: FEDERICA GRASSI/GETTY IMAGES, EQROY/SHUTTERSTOCK, JERRY HOLT/STAR TRIBUNE VIA GETTY IMAGES

Fillmore Auditorium (p157)

BEST OUT-THERE ART EXPERIENCES

Explore Yayoi Kusama's pumpkin, Olaf Eliasson's *One-Way Color Tunnel*, and sixth-floor video installations at ❶ **SFMOMA** (p86).

❷ **Minnesota Street Project** (p184) keeps art fresh with eye-opening gallery shows, indie popup art fairs, and First Saturdays art openings.

❸ **Catharine Clark Gallery** (p189) unfolds like origami, with gallery nooks for mesmerizing video art, tactile book arts, and limited-edition artworks.

See poster art fresh from the silkscreens at ❹ **Haight Street Art Center** (p217) – plus 60 years of iconic handbills, posters and photos from SF's music scene.

No matter what show you see at the ❺ **Fillmore** (p157), gallery posters covering 60 years of music history will rock your world.

PARADE ON

SF throws extravagant parades to celebrate San Franciscans being exactly who they are – proud of their immigrant roots, chosen families and civil rights achievements. Can't tell who's in the parade and who's an onlooker? That's the point – by cheering each other on, the parade becomes a community, that becomes a parade, that becomes a community.

Bursting with Pride

The world's queer capitol overflows with **Pride** (p94; pictured), filling June with events and multiple parades – including the **Trans March**, **Dyke March** and million-strong **Pride Parade**.

Dancing with Lions

A 288ft dragon (pictured) stars in SF's **Chinese New Year Parade** (p118), manuevered by 150 martial artists – but the crowd goes wild for the littlest lion dancers.

Poetry in Motion in the Mission

Join **Carnaval** (p168) conga lines, hear singing in the streets at **Flor y Canto** (p175), and celebrate the ancestors on **Dia de los Muertos** (p168).

FROM LEFT: SUNDRY PHOTOGRAPHY/SHUTTERSTOCK, MARIUSZ S. JURGIELEWICZ/SHUTTERSTOCK, SHEILA FITZGERALD/SHUTTERSTOCK

Participant at the Pride Parade (p94)

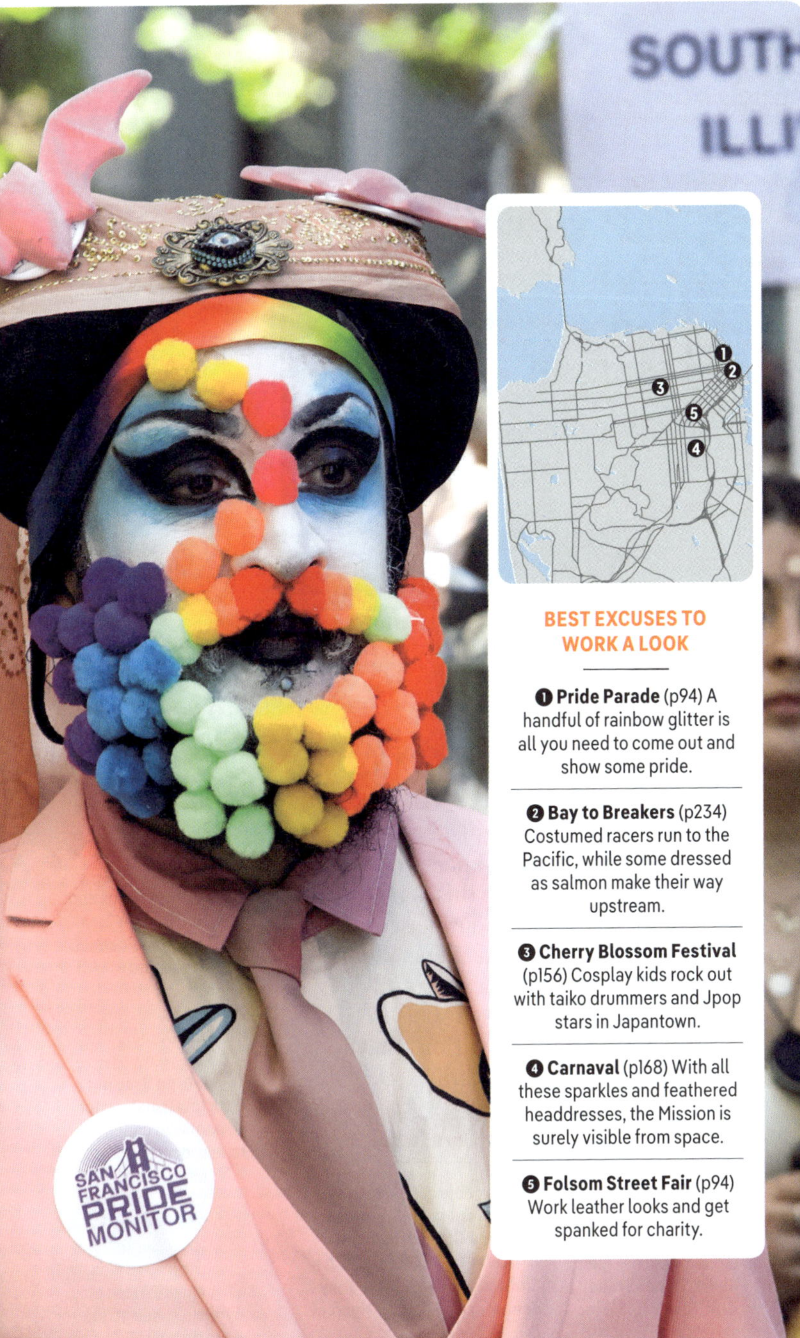

BEST EXCUSES TO WORK A LOOK

❶ **Pride Parade** (p94) A handful of rainbow glitter is all you need to come out and show some pride.

❷ **Bay to Breakers** (p234) Costumed racers run to the Pacific, while some dressed as salmon make their way upstream.

❸ **Cherry Blossom Festival** (p156) Cosplay kids rock out with taiko drummers and Jpop stars in Japantown.

❹ **Carnaval** (p168) With all these sparkles and feathered headdresses, the Mission is surely visible from space.

❺ **Folsom Street Fair** (p94) Work leather looks and get spanked for charity.

JACK-SOOKSAN/SHUTTERSTOCK

Dolores Park (p168)

PEAK ROMANCE

Your heart beats faster, your knees go weak, your palms get sweaty – either this is true love, or you're climbing one of San Francisco's 40-plus hills. Pause to admire the scenery along garden-lined stairways, over parrot-filled treetops, past Victorian peaked roofs to the sparkling bay. Glorious – next time, maybe you'll hop a cable car.

Shout It from the Hilltops

Hike **Francisco Street Steps** (p137) to benches built for two – popular for proposals – then climb **Filbert Street Steps** (p137) to **Coit Tower** (p136) for swoon-worthy views.

Cable Cars to the Stars

Hop a cable car to **Masonic Auditorium** (p43) shows, **Grace Cathedral** (p145) concerts, and cocktails at the **Fairmont** (p146), where Tony Bennet sang 'I Left My Heart in San Francisco.'

BEST SMOOCH-WORTHY EXPERIENCES

Watch the Castro's rainbow lights glow as the sun sets over ❶ **Corona Heights Park** (p201).

At ❷ **Alamo Sq** (p162), peek over the shoulders of 'Painted Lady' Victorian mansions as the city rolls out like a carpet beneath you.

Shipwrecks, wind-sculpted evergreens and stunning Golden Gate vistas reward romantics at ❸ **Lands End** (p233).

Wax poetic atop Russian Hill with Golden Gate Bridge views from ❹ **George Sterling Park** (p147), named for the poet who called San Francisco 'the cool, grey city of love.'

Sit atop ❺ **Dolores Park** (p168) above sunbathers, picnickers and kids swarming the Aztec play pyramid to see all the way to the twinkling bay.

Transamerica Pyramid (p98)

BEST SCI-FI EXPERIENCES

Art, science and technology boundaries blur at ❶ **Gray Area's** (p173) futuristic, mind-expanding events.

Join the future already in progress at the ❷ **Exploratorium** (p72), where MacArthur Genius inventors build interactive experiments exploring human perception.

Watch SFFILM Festival sci-fi movie premieres at the Letterman theater in the ❸ **Presidio** (p58), built by George Lucas as ILM's *Star Wars* screening room.

William Pereira's sci-fi concrete rocket ❹ **Transamerica Pyramid** (p98) is so iconic, Godzilla politely sidestepped it in the 2014 remake.

❺ **Salesforce Tower** (p102) is capped with artist Jim Campbell's *Day for Night*, a rotating digital art installation featuring SF talents - local dancers, high-school animators, Bay tides and towering drag queens.

SCI-FI SCENERY

You've probably seen movies where aliens, Godzilla or genetically enhanced apes roam San Francisco streets – and when you see the futuristic scenery here, those sci-fi movies don't seem that far-fetched. Between self-driving cars, art experiments and concrete rocket pyramids, San Francisco is a comic-book fantasy come to life.

Outlandish Landmarks

Hop a self-driving Waymo to see the retro-futurist **Transamerica Pyramid**, **Salesforce Tower**'s nine-story-high digital projections, and people drifting across Fog Bridge into the **Exploratorium**.

Future Visions

Glimpse the future at **Gray Area** cyberpunk fests, sci-fi art at **Cartoon Art Museum** (p71) and **SFMOMA** (p86) – then discuss over newfangled old fashions at **The Interval** (p68).

TASTE SENSATIONS

With 46 global cuisines packed into seven miles, San Francisco is like a greatest-hits compilation with no skips. With under a million people, SF holds the most Michelin stars of any US city, and the third most James Beard Awards. Yet many local chefs have been unaccountably overlooked for awards – luckily, you're about to discover them.

FROM LEFT: SHEBEKO/SHUTTERSTOCK, JEJIM/SHUTTERSTOCK, RONNIE CHUA/SHUTTERSTOCK

Global Greatest Hits

Sample Uzbek *manti* (beef dumplings) at **Sofiya** (p150), Northern Iranian *katte morgh* (pomegranate chicken) at **Komaaj** (p179), and Cambodian *lok lak* (shaking beef) at **Lunette** (p101).

Some of Everything

Why decide? The **Ferry Building** (p100) is flanked by farmstands and food vendors Tuesdays, Thursdays and Saturdays, and **Spark Social** (p184; pictured) features 25 to 30 food vendors – plus minigolf.

Outlandish Dishes

Explore entirely new cravings: Peking duck pizza at **Outta Sight** (p110), 'progressive Indian' wild-mushroom dosa at **Rooh** (p97) , and crispy MSG (mushroom/shrimp/garlic) chicken at **Mamahuhu** (p235).

Ferry Building (p100)

BEST TASTING MENUS

❶ **San Ho Won** (p175) A parade of flavors, from punchy *banchan* (Korean sides) to *jebi churi* beef filet that rocks tastebuds like a marching band.

❷ **Rich Table** (p218) Feel clever by association with ingenious Californian signature dishes like *cacio e pepe* with Pacific sea urchin.

❸ **Azalina's** (p110) Chef/owner Azalina Eusope keeps her seasonal menu under $100, featuring Malaysian shrimp *laksa* (noodle soup).

❹ **Mister Jiu's** (p121) Chef/owner Brandon Jew brings pristine ingredients to Chinatown's historic banquet hall, setting a party mood with Sonoma Peking duck.

❺ **Acquerello** (p150) Pure romance in a former wedding chapel, with rare Italian wines and lovingly handmade pasta lavished with truffle marsala.

DRAG ACROSS SF

Nowhere does drag quite like San Francisco, where performers have entertained in drag since the gold rush. Between shows, SF's drag queens, kings and nonbinary royals stay busy running for office, fundraising for public-health initiatives, reading at drag story hours, and winning hearts and civil rights victories with false lashes and true courage.

FROM LEFT: BRIGITTE MERLE/GETTY IMAGES, JOSIE NORRIS/THE SAN FRANCISCO CHRONICLE VIA GETTY IMAGES, NIC COURY/AFP VIA GETTY IMAGES

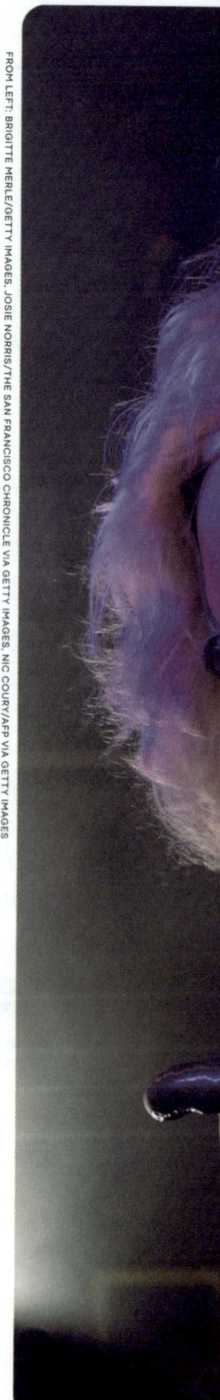

All Hail the Empress

Rainbow Honor Walk (p196) starts with WWII veteran and drag hostess Jose Sarria, America's first out gay candidate for office, who declared herself Absolute Empress of San Francisco in 1964.

Only-in-SF Drag

Forget everything you know from *RuPaul's Drag Race*: SF drag is outlandishly original at **Oasis**, too wild for TV at **The Stud** (p94; pictured), and completely unpredictable at **Aunt Charlie's**.

DIY Drag

Get in drag with assists from the drag-couture experts at **Piedmont Boutique** (p217), big wigs and outlandish notions from **Cliff's Variety** (p203), and vintage fabulousness from **Community Thrift** (p183).

Drag queen, Oasis (p94)

BEST DRAG EXPERIENCES

❶ **Oasis** (p94) keeps audiences gagging for more drag cabaret with Amy Winehouse tributes, *Star Trek* spoofs, original Mall Drag revues, and drag-superstar DJ dance parties.

Easter Sunday is iconic at ❷ **Hunky Jesus Contest** (p270), the fundraising drag contest by SF's charitable drag nuns, the Sisters of Perpetual Indulgence.

When Peaches Christ hostesses at ❸ **Chan National Queer Arts Center** (p173), look out – the crowd goes wild for drag punk pride.

Towering wigs poke through fog at ❹ **Pride** (p94), SF's defiantly joyous celebration for LGBTQ+ community, friends and allies.

Yes, the looks are thrown together and the queens are winging it at ❺ **Aunt Charlie's** (p286) – that's why you can't look away.

WITH KIDS

San Francisco has the fewest kids per capita of any US city – yet many locals dedicate their careers to entertaining and educating kids, from Pixar animators to aquarium marine biologists. Every SF neighborhood offers kid-friendly attractions – especially if they're into sci-fi, skateboards, art, wildlife, gadgets, sports, comics and/or adventure.

FROM LEFT: ANDY SUTHERLAND/SHUTTERSTOCK, GILBERTO MESQUITA/SHUTTERSTOCK, ANTON_IVANOV/SHUTTERSTOCK

SF Wildlife Encounters

Chase butterflies through the Rainforest Dome at the **California Academy of Sciences** (p226), bark back at **Pier 39** (p71) sea lions, and brave the shark tunnel at **Aquarium of the Bay** (p75; pictured).

Double Dare Ya

Join freaky scientific experiments at the **Exploratorium** (p72; pictured), plot your escape from **Alcatraz** (p238), and enter submarine stealth mode aboard the **USS Pampanito** (p79).

Energy to Burn

Create a kid-triathalon: bike **Golden Gate Park** (p224), paddle **Blue Heron Lake** (p227), then gear up at **Mission Skateboards** (p181) and hit **Potrero del Sol/ La Raza Skatepark** (p181).

California Academy of Sciences (p226)

BEST EXPERIENCES FOR KIDS

Discover superpowers you never know you had and explore weird science at the hands-on ❶ **Exploratorium** (p72).

Hang out with butterflies, penguins, alligators and real-life scientists at the ❷ **California Academy of Sciences** (p226).

Meet comic-book heroes at the ❸ **Cartoon Art Museum** (p71).

A climbing wall, swings, daredevil hillside slides and a vintage carousel await at ❹ **Golden Gate Park playground** (p227).

❺ **Yerba Buena Fun Zone** (p88) is action-packed with a bowling alley, ice rink and carousel.

FOR FREE

The best things in life and San Francisco are free – including spirits and speech, thanks to decades of dedicated local efforts. San Francisco loves throwing free festivals, concerts and shows, several of San Francisco's landmark attractions are free, and you can roam freely along city beaches, parks and the Golden Gate Bridge (p56).

FROM LEFT: WONDERLUSTPICSTRAVEL/SHUTTERSTOCK, CONOR P. FITZGERALD/SHUTTERSTOCK, LARRY ZHOU/SHUTTERSTOCK

Free Museum Access

See how 150-year-old machinery works at the **Cable Car Museum** (p144; pictured), discover art deco mosaics at the **Maritime Museum** (p75), and don't miss free days at SF art museums.

Free Peak San Francisco Moments

Celebrate your right to read freely at **City Lights Books** (p130), catch free **Giants** (p97; pictured) baseball on the Embarcadero, and see free dragstavaganzas in **Dolores Park** (p168).

Free Peeks Inside SF Landmarks

See censored murals inside **Coit Tower** (p136), never-used cannons at **Fort Point** (p60), and defunct nuclear bunkers at **Fort Funston** (p231) – and watch history unfold at **City Hall** (p115).

Stern Grove Festival (p232)

BEST FREE CONCERTS

❶ **Stern Grove Festival** (p232) brings free marquee acts to SF's natural amphitheater, from funk to punk and pop to opera.

Catch ❷ **Hardly Strictly Bluegrass** (p225) headliners like Elvis Costello, Gillian Welch and banjo legend Béla Fleck plus 100 other acts for free in Golden Gate Park.

Follow smoke signals to ❸ **420 Festival** (p225) with free music and free giveaways for adults with ID.

Rockers, DJs and hip-hop heroes give free shows in-store at ❹ **Amoeba Music** (p212).

The heart of the city beats with free concerts in front of City Hall at the ❺ **Civic Center Soundtrack** (p115).

UNDER THE RADAR

Misleading names, hidden entries, tricky hours, no website: some of SF's best discoveries are deliberately hard to find. Smartphones are discouraged at SF's low-key bars, restaurants and arts venues, so everyone can live in the moment – feel free to pogo at a Bottom of the Hill punk show or freestyle at Golden Sardine (p135) poetry nights.

Underground Music Scene

Punk's roaring back at historic **Mabuhay Gardens** (p127) and **Savoy Tivoli** (p129) – and flaring up again at **Bottom of the Hill** (p190; pictured), **The Knockout** (p191), and **Thrillhouse Records** (p191).

Speakeasies

You'll need a token to enter **The Pawn Shop** (p96) restaurant, a password ('books') for **Bourbon & Branch** (p110; pictured) bar, and a quarter for **Free Gold Watch** (p214) arcade.

Alternative Art Spaces

Who knew contemporary art stars awaited discovery at community-run **Adobe Books** (p174), nonprofit **Edge on the Square** (p118) and an ex-factory called **Minnesota Street Project** (p184)? You did.

FROM LEFT: SABRINA DALBESIO/LONELY PLANET, HANS KWIOTEK/SHUTTERSTOCK, BRYAN MIN/SHUTTERSTOCK

Labyrinth, Lands End (p233)

BEST SF INSIDER EXPERIENCES

Duck into the sea cave at ❶ **Lands End** (p233) and emerge to end-of-the-world views.

After 8pm at ❷ **Dalva** (p183), duck into Hideout for off-the-menu cocktails and unannounced events.

See the Golden Gate Bridge vista you won't find on postcards: from the roof at ❸ **Fort Point** (p60), you'll get an eyeful of the bridge's riveted orange underbelly.

Don't book, don't call, don't attempt takeout – just line up on a Japantown corner for soba at ❹ **Sobakatsu** (p159).

Walk to the end of the Marina yacht jetty, and when you see a tube among tombstones, lean down and listen to the bay: you've found the ❺ **Wave Organ** (p67).

Perfect Days

Bliss is easy to find in this 7x7-mile city. A day or two is all you need to engage your senses with breathtaking art, foot-stomping concerts, mouthwatering meals, and belly-laugh comedy.

F-line streetcar (p30)

BENJAMIN HEATH FOR LONELY PLANET

DAY 1

Wander Chinatown byways for bubble tea, art breakthroughs at **Edge on the Square** (p118) and incredible true stories at the **Chinese Historical Society of America** (p119). Find your fortune at **Golden Gate Fortune Cookies** (p120), and go gourmet with cookbooks from **On Waverly** (p122) and **Wok Shop** (p122) equipment.

Lunch Go traditional dim sum at **Hang Ah Tea Room** (p123), or get creative at **Osmanthus Dim Sum Lounge** (p121).

Hop the Powell-Hyde cable car to Fisherman's Wharf to glimpse the hidden art deco treasures at the **Maritime Museum** (p75), meet **Cartoon Art Museum** (p71) comic-book heroes, battle Space Invaders at **Musée Mécanique** (p71), and bark back at Pier 39 **sea lions** (p71).

Dinner Enjoy waterfront sunsets and SF's signature seafood cioppino at **Scoma's** (p80).

Jump on the cable car to North Beach for your preferred entertainment: uncensored comedy at **Cobb's** (p132), spur-rattling cocktails at **Comstock Saloon** (p129), or roaring punk rock at **Mabuhay Gardens** (p127).

DAY 2

Your next epic adventure begins at the **Exploratorium** (p72), where hands-on exhibits dare you to stop time, sculpt fog, and dive headfirst into total darkness in the Tactile Dome.

Lunch Go gourmet by the bay at SF's local food showcase: the **Ferry Building** (p100).

Ready to time-travel? Cover 150 years of cutting-edge, multi-media art at **SFMOMA** (p86), or meander through millennia of Asian art treasures at the **Asian Art Museum** (p108).

Dinner Get the star-chef treatment with the multicourse meal of a lifetime at **Benu** (p96), or à la carte seasonal sensations at **Rich Table** (p218).

Cheer for virtuosos performing live at one of SF's world-renowned downtown music venues: **SFJAZZ** (p220), **SF Opera** (p111), **San Francisco Symphony** (p110) and **Great American Music Hall** (p114). Toast your epic day with rare rum drinks at Smuggler's Cove – or head to SoMa clubs to see where the night takes you next.

DAY 3

Start in **Golden Gate Park** (p224), with year-round flowers at **San Francisco Botanical Garden** (p225) and **Conservatory of Flowers** (p225), and handmade wonders at the **de Young Museum** (p224). If it's foggy, warm up with butterflies inside the Rainforest Dome at the **California Academy of Sciences** (p226) – if it's sunny, head to **Ocean Beach** (p234) to beachcomb along the Pacific.

Lunch Enjoy Chinese American diner classics reinvented with fresh ingredients at **Mamahuhu** (p235).

Even when it's foggy in the park, the sun is probably shining in mural-lined **Balmy Alley** (p180). Head down **Calle 24** (p176) for more mural-covered local landmarks – bookstores, skateshops, cafes, *panaderías* (bakeries) – until your rumbling stomach announces it's ready to take on a Mission burrito.

Dinner Get the definitive Mission burrito at **La Taqueria** (p169).

Post-burrito, take a late-afternoon disco nap in **Dolores Park** (p168) – but don't miss showtime at **Chan National Queer Arts Center** (p173), movies at **Roxie Cinema** (p178) or drag at **Oasis** (p94). Follow rainbow-lit sidewalks to Castro clubs, or end your night toasting to new friends at historic Mission bars.

WHEN TO GO

Anytime you're free, San Francisco is ready to show you the time of your life – just remember to throw on a coat, and maybe some glitter.

Whenever you arrive, you're right on time to see San Francisco put on a show. Year-round, there are film festivals, major music events, art openings, theater premieres and cultural celebrations. In this multicultural, interfaith city, festive holiday lights illuminate long nights from Halloween through Lunar New Year, Holi, Nowruz, Ramadan, Passover, Easter and Solstice – some San Franciscans just keep them up year-round, because why not? No matter what you're celebrating, San Franciscans will gladly celebrate with you – and if it means we get to dress up and eat tasty treats, even better. Hotel rates fluctuate wildly from summer peaks (June to July) to low season (January to February) – but you'll find that San Francisco takes a nonconformist approach to the seasons (and everything else). Summer can feel wintry, fall feels like summer, and winter blooms like spring. Might as well just come when the spirit moves you, and join San Francisco in full swing.

I LIVE HERE

SF'S RIOT PARTY

Honey Mahogany is SF's Transgender District co-founder, Oasis (p94) star, and the nation's first African American trans woman Democratic Committee chair. *@honeymahogany*

The first LGBTQ+ uprising was 1966 Compton's Cafeteria Riot, when trans women fought police harassment at Turk and Taylor, where we hold our **Riot Party** (at the end of SF's Transgender History Month). Down the block you'll find drag at **Aunt Charlie's** (p286), **GLIDE** (p104) doing incredible work for housing stability, and art-house theater **CounterPulse** (p113).

Golden Gate Bridge (p56)

FROM LEFT: ANDREW ZARIVNY/SHUTTERSTOCK, FRANCESCO CANTONE/SHUTTERSTOCK

MICROCLIMATES

When it's blustery at **Ocean Beach** (p234), hop the bus to the Castro, Mission or Dogpatch – the weather can be sunny and up to 25°F warmer in these districts on the city's sheltered side.

Weather Through the Year

JANUARY	FEBRUARY	MARCH	APRIL	MAY	JUNE
Avg. daytime max: **57°F**	Avg. daytime max: **61°F**	Avg. daytime max: **64°F**	Avg. daytime max: **66°F**	Avg. daytime max: **67°F**	Avg. daytime max: **70°F**
Days of rainfall: **11**	Days of rainfall: **11**	Days of rainfall: **10**	Days of rainfall: **6**	Days of rainfall: **4**	Days of rainfall: **2**

FOGGY SUMMER DAYS

San Francisco's marine layer can put a damper on beach plans and breezy summer outfits from May Gray days to chilly Fogust. But this is also the height of San Francisco's festival season, so determined San Franciscan partiers throw on their feathers, leathers and glitter and dance until the goosebumps go away.

Party in the Streets

San Francisco will not rest until every joyous occasion is thoroughly celebrated. Here **Lunar New Year** (p118) and **Pride** (p94) are each month-long celebrations, capped by spectacular parades with thousands of performers and participants – and up to half a million people cheering them on. Between parades, San Francisco street parties blur the lines between performers and audiences, giving everyone an excuse to dress up, show out and party down. From April through October, San Francisco neighborhoods take turns throwing epic street parties. Highlights include Japantown's flower-powerful **Cherry Blossom Festival** (p156) in April, the Mission's feathered and fabulous **Carnaval** (p168) in May, poetic **North Beach Festival** in June, kinky **Dore Alley Fair** in July, hippie **Haight Street Fair** (p210) in September, and rainbow-glow **Castro St Fair** in October.

I LIVE HERE

LITQUAKE

Scott James is a Litquake board member and the author of *Trial by Fire* and *SoMa*. His work has appeared in *The New York Times*. *@scottjameswriter*

Litquake (p174) includes literary stars and complete unknown. The final night's Lit Crawl takes over the Mission neighborhood with dozens of events at bars, pizza joints and laundromats in a literary pub crawl. My favorite moment: reading in a barbershop while customers got haircuts! Mixing words and weird is so Litquake.

Outdoor Music Festivals

To San Franciscans, every open space looks like a promising concert venue. Every summer for almost 100 years, a sleepy redwood and eucalyptus grove in the Outer Sunset has roared with cheers for free **Stern Grove** (p232) concerts. Golden Gate Park's grassy Polo Fields made hippie history as the site of the 1967 Human Be-In, and now these grounds are regularly rocked by SF megafestivals **Outside Lands** (p225) and free **Hardly Strictly Bluegrass** (p225). Nearby at the San Francisco Botanical Garden, pianists serenade the plants during Flower Piano. Across the park, Hippie Hill provides a fitting backdrop for jam bands April 20th at the **420 Festival** (p225). For year-round musical events in parks and public plazas citywide, check the calendar at sfrecpark.org.

Ocean Beach (p234)

FALL, AKA SF SUMMER

When summer ends elsewhere, SF is just warming up. Now's the time for sunny beach days, harvest food festivals, and crush season in Napa (p255) and Sonoma Valley (p255) – plus street fairs and outdoor concerts across town.

JULY	AUGUST	SEPTEMBER	OCTOBER	NOVEMBER	DECEMBER
Avg. daytime max: **70°F**	Avg. daytime max: **70°F**	Avg. daytime max: **72°F**	Avg. daytime max: **67 °F**	Avg. daytime max: **60°F**	Avg. daytime max: **56°F**
Days of rainfall: **1**	Days of rainfall: **1**	Days of rainfall: **1**	Days of rainfall: **4**	Days of rainfall: **7**	Days of rainfall: **10**

FROM LEFT: GG-FOTO/SHUTTERSTOCK, ENTERTAINMENT PICTURES/ALAMY

Pier 39 (p71)

GET PREPARED FOR SAN FRANCISCO

Useful things to load in your bag, your ears and your brain.

Clothes

Wear layers Even when it's sunny out, bring a warm, wind-resistant outer layer – especially when you're headed to the coast or the Avenues, where the fog tumbles through the streets by the late afternoon.

Costumes San Franciscans take any excuse to throw on wigs and fun fur, and take particular pride in drag and custom-made costumes – whether that's for Pride, Burning Man, Halloween, Sunday tea dances, or just a random Wednesday.

Every day is casual Friday Even at work, Californians dress casually – jeans were invented here – and suits are mostly for bankers and funerals.

Leather Pack your chaps: San Francisco is home to the world's first designated Leather & LGBTQ Cultural District (p93), and kinkwear is standard at Folsom Street Fair (p94), Dore Up Your Alley Fair, and SoMa Leather District clubs.

Manners

Don't stare, no matter how little or how much extra someone is wearing.

Ask before taking a photo you intend to share – California has strict laws protecting image-usage rights.

Put phones away to enjoy restaurant meals, movies and live shows where video isn't allowed.

Calling a person may be considered intrusive, even if they gave you their number – text first.

READ

A Coney Island of the Mind (Lawrence Ferlinghetti; 1958) Poems capturing SF's joyous chaos inspired global counterculture movements.

Slouching Towards Bethlehem (Joan Didion; 1968) Didion's scorching truth burns through SF fog during the Summer of Love.

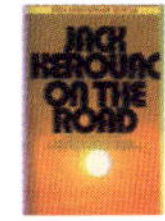

On the Road (Jack Kerouac; 1957) Banged out in a San Francisco attic, Kerouac's travelogue set postwar America free.

The Joy Luck Club (Amy Tan; 1989) SF immigrant stories play out across four generations of mothers and daughters in Tan's epic novel.

Words

420 was coined in the Bay Area c 1971, declaring 4:20pm as International Bong Hit Time; also refers to SF's 420 Festival (p225).

The City is how Bay Area residents refer to San Francisco.

Dude is a prime example of expressive, tonal, surfer-influenced SF slang. How you say it changes its meaning: 'duuuuuude' can mean 'I couldn't agree more' (especially with a chuckle), while 'Dude!' is another way to say 'Watch where you're going, jerk' and 'dude...' expresses empathy, like 'so sorry.'

Frisco is the nickname legendarily banned by SF's self-appointed 19th-century Emperor Norton – now used by rappers and comedians to get a rise out of local crowds ('What's good, Frisco?!?!')

Hella is a Bay Area way to say extremely, as in 'hella spicy.'

Karl the Fog is the affectionate name for SF's enduring marine layer – and its snarky social-media presence.

Queer is how many in the LGBTQ+ community refer to LGBTQ+ culture, reclaiming a historic slur – as in SF's Chan National Queer Arts Center (p173) – though some who remember its derogatory use may not appreciate hearing it from people outside the community.

San Fran is the nickname that makes locals shudder, and flags speakers as outsiders.

WATCH

Milk (Gus Van Sant; 2008; pictured) Sean Penn won an Oscar for portraying California's first openly gay elected official.

Tales of the City (Alastair Reid; 1993) Laura Linney unravels mysteries in SF's swinging '70s disco scene.

Chan Is Missing (Wayne Wayne; 1982) When Chan disappears, two cabbies realize they don't know Chan, Chinatown or themselves.

The Maltese Falcon (John Houston; 1941) Dashiell Hammett's SF detective is played by Humphrey Bogart and his fedora.

Harold & Maude (Hal Ashby; 1971) The Conservatory of Flowers and Sutro Baths make apt backdrops for May to December romance.

LISTEN

Take Five (Dave Brubeck Quartet; 1959) SF's piano virtuoso and laid-back saxophonist Paul Desmond defined West Coast cool.

The Avengers Live at Winterland (The Avengers; 1978) Penelope Houston proves an impossible act for Sex Pistols to follow.

Sly Lives! (Sly and the Family Stone; 2025) SF's iconic band shaped '60s psychedelic rock, '70s funk and '90s hip-hop.

American Beauty (The Grateful Dead; 1970) Inspires SF road-trip singalongs with hits like 'Ripple', 'Box of Rain', and 'Truckin''.

FROM LEFT: KENISHIROTIE/SHUTTERSTOCK, IV-OLGA/SHUTTERSTOCK, SHEILA FITZGERALD/SHUTTERSTOCK

San Francisco International Airport (SFO)

GETTING THERE

The Bay Area has three busy international airports: San Francisco (SFO), Oakland (OAK) and San Jose (SJC). You may find flight deals to OAK or SJC – but be sure to factor in additional transit time, cost and hassles to reach San Francisco proper. By car, San Francisco is a 25- to 60-minute, 14-mile trip north from SFO on Hwy 101; BART rides are cheaper and faster.

BART

Bay Area Rapid Transit *(BART; bart.gov)* trains take you from SFO to SF downtown in 30 minutes, departing from the BART station at the International Terminal. Purchase a reloadable physical Clipper card at BART kiosks, or download the scannable **Clipper app** *(clippercard.com)* for use on SF transit including BART, Muni streetcars and ferries.

Rideshare

SF-invented ride-share services such as **Lyft** and **Uber** serve SFO. Download the app in advance and ensure you'll have battery power and wi-fi or cell coverage to use it. Ride-shares depart from designated areas on Level 5 of the domestic parking garage.

Taxis

Taxis to downtown San Francisco depart from designated zones outside the lower-level baggage-claim area at SFO. To book in advance, download the **Flywheel app** *(flywheel.com)*.

FROM THE AIRPORT TO THE CITY CENTRE

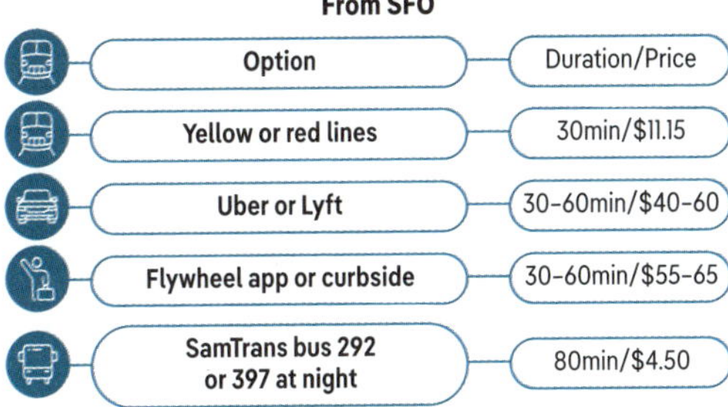

From SFO

Option	Duration/Price
Yellow or red lines	30min/$11.15
Uber or Lyft	30-60min/$40-60
Flywheel app or curbside	30-60min/$55-65
SamTrans bus 292 or 397 at night	80min/$4.50

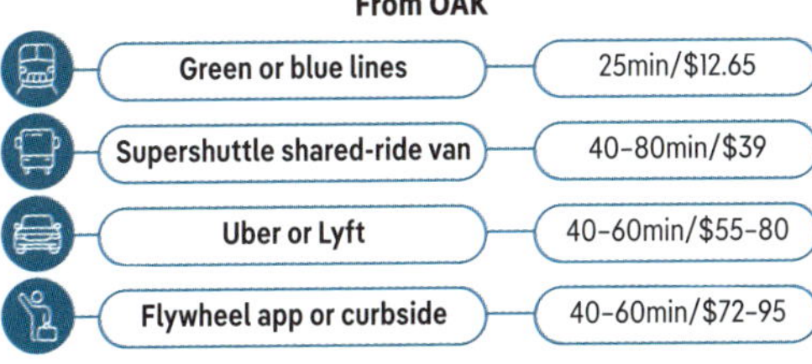

From OAK

Option	Duration/Price
Green or blue lines	25min/$12.65
Supershuttle shared-ride van	40-80min/$39
Uber or Lyft	40-60min/$55-80
Flywheel app or curbside	40-60min/$72-95

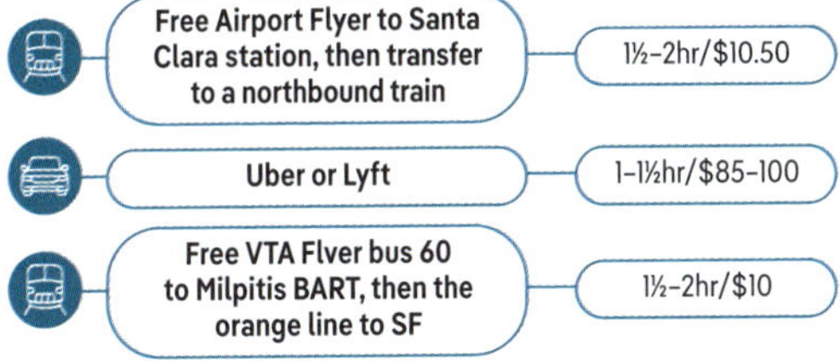

From SJC

Option	Duration/Price
Free Airport Flyer to Santa Clara station, then transfer to a northbound train	1½-2hr/$10.50
Uber or Lyft	1-1½hr/$85-100
Free VTA Flyer bus 60 to Milpitis BART, then the orange line to SF	1½-2hr/$10

TIP

Add the Bay Area transit **Clipper Card** *(clippercard.com)* to your digital wallet to pay for rides with your mobile device or smartwatch – or pay $3 extra to buy a physical Clipper Card from BART station vending machines.

OTHER POINTS OF ENTRY

Train

Amtrak *(amtrak.com)* serves SF via Emeryville (near Oakland), with Thruway 99 bus connections to SF's **Salesforce Transit Center**. Amtrak's **Coast Starlight** runs from Los Angeles to Seattle via Emeryville/Oakland (35 hours; from $292); **California Zephyr** connects Chicago and Emeryville (51 hours; from $302).

Car

Driving in San Francisco means navigating hills, one-way streets and nonstop traffic, except in the middle of the night. If you arrive by car or motorcycle, plan to park your car until it's time to leave, and get around with public transit, ride-shares, bicycles or taxis.

Bus

Daily **Greyhound** buses *(greyhound.com)* connect SF with Los Angeles (from $39, eight to 12 hours), Truckee (from $32, 5½ hours) near Lake Tahoe and other scenic destinations. **Green Tortoise** *(greentortoise.com)* organizes trips along the California coast and to national parks via biodiesel-fueled sleeping coach.

ANDREY BAYDA/SHUTTERSTOCK

Cable car

GETTING AROUND

Scenic San Francisco is best seen by cable car, streetcar, bicycle, skateboard and on foot. If you start to flag on uphill climbs, hop Muni or rideshare. Parking is hard to find and not cheap – plus tickets are steep. Avoid driving until it's time to leave town.

Cable Car

San Francisco's original steampunk trolley is a total joyride – no seat belts, no airbags, no digital dashboard. Sit on a wooden bench or hang onto a creaking leather strap, and brace for downhill slides. Cable cars are scenic, slow and frequent, from 7am to about 11pm daily. Single rides cost $9; for more than one ride, get a Muni Visitor Passport (one-/three-/seven-day pass $15/35/47).

Muni Metro & Streetcar

Schedules vary by line and service – vintage F-line streetcars are charming but slow – and service is infrequent after 9pm. Muni Metro lines run underground downtown; see sfmta.com for station locations.

Key Muni Metro & Streetcar Lines

F – Vintage streetcars run from Fisherman's Wharf and Embarcadero down Market to the Castro.

J – Downtown to the Mission, Castro and Noe Valley.

K, L, M – Downtown to the Castro and the Sunset.

N – Caltrain and SBC Ballpark to the Haight, Golden Gate Park and Ocean Beach.

Cable Car Lines

California Street runs east–west along California St, from the Market St terminus through Chinatown to Van Ness Ave. It's the least-traveled route, with the shortest queues.

Powell-Mason runs from the Powell St cable-car turnaround past Union Sq, turns west along Jackson St, then heads north toward Fisherman's Wharf; southbound, it takes Washington St.

Powell-Hyde is the most picturesque route, following the Powell-Mason line until Jackson St, where it turns down Hyde St to Aquatic Park; southbound, it takes Washington St.

T – Chinatown to Caltrain, Dogpatch and Bayview.

BART

Bay Area Rapid Transit *(BART; bart.gov)* trains link SF to the East Bay, SFO and Millbrae, where it connects with Caltrain. Within SF, BART is the fastest way to get from downtown to the Mission district.

Bicycle

Bike-sharing is available citywide through **Lyft's Bay Wheels** *(lyft.com/bikes/bay-wheels)*; bring your own helmet. Locate an available bicycle nearby, then use your digital Clipper Card or Lyft app, scan the QR code, and unlock it.

Check the **San Francisco Bicycle Coalition** *(sfbike.org)* for maps, information and local laws regarding cyclists. Bicycles can be taken on BART, but not the first car, crowded trains, or in the first three cars during weekday rush hours.

Bus

Muni buses display their route number and final destination; routes with an X or R are limited-stop or express services; Owl routes run after midnight.

Three other Bay Area public-bus systems connect San Francisco to the rest

TIP

Hang on to your ticket, even if you're not planning to use it again – if you're caught without one by the transit police, you're subject to a $130 fine.

PUBLIC TRANSPORTATION ESSENTIALS

Muni Stops

A detailed **Muni Street & Transit Map** is available free online *(sfmta.com)*. Some Muni bus and streetcar stops have a sheltered bench; others are indicated by a street sign and/or a yellow-painted stripe on a lamppost with the route number/letter.

Ways to Pay

You can pay digitally or use a reusable plastic Clipper Card for most San Francisco transit options, including cable cars. You can still use cash and paper tickets for Muni rides, with some limitations.

Cash Fares

Fares can be paid in cash on cable cars, Muni buses and surface Muni streetcars (not underground metro); exact change is required.

Muni Visitor Passports

For frequent use of Muni streetcars, metro, buses and cable cars, get a **Muni Visitor Passport** *(sfmta.com; one-/three-/seven-day pass $15/35/47)*. You can add a Muni Passport to your Clipper Card through the website or at a Clipper Card machine at BART and Muni metro stations.You can also purchase one at the Muni kiosks; see sfmta.com for exact locations.

Clipper Card

Most Bay Area public transit accepts digital or physical **Clipper Cards** *(clippercard.com)*, including Muni, BART, Caltrain and San Francisco Bay Ferry. Clipper cards automatically deduct fares and apply transfers – only one Muni fare is deducted per 90-minute period. Add the Bay Area transit Clipper Card to your digital wallet to pay with your mobile device, or pay $3 to buy a physical Clipper Card from machines at BART or Muni metro stations. You'll need to tap your Clipper Card on a scanner to enter – and exit – BART, ferries and Caltrain. If your Clipper Card value is less than needed to exit, use a station Addfare machine to pay the remainder.

Ticket Machines & Kiosks

Clipper Card machines are located at BART and Muni metro stations. Paper Muni tickets that are good for 90 minutes of travel for Muni metro, streetcar and buses can be purchased from ticket machines at Muni metro stations or Muni kiosks; see sfmta.com for exact locations. You can purchase individual cable-car-ride tickets at cable-car turnaround kiosks.

of the Bay Area, all of which accept Clipper Cards:

AC Transit *(actransit.org)* buses connect SF to East Bay destinations at Salesforce Transit Center.

Golden Gate Transit *(goldengate.org)* connects SF to Marin ($8.50–9.75) and Sonoma county ($14.50).

SamTrans *(samtrans.com)* buses connect SF to SFO and the South Bay.

Rideshare

Rideshare services Lyft and Uber were founded in SF, and they're widely used – expect to wait and/or pay a premium during peak-use times, including rush hour, weekend nights or after conferences or events. Off-peak fares within SF range from $7 to $23 for a direct-to-destination ride.

Taxi

Taxi fares are about $3.25 per mile; meters start at $4.15, and there's no surge pricing at peak times. Add 15% to the fare as a tip ($1 minimum). For quickest service in San Francisco, download the **Flywheel app** *(flywheel.com)*.

If you need to call a cab, **Green Cab** *(greencabsf.com; 415-626-4733)* dispatches fuel-efficient hybrids. **Homobiles** *(homobilessf.org; 415-574-5023)* provides secure, reliable, donation-based, 24/7 transportation by and for the LGBTQ+ community; text for fastest service.

Ferry

Ferries provide scenic boat rides across the bay. **San Francisco Bay Ferry** *(sanfranciscobayferry.com)* departs from SF's Ferry Building to Oakland, Alameda, Richmond and Vallejo. **Golden Gate Transit** *(goldengate.org)* runs ferries from the Ferry Building to Larkspur, Sausalito, Tiburon and Angel Island, plus game-day ferries to Warriors and Giants games; bicycles permitted. **Blue & Gold Fleet** *(blueandgoldfleet.com)* operates ferries from Pier 41 to Sausalito and Alcatraz.

Walking

Limber up: San Francisco has 40-plus hills for you to summit, with stairway hikes leading to vista points and Golden Gate Bridge views. The Bay waterfront is flat and scenic from Dogpatch to Crissy Field, and Golden Gate Park stretches over 50 blocks to Ocean Beach. When you walk around at night, bear in mind that although San Francisco has low rates of violent crime compared to other major US cities, you should still apply your street smarts and pay attention to your surroundings. If you're alone at night in an unfamiliar area that isn't well lit, consider ridesharing instead of walking or waiting for a bus.

TIP

If you must drive, avoid rush hours: 7:30am to 9:30am and 3:30pm to 6:30pm Monday to Friday. Before heading to any bridge, airport or other traffic choke-point, call 511 for a traffic update.

Car & Motorcycle

If you can, avoid driving in San Francisco: heavy traffic is a given, street parking is harder to find than true love, and meter readers are ruthless. To locate public parking garages and check prices (typically $5–8/hr or $40–46/day), see sfmta.com/garages-lots. If you're towed, you'll need to pay for fines and towing retrieve your car from **Autoreturn** *(autoreturn.com)*.

For route planning and schedules, consult transit.511.org.

Key Muni Bus Routes

22 Fillmore runs from Dogpatch (Potrero Hill), through the Mission, Haight and Pacific Heights to the Marina.

33 Ashbury runs from San Francisco General Hospital through the Mission, Castro and Haight, past Golden Gate Park to the Richmond District.

38 Geary runs from Salesforce Transit Center, along Market to Geary Blvd, through downtown, the Tenderloin, Japantown and the Richmond District to Ocean Beach.

7 Haight runs from Salesforce Transit Center along Market to Haight St, along the south side of Golden Gate Park through the Sunset District to Sunset Dunes park.

IV-OLGA/SHUTTERSTOCK

DRIVERLESS CARS

The first time you spot a car cruising through San Francisco with no one in the driver's seat, you may do a double take – until you remember that this is SF, where driverless cars have been navigating city streets for more than a decade. Robotaxi service is now available in San Francisco from **Waymo** *(waymo.com)*, aka Google's self-driving car fleet. To try it, download the Waymo One app, and use it to call a self-driving Waymo – typically a white Jaguar I-PACE model with a LiDAR sensor laser array on the roof – to pick up/drop off up to four passengers. Waymo is currently slightly costlier than rideshares from Lyft or Uber – but on the other hand, there's no driver to tip. Currently Amazon's boxy, steering-wheel-less **Zoox** *(zoox.com)* robotaxi is also running test runs in San Francisco.

TRAVEL COSTS

Muni streetcar/ metro/bus
Fares are **$3** cash or with a Metro ticket, or **$2.75** with a reloadable Clipper Card; included with Muni Visitor Passport (one-/ three-/seven-day pass $15/35/47).

Cable car
$9 per ride; included with Muni Visitor Passport.

BART
Clipper Card fare from Mission 24th stop to Embarcadero is **$2.40**; not included with Muni Visitor Passport.

ACCESSIBILITY

Bay Area transit companies offer wheelchair-accessible service and travel discounts for travelers with disabilities. **San Francisco Bay Area Regional Transit Guide** *(511.org/transit/accessibility)* covers accessible transit options for people with disabilities. **Muni** *(sfmta.com/muni-access-guide)* also provides detailed information on its wheelchair-accessible bus routes and streetcar stops.

Independent Living Resource Center of San Francisco *(ilrcsf.org)* is a disability advocacy and support organization that provides helpful travel tips, including information about accessibility on public transit, in hotels and at other local facilities.

For accessible outdoor adventures, **San Francisco's Environmental Traveling Companions** *(etctrips.org)* organizes top-notch whitewater rafting, kayaking and cross-country skiing trips in California for people of all ages with disabilities.

FANFO/SHUTTERSTOCK

Cioppino

DINING OUT

SF packs flavor into seven sq miles, with three culinary advantages: organic local ingredients, deep immigrant influences and wild imagination.

Visitors from around the world are surprised to discover truly original San Francisco dishes that somehow taste like home. San Franciscans from around the world work side by side to feed the community something delicious – Salvadoran *pupusas* (tortilla pockets), Irish soda bread, Palestinian mezze, Korean barbecue, plus inventive remixes of classics. San Francisco's adventurous eaters are receptive to tasty food of all kinds: tamales, chow mein and omelettes have been SF staples since the 1850s.

Global influences and local ingredients shine on the plate here: Chef Alice Waters set the Bay Area standard for organic, sustainable food in 1971 at **Chez Panisse**, inspiring the global Slow Food movement and generations of SF restaurateurs. Today San Franciscans follow mom-and-pop food purveyors as they evolve from bar pop-ups and farmers market stands to Insta-famous food trucks and acclaimed restaurants. For a taste of what's on the menu where, see **California Migration Museum's SF Melting Spots Map** *(meltingspots.calmigration.org/map)*. Congratulations: you're right on time for dinner.

The Taste of Immigrant Success

Food and Wine named San Francisco America's top city for multicultural dining, packing 46 global cuisines into a 7x7-mile city. There's a reason for this global gourmet scene: an official Sanctuary City since 1989, San Francisco has long been a safe

Classic San Francisco Dishes

LOCAL OYSTERS
Indigenous Ohlone staple, sourced at Hog Island.

HANGTOWN FRY
Gold-rush-style oyster omelettes at Brenda's French Soul Food.

NOODLES
Organic buckwheat soba inspires slurping at Sobakatsu.

SONOMA DUCK
Sonoma-raised, Peking-style duck at Mister Jiu's.

place to call home, start small businesses, and celebrate cultures and cuisines. San Francisco's nonprofit restaurant incubator **La Cocina** has helped more than 150 immigrant-owned and women-run businesses launch— so you can enjoy Pali-Cali flatbread at **Reem's** (p179), multicourse Malaysian at **Azalina's** (p110), fried chicken and bubbles at **Minnie Bell's Soul Movement** (p160), Nepalese *momos* (dumplings) at **Bini's Kitchen** (p92), and more on La Cocina's **Dream Destination Map** *(lacocinasf.org/bornatlacocina)*. California's immigrant farmers and farm workers supply 14 weekly farmers markets city-wide – including year-round **Ferry Building** (p100) and **Heart of the City** (p115) markets – so chefs never run out of fresh inspiration. SF cuisine thrives with immigrant contributions – from farmers and farm workers to chefs and line cooks, and generations of family restaurateurs – plus appreciative eaters like you.

Dim Sum

Since one in three San Franciscans identifies as Asian, SF's go-to comfort foods aren't just burgers and pizza – though you'll find plenty of those – but also kimchi, tandoori and, above all, dim sum. Dim sum is Cantonese for what's known in Mandarin as *xiao che* ('small eats'). At traditional dim-sum places like **Hang Ah Tea Room** (p119), steaming baskets are opened with a flourish to reveal plump dumplings and fluffy *bao* (buns), accompanied by platters of garlicky greens and for dessert, jiggly egg-custard tarts and toasted sesame balls with sweet bean paste.

If you prefer to cut to the chase, step up to the counter at Chinatown's **Good Mong Kok** (p119) or **Dim Sum Bistro** (p119) and get dumplings to go, straight from the steamer. Expect queues for traditional dim-sum hot spots in Chinatown and along Geary St and Clement St – for dumplings made to order without the wait, head to Irving St around 22nd Ave for store-front dumpling specialists, including **Mini Potstickers** (p231).

At SF's genre-defying dim sum innovators like **China Live** (p121), **Dragon Beaux** (p236) and **Palette Tea House** (p78), you'll find creative, succulent dumplings that rival most fine-dining tasting menu signatures. For critically acclaimed Chinese-inspired, California-fresh takes on small-plate dining, book inventive **Four Kings** (p122) or fusion sensation **State Bird Provisions** (p157).

GARAGE38/SHUTTERSTOCK

mochitsuki

CELEBRATE WITH FOOD

SF Restaurant Week *(sfrestaurantweek.com)* Chase away winter blues with meal deals at 100-plus SF restaurants, including multicourse fixed-price lunches and dinners.

Kung Pao Kosher *(koshercomedy.com)* A SF holiday tradition for over 30 years, Kung Pao Kosher is a Chinese feast and Jewish comedy marathon in a Chinatown banquet hall at Christmas.

Dia de los Muertos (p168) Altars offer favorite foods to dearly departed across the Mission – including sweet *pan de muerto* and savory *mole* (sauce) – and Mission Cultural Center hosts 'Mole to Die For' competitions.

Cherry Blossom Festival (p156) Japantown dishes out ramen, grills yakitori skewers, and hosts *mochitsuki*, the mochi-pounding ceremony turning rice into treats with massive mallets.

CIOPPINO	DUMPLINGS	BURRITO	DUNGENESS CRAB
Bowls of seafood taste deep as the Pacific at Scoma's.	Hang Ah Tea Room has served Cantonese classics for a century.	La Taqueria loads theirs with slow-cooked beans, meat and just-made salsas.	Roasted whole with garlic noodles at Thanh Long.

Golden Boy (p129)

CHRIS ALLAN/SHUTTERSTOCK

FANTASTIC FLATBREAD

San Francisco is known globally for sourdough (see p290), with a distinctive tang from *lactobacillus sanfranciscensis* – but there's also a loyal local following for focaccia, the pillowy-on-top, crunchy-on-bottom flatbread introduced to SF by Genovese immigrants more than a century ago. Today you can get focaccia hot from the 100-year-old oven at **Liguria Bakery** (p129), sizzling with garlicky clams at **Golden Boy** (p129), stuffed with cheese at **Cotogna** (p98), or loaded with salami hot from the panini press at **Molinari** (p137). But SF's love for flatbreads knows no bounds – current local obsessions include crispy, light *pinsa* at **Montesacro Pinseria** (p94), soulful sumac-spiced Palestinian flatbread at **Reem's** (p179), buttery *paratha* with Point Reyes blue cheese at **Besharam** (p184), and griddled *tawa* bread at **Yemen Kitchen** (p105).

SF Roots Cuisine

Tax and tip (obligatory) add about 35% to SF restaurant bills.

The food other cities call crossroads or fusion cuisine has another name here: San Francisco roots cuisine. Foraged ingredients and trade-route flavors may seem trendy, but they've been local cooking staples since long before San Francisco was established. For millennia, indigenous Ohlone, Miwok, Wappo, Patwin and Yokut people communicated in 40 different languages around the Bay Area, sharing information about hunting and gathering spots, crop cultivation and food preparation – until colonization and introduced diseases devastated indigenous California. Today, Bay Area chefs honor indigenous Californian foodways with their sustainable practices and ingenious use of seasonal, local ingredients. If you don't see sourcing footnotes or mentions of sustainable, local, organic ingredients on the menu, ask – any SF restaurant should be proud to share where and how your food was sourced.

Before the gold rush, early arrivals to the Bay Area included Filipino sailors, French and Russian trappers, Spanish monks, Mexican ranchers, and Chilean and Peruvian farmers – each bringing food traditions you can taste today in creative San Franciscan fare. **Californios** (p94) brings deeply rooted flavors to exquisitely presented dishes, **Abacá** (p78) turns Filipino flavors all the way up in new Californian brunch hits, and acclaimed chef Dominique Crenn celebrates Californian coastal cuisine with French technique at **Atelier Crenn** (p69).

Over the 175 years since people from around the world rushed to San Francisco in the hopes of finding gold, a world of flavors have blended together on plates here – and when chefs strike the right

ESSENTIAL SF DESSERTS

CHOCOLATE

The gold rush brought on a sugar rush c 1852 at **Ghirardelli** (p75) – get the hot fudge sundae.

FORTUNE COOKIES

Invented for SF's Japanese Tea Garden – get yours hot off the press at **Golden Gate Fortune Cookies** (p120).

KOUIGN-AMANN

Pastry chef Belinda Leong introduced SF to its new favorite pastry at **b. patisserie** (p164), pronounced 'Queen Ahh-Man.'

CULT ICE CREAM

Original flavors made with organic local cream – notably the salted caramel at **Bi-Rite Creamery** (p178).

balance, they tap into a motherlode of flavor. Enjoy your own eureka moment as you taste global influences and California ingredients at Korean-inflected **Benu** (p96), Mediterranean flavors at **Dalida** (p69), Fillmore-psychedelic Thai at **Nari** (p157), and Chinese American diner fare at **Mamahuhu** (p235). For more on SF's elevated Asian cuisines, see p287.

Romantic Restaurants

Date night is definitely delicious in San Francisco, with the most Michelin-starred restaurants of any US city. But since this town also has the most restaurants per capita, how do you decide? Instead of starting with a cuisine or location – all cuisines get romantic and fancy here, and rideshare can get you anywhere in this small city – consider how much you want to spend, then check this guide to find intriguing restaurants in that price bracket, and finally, see where reservations are available.

Reservations are a must at popular San Francisco restaurants – the sooner you make them, the better options you'll have. Most restaurants have online reservations through their websites, **OpenTable** *(opentable.com)*, **Resy** *(resy.com)* or **Tock** *(exploretock.com)*. If the system shows no availability, call the restaurant directly – some seats may be held for early-evening walk-ins, and there may be last-minute cancellations or room at the bar. Landmark restaurants like **Chez Panisse** (p34) and small, celebrated SF bistros like **Benu** (p96), **Rich Table** (p218), **Boulevard**, **State Bird Provisions** (p157), **Four Kings** (p122) and **Frances** (p197) offer limited seating, so call a month ahead and take what's available.

If you don't have a reservation, your best bets for a walk-in table are restaurant-dense areas like Calle 24 or Valencia St (in the Mission), Japantown, Polk St (in Russian Hill), Clement St (in the Avenues), Hayes Valley, Chinatown or North Beach. Go early (5pm-ish) or eat late (after 9pm).

No matter where you go for SF date nights, expect service that's well-informed and friendly, never snooty. Mention any dietary limitations when reserving, and you should be cheerfully accommodated. Nice jeans are acceptable and personable interactions appreciated for good vibes all around.

BENJAMIN HEATH FOR LONELY PLANET

Golden Gate Fortune Cookies (p120)

SABRINA DALBESIO/LONELY PLANET

Elixir (p183)

BAR OPEN

No matter what you're having, SF cafes, bars and clubs will oblige, serving local roasts, California wines, Bay-distilled spirits and zero-proof aperitifs with pride.

Through 150 years of booms and busts, San Francisco never lost its thirst. San Francisco's swaggering saloons have survived earthquakes and brawls, fires and raids – and the city's cafes have admirably performed the daunting task of rousing everyone the morning after. Adventurous drinking is abetted by bartenders who continue gold-rush traditions with potent drinks in vintage glassware – and added mocktails to modern menus to make getting up tomorrow a bit easier, though espresso remains obligatory. Craft is a given: bartenders brew their own bitters, club DJs invent their own software, and baristas pour their hearts into foam-art hearts.

Signature Cocktails

When you recognize SF drink historians by their vintage barware and Old Tom gin selections, trust them to make you an SF signature – maybe a gold rush-era Pisco Punch, or Prohibition-era 'house cappuccino.' All that authenticity-tripping over cocktails may sound self-conscious – but after strong pours at SF's Western saloons, speakeasies, and tiki bars, consciousness is hardly an issue.

For spur-rattling Wild West cocktails, order a deceptively dainty Martinez at **Comstock Saloon** (p126) or a citrusy Lavender 75 at **Devil's Acre** (p131), a surefire cure for scurvy and/or sobriety. **Elixir** (p183) is the Mission's oldest saloon and SF's first certified green bar, delivering

Best SF Drinking Spots

TRICK DOG
For provocatively themed cocktails.

PLOUGH & STARS
For Guinness and bluegrass.

WILD SIDE WEST
For toasting the end of patriarchy.

LAST RITES
For party crashing.

a powerful Pisco Punch that tastes like trouble circa 1858. **Homestead** (p181) has supplied adult beverages since 1902 – during Prohibition, they served soda with hooch stashed in secret drawers – plus peanuts to offset potent seasonal gimlets.

Arrive before the jazz combo starts swinging at **Stookey's Club Moderne** (p146) to secure your Corpse Reviver and strike up conversation with a veiled femme fatale – regulars are real characters at this noir-novel bar. Look for the deliberately misleading 'Anti-Saloon League' sign to find **Bourbon & Branch** (p110), where you'll need a password to enter ('books'). Vintage neon points the way into the grotto doorway at 1937-vintage **Li Po** (p126), creator of the original Chinese mai tai, and host to poets and philosophers holding forth under the golden Buddha.

Pacific trade winds blow strong through happy hours at SF's trendsetting tiki hot spots **Last Rites** (p202), **Smuggler's Cove** and **Zombie Village** (p110) – but the **Tonga Room** (p148) still sets the standard, serving Hurricanes while hurricanes blow over the pool. Trade winds blow east–west at **Copra** (p157), where the decolonized bar mixes independent, small-batch Indian and Barbadian rums with Portland's Flora Green liqueur in the city's finest daiquiri. For fresh takes on spice-route cocktails, hit **Pacific Cocktail Haven** (p111) for coconut-washed, pandan-green Leeward Negronis.

Expand mocktail horizons at the Marina's Better Sunday (p69) and New Bar (p69).

Wine

To taste the good stuff, you don't need to commit to a bottle or escape to Wine Country – most restaurants and bars proudly serve local wine by the glass. Plan Napa/Sonoma getaways for fall, when you can taste new releases and score harvest specials.

North Beach is prime year-round for wine among new friends, thanks to delightful wine/cheese pairings at **Little Vine** (p135), raucous poetry/wine nights at **Golden Sardine** (p135), and blissful days of wine and song at **Belle Cora** (p135). At **Friend of a Friend** (p135), urban farmer/winemaker/co-owner Christopher Renfro pours rare finds from sustainable producers – plus his own SF wine, made from grapes grown under a SF freeway.

For dream food/wine pairings, join downtown crowds at **Verjus** (p98) and the Ferry Building's

SVETLANASF/SHUTTERSTOCK

Buena Vista Cafe (p79)

NEED TO KNOW

Smoking isn't legal indoors. Many Castro and Mission bars have smoking patios or backyards – including **El Rio** (p172), **Wild Side West** (p169) and **Zeitgeist** (p181). Otherwise, you'll be puffing on the sidewalk. Pot's legal in SF, but secondhand smoke is still unwelcome. Vaping is subject to mockery.

Downtown and SoMa bars draw happy-hour crowds from 4pm to 7pm; otherwise, bars are hopping by 9pm, with last call 10:30pm to 11:30pm weekdays and 1:30am weekends. Clubs kick in around 10pm and many close at 2am – check before you invest in cover.

Happy-hour specials run \$3 to \$6 for beer, \$7 to \$10 for well drinks, and \$10 to \$15 for specialty cocktails. With a \$1 to \$2 tip per drink, bartenders return the favor with heavy pours next round – that's why it's called getting tip-sy.

QBAR
For finding family among strangers.

SMUGGLER'S COVE
For thirsty pirates.

STOOKEY'S CLUB MODERNE
For swell dames and hep cats.

MARTUNI'S
For martinis and singalongs.

Juanita MORE!

EVENTS CALENDAR

Bay Area Reporter *(ebar.com)* Free LGBTQ+ community newspaper since 1971, with stellar event listings.

SF Station *(sfstation.com)* Besides neighborhood flyers and community notice boards, this is the best source for underground event listings.

Funcheap SF *(sf.funcheap.com)* Well-curated list of cheap or free events in and around SF.

Juanita MORE! *(juanitamore.com/events)* SF's Absolute Empress and drag hostess fundraises for the LGBTQ+ community with fab parties and public events.

Comfort and Joy *(cnj.world)* The Radical Faeries collective brings queer magic to New Years, Burning Man and other major SF holidays.

Hog Island Oyster Company (p101). In the Avenues, **Bettola** (p236) pairs top-value Italian wines with housemade lasagne, and **Palm City** (p230) serves natural wines with hoagies.

Top sommeliers pour in Dogpatch – **Ungrafted** (p187) offers inspired pairings with savory flatbreads, and **Dig** (p187) features deep cuts of wine, sake and vinyl. **Domaine SF** (p187) sells small-scale sustainable wine for picnics at Crane Cove Park – including nonalcoholic rosé you could actually drink all day.

To enjoy wine before/after Hayes Valley jazz, operas or symphonies, choose your own adventure: enter the garden at **Birba** (p219) for old- and new-world selections, duck into the well-curated wine speakeasy at **Hotel Biron** (p219), or hit **Millay** (p219) for sustainable staff picks – by female winemakers, biodynamic, zero-intervention wines – with Japanese snacks.

Beer

SF's first brewery (1849) was built before the city was, and beer has been a staple ever since – you'll find it on the menu everywhere, from top restaurants to leather bars. Drink in the great outdoors at **Zeitgeist** (p181), **Beach Chalet** (p234) and **Casements Bar** (p173). For queer cheers over beers, hit the legendary **Wild Side West** (p169), **The Eagle** (p94), **The Stud** (p94) and **Lone Star Saloon** (p94) – plus wherever else you feel so inspired here in the out-and-proud capital of the world, where even mostly straight Marina bars display rainbow and trans pride flags.

To toast San Francisco like a local, go with seasonal specials from SF's signature brewpubs: **21st Amendment Brewery**, **Fort Point** (p64), **Magnolia Brewery** and **Woods Outbound** (p230). If you're inspired to brew your own, check out meetups with local brewers at the **SF Brewers' Guild** *(sfbrewersguild.org)* or brewing classes at **WorkshopSF** (p210).

BEST DEEP DIVES

SPECS
For epic nights of tall tales.

ROYAL CUCKOO ORGAN LOUNGE
For low-key musical mayhem.

LI PO
For finding life's meaning in mai tais.

AUB ZAM ZAM
For crisp martinis with shaggy hippies.

Cafes

When SF couples break up, the thorniest issue is: who gets the cafe? San Franciscans are fiercely loyal – especially in the Mission, Hayes Valley and North Beach. When using free cafe wi-fi, remember: order something every hour, leave a tip, and don't leave laptops unattended. Phone calls are many baristas' pet peeve, but texting is fine. A drip coffee costs $3 to $5, and espresso drinks $4 to $7.

Some cafes are major neighborhood scenes – **Manny's** (p174) keeps a packed events calendar, **Caffe Trieste** (p133) throws accordion jams, and jazz combos practically live at **Cafe International** (p214). Other cafes attract coffee connoisseurs, including **Ritual Coffee Roasters** (p174), **Sightglass Coffee** (p95), **Andytown Coffee** (p230), **Equator Coffee** (p69), and **Blue Bottle Coffee**. For a caffeinated cultural experience, go for Yemeni coffee at **Finjan Qahwa** (p174), Turkish coffee at **Telve Coffee Shop** (p69), or farm-direct Costa Rican coffee at **Coffee Bodega** (p69).

Clubs

DJs set the tone at clubs in SF, where the right groove gets everyone on the dance floor – blending gay and straight in a giddy motion blur. Many clubs charge $10 to $30 (often cash) at the door, unless you show up before 10pm or join the club's online guest list. You'll usually only wait 15 minutes to get in anywhere, unless you're stumbling drunk. Last call at many clubs is around 10:30 weeknights and 1:30am weekends; many close around 2am, though **EndUp** (p96) rages until dawn on weekends.

Here's the lowdown on hot spots: Mission clubs include **Bottom of the Hill** (p190) for punks, **Jolene's** (p169) for lesbians, and **El Rio** (p172) for everybody; SoMa features retro nights at **Cat Club** (p96), leather daddies at **The Stud** (p94), and drag-star DJs at **Oasis** (p94); the Castro offers **QBar** (p201) for company, **440 Castro** (p199) for hookups, and **Cafe du Nord** (p201) for singer-songwriters; and the Haight means Prince/Michael dance-offs at **Madrone Art Bar** (p217) and roller boogie at **Church of 8 Wheels** (p218).

PAUL CHINN/THE SAN FRANCISCO CHRONICLE VIA GETTY IMAGES

Casements (p173)

FROM LEFT: AGWILSON/SHUTTERSTOCK, LET GO MEDIA/SHUTTERSTOCK

Performers, Great American Music Hall (p114)

SHOWTIME

Spend a night on the edge of your seat at a history-making SF venue.

SF ranks among the top five US cities for the number of creative types per square mile – and when they hit the stage, look out. SF's soundtrack isn't a playlist or a podcast – San Franciscans still prefer live music and performance in legendary venues, and that support attracts major global talent. Though SF has world-class opera, orchestra, jazz, sports and theater, the scene isn't all about marquee names or sit-down shows: here you can see cutting-edge music, drag, comedy and film-festival premieres in historic hotspots for the price of a movie. SF has specialized in deliciously subversive, unpredictable and uncensored entertainment since the 1930s – and you're right on time to catch SF's next wave of fearless talent. Brace for impact at underground punk, drag, comedy and jazz shows, now staging roaring comebacks in restored venues in North Beach, Chinatown, Mission and Downtown. Check KQED's **The Do List** *(kqed.org/arts/program/the-do-list)* for an excellent selection of upcoming performing-arts events.

Opera & Classical

Since the gold rush, San Francisco has gone wild for opera divas – and vice versa. When the city was leveled by the 1906 Great Quake, divas from around the world rushed to SF at their own risk to perform for free in ruined streets, bringing the city back to its feet. The city raised funds to rebuild City Hall by promising San Franciscans an opera house alongside it – today, **SF Opera** (p111) rivals New York's Metropolitan for scale and ambition, launching original works at **War Memorial Opera House**

Best Venues

SFJAZZ CENTER Top global talents reinvent standards and improvise live.

FILLMORE AUDITORIUM Rock-legendary since the '60s, with psychedelic posters to prove it.

SAN FRANCISCO OPERA World-class divas bring down the house at global premieres.

GREAT AMERICAN MUSIC HALL Marquee acts in a baroque former bordello.

(p112). During its September-to-June season, SF Opera offers affordable opera tickets starting from $28. Between seasons, SF Opera gives free shows at **Stern Grove Festival** (p232) and at Opera Out of the Box events, and throws **Pride** (p94) shows, Opera balls and Adler Fellows young artists showcases.

The multi-Grammy Award–winning **San Francisco Symphony** (p110) performs in **Davies Symphony Hall**, which looks like a cruise ship but sounds like a dream, no matter where you're sitting in seats that encircle the stage. Terrace seats behind the stage go for a song (from $25), for up-close views of musicians facing the conductor. **San Francisco Performances** *(sfperformances.org)* hosts world-class classical performances at **Herbst Theater** (p113), and **Noontime Concerts** *(noontimeconcerts.org)* offers free musical lunch breaks around SF; check **SF Classical Voice** *(sfcv.org)* for classical and choral performances.

Headliners & Indie Acts

Ever since **Fillmore Auditorium** (p157) launched 1960s psychedelic rock, SF has attracted big names. Global headliners play major venues here, including the Fillmore, **Masonic Auditorium**, **Bill Graham Civic Auditorium** (p114) and **Warfield** (p114). But marquee names also play SF's smaller historic venues, including **Regency Ballroom**, **August Hall** (p114), **Boom Boom Room** (p156) and **Great American Music Hall** (p114).

Outside Lands (p225) is Coachella's cool cousin, with three days of headliners and partying in **Golden Gate Park** (p224). California's roots music shares center stage with stars across genres at SF's free **Hardly Strictly Bluegrass** (p225) festival, and the free **Stern Grove Festival** (p232) features greats from funk to pop. For dance music, check out the **Portola Festival** *(portolamusicfestival.com)* and lineups at the **Midway** (p188).

Eclectic SF clubs like the **Independent** (p157) and **Chapel** (p174) host hip-hop, alt-pop, and singer-songwriters. Meanwhile, punk's not dead at **Bottom of the Hill** (p190), **Mabuhay Gardens** (p127) and **The Knockout** (p191).

Jazz

Global jazz talents are in residence year-round at **SFJAZZ Center** (p220), America's largest jazz center, featuring brilliant sound, clear stage views, appreciative audiences and potent cocktails. For a century, jazz greats made music history with shows performed and recorded in North Beach, Tenderloin, Japantown and the Fillmore – now you get to see what's next at SF jazz clubs **Keys Jazz Bistro** (p127), **Black Cat** (p114), **Stookey's Club Moderne** (p146), **Dawn Club** (p114), **Sheba Piano Lounge** (p156), **Scopo Divino** (p156) and **Mr Tipple's Recording Studio** (p114).

Theater & Performance

Broadway-bound shows and musicals do test runs in San Francisco – catch them here first at historic **Orpheum** (p113), **Golden Gate** (p113) and **Curran** (p113) theaters. **American Conservatory Theater** (p113) stages

Orpheum (p113)

OASIS
Drag so outrageous, you'll laugh until you cough up glitter.

AMERICAN CONSERVATORY THEATER
Breakthrough original shows, plus experimental works at Strand Theater.

CHAN NATIONAL QUEER ARTS CENTER
Often eclectic, always electric, from Gay Mens Chorus to punk drag.

SAN FRANCISCO SYMPHONY
Sets the tempo for modern classical music.

world premieres of original works by major playwrights – before winning Tonys and a Pulitzer, *Angels in America* got its wings here. **Magic Theatre** (p65) launches original works by artists in residence, and **Brava Theater** (p173) showcases new works by women and queer playwrights. If you prefer summer theater free and outdoors, you're in luck: **San Francisco Mime Troupe** (p168) stages free musical-comedy satire in Dolores Park, while the **SF Shakespeare Festival** performs gratis across from the **Ferry Building** (p100) in Sue Bierman Park.

Drag

To keep SF drag fresh after 175 years of shows – through police raids, world wars and pandemics – SF drag queens put in the werk. Lines wrap around the block to see drag stars perform, especially **Oasis** (p94), **Beaux** (p204), and soon the restored **Castro Theatre** (p196). **Chan National Queer Arts Center** (p173) is home to San Francisco Gay Men's Chorus, and hosts drag extravaganzas like Peaches Christ's iconic Punk Pride. Any Mission, Castro, Tenderloin or SoMa bar worth its zip code has at least occasional drag shows – shambolic, wildly unprofessional, wholly unpredictable art drag is a beloved SF anti-institution. For regularly irregular SF drag, check calendars at **Aunt Charlie's** (p286) and **The Stud** (p94).

Comedy & Spoken Word

Comedian Lenny Bruce famously got arrested for his SF stand-up act in 1961, but was acquitted – and comedians keep SF entertained with fresh, risky new material. To see comedy legends test new material for their next HBO specials and catch rising star comics, head to **Cobb's Comedy Club** (p132) and the **Punch Line** (p114). Feeling brave? Join **BATS Improv** (p65) comedy workshops and hit open-mic nights in North Beach, the Haight and the Mission.

SF keeps the laughs coming with uproarious drag comedy cabaret at **Oasis** (p94), poignantly funny **Marsh** (p173) monologues, and comedy showcases at **Brava Theater** (p173). For uproariously true SF stories, check out annual **Litquake** (p174), **San Francisco Main Library** (p115) events and raucous **Booksmith** (p214) readings.

Dance

SF supports the longest-running US ballet company, **San Francisco Ballet** (p112), and multiple independent troupes

DIEGO GRANDI/SHUTTERSTOCK

Castro Theatre (p196)

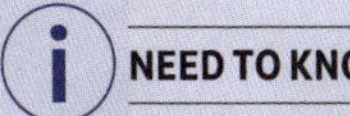

NEED TO KNOW

Listings & Costs
Theatre Bay Area *(theatrebayarea.org)* lists shows for 100-plus theater companies. **SHN** *(shnsf.com)* lists SF Broadway shows. Major shows run $35 to $150; try for bargain same-day tickets. Indie theater tickets cost $10 to $50.

Buying Tickets
Book sports tickets through team websites. Concert and sports tickets may also be available through **SeatGeek** *(seatgeek.com)* or **Ticketmaster** *(ticketmaster.com)*.

Sold-Out Shows & Events
For sold-out shows and sports events, search **Stubhub** *(stubhub.com)* or the 'Tickets' category on **Craigslist** *(craigslist.org)*.

ENTERTAINMENT BY NEIGHBOURHOOD	
The Presidio, Marina & Fisherman's Wharf	Independent theater and cinema.
Downtown, Civic Center & SoMa	Symphony, opera, theater, drag, jazz, ballet, pop and comedy.
Chinatown & North Beach	Comedy, punk, jazz, Cantonese opera and spoken word.
Japantown, the Fillmore & Pacific Heights	Marquee bands, jazz, hip-hop, singer-songwriters and taiko drumming.
The Mission, Dogpatch & Potrero Hill	Indie cinema, punk, dance, folk, theater, EDM and spoken word.
The Castro	Comedy, drag and queer premieres.
The Haight & Hayes Valley	Jazz, indie bands and street musicians.
Golden Gate Park & the Avenues	Festivals and free concerts.

at **Yerba Buena Center for the Arts** (p88), including **Alonzo King Lines Ballet** (p88). Experimental styles are championed at **Oberlin Dance Collective** (ODC; p173) and you can pick up some new moves at their ODC Dance Commons. **Dancers' Group** *(dancersgroup.org)* keeps a comprehensive dance calendar.

Spectator Sports

Sports fans, you're in luck: you've got 81 chances each year to see the SF Giants play baseball on their home turf at **Oracle Park** (p97), aka **Giants Stadium**, and you can watch the Golden State Warriors play NBA basketball at state-of-the-art **Chase Center** (p186). American football fans aren't quite so lucky: to catch the San Francisco 49ers in action, drive an hour south to Santa Clara's Levi's Stadium. The *San Francisco Chronicle (sfgate.com)* provides complete sports coverage.

Film

Cinemaniacs adore SF's vintage deco movie palaces, including the **Roxie** (p175), **Balboa** (p235) and **Presidio** (p69) cinemas. For major releases and cult classics with drinks and dinner, head to **Alamo Drafthouse** (p178). Beyond the **SF International Film Festival** *(sffilm.org)*, the city hosts LGBTQ+ **Frameline Fest** *(frameline.org)*, **Asian American** *(caamedia.org)*, **Jewish** *(jfi.org)* and **Arab** *(arabfilminstitute.or)* film festivals. For new, not-yet-distributed indie films year-round, check calendars at the **Roxie** (p175), **Four Star** (p235) and **Artists' Television Access** (p175). Most tickets cost $12 to $18.

FROM LEFT: JEJIM/SHUTTERSTOCK, WALTER CICCHETTI/SHUTTERSTOCK

Piedmont Boutique (p217)

SHOP

Of course you'll want something to remember your time here – and when admirers ask where you got such a fabulous item, you get to say, 'I found it in San Francisco...' Major flex.

All San Francisco's tricked-out dens, fabulous ensembles and well-stocked spice racks don't just pull themselves together – San Franciscans scour the city for them. Eclectic originality is SF's signature style, and local designers and vintage shops provide options galore along SF's most boutique-studded streets: Haight, Divisadero, Valencia, Hayes, Grant, Fillmore, Clement, Chestnut and Polk. San Francisco treasure hunts come with unique perks: while shopping you can watch fish theater, pick up home-design hacks, and trade fashion tips with drag icons. What you won't find here are standard downtown shopping malls, with chain stores and megastore anchor tenants. San Francisco has long been a hub for e-commerce – Instacart, Square, Shopify and DoorDash were all founded here – so unless retailers offer a unique experience or host local events, San Franciscans tend to order online or shop their neighborhood stores. But watch this space: with 47 city-sponsored retail pop-ups opening downtown, small businesses are staging a comeback, and reinventing brick-and-mortar shopping experiences.

Local Makers & Designers

San Francisco designer flagships and studio-showrooms give you a glimpse inside some of SF's most creative minds.

Best Only-in-SF Scores

NOOWORKS
Those trippy 'wormiverse' pattern coveralls are meant for SF stage-diving.

CREATIVITY EXPLORED
Rep SF with SF artist Laron Bickerstaff's SFMOMA sign-language tees.

CASE FOR MAKING
Watercolor palettes handmade in SF to capture Ocean Beach sunsets.

OPEN EDITIONS
Dodge torpedoes in SF artist Stephanie Syjuco's battleship-dazzle-pattern hoodies.

Nooworks (p182) is a colorful explosion of local-artist-designed prints in garments of all shapes and sizes, and the **Zuri** (p157) collective dazzles with limited-edition tunics printed with chickens, pretzels, fireworks – all ethically and sustainably made in Kenya. **Mollusk** (p230) is a surf shop, gallery, bookstore and surfboard-maker studio all in one, while **Piedmont** (p217) is one-stop shopping for drag, whether you're making your debut as a mermaid or a sailor.

Curated showcases of local artists and designers combine two favorite local pastimes: gallery-hopping and indie-boutique shopping. For inspired choices, don't miss **On Waverly** (p122) for risograph prints, iron-on patches and plushies by SF designers; **Park Life** (p237) for hand-painted books and Aesthetics team tees; **In the Black** (p159) for Black Excellence candles and guitar purses by Black designers; **Queer Arts Featured** (p200) for LGBTQ+ art and tarot decks; **Open Editions** (p182) for hoodies, bandanas and blankets by SF artists; and Exit Store at **Catharine Clark Gallery** (p189) for coffee-table books, statement jewelry and limited-edition works by major SF art stars.

Mix shopping with sightseeing at SF museums that proudly feature local designers: the **de Young Museum** (p224) hosts maker showcases, the **Museum of Craft & Design** (p186) store includes locally handmade ceramics and textiles, and the **SFMOMA** (p86) store features jewelry by local designers plus limited-edition merch designed by Bay Area artists.

To see what local makers have been dreaming up lately, don't miss **West Coast Craft** *(p67; westcoastcraft.com; mid-June and mid-November)* and **Art Market San Francisco** *(artmarketsf.com; last weekend in April)*, and biannual **Renegade Craft Fair** *(p67; renegadecraft.com)*, all held at **Fort Mason Center** (p65). To catch rising-star designers and makers between fairs, check out upcoming pop-ups through SF's **Vacant to Vibrant** *(vibrantsf.org/all-popups)* residency program.

Eclectic Decor

If you need a change of scenery, you've come to the right place – no other city looks quite like SF, and and you can take that look home with you. Downhill from the Painted Ladies of **Alamo Sq** (p162), Victorian-lined Divisadero delivers design inspiration at **Rare Device** (p165) with handcrafted ceramics and local art, and handmade housewares with lush textures from **Perish Trust** (p165), from terra-cotta candelabras to wind-sculpted driftwood brooms. For that signature piece that ties the whole room together, **ATYS** (p70) offers options – from fiber art woven in SF to clocks made of moss. To recreate mellow Mission days back home, **Gravel & Gold** (p183) provides hand-printed pillows, beach-shack design books, and hanging lounge chairs.

But what to put on the walls? Poster art has been SF's signature since the '60s, and you can still find original psychedelic Fillmore posters at **San Francisco Rock Posters** (p135) – or get new ones hot off the press at **Haight Street Art Center** (p217). For affordable works by rising artists, head to

Heath Ceramics (p101)

CITY LIGHTS BOOKS
Browse SF Poet Laureates in the designated Poet's Chair.

HEATH CERAMICS
Your favorite SF restaurant's plates were probably made here.

ATYS
Knives with handles made from repurposed Golden Gate Bridge steel.

826 VALENCIA
Fill blowfish tote bags with freshly published writing.

bookstore back-room galleries at **Adobe Books** (p174) and **Medicine for Nightmares** (p175).

For outdoor inspiration, head to **San Francisco Botanical Garden** (p225) – then at the on-site store, pick up gardening guides, botanically themed prints, tea towels, seeds and gardening supplies galore. Garden parties practically plan themselves at **Cliff's Variety** (p203), with all-weather disco balls, programmable LED light displays, and streamers and tiaras for every occasion.

Vintage Scores

Choose your decade: in SF, you can rock that look, seek out that soundtrack, and change up your decor accordingly. You never need an excuse to rock vintage here, but vintage-fabulous fits right in at **Pride** (p94), SF street fairs, and festivals like **Outside Lands** (p225) and **Hardly Strictly Bluegrass** (p225). Your first stop is the Haight to find your era at **Decades of Fashion** (p211), maxis and mod looks at **Fuzz & Sway** (p212), and western wear and rocker style at **Held Over** (p211).

For rare finds at reasonable prices, head to **Love Street Vintage** (p237) for psychedelic aloha shirts and hippie heirloom silver jewelry, or **Crossroads** (p157) on Fillmore for current designer finds for a steal (check the back racks). **Vacation** (p134) has prime finds from every decade, ready to rock onstage – from glitter platforms and dead-stock denim to punk concert tees.

You'll find the soundtrack for that look at **101 Music** (p135), though it may take some digging through crates of vinyl and cassettes. **Thrillhouse Records** (p191) is nonprofit and volunteer-run, which is why you're about to score a deal on rare live albums by jazz greats and Japanese-issued punk EPs. If you can't find the album you're looking for anywhere, it's probably waiting for you at **Amoeba** (p212).

Change your decor to match your new/old sound and look at **Community Thrift** (p183), where you can load up on stoneware mugs and paintings of SF circa 1973 – proceeds benefit Bay Area nonprofits. Nostalgia comes naturally at **Landline** (p183), where bar carts are perfectly stocked

SEYHAN AHEN/SHUTTERSTOCK

Amoeba Music (p212)

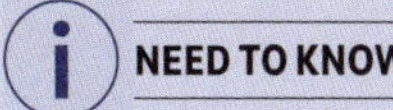

NEED TO KNOW

Sales Tax
Combined SF city and California state sales taxes tack 8.625% onto the price of your purchase. This tax is not refundable.

Opening Hours
Most stores are open daily from 11am to 5pm or 6pm, though some stay open later on weekends. Stores in the Mission and Haight tend to open later and keep erratic hours – call ahead.

Returns & Gift Certificates
Try before you buy and ask about returns – many stores offer returns for store credit only. When in doubt, consider a gift certificate; in California, they never expire, and you can often use them online.

SHOPPING BY NEIGHBOURHOOD

The Presidio, Marina & Fisherman's Wharf	Gear, gifts, clothing, wine and design in the Marina.
Downtown, Civic Center & SoMa	Museum shops, global brands and Apple's flagship store.
Nob Hill & Russian Hill	Vintage and indie boutiques in Russian Hill's Polk Gulch.
Japantown, Fillmore & Pacific Heights	Home design, stationery, toys, accessories and anime in Japantown; haute resale, designers and decor in Pacific Heights.
The Mission, Dogpatch & Potrero	Local makers, bookstores, indie art galleries, artisan foods, dandy style and vintage galore.
The Castro	Decor, fashion and queer pride accessories.
The Haight & Hayes Valley	Design boutiques, decor and gourmet treats in Hayes Valley; vintage, music and skate gear in the Haight.

for Rat Pack visits and shelves of novelty bakeware feed layer-cake ambitions.

For the Person Who Has Everything

You're in luck: unique is what San Francisco does best, and the hunt is its own adventure. Stop by **826 Valencia** (p175) for pirate supplies, and duck behind the velvet curtain to watch ichthyoid antics in the Fish Theater. Pop into the **Exploratorium** (p72) for a tumble through the Tactile Dome, and pick up a pocket microscope, portable luminescence lab, and build-your-own dinosaur kits to bring experiments home.

San Francisco is full of novel ideas – just check out the signed graphic novels at **Isotope** (p220), the Gender-Funky Sci-Fi section at **Fabulosa Books** (p197), censored novels at **Bound Together Anarchist Book Collective** (p214), and 'I've Been Killing Slimes for 300 Years and Maxed Out' and other multilingual manga at **Kinokuniya Books** (p158).

For something new to do, browse the game library at **Gamescape** (p220), find SF-designed decks at **Mission Skateboards** (p181), or pick up a 9ft paper dragon from **Chinatown Kite Shop** (p121). The Pacific Ocean probably won't fit in your suitcase, but surf tees from **Aqua Surf Shop** (p230) will, and **Foggy Notion** (p236) supplies Pacific salt scrubs and un-washing powder for Ocean Beachy hair. If you're fresh out of ideas, leave the gifting to the pros at **Nikoniko Gifts** (p70), where thoughtfully wrapped mystery gifts deliver the element of surprise.

SAN FRANCISCO

THE GUIDE

Chapters in this section are organised by neighborhood. Neighborhoods are delineated by a specific local character or identity, where you'll find unique specific experiences, local insights, insider tips and expert recommendations.

Saints Peter and Paul Church and Russian Hill (p140)
TUPUNGATO/SHUTTERSTOCK

NEIGHBORHOODS AT A GLANCE

Find the neighborhoods that tick all your boxes.

The Presidio, Marina & Fisherman's Wharf (p54)

Along SF's northern waterfront, army outposts become public parks, boutiques replace cow pastures, and sea lions bump aside yachts.

Japantown, Fillmore & Pacific Heights (p152)

Making history, music and dinner for over a century, with the Victorians, psychedelic posters and acclaimed restaurants to prove it.

The Haight & Hayes Valley (p206)

Hippie idealism lives in Haight's psychedelic murals and bookshops, while off-duty jazz legends and Zen monks drift down Hayes sidewalks.

Golden Gate Park & the Avenues (p222)

Surfers and gourmet adventurers meet in foggy avenues around Golden Gate Park for priceless art, cult-classic cinema and memorable meals.

Golden Gate Bridge
The Presidio
Presidio Pkwy
California St
Point Lobos Ave
Geary Blvd
25th Ave
Balboa St
Park Presidio Blvd
Turk Blvd
Fulton St
de Young Museum
California Academy of Sciences
Stanyan St
Ocean Beach
Golden Gate Park
Lincoln Way
Great Hwy
Sunset Blvd
Noriega St
Noriega St
19th Ave
Fanning Way
Woodside Ave
Dewey Blvd
Taraval St
Portola Dr
Vicente St
0 2 km
0 1 miles

Nob Hill & Russian Hill (p140)

Cloud nine can't compare to these hills, where cable cars climb to scenic parks and iconic lounges.

Chinatown & North Beach (p116)

Noodles, poetry and art by day – legendary jazz, comedy, punk, and Cantonese and Italian opera at night.

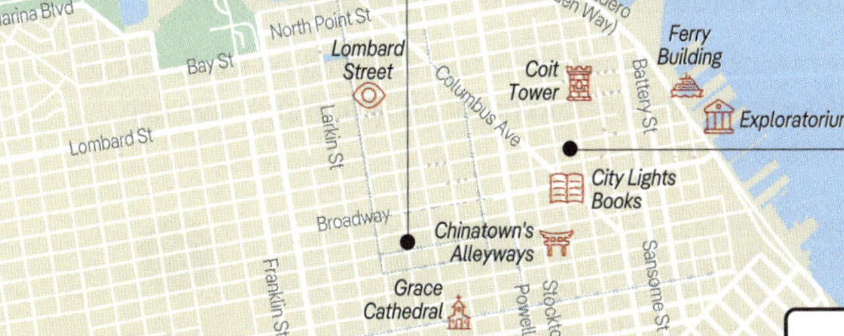

Downtown, Civic Center & SoMa (p82)

Luring crowds with dazzling museum shows, killer cocktails, fabulous food and kinky clubs.

The Castro (p192)

Head over rainbow crosswalks into the world's premier gayborhood, where the community meets to make history, make out, or both.

The Mission, Dogpatch & Potrero (p166)

Chill at Mission bookstores and bars, find inspiration by Dogpatch docks, and crash Potrero art openings and punk shows.

Researched by
Alison Bing

THE PRESIDIO, MARINA & FISHERMAN'S WHARF

BEYOND THE ICONIC BRIDGE, EXPECT THE UNEXPECTED

Make a grand entrance to San Francisco through the Golden Gate Bridge and follow the waterfront to nature hikes, immersive art, scientific marvels and more.

For centuries, Golden Gate Strait was the main entrance to San Francisco – note the shipwrecks dotting its shores. Luckily, the Golden Gate Bridge now offers easier entry, and spectacular views besides. Enter the Presidio military base that's now a coastal preserve to spot only-in-SF sights: rare shorebirds on a former airstrip, priceless sculptures hidden in the woods, and goosebumps galore on the clothing-optional end of blustery Baker Beach. To the west, the Marina has deco arthouse cinemas alongside sports bars, chic boutiques in a former cow pasture, and a waterfront fort overflowing with art. At Fisherman's Wharf, you'll meet lazy sea lions, legendary cartoonists, pinball wizards, scientific geniuses, and oh yes, salty sailors.

INCLUDES

FROM LEFT: LEONID ANDRONOV/SHUTTERSTOCK, BENJAMIN HEATH FOR LONELY PLANET.

Above: Crissy Field (p59); Right: Pier 39 (p71)

See page 259 for places to stay in The Presidio, Marina & Fisherman's Wharf.

0 — 2 km
0 — 1 miles
San Francisco Bay
1 Golden Gate Bridge
2 Crissy Field
3 Exploratorium
4 Walk the Wharf
5 Tunnel Tops Park
FISHERMAN'S WHARF
THE MARINA
RUSSIAN HILL
PRESIDIO
COW HOLLOW
Mountain Lake Park
Strawberry Hill
101
1
Marina Blvd
Presidio Pkwy
Lincoln Blvd
Bay St
Lombard St
North Point St
Columbus Ave
The Embarcadero
Broadway
Sansome St
Powell St
Franklin St
Presidio Ave
California St
Pine St
Market St
1st St
2nd St
3rd St
Bush St
Geary Blvd
Gough St
Van Ness Ave
Geary St
Turk St
Mission St
Howard St
Folsom St
6th St
James Lick Skwy
4th St
5th St
Park Presidio Blvd
Golden Gate Ave
8th St
9th St
10th St
Balboa St
Fell St
Fulton St
Divisadero St
Masonic Ave
Oak St
Central Fwy

Highlights

❶ Golden Gate Bridge

Pose for photos at SF's iconic landmark, while mists swirl overhead and sailboats drift underfoot. **p56**

❷ Crissy Field

At this airstrip turned wildlife sanctuary the preferred pastimes are kite-flying, birdwatching and lollygagging. **p59**

❸ Exploratorium

Make your own discoveries with fascinating immersive exhibits, including the trippy Tactile Dome – plus mad-scientist cocktails. **p72**

❹ Walk the Wharf

Hang out with sea lions, sailors, superheroes and Space Invaders along SF's wildest waterfront. **p76**

❺ Tunnel Tops Park

Enjoy leisurely park picnics with panoramic views of Golden Gate Bridge, while commuter traffic zooms underground. **p57**

Getting Around

Bus

MUNI buses connect the Wharf, Marina and Presidio with points beyond, Golden Gate Transit crosses the bridge, and Presidio GO shuttles cover Presidio parks.

Walking

The best way to see Fisherman's Wharf and Presidio nature trails is at your own pace, with frequent stops for entertainment and photos.

Bicycle

Cover the waterfront on rental bikes with pickups at the Presidio and/or Wharf – but book ahead on weekends.

JON BILOUS/SHUTTERSTOCK

TOP EXPERIENCE

Golden Gate Bridge

No other bridge puts on a show like this. Morning mists lift to reveal the Golden Gate Bridge, glowing orange-red against blue skies. Stick around for the late-afternoon grand finale, when fog tumbles acrobatically over the bridge. As commuter traffic disappears into the fog, look up: you'll spot deco towers floating above the clouds. Magic.

DON'T MISS

- Foggy afternoon disappearing acts
- Bridge-view Presidio picnics
- Welcome Center displays
- Crossing the span
- Batteries to Bluffs Trail
- Fort Point rooftop views

Iconic Design

It's hard to picture San Francisco without its iconic art deco suspension bridge, but the US War Department almost nixed this design. To ensure safe passage for ships from the Pacific Ocean into the San Francisco Bay, the navy wanted a chunky concrete bridge painted black with caution-yellow stripes.

Local architects Gertude Comfort Morrow and Irving Morrow realized that ships may pass in the night, but San Franciscans would have to live with the bridge every day. Working with engineer Joseph B Strauss, the Morrows submitted a counterproposal to harmonize with the natural environment: a sleek suspension bridge painted a signature shade called

PRACTICALITIES

● goldengate.org ● vehicle toll northbound free, southbound $9.50
● Welcome Center: 9am-6pm

International Orange. Even though the War Department owned the land on either side, the City of San Francisco gave their ingenious orange art deco bridge design the green light.

Death-Defying Feats

Before the War Department could insist on an eyesore, laborers dove into treacherous riptides to sink bridge foundations in 1933. They faced tight city deadlines, and many skeptics besides. Could anyone actually build a bridge across the treacherous Golden Gate Strait, where shipwrecks dot the shores? Builders braved powerful ocean currents and blustery winds, and despite standard-setting safety measures – including mandatory hard hats and reinforced safety nets that saved the lives of 19 workers who fell from bridge scaffolding – 11 builders lost their lives during construction. Today a plaque at the bridge's southern entrance honors their courage and extraordinary achievement: a soaring suspension bridge stretching 1.7 miles across the bay.

Stop by the **Golden Gate Bridge Welcome Center** to witness precarious construction work in progress, captured in jawdropping vintage photos – riveters balance atop swaying cables 80 stories high, while divers plummet 110ft underwater with only a rubber hose for air. Take a moment to admire the bridge's signature color, still touched up by a daredevil crew of 34 painters suspended from 764ft suspension towers.

Unbelievable Bridge Views

Sunny days are best to get the full effect, as red-orange towers pierce blue skies above the sparkling waters of the Golden Gate. To make the most of SF's rare hot days, pack a picnic and head to the beach at **Crissy Field** (p59) or **Baker Beach** (p59) for spectacular bridge views. Panoramic Golden Gate Bridge views that were once interrupted by traffic are now revealed at the new **Tunnel Tops Park**, with strategically placed benches that look like driftwood carved from fallen cypress trees.

For an adventurous approach, hike the **Batteries to Bluffs Trail** (p59) above Baker Beach to the **Golden Gate Overlook**, pausing along the uphill climb for breathtaking ocean-to-bay views at the **Pacific Overlook**. Or head to the roof of **Fort Point** (p60) for positively riveting close-up views of the iron bolts and trusses holding up the Golden Gate Bridge. Listen to bridge traffic thumping overhead: that's SF's heartbeat. Don't get discouraged by bad weather – the bridge saves its most dramatic looks for cloudy days, when mist swirls around the deco towers. Fog aficionados don raincoats to watch the marine layer roll past Marin's **Vista Point**, on the bridge's northern end. Or you can stay dry and watch acrobatic fog feats over fair-trade coffee at the **Round House Café**, the circular art deco diner built by Golden Gate Bridge ironwork engineer Alfred Finnila in 1938.

SCENE-STEALING CAMEOS

Cinema buffs know Hitchcock was right: seen from below at Fort Point, the bridge induces a thrilling case of *Vertigo*. Trekkies will be relieved that despite alien attacks by Klingons and Breen on *Star Trek*, the bridge remains remarkably intact. Superman and James Bond may survive bridge high-wire acts, but can the bridge survive Godzilla, Sharknados and an entire *Planet of the Apes*? Tune in to find out.

TOP TIPS

- Even when sun shines on SF, it's probably damp and chilly on the bridge. Wear a water-resistant outer layer.
- If you get cold or tired walking across the bridge, catch any Golden Gate Transit bus back from the northern toll plaza.
- Cycling is faster than walking, though bike traffic gets hectic on weekends. The nearest bike rentals are in the Presidio at Sports Basement or Lyft bikeshare docks. Bicycles and e-bikes are allowed on bridge sidewalks, but not skateboards, electric scooters or skates.
- Volunteer City Guides lead free bridge tours ($20 donation suggested) most Sundays and Thursdays at 11am, departing from outside the Welcome Center.

FRANKIE WO/SHUTTERSTOCK

Walking trail, the Presidio

TOP EXPERIENCE

The Presidio

Spies, Yoda, Andy Goldsworthy sculptures, Walt Disney drawings: SF's best-kept secrets are revealed along Presidio hiking paths. After two centuries of preparing for invasions that never arrived on these shores, this retired military base is now a panoramic public park packed with attractions – including sweeping Golden Gate Bridge views previously only seen by top brass and passing commuters.

DON'T MISS

- Tunnel Tops Park
- Crissy Field
- Fort Point
- Baker Beach
- Andy Goldworthy's *Spire*
- Batteries to Bluffs Trail
- Military Intelligence Service Historic Learning Center

Back to Nature

'Presidio' means fort in Spanish – but in San Francisco, it's a playground. What started in 1776 as a Spanish military post built by conscripted Ohlone people officially retired from military duty in 1996, when President Clinton signed the Omnibus Parks Act. To the obvious delight of shorebirds, puppies and people, the **Presidio of San Francisco** is now a national park.

After decades of painstaking habitat restoration, nature is fully in command in this rare urban park where wildlife outnumbers people. More than 900 native plant species now thrive across nearly 1500 acres of woodlands, dunes and wetlands – attracting more than 300 bird species, 100 butterfly species, sundry

PRACTICALITIES

● presidio.gov ● free park entry ● Visitor Center: 10am-5pm

MARIO LINGE/SHUTTERSTOCK

Baker Beach

turtles, salamanders and lizards (but no venomous snakes), and the occasional shy coyote. To allow wildlife to thrive in the park, commuter traffic was rerouted underground – revealing glorious views clear across the bay. The **Tunnel Tops Park** instantly became the prime Presidio picnic spot, with driftwood-shaped benches and tables offering sweeping views of the Golden Gate Bridge.

On rare hot days, race the crowds to **Baker Beach**, the sandy Presidio cove with spectacular views of the Golden Gate framed by wind-sculpted pines – plus nude sunbathing behind the rocks on the clothing-optional, gay-friendly, no-photography-allowed north end. Picnickers and sand-castle architects stick to the sandy south end, nearer parking. Yes, the currents are strong and water is c-c-cold – but there's no better place to get back to nature in the city.

GOLDSWORTHY'S NATURAL WONDERS

Above Inspiration Point, you'll spot an unusual formation that seems entirely natural, yet artful: you found ***Spire***, a contemporary sculpture Andy Goldsworthy created from 37 reclaimed Presidio cypress trunks. *Spire* was intended to disintegrate over time, but when it was damaged by fire, San Franciscans volunteered to restore and reinforce it. For more Goldsworthy, follow Lover's Lane Trail past his zigzagging ***Wood Line***, and duck into the Presidio Officer's Club to view his ***Earth Wall***.

Happy Trails

Hiking adventures begin at the informative **Presidio Visitors Center**, where you can get your bearings and pick up trail maps. For a moderately challenging and truly inspiring hike, follow the Ecology Trail through redwood groves and spring wildflower meadows to **Inspiration Point** for bird's-eye views across the Bay, then push onward to reach the Presidio's artistic pinnacle: Andy Goldsworthy's *Spire*, made from reclaimed cypress trees. Adventurous hikers take on the **Batteries to Bluffs Trail**, heading uphill above **Baker Beach** (p59) to splendid **Golden Gate Bridge** (p56) vistas.

Or just follow the lead of San Franciscan regulars to **Crissy Field**, and stroll, jog, bike, skate or roll along scenic, flat, wheelchair-accessible paths. The strip where military planes once zoomed in for landings is now a reclaimed tidal marsh, where bird-watchers perch on strategically positioned benches.

SHOTS NOT FIRED

Over two centuries, the Presidio stood armed and ready for invasions that never arrived on its shores. Control of this military outpost passed from Spain to Mexico to the US without a single battle on these grounds. Fort Point mounted 102 cannons to fight the US Civil War, but Confederate ships never made it this far. Battery Bluff guns weren't fired in WWI, the Presidio's Western Defense Command wasn't bombed during WWII, and Cold War Nike nuclear missile operations in Battery Caulfield were quietly suspended in 1974. When San Franciscans throw peace signs, we really mean it.

Further along the coastal path, puppies chase kite-fliers across a grassy lawn and windsurfers skim bay waters along **East Beach**. Pick up the **Bay Trail** to reach **Fort Point** (p60) and head over the Golden Gate Bridge, or stop at certified-green cafe **Warming Hut** to browse California field guides and warm up with fair-trade coffee.

Drama at Fort Point

Wander Presidio woodlands and beaches, and you'll discover an absolute treasure trove of military secrets hiding in plain sight. Tucked beneath the Golden Gate Bridge is **Fort Point** *(free; 10am-5pm Fri-Sun)*, a triple-decker brick fortress built by the US military in 1861 on the grounds of an abandoned Spanish fort. At the eye-watering cost of more than $100M in today's terms, then-cutting-edge iron cannons were installed here just in time to protect the bay against certain invasion during the Civil War...or not, as it turned out. Though it quartered up to 500 soldiers at its peak, Fort Point never saw military action – unless you count recent *Macbeth* performances here by an all-female cast. The cannons quickly became obsolete, and the fort was abandoned – but not entirely forgotten.

Movie buffs recognize Fort Point from the suspenseful finale of Alfred Hitchcock's *Vertigo*, when Kim Novak leaps to certain death into the bay...or not, as it turned out. Today Fort Point embraces its dramatic side with action-packed historical displays, knockout roof-deck bridge views, and immersive art installations like the *Immigrant Yarn Project,* where 600 knitters outfitted the fort's massive pillars in cozy, colorful knits honoring the many immigrant soldiers who served here. Check the park schedule for on-site theater shows and interpretive

PHOTO BY MIKE SHAW/GETTY IMAGES

Fort Point under Golden Gate Bridge

history events, including spooky Saturday-night candlelight tours in winter (reservations required).

Hidden History in the Presidio Officers' Club

The historic **Presidio Officers' Club** was long off-limits to civilians – but now you can witness hidden military history in the room where it happened. During recent restorations here, archaeologists uncovered original Spanish colonial adobe walls built by Ohlone conscripts in 1810. Today the Officer's Club showcases the Presidio's history, tracing its roots as ancestral Ohlone homeland for 10,000-plus years and its 250 years of military service to Spain, Mexico and the US. The adjoining **Heritage Gallery** *(free; 11am-4pm Fri-Sun)* hosts special exhibitions – including an immersive exhibit acknowledging the Presidio's pivotal role in the unjust incarceration of 120,000 Japanese Americans during WWII as supposed 'enemy aliens' in accordance with US Executive Order 9066. Chilling 1942 posters ordered 'all persons of Japanese ancestry' to report to the Presidio, where they were sent to remote prison camps for the duration of the war. San Francisco-based Japanese American Citizens League immediately demanded redress for civil rights violations, laying the legal groundwork for the US Civil Rights Movement.

Military Secrets, Revealed

The next chapter of this story unfolds just downhill from the Presidio Officers' Club, at low-profile **Building 640** – the top-secret WWII spy-craft school unveiled to the public as the **Military Intelligence Service Historic Learning Center** *(njahs.org/building-640; adult/kids $10/free; noon-5pm Sat & Sun).* Select Japanese American soldiers lived and trained in this drafty bunkhouse as code-breakers and spies for high-risk intelligence missions to WWII battlegrounds. Fascinating exhibits show how the Japanese American 442nd regiment became the most decorated unit in US history, while their families were incarcerated – and how the JACL finally won an unprecedented apology from the US government for the wrongful incarceration of Japanese Americans, 43 years after the war ended.

When WWII Western Defense Command ceased operations at the Presidio in 1945, the gun batteries along **Battery Bluff** fell into disuse. But top-secret Cold War missions continued in the Presidio, with Nike nuclear missile command at **Battery Caulfield** and top brass flown in for secret meetings at **Crissy Field** – including former USSR President Mikhail Gorbachev, who later established a peace institute in the Presidio. Since the Presidio became a park in 1996, its concrete bunkers are abandoned – but the Presidio's **San Francisco National Cemetery** is immaculately maintained, with 30,000 headstones on a lush green hillside offering stark reminders of the human costs of war. Downhill, handmade headstones in the **Presidio Pet Cemetery** commemorate military family pets that served their last tour of duty, including Blinky and Stinky.

TOP TIPS

- Forgot to pack a picnic? No problem: **Presidio Pop Up** food and drink trucks line the former Parade Grounds weekdays from 9am to 3pm, and weekends from 9am to 4:30pm.
- If you'd rather catch your own lunch, try your luck right under the Golden Gate Bridge on Torpedo Wharf. No license is required for fishing here; check posted catch limits. Watch and learn from local anglers, who catch prized sole and sniggle eels here in season.
- Presidio park rangers tell incredible true stories at free 4pm Tunnel Tops Campfire Talks, introducing legendary locals whose footsteps you're walking in – including indigenous healers, Buffalo Soldiers and Cold War spies.

The Presidio

Beyond hiking, biking and historic sites, the Presidio offers unusual attractions: an airplane hangar full of trampolines, vintage bowling alley, a showcase of Disney drawings, *Star Wars* selfies and film-festival premieres.

TAKING TRANSIT

Use **Muni** buses to/from/around the Marina and Wharf, and **Presidio GO** (p55) shuttles around the Presidio. **Golden Gate Transit** buses cross the bridge, connecting Marin, the Marina and downtown. Rideshares can get lost in the Presidio, where cell signals vary.

R&R in the Presidio

Go play in an ex-army outpost

Now that the Presidio has retired from military duty, rest and recreation opportunities abound here. Civilians can throw strikes at the post's **Presidio Bowl** *(presidiobowl.com; per lane up to 6 people before 6pm weekdays/weekends $55/75, after 6pm weekdays/weekends $75/85; shoe rental $7.50)* bowling alley or bounce off walls inside an ex-airplane hangar lined with trampolines called the **House of Air** *(houseofair.com; 1hr adult/child from $20/15)*. The posts's former PX (provisions warehouse) is now a **Sports Basement** *(sportsbasement.com)* that stocks bikes, wetsuits and other sporting equipment to rent, buy or trade. The Presidio also has the city's biggest play space, at Tunnel Tops Park: **Outpost Playground**, wildly popular for its nature-themed play structures, water features, nearby food trucks, picnic facilities and clean bathrooms.

Discover Presidio Movie Magic

See movie classics in the making

Fans of fairy-tale heroines and Jedi sci-fi legends, you've come to the right place. Anyone who can hum along with at least one animated Disney movie (aka everyone), head to the **Walt Disney Family Museum** *(waltdisney.org; adult/student/child $25/20/15)* to see how your favorites were made. Interactive exhibits showcase original Disney designs, from early animation cels to a scale model of Disneyland – courtesy of Walt's daughter Diane Disney Miller – plus major showcases of the trailblazing women designers who made Disney magic. Check online for upcoming screenings of rare cartoons onsite and hands-on animation workshops.

At the edge of the Presidio, *Star Wars* creator George Lucas transformed a former military hospital into Luscasfilm HQ. The LEED Gold-certified sustainable **Letterman Campus** keeps a deliberately low profile, but you'll spot fans taking selfies by the **Yoda fountain** out front. When the building is

HIGHLIGHTS
1 Crissy Field
2 Golden Gate Bridge
3 The Presidio

SIGHTS
4 Fort Point
5 Military Intelligence Service Historic Learning
6 Presidio Officers' Club
7 Tunnel Tops Park
8 Walt Disney Family Museum

ACTIVITIES
9 House of Air
10 Presidio Bowl

SLEEPING
11 Inn at the Presidio
12 Lodge at the Presidio

EATING
13 Borsch Mobile
14 Dalida
15 Kabob Trolley
16 Señor Sigsig
17 Warming Hut

DRINKING & NIGHTLIFE
18 Fort Point Beer
see 4 Round House Café

SHOPPING
19 Sports Basement

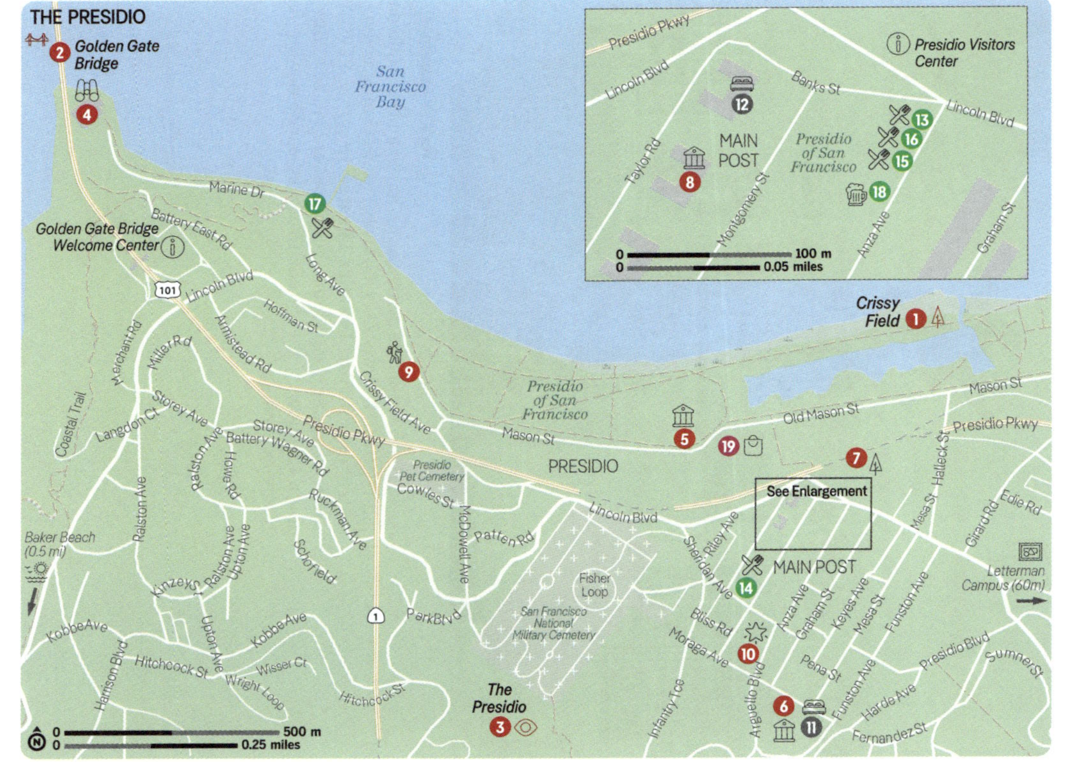

Yoda fountain (p62)

open, check out movie memorabilia in the lobby – and consult the **SFFILM** website (sffilm.org) for festival screenings in its state-of-the-art **Premier Theater**. In spring, SFFILM also screens free classic films shot in and around SF at **Sundown Cinema** on the Parade Grounds; check website for upcoming events.

EATING IN THE PRESIDIO: FOOD TRUCKS TO CHASE

Borsch Mobile: Ukranian comfort food like borscht and potato dumplings warm the belly on a blustery day. *hours vary* $

Señor Sigsig: Filipino-style saucy, succulent meats and adobo garlic rice folded into a burrito – lunch is a wrap. *hours vary* $

Fort Point Beer: Brews crafted just uphill go down even easier on sunny Presidio Parade Grounds with Dungeness crab rolls. *hours vary* $

Kabob Trolley: Get your pick of Afghan-spiced meats described as 'hella Halal' packed into sliders, wrapped into gyrritos, or piled on fries to share... maybe. *hours vary* $

The Marina

Cows once grazed these coastal marshes – until the city built a futuristic fairground here for the 1915 Panama-Pacific International Expo. Deco cinemas, indie boutiques and picturesque parks popped up around the fair, making space in the Marina for grand plans and good times that keep coming, more than a century later.

Showtime at Fort Mason

Watch talents launch in waterfront waterhouses

San Francisco takes subversive glee in turning military installations into civilian playgrounds. **Fort Mason** *(fortmason.org; free)* was an embarkation point for WWII troops, but today it launches cutting-edge theater and comedy. Pushing boundaries since 1967, **Magic Theatre** *(magictheatre.org; tickets sliding scale $35–75)* stages breakthrough works by provocative playwrights, including premieres of original commissioned works like *Jerry Garcia in the Lower Mission*. The Magic houses stunning new murals, artistic residencies for **Campo Santo**, **Lorraine Hansberry Theatre** and **Play On! Shakespeare** – plus freeform jazz-worship services for SF's legendary **St John Coltrane Church**. Next door, **Bay Area Theater Sports** *(aka* **BATS Improv**; *improv.org; tickets adult/student $25/20)* dares you to suggest plot twists for raucous improvised comedy shows performed in a range of styles: madcap musicals, SF rom-coms, B-movie sci-fi and more. Feeling brave? Take center stage at three-hour introductory improv workshops or weekend intensives like improvised Shakespeare. Book tickets and workshops online; classes fill quickly.

ST JOHN COLTRANE

'There's music in his name,' proclaims the reverend at **African Orthodox Church of St John Coltrane,** SF's church dedicated to the jazz legend since 1969. Sunday mass kicks off with a joyous jam session in the Magic Theatre at 11am, and all are invited to participate – if you have an instrument to play or a groove in your soul, bring it.

Coltrane was officially canonized by the African Orthodox Church in 1982, and the church commissioned spectacular icons by San Francisco painter Mark Dukes depicting Coltrane in glory – with a gold halo, an unwavering gaze, and fire coming out of his saxophone. A St Coltrane icon takes pride of place at Mass, and even nonbelievers leave feeling *A Love Supreme*.

Make Art, Not War

Find artistic inspiration in military storehouses

During WWII, Fort Mason shipped out 23 million tons of wartime supplies – but now its storehouses supply artistic inspiration to 1.4 million visitors annually. Dockside nonprofit **SF Camerawork** *(sfcamerawork.org; free)* has showcased next-wave photographers since 1974, while **Haines Gallery** *(hainesgallery.com; free)* represents leading global contemporary artists like Andy Goldsworthy and Ai Weiwei. **Arion Press** *(arionpress.com; free)* showcases limited-edition, letterpress art books featuring collaborations by leading poets and artists. The former pier warehouse now known as **Herbst Pavilion** includes arts-and-craft fairs among its arsenal of

- **SIGHTS**
  - 1 Arion Press
  - 2 Fort Mason Center
  - 3 Haines Gallery
  - 4 SF Camerawork
  - 5 Wave Organ
- **SLEEPING**
  - 6 Hotel del Sol
  - 7 Infinity Hotel
  - 8 Marina Motel
  - 9 Union Street Inn
- **EATING**
  - 10 A16
  - 11 Atelier Crenn
  - 12 Blue Barn Gourmet
  - 13 Causewell's
  - 14 Greens
  - 15 Italian Homemade
  - 16 Izzy's Steakhouse
  - 17 Komeya No Bento
  - 18 La Fromagerie
  - 19 Lucca Delicatessen
  - 20 Viva Goa
- **DRINKING & NIGHTLIFE**
  - 21 Better Sunday
  - 22 California Wine Merchant
  - 23 Coffee Bodega
  - 24 Equator Coffee
  - 25 For the Record
  - 26 New Bar
  - 27 Radhaus
  - 28 Telve Coffee Shop
  - 29 The Interval
- **ENTERTAINMENT**
  - 30 BATS Improv
  - 31 Herbst Pavilion
  - 32 Magic Theatre
  - 33 Marina Theatre
  - 34 Presidio Movie Theater
- **SHOPPING**
  - 35 Aggregate Supply
  - 36 ATYS
  - 37 Books Inc
  - 38 Flax Art & Design
  - 39 Fort Mason outdoor markets
  - 40 Marine Layer
  - 41 Nikoniko Gifts
  - 42 Pillowtrip
  - 43 Pyarful
- **TRANSPORTATION**
  - 44 Golden Gate Bridge Bike Rental

events, with annual highlights including **FOG Design+Art** *(fogfair.com; admission $35–40)* in winter, **San Francisco Art Fair** *(sanfranciscoartfair.com)* in spring, and **Renegade Craft** and **West Coast Craft** *(westcoastcraft.com; free)* fairs in both summer and fall – plus monthly West Coast Craft pops-up in Fort Mason's parking lot (see their website for dates). Feeling inspired? Make your own with art-and-craft supplies from **Flax Art & Design**, well-stocked with top-notch watercolors, pens, oils, notebooks, canvas and more.

PRIME PICNIC SPOTS

On windy days, picnic blankets tend to blow away along the Marina waterfront. For more sheltered spots, head to the Presidio to nab bay-view tables alongside the **Presidio Visitors Center** (p59) and at **Tunnel Tops** (p59).

Brunch with Bridge Views

Chew the scenery at Greens

Since 1979, Fort Mason's ex-army mess hall has been commandeered by women star chefs, inventing flavor-bomb vegetarian dishes with organic ingredients from Marin's Buddhist Green Gulch Farm. Reserve ahead for bayfront tables at **Greens** *(greensrestaurant.com)* with breathtaking Golden Gate Bridge views, savor bar bites with Buddha-hand-infused cocktails at JB Blunk's reclaimed-redwood-stump tables, or get boxed lunches to enjoy on the docks of the bay.

Strike Poses at the Palace of Fine Arts

Photobomb prom photos at SF's best backdrop

Like many a fine romance, the **Palace of Fine Arts** *(palaceoffinearts.com; free)* was a folly that wasn't expected to last. The California Arts and Crafts Movement's leading architect Bernard Maybeck originally built this Greco-Roman ruin in plaster for the 1915 Panama-Pacific International Expo, but San Francisco decided to keep the Palace after the fair, and eventually recast it in concrete. Join shy prom dates and shivering brides posing for photos under the Rotunda frieze, showing 'art under attack by materialists, with idealists leaping to her rescue' – a timeless sentiment.

Listen to the Wave Organ

Hum along with the Bay

Follow a trail past yacht-club docks along a jetty poking into the Bay, and you'll discover an aural oddity: the **Wave Organ** *(exploratorium.edu; free)*. Eerie sounds wheeze from repurposed

EATING IN THE MARINA: FIVE-STAR PICNIC SUPPLIES

Lucca Delicatessen: Italian deli classics since 1929 – mighty meatball sandwiches, minestrone soup, and spicy-salami Calabrian subs with rustic Chianti. *9am-6pm* $

Komeya No Bento: Proper Japanese bento (lunchbox): salmon or duck breast, sushi rice, dashi broth and side salads. *11:30am-2:30pm & 5-6:30pm Tue-Sat* $

La Fromagerie: Classic French sandwiches: Parisien ham and Gruyere cheese, or Toulouse duck with manchego. *11am-6pm Mon & Tue, from 10am Wed-Sun* $

Fort Mason outdoor markets: Sunday farmers markets bring readymade food vendors *(9:30am-1:30pm)*; Friday nights feature food trucks and local makers *(4-9pm)*. $

WALTER CICCHETTI/SHUTTERSTOCK

Palace of Fine Arts (p67)

BIKING THE MARINA

Covering the waterfront is easy on a rental (e-)bike - book online or pickup at **Golden Gate Bridge Bike Rental** *(goldengatebridgebikerentals.com; per day bike/e-bike $45-65/$89-119)* or **Sports Basement** (p62). Use the Lyft app to locate bikes at Marina and Presidio Bay Wheels bike-sharing stations *(lyft.com/bikes/bay-wheels)*.

SF cemetery marble statues and PVC plumbing parts, ingeniously reconfigured into acoustic sculpture by Exploratorium artists Peter Richards and George Gonzalez. Depending on the waves, winds and tide, the installation sounds like humming from a cook in a noisy kitchen or spooky heavy breathing on a prank phone call.

Get Equipped on Chestnut Street

Gear up for hikes and date nights

It's Murphy's law, San Francisco-style: once you reach the waterfront, you realize you're missing something. Whether that's an outer layer, California field guide, or date-worthy shirt, Chestnut St boutiques have you covered. Take the edge off coastal breezes at **Marine Layer** *(marinelayer.com)*, local designer of classic made-in-California chore coats and that ingenious 'shacket' (heavyweight flannel overshirt) you'll spot on Crissy Field surfers. For your Presidio birdwatching, botany

DRINKING IN THE MARINA: BEYOND SPORTS BARS

The Interval: Lose track of time over International Orange aged-gin aperitifs. *5-10pm Mon, 10am-11pm Tue-Fri, 5-11pm Sat, 3-10pm Sun*

California Wine Merchant: Nonstop block party for 50-plus years, pouring 50 well-chosen wines by the glass/half-glass. *1-10pm Mon-Wed, to 11pm Thu-Sat, 2-7pm Sun*

For the Record: Retro-dream den with disco balls, DJs spinning vinyl, and EP-style menus of radio-hit cocktails. *5pm-midnight Tue-Thu, to 2am Fri, 3pm-2am Sat*

Radhaus: Bavarian beer hall serving brats, schnitzel and Oktoberfest vibes. *noon-8pm Mon, to 3:30pm Wed, to 9pm Tue, Thu & Fri, 11am-10pm Sat, 10am-8pm Sun*

and beach adventures, pick up handy field guides and riveting beach reads by local authors at independent **Books Inc** *(booksinc.net)*. Look sharp yet casual for Marina meetups with **Aggregate Supply** *(aggregatesupplysf.com)* California-cool fits – Eat Dust Oakland chinos, breezy Rachel Comey top, Clare V. woven bag, done.

Marina Movie Palaces

Catch arthouse features in deco cinemas

Mall multiplexes come and go, but San Francisco's vintage neighborhood cinemas still showcase the city at its best: artistically inclined, technologically advanced, community oriented and fiercely independent. Since 1937, the **Presidio Movie Theater** *(lntsf.com; adult/child $17/14)* has entertained SF crowds – and they keep coming to this independent, local, family-owned cinema for current blockbusters, acclaimed arthouse films, **SFFILM Fest** premieres, and free NBA games on the big screen whenever the Warriors are in it to win it (read: always). Buy tickets online or at the booth under the Streamline Moderne marquee, and claim a cushy seat in this remodeled four-plex, with a velvet-swagged main auditorium, two upper theaters and one cozy screening room. The Lee family also runs the Spanish deco **Marina Theatre** *(lntsf.com; adult/child $17/14)* with an equally eclectic calendar: Oscar contenders, rom-coms, global film-fest favorites, Met Opera livestreams, and occasional live stand-up comedy. Chilly Marina days call for bargain matinees and indie movie binges.

Enjoy Alcohol-Free Happy Hours

Raise toasts with tasty mocktails

To celebrate today with no regrets tomorrow, nonalcoholic (NA) party beverages are all the rage in San Francisco. On Union St alone, two alcohol-free package stores stock new 0ABV (zero alcohol by volume) beverages far more exciting than that sparkling apple juice you may remember from some kid's birthday. Thanks to the **New Bar** *(thenewbar.com)*, you can call for a toast with frothy, zesty Priva Pave NA sparkling wines from Italy, enhance taco Tuesdays with Ghia's margarita-esque lime-and-salt NA apertitif, and enjoy happy hour anytime with St Agrestic's NA 'phony Negroni.' **Better Sunday** *(abettersunday.com)* calls itself a 'Feel-good bottle shop and social club,' where you can buy and sip Fieldwork NA

BEST MARINA DINNER DATES

Dalida (Map p63): *Top Chef* Laura Ozylimaz brings sumptuous Mediterranean flavors to the Bay – Istanbul stuffed mussels, Aleppo roast chicken, Yemeni lamb stew, mmmm. *11:30-2pm & 5-9pm Fri-Wed, 11am-2pm Thu* **$$**

Atelier Crenn: Triple-Michelin-starred Dominique Crenn creates edible art inspired by SF's seafaring legends and her own Sonoma farmstead. *5-9pm Tue-Sat* **$$$**

A16: Romance is ably assisted by James Beard Award–winning wood-fired pizzas, house-cured salami, and a deep Italian wine list. *5-9pm Mon-Thu, noon-9:30pm Fri-Sun* **$$**

Izzy's Steakhouse: Forget rings – for 40-plus years, SF's surest sign of commitment is sharing The Gomez, Izzy's plump prime rib with gooey Ilaicise potatoes. *5-9:30pm Mon-Fri, from 4pm Sat & Sun* **$$$**

DRINKING IN THE MARINA: GREAT COFFEE BREAKS

Equator Coffee: Get fair-trade espresso at Fort Mason's gatehouse, and catch rays in sheltered outdoor seating. *6:30am-5pm Mon-Fri, from 7am Sat & Sun*

Dynamo Donut & Coffee: Power hikes with Proyecto Diaz coffee and donuts in SF flavors, from berry Pride to May the Fourth chocolate. *8am-1pm Wed-Fri, to 4pm Sat & Sun*

Coffee Bodega: Beans grown, roasted and delivered directly from Costa Rican cooperatives make sensational coffee. *8am-4pm Mon-Fri, 9am-5pm Sat, 9am-4pm Sun*

Telve Coffee Shop: Coffee breaks become major events over cardamom-spiced Turkish coffee brewed in *cezve* (brass pots). *7am-7pm Sun-Thu, to 9pm Fri & Sat*

PARTY OF THE CENTURY

San Francisco was rebuilt after the 1906 earthquake. To celebrate its comeback and the opening of the Panama Canal, SF invited the world to an epic party: 1915's **Panama-Pacific International Expo**.

Minor hitch: SF wasn't big enough to host everyone. Landfill extended the northern shoreline to accommodate fairgrounds spanning almost 400 square city blocks.

PPIE had it all: the 435ft Tower of Jewels, glittering with 100,000 cut-glass gems; flashy technology, including a 14-ton Underwood typewriter; eyebrow-raising modern painting and sculpture at the Palace of Fine Arts; and forward-thinking events, including the International Conference of Women Workers to Promote Peace. The party was a smash – and technology, art and peace are perpetually in progress in San Francisco.

craft brews and Ethic NA social tonics – including NA sparkling apple tonic with hints of lychee and hibiscus that easily outclasses average apple juice. With suggestions from upbeat Better Sunday staff, you can host your own *White Lotus*–style wellness retreat (minus the murders) with NA 'adaptogenic beverages' infused with mushrooms (not that kind) and herbs (also not that kind). Cheers to your health!

Shop Cow Hollow

Gather gifts for all occasions

San Francisco's former cow pastures are now fertile grounds for clever Union Street gift boutiques. When San Francisco hosts go above and beyond, gracious guests thank them with ingenious host gifts from **ATYS** *(atysdesign.com)*: green-wall clocks made of moss, psychedelic fiber-art grids woven in San Francisco, and steak knives with International Orange handles made of reclaimed steel from the Golden Gate Bridge. At **Pyarful** *(pyarful.com)* playful South Asian-inspired gifts and stationery need no official occasion for greeting cards with tea proclaiming 'Chai miss you,' fridge magnets with upbeat cauliflower urging 'Gobi awesome today,' and badges of honor bragging 'Didn't become a doctor.' Perfect the art of gifting at **Nikoniko Gifts** *(shopnikoniko.com)*, Union St's Japanese and Korean heritage boutique lined with gift suggestions: goldfish-shaped welcome soap, sleek foot spa kits, gourmet pet treats, and themed gift bundles wrapped in elegant furoshiki cloths. For a one-of-a-kind gift, resident sewing wizard Frances Wolff at **Pillowtrip** *(instagram.com/pillowtrip)* can turn any fabric into a keepsake pillow – including that glittery rainbow 'fit you rocked at Pride, or the Warriors jersey you got signed at the stadium.

EATING IN THE MARINA: NOT-SO-FAST FOOD

Blue Barn Gourmet: Prime California produce with gourmet fixings – artisan cheeses, caramelized onions and heirloom tomatoes. *11am-8pm* $

Viva Goa: Tangy, warming Goan favorites – prawn *xacuti* (toasted-coconut curry), pillowy naan, made-to-order samosas. *11am-3pm & 5-10pm Tue-Sat, 5-10pm Sun* $

Italian Homemade: Chefs roll fresh pasta and serve with your choice of sauce – including proper pork-and-beef bolognese. *11am-9:30pm Sun-Thu, to 10pm Fri & Sat* $

Causewell's: Come for 'fancy-pants burgers' – local beef with pork confit, melted onions and taleggio cheese. *11am-9pm Tue-Fri, 10am-10:30pm Sat, 10am-9pm Sun* $$

Fisherman's Wharf

Wharf attractions draw visitors year-round for action-packed afternoons: check out the sea lions, meet comic-book heroes, dance with manta rays, catch your own dinner, and toast sunsets on Bay cruises.

Game On at Musée Mécanique

Play vintage games at SF's Wild West arcade

The massive boatshed at Pier 45 can scarcely contain this sprawling, mind-blowing collection of 300-plus vintage mechanical amusements. Giant, freckle-faced Laughing Sal has freaked out kids for over a century, but don't let this manic mannequin deter you from the **Musée Mécanique** *(musee mecanique.com; entry free)*, the best arcade west of Coney Island. For less than a buck, you can battle Space Invaders, get your fortune told by an all-seeing wizard, peep at belly dancers through a vintage Mutoscope, or be hypnotized by a Ferris wheel made entirely from toothpicks.

Meet Superheroes at the Cartoon Art Museum

Get up close and personal with comic legends

Founded on a grant from Bay Area cartoon legend Charles M Schultz of *Peanuts* fame, the **Cartoon Art Museum** *(car toonart.org; adult/child $10/4)* showcases cartoon classics from Batman blockbusters to Calvin & Hobbes strips. But these curators aren't afraid of the dark or serious subjects, either, showcasing Ukrainian political cartoons, Edward Gorey's Goth monsters, SF feminist comics trailblazer Trina Robbins, and Wahab Algarmy's stories of growing up Muslim by the Bay. Events are rare opportunities to mingle with comic legends, local Pixar Studios animators, and obsessive comic collectors.

Family Fun on Pier 39

Choose your own bayside adventure

Sea lions aren't the only ones who enjoy sunny days out at **Pier 39** *(pier39.com; free)*. Families flock to this boardwalk for amusement-park atmosphere without the prohibitive entry fees – and though the souvenir shops and fast-food chains may seem un-San Francisco, you'll find quirks galore on the pier

Continues on p75

SAN FRANCISCO'S FAVORITE SEA-LEBRITIES

Sea lions took over San Francisco's most coveted waterfront real estate in 1990, and have been making a public display of themselves ever since.

Night and day they canoodle, belch, scratch and gleefully shove one another off the docks. They don't seem to mind human visitors or photos, as long as you keep your distance – at least 50ft away is recommended by local Marine Mammal Center biologists – and remember that it's illegal to feed them.

Up to 2100 sea lions at a time converge on Pier 39's K dock from July to May, and whenever else they feel like sunbathing – California law requires yacht owners to relinquish valuable dock slips to accommodate them.

IV-OLGA/SHUTTERSTOCK

TOP EXPERIENCE

Exploratorium

Can you stop time, sculpt fog or make sand sing? At San Francisco's living laboratory of science and human perception, you'll discover superhuman abilities you never knew you had – and emerge from the hands-on exhibits with a renewed sense of wonder.

DON'T MISS

- Tactile Dome
- Glimpses into the Tinkering Studio
- Fog Bridge
- After Dark events
- Plankton paintings
- *Visualizing the Bay* exhibit

Mind-Expanding Experiences

Is there a science to skateboarding? How big is your blind spot? Can plankton make art? You have questions about life's mysteries, and the **Exploratorium** is here to help you find answers. Designers of the Exploratorium's 700-plus hands-on exhibits have won MacArthur Genius grants for inventions that engage all the senses: try on a static-electricity punk hairdo, send whispered messages to strangers across the room, or dance with your own rainbow shadows in a light-refraction room. Combining science with art, these interactive exhibits reveal the fascinating sides of familiar phenomena – and nudge you to question what you think you know.

PRACTICALITIES

● exploratorium.edu ● Exploratorium entry adult/youth $40/30, After Dark $23, Tactile Dome $16 ● 10am-5pm Mon-Sat, noon-5pm Sun; After Dark 6-10pm

The Tactile Dome

The Exploratorium's most popular exhibit is also the trippiest: the **Tactile Dome**. Slip off your shoes and step inside this mysterious geodesic dome, and suddenly you're enveloped in total darkness. You'll have to rely on your senses of adventure and touch to guide you through an elaborate labyrinth, with new textures at every turn. Slide, climb and feel your way through this highly tactile maze to emerge exhilarated and triumphant, with hands tingling. Originally created in 1971 by Dr August Coppola (aka brother of filmmaker Francis Ford Coppola, dad of actor Nicholas Cage, and uncle of director Sophia Coppola), the dome has been through a few iterations – people got naked in the original one, and it was hard to clean – and helpful staff are on hand to handle any minor freakouts. Advance reservations and a separate ticket are required; book ahead. Bring socks, and prepare to have them knocked off.

A Showcase for Experimental Thinking

The Exploratorium's mind-bending science exhibits are inspired by founder Frank Oppenheimer, a physicist who worked on the atom bomb with his brother Robert (featured in the movie *Oppenheimer*), but was blacklisted during the McCarthy era and barred from scientific research. He dedicated the rest of his life to promoting science in the public interest, teaching at public high school and founding the Exploratorium in 1969 in the **Palace of Fine Arts** (p67) exhibition hall.

But as ongoing experiments continued in the in-house **Tinkering Studio**, the Exploratorium started to outgrow its venue. Leading scientists put their heads together, and came up with a wildly inventive solution for the Exploratorium: a purpose-built, solar-powered space on a glass-walled pier jutting over San Francisco Bay. Today the Exploratorium houses 9 acres of exhibits across Pier 15 – including the mysterious **Fog Bridge** and other outdoor exhibits you can explore free of charge, 24 hours a day. National Oceanic and Atmospheric Administration (NOAA) also hardwired the pier with sensors delivering real-time data visualizations of weather, wind and tides, so you can see San Francisco Bay from the inside out.

AFTER DARK

The Exploratorium's not just for kids: at After Dark Thursdays, 18-plus crowds bond over glow-in the-dark mad-scientist cocktails, technology-assisted sing-alongs and eye-opening special exhibits. Book ahead to witness awe-inspiring events like *Kinematic/Kinesthetic*, an epic performance by dancers with and without disabilities using dynamic mobility devices like telescoping crutches and robotic appendages.

TOP TIPS

- Continue Exploratorium experiments at home with gear and gifts from the Exploratorium's gift shop – including maker kits, chemistry sets, solar-powered robots, circuitry for babies (yes, really), and books for curious readers of all ages.
- For quick bites and a jolt of caffeine, stop by the **Seismic Joint Cafe** *(10am-3pm Tue-Fri, to 5pm Sat & Sun)* near the entrance to enjoy outdoors.
- At the end of the pier, the Exploratorium's scenic waterfront **Seaglass Restaurant** *(11am-3pm Sun & Tue-Sat, 6-9:30pm Thu)* serves sit-down, locally sourced lunches and scientifically inspired cocktails at Thursday After Dark events.

SIGHTS
1 Aquarium of the Bay
2 Bill Chester Longshoremen's Union Hall
3 Cartoon Art Museum
4 Maritime Museum
5 Musée Mécanique
6 Pier 39
7 San Francisco Carousel
8 SS Jeremiah O'Brien
9 USS Pampanito

ACTIVITIES
10 Adventure Cat
11 Blue & Gold Fleet
12 Lovely Martha fishing trips
13 Red & White Fleet
14 Sea Forager Expeditions

SLEEPING
15 Argonaut Hotel
16 Kimpton Alton

EATING
17 Abacá
18 Board & Drink
19 Codmother Fish & Chips
20 Eagle Cafe
21 Fisherman's Wharf Crab Stands
22 Fog Harbor Fish House
23 In-N-Out Burger
24 Palette Tea House
25 Scoma's
26 Surisan
27 Tanguito
28 The Original Ghirardelli Chocolate & Ice Cream Shop

DRINKING & NIGHTLIFE
29 Buena Vista Cafe
30 Sweetie's Art Bar

INFORMATION
31 California Welcome Center

Continued from p71

if you know where to look. Make music as you climb giant piano keys on the interactive **Musical Stairs**, and head to the second-floor **California Welcome Center** for discounted tickets, boat cruise schedules, and local travel tips from savvy staff (pro tip: the **Pier 39 parking garage** roof is prime for photo-ops, with panoramic Bay views).

At Pier 39's not-for-profit, Smithsonian-affiliated **Aquarium of the Bay**, *(aquariumofthebay.org; adult/child $28/20)* you can visit 24,000 aquatic creatures in their homes underwater – walk through shark tanks, be hypnotized by jellies, wave back at rescued river otters, and join a fish-feeding frenzy here. On the pier's bayside end, your chariot awaits at the antique **San Francisco Carousel** *(10am-8pm, $6 per ride)* twinkling with 1800 lights and hand-painted with local landmarks. Make it a game to see how many you recognize besides the Golden Gate Bridge, and the winner scores favorite local treats: **Trish's Mini Donuts** *(10am-9pm)* and/or California strawberries from the **Vlahos family fruit stand** (spring to fall).

Go Deco at the Aquatic Park Bathhouse

Immerse yourself in art at SF's landmark bathhouse

A monumental hint to sailors in need of a scrub, this ship-shaped 1939 Streamline Moderne landmark is decked out with gloriously restored marine-themed masterpieces that upstage rotating **Maritime Museum** *(maritime.org; free)* exhibits. Each floor features original 1930s artworks by leading Works Progress Administration (WPA) artists: the lobby is awash in surreal underwater murals by Ann Sonia Medalie and Hilaire Hiler, Beniamino Bufano's playful seal and toad sculptures are mezzanine mascots, and the top floor showcases tugboat murals and wavy terrazzo floors by Shirley Staschen and Richard Ayer.

But pride of place here goes to Black avant-garde sculptor Sargent Johnson, who created the stunning carved green-slate marquee doorway as well as the veranda's mesmerizing aquatic mosaics with Moroccan mosaic artist Mohammed Zyani. To protest plans to include a private casino in this public facility, Johnson deliberately left unfinished the mosaics on the eastern side. Johnson won: the east wing is now a senior center. Almost 150 years after Aquatic Park was proposed as a bayside retreat for all, this co-ed bathhouse and its diverse crew of visionary artists still seem ahead of their time.

SF'S RIVAL SWIMMING CLUBS

Dip a toe in Aquatic Park's bone-chilling waters, and you might wonder: do people actually swim here? Yes, and they've been doing it for 150 years.

Bay swimming and rowing clubs formed in the 1870s – because misery apparently loves company, not to mention strong drink.

Two neighboring clubs remain at Aquatic Park: South End Rowing Club (founded 1873) and the Dolphin Club (founded 1877). Their century-plus rivalry peaks at wintertime polar bear swims and annual 1.5-mile Alcatraz Sharkfest Swim – not for the faint-hearted or cold-toed.

The occasional rogue sea lion has been known to nip at swimmers' heels in the cove, so give them a wide berth and don't try to race them – with swimming speeds reaching 30mph, sea lions easily beat Olympians.

EATING AT THE WHARF: QUICK BITES

The Original Ghirardelli Chocolate & Ice Cream Shop: SF's original c 1852 chocolate company. *9am-midnight Wed-Sat, to 11pm Sun-Tue* $

Eagle Cafe: Brunch with SF perks: crab Benedicts, sourdough French toast, affordable kids' menu, plus eagle's-eye views over Pier 39. *8am-3pm* $$

Tanguito: Hole-in-the-wall serving hearty Argentine fare – chicken empanadas – at outdoor tables. *11:30am-6:30pm Tue-Fri, noon-7:30pm Sat, noon-6pm Sun* $

In-N-Out Burger: Follow the '50s bent-arrow logo for prime chuck beef burgers, fries and shakes, with ingredients you can pronounce. *10:30am-1am Sun-Thu, to 1:30 Fri & Sat* $

WALKING TOUR

Explore the Wharf's Wild Side

Brace for an action-packed afternoon along SF's wharf. Wander along the wharf, where you can take selfies with sea lions, stare down sharks, hop a submarine, and swap stories with sailors over spiked coffee. Yes, the wharf can get touristy – its family-friendly attractions draw all-age crowds most weekends – but this 45-minute, half-mile walk reveals its wild side.

1 Sea Lions at Pier 39

Take a selfie with SF's favorite sea-lebrity guests. When sea lions took over **Pier 39** (p71) docks in 1990, California recognized their squatters' rights – they were here first, after all – and yacht owners got bumped to accommodate a barking bunch of slapstic comedians as neighbors. Keep a safe distance – they may be adorable, but sea mammals can get territorial.

The Walk Cross over to the east side of Pier 39, and head for dry land. Just before you reach it, your next stop is on the left-hand side.

2 Aquarium of the Bay

Walk underwater at the **Aquarium of the Bay** (p75) – descend into underwater chambers lined with glowing jellyfish tanks, then step into glass tubes jutting deep into San Francisco Bay. Suddenly you're surrounded by marine life – sharks circle overhead, while manta rays perform underwater ballets.

The Walk Emerge from the deep and return to dry land. Head away from the tides of tourists strolling the Embarcardo and turn onto North Point St.

BENJAMIN HEATH FOR LONELY PLANET

Sea lions

❸ Bill Chester Longshoremen's Union Hall

This unusual hexagonal building is still-active **Bill Chester Longshoremen's Union Hall,** named for SF's trailblazing 1930s Black union leader. Front windows showcase signs from SF's 1934 strike that set historic standards for fair pay, safety and working hours. But this hall is known globally for hosting one epic party: 1966 Trips Festival. Fresh from testing government-issued LSD for the CIA, novelist Ken Kesey spiked punch with it. The rest is hippie history: Trips Festival promoter Bill Graham founded rock-legendary Fillmore Auditorium, featuring Trips Festival performers the Grateful Dead. Festival organizer Stewart Brand hallucinated a military computer shrunk to palm-size, bringing computing power to the people. Forty years later, Steve Jobs thanked Brand for the inspiration.

The Walk Behind the hall, turn right at Beniamino Bufano's serene statue of the city's patron St Francis.

❹ USS Pampanito

Enter stealth mode at Pier 45 inside **USS Pampanito** (p79), a 1943 submarine that survived WWII to tell hair-raising tales of torpedo battles and deep dives in onboard audio tours. Head below decks to inspect polished instruments and impossibly close quarters – if you get claustrophobic, surface for deck views.

The Walk For more action, head into the Pier 45 boatshed.

❺ Musée Méchanique

Cheap thrills await inside vintage arcade **Musée Mécanique** (p71). For a buck, start a Wild West saloon brawl, race antique roadsters, and save the planet from asteroids.

SUSTAINABLE SEAFOOD

Sustainability is always top of mind at Fisherman's Wharf, so don't be shy about asking where and how your dinner was caught, and make dining decisions accordingly.

To consider your options and find best local choices for every season, consult California's nonprofit Seafood Watch Guide online *(seafoodwatch.org)*. Ocean-friendly menu items on the 'Super Green List' include pole-and-line-caught albacore tuna, and farmed oysters, clams, mussels and rainbow trout.

Local, seasonal 'Best Choices' include Petrale sole, Pacific sand dab, California squid, and Pacific pole-and-line-caught skipjack tuna. Local specialties like Dungeness crab, Pacific halibut and wild Pacific salmon are seasonally available, only when the California Department of Fish and Wildlife deem fishing conditions low-risk for aquatic ecosystems.

Fishing at the Wharf

Score the catch of the day

At the foot of Pier 45, behind crab stalls number 8 and 9, you'll spot swinging doors with a porthole and a mysterious sign: 'Passageway to the Boats.' You've found SF sailors' secret passageway to the Wharf's working fishing docks. On weekends, follow SF's savvy gourmet grandmas to boats selling the catch of the day directly to the public at no markup – some even clean and filet for you.

Would you rather be fishing than sightseeing? That can be arranged – several fishing boats docked between Piers 45 and 47 also run charters and fishing trips. For over a century, four generations of the Rescino family have fished these waters on their boat the **Lovely Martha** *(lovelymartha.com; fishing trips half/full day $150/200, Bay cruises $15)*, so they know just how and where to hook halibut, bass and salmon in season. Book half- or full-day trips and get your California fishing license via Lovely Martha's website.

If you love seafood but worry about getting seasick on boats, try sea foraging instead. Former Pacific fisheries manager and James Beard Award–winning sea forager Kirk Lombard runs 'from hook to cook' **Sea Forager Expeditions** *(seaforager.com)*, where you fish and forage ingredients around SF to assemble into a sustainable seafood feast. To hear sailors' stories too salty to print, don't miss Kirk's deliciously scandalous **Real Fisherman's Wharf Scallywag Tour** *(foraging expeditions $79–159, wharf walking tour $29)*.

You might feel moved to ask the universe to keep the boats safe and the sustainable seafood coming – and you'll see locals doing exactly that on Saturdays from 11am to 1pm at the non-denominational **Fisherman and Seamen's Memorial Chapel**. You'll recognize this little wooden chapel at the end of the pier by its stout *campanile* (bell tower) and ship's-wheel stained glass over the door. Every autumn since 1935, San Francisco's Italian American community converges here to celebrate **Madonna del Lume** *(Madonna of the Light; sfitalianheritage.org)* with a boat parade and blessing of the fleet. As SF old-timers say: *Vivi i pescatori!* (Long live the fisherfolk!)

EATING AT THE WHARF: BRUNCH

Abacá: SF's original Filipino soul food – including fried chicken and pandan waffles. *7-9am & 5-9pm Mon, Tue, Thu & Fri, 8am-1:30pm & 5-9pm Sat & Sun* $$

Palette Tea House: Settle into banquettes for swanky dim sum – wagyu-steak potstickers, lobster dumplings, Iberico pork bao. *11:30am-7:30pm Sun-Thu, to 8pm Fri & Sat* $$

Board & Drink: Go savory and sweet: *shakshuka* on sourdough or deconstructed lox bagel, plus brioche French toast or waffles. *8am-1:30pm Thu-Mon* $

Surisan: Take the edge off SF fog with Cal-Korean specials – ricotta pancakes, savory *pajun* pancakes with shrimp and bacon, matcha mojitos. *9am-2pm & 5-9pm* $

Fisherman and Seamen's Memorial Chapel

Enter Stealth Mode on USS Pampanito

Board a WWII submarine

Explore a restored submarine that did six tours of WWII duty and survived to tell the tale. The award-winning audio tour will have you holding your breath as you hear submariners' stories of sudden attacks and tense moments in underwater stealth mode aboard the **USS Pampanito** *(maritime.org; adult/child $25/10)*. All those shiny brass knobs and mysterious hydraulic valves make modern technology seem boring – plus the vintage 1943 USS *Pampanito* survived deep dives up to 600ft, which is far more than you can say for your smartphone. Blink and you might miss the tiny galley kitchen that fed a crew of 80, complete with built-in ice-cream maker. Mind your head as you explore tight quarters below decks, and resurface ready for shore leave in San Francisco.

DRINKING ON THE WHARF: DRINK LIKE A SAILOR

Buena Vista Cafe: Old saloon slinging Irish coffee to naval officers, cannery workers and Food Network stars. *9am-11pm Sun-Thu, to midnight Fri & Sat*

Scoma's Lounge (p80)**:** Boats dock outside this landmark bar for SF's finest Manhattan, barrel-aged for 1965 nights to honor Scoma's 1965 opening. *noon-9pm*

Sweetie's Art Bar: Iron chandeliers and jazz combos swing at this pirate's den serving legit navy-strength gin slings, draft hazy IPA and thin-crust pizza. *4:30-10:30pm*

Pier 23: Mingle with artists and sailors in the gallery while you wait your turn for local brews, fish tacos and crabcakes on the bayfront patio. *11:30am-6pm Wed-Mon*

ROSIE THE RIVETER & FRIENDS

During WWII, women and men came to the SF Bay to serve as shipbuilders, including 50,000 Black men and women. You may recall the poster of muscle-flaunting Rosie the Riveter proclaiming 'We Can Do It' – the model was Bay Area naval worker Naomi Parker Fraley.

Twenty to 25 percent of Bay Area shipyard workers were women, often assigned 'less skilled' jobs – including welding and computer programming. Bay Area shipbuilders worked long hours to turn the tides of WWII, building an entire ship every day– nearly half of all US military cargo ships were built by the Bay, plus one in five warships.

Post-war, these essential workers suddenly became unemployed. By the 1950s, Bay Area women were staffing a new local industry: silicon-chip manufacturing.

All Aboard SS Jeremiah O'Brien

See the last WWII Liberty Ship in action

Battleships get the glory in WWII movies, but Liberty cargo ships like the **SS Jeremiah O'Brien** *(ssjeremiahobrien.org; adult/child/family $20/10/45)* did some seriously heavy lifting. This original 1943 armed Liberty cargo ship survived seven WWII tours of duty equipping Allied forces in the UK, India, South America and Australia – plus 11 trips to supply the D-Day Allied invasion at Normandy. When its missions were complete, the *O'Brien* was mothballed and scheduled to be scrapped – until former Liberty ship sailors recognized the life and purpose left in this mighty ship.

Veterans and volunteers restored the *O'Brien* to working condition as a memorial to Bay Area shipbuilders, Merchant Marines and navy seamen who built, ran and defended armed Liberty ships. Today the *O'Brien* is docked at Pier 35 and open to visitors daily (except US holidays). On the third Saturday and Sunday of the month, crew fire up the 2500-horsepower steam engine so visitors can feel its power and witness the huge propeller in action.

Sail Away on the Bay

Cruise to the Golden Gate and beyond

When the fog lifts and sun twinkles across the bay, there's only one thing better than strolling the waterfront: getting out on the water. But do you want to get there by sailboat or cruiser, by day or at sunset, with or without booze? Whatever floats your boat, the Wharf has you covered.

To skim across the bay with the wind in your hair and a trampoline for kids, book a catamaran trip with **Adventure Cat** *(adventurecat.com)*. Their 'Sail and Jail' package makes escapes to and from Alcatraz way more fun, and their 1½ hour sunset cruises whisk you to the Golden Gate Bridge and back with a drink in your hand *(cruise adult/child $75/35, sunset incl drink weekdays/weekends $90/80, Sail and Jail $125)*.

How many marriage proposals have happened on the Red & White sunset cruise? Hard to say – the family-owned **Red & White Fleet** *(redandwhite.com; cruise adult/child 60min $39/29, 90min $48/36, sunset $58/38)* has been running sightseeing cruises since 1892, and ring boxes just keep popping. Red and White's classic booze cruise drifts past Alcatraz to the Golden Gate Bridge on modern triple-decker boats complete

EATING AT THE WHARF: FRESH SEAFOOD

Scoma's: Fishing boats out front supply ultra-fresh 'pier-to-plate' classics – crisp Dungeness crab cakes, creamy shrimp Louie salads. *noon-9pm* $$$

Codmother Fish & Chips: Crisp, fried-to-order Pacific cod with malt vinegar or tartar sauce plus garlic fries at outdoor tables. *11:30am-6pm Sun-Thu, to 7pm Fri & Sat* $

Fisherman's Wharf Crab Stands: Steaming cauldrons of Dungeness crab at Pier 45 sidewalk crab-stands are ready for feasts. *11:30am-9pm winter through spring* $

Fog Harbor Fish House: Brilliant Bay views frame sustainable faves like petrale sole, Pacific cod and Dungeness crab – flavors shine through. *11am-9pm* $$

JAVEN/SHUTTERSTOCK

Red & White Fleet ferry

with full bar and snacks – you can bring your own crab salad feasts from the Wharf.

The most economical way across the Bay is **Blue & Gold Fleet** *(blueandgoldfleet.com; ferry rides adult/child $14.75/9, 90min sunset tour $50/33)*, which operates regular ferry services to Sausalito and the East Bay from Pier 41 on big, wheelchair-accessible boats with wraparound windows, ample bathrooms and full-service bars. Blue & Gold also runs the world's first zero-emissions, all-hydrogen-powered ferry, plus seasonal sunset cruises with audio narration in nine languages.

PACIFIC WHALE-WATCHING

If your dream boat trip is part rom-com, part Moby Dick, consider Pacific whale-watching expeditions with Oceanic Society *(oceanicsociety.org; $300)*. During migration seasons, naturalist-led, all-day cruises depart from near the **Wave Organ** (p67) at the Marina yacht harbor; book ahead.

Researched by
Margot Seeto

DOWNTOWN, CIVIC CENTER & SOMA

BIG BUILDINGS, BIG CHANGES

In eastern San Francisco, Downtown encompasses Union Square, Civic Center and the Tenderloin, South of Market (SoMa), Financial District (FiDi), and parts of Mission Bay.

Downtown has all the urban amenities: art galleries, swanky hotels, first-run theaters, malls and entertainment megaplexes. Civic Center is a zoning conundrum, with great performances and Asian art treasures on one side of City Hall and dive bars and soup kitchens on the other. SoMa's high tech landscape is fickle but still present (Twitter/X has left the building, literally) – others like it for high art, but everyone gets down and dirty on the dance floor.

INCLUDES

FROM LEFT: NICKOLAY STANEV/SHUTTERSTOCK, BENJAMIN HEATH FOR LONELY PLANET

Above: Ferry Building (p100); Right: Sweet treat, Ferry Building

See page 259 for places to stay in Downtown, Civic Center & SoMa.

Highlights

1 Ferry Building

Graze the Northern California food scene at this showcase for the Bay Area's food purveyors and farmers. **p100**

2 San Francisco Museum of Modern Art

Get lost in mesmerizing installation art at SFMOMA that tripled its size in 2016. **p86**

3 San Francisco Symphony

The Grammy-winning symphony carries on the legacy of former conductor Michael Tilson Thomas. **p110**

4 Asian Art Museum

See all the way across the Pacific via the museum's treasures of both ancient and contemporary art from the Asian diaspora. **p108**

5 Embarcadero

Wander south for people-watching, historic watering holes, peeks at Giants games, and dazzling nighttime views of the Bay Lights. **p103**

Getting Around

Muni & BART

Buses , metro lines J, K, L, M, N, and T, and F-Market streetcars serve the area. BART shares Muni Downtown stations, connecting to the greater Bay Area.

Cable Car

Powell-Hyde and Powell-Mason lines link Downtown with the Wharf; the California St line runs perpendicular, over Nob Hill.

Ferry

Ferries connect the Ferry Building (p100) to Treasure Island, Angel Island/Tiburon, North Bay and East Bay.

Union Square

Union Square's image as a main tourist hub with shopping and hotels galore had been challenged by the pandemic. However, it's still a top place to stay – home to the Powell cable car turnaround and new pop-ups.

MAYA ANGELOU

Famed poet and civil rights activist Maya Angelou had talents beyond writing, including singing, acting, and dancing. Then there's the legend of her being the first Black cable car operator – not entirely true, but Angelou still had a pioneering transportation role in San Francisco.

The teenage Angelou moved with her family to the Bay Area in the 1940s, which coincided with the WWII labor shortage that opened up jobs to people of color and women (still with much discrimination).

Angelou became one of the first Black female electric streetcar conductors in SF for Muni's then-competitor, Market Street Railway (think streetcars instead of cable cars), a feat that garnered her a lifetime achievement award from the Conference of Minority Transportation Officials in 2014.

Ride All Three Cable Car Lines

Max out your visitor ride pass

Cable cars almost disappeared in 1947, but the city came to its senses and eventually designated the system a National Landmark in 1964. What would San Francisco be without them? Part of the city's Muni system *(sfmta.com/getting-around/muni/cable-cars, $8 single, $13 1-day Muni passport)* since 1944 (but here since 1873), SF's cable cars are the only manually operated cable car system in the world, with more than 254,000 passenger trips per month. Why not ride all the lines in a day? It won't take as long as you think, with each one-way ride clocking in around 15 minutes. The longest part may be waiting at the turnarounds, which are more crowded than hopping on mid-route. The upside to the wait is that riders can see staff manually turn the cars around on wooden platforms. Seasoned operators and conductors are helpful, with a dry sense of humor.

Ride north-south up and down the hills on both the Powell/Hyde and Powell/Mason lines, starting at the **Powell St Cable Car Turnaround**, which take riders between downtown's skyscrapers, through culture-filled Chinatown (p118), past Nob Hill's Fairmont Hotel (p146) and Grace Cathedral (p145) and end at the tourist attractions of Fisherman's Wharf (p71). Most visitors stick to these lines, but there's a third line that tends to be less crowded — the east-west California St beginning from the **California St Cable Car Turnaround**, that runs between Van Ness Avenue in Nob Hill and Davis Street in FiDi (p98). It passes many of the same landmarks, with the addition of Polk Gulch and more of FiDi.

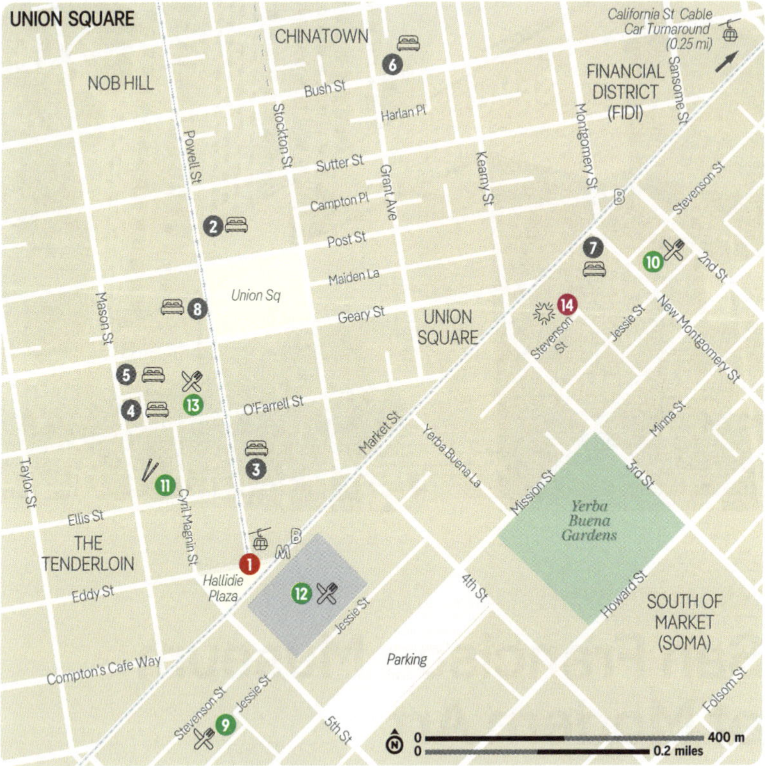

UNION SQUARE

SIGHTS
1 Powell St Cable Car Turnaround

SLEEPING
2 Beacon Grand
3 citizenM San Francisco Union Square
4 HI San Francisco Downtown
5 Hotel Nikko
6 Orchard Garden Hotel
7 Palace Hotel
8 Westin St Francis Hotel

EATING
9 Burma Love
10 House of Shields
11 Kin Khao
12 Mashaallah Pakistani Halal Food Restaurant
13 The Halal Guys

ENTERTAINMENT
14 Dawn Club

EATING NEAR POWELL STATION: OUR PICKS

Mashaallah Pakistani Halal Restaurant: Food court stand with sit-down-quality grilled meats, worth the 10-minute wait. *10am-8pm* $

Burma Love: Contemporary offshoot of the famed Burma Superstar. Try the crunchy tea leaf salad. *11:30am-9:30pm Sun-Thu, to 10pm Fri & Sat* $$

Kin Khao: Michelin-starred Thai cuisine highlighting Californian ingredients inside the Parc 55 Hotel. *11:30am-2pm, 5:30-9pm Sun-Thu, to 9:30pm Fri & Sat* $$$

The Halal Guys: A brick-and-mortar outpost of NYC's famous meat-and-rice Halal carts with NYC hours to match. *10am-3am Sun-Tue, to 5am Wed-Sat* $$

ANNE CZICHOS/SHUTTERSTOCK

TOP EXPERIENCE

San Francisco Museum of Modern Art

Expand your mind at **SFMOMA**, where boundary-pushing modern and contemporary masterworks sprawl over seven floors. The top 6th and 7th floors feature cutting-edge installations. Get an eyeful of Warhol's pop art on the 5th floor. Head to the 2nd floor for iconic works by Frida Kahlo and Henri Matisse, plus pieces by local artists throughout the museum.

DON'T MISS

- Alexander Calder: Dissonant Harmony
- Afterimages: Echoes of the 1960s
- 1900 to Now: SFMOMA's collection
- Special Exhibitions
- Bay Area Walls
- The Living Wall

Alexander Calder: Dissonant Harmony

The crowd-pleasing mobiles and metal sculptures of abstract artist Alexander Calder occupy part of the 3rd floor. Kinetic and whimsical, Calder's elements were actually always painstakingly thought-out. SFMOMA's collection includes the multi-colored *Lone Yellow* and the spellbinding movements of *Quatrro Pendulati*. Outside the Calder gallery is the impressive Living Wall.

PRACTICALITIES

● sfmoma.org ● adult/child $30/free ● 10am-5pm Fri-Tue, noon-8pm Thu, closed Wed

Afterimages: Echoes of the 1960s from the Fisher and SFMOMA Collections

The 5th floor collection presents some of the greatest hits of Pop Art, including Andy Warhol's electrically colored prints of celebrities and Ellsworth Kelly's joined-up canvases of unevenly shaped, bold colors. The pieces push the idea that the consciousness-shifting art movements of the 1960s are still relevant today.

1900 to Now: SFMOMA's collection

Rotating experimental works and masterpieces from its massive collection, SFMOMA encourages viewers to constantly re-examine the contradictions and interpretations of some of the greatest works of our time. Ponder the evolution of Diego Rivera's boldly colored works from the Cubist period to Post-Impressionist and beyond, and peruse Georgia O'Keeffe's interpretations of nature and the feminine through her technique of combining fine charcoal lines with paint.

Special Exhibitions

While the permanent collection pieces are rotated out to keep things fresh, the special exhibits provide a reason to visit the museum with each trip to SF. A retrospective of longtime SF resident, activist and artist Ruth Asawa, shared the evolution of her prolific art career, crafting hypnotically curved wire art. It also featured an outdoor garden in honor of her love of the hobby, and a version of her own living room that served as both her art studio and central family gathering space with her husband and six children. Other special exhibits have included the disorienting mirrored 'infinity' rooms of Yayoi Kusama, inclusivity in skateboard culture curated by local skate collective Unity, Ragnar Kjartansson's immersive video installation of his friends playing music in an old mansion, and Kara Walker's Octavia Butler-inspired sculpture exhibit that combined medieval mechanisms with ideas of transforming trauma.

Bay Area Walls

As a series of commissioned murals painted by local artists that span the 2nd, 3rd, and 5th floors, Bay Area Walls addresses current issues, and changes every few years. Get in the Game: Sports, Art, Culture – the series that debuted in 2024 – features graphic novel-style murals in Gene Luen Yang's *Bay Area Hoops,* depicting the story of three basketball players from local teams, including NBA darling Steph Curry. Jenifer K Wofford's *VMD* has pioneering Filipina Olympic diver Victoria Manalo Draves (born and raised in SoMa) captured in a vividly colored pike position, whereas David Huffman's *Portals* incorporates his recurring basketball court motif with otherworldly landscapes.

GREEN SPACES

While the high ceilings of SFMOMA's galleries aren't claustrophobic, it's still refreshing to have a few green respites during one's visit. On the 3rd floor is the Living Wall – the largest of its kind in the US. It is 30 feet high and contains more than 19,000 plants, including wild huckleberry and fragrant pink flowering currant. On the rooftop patio of Cafe 5 on the 5th floor there is a sculpture garden.

TOP TIPS

- Free general entry in on the first Thursday of the month (special exhibitions cost $10 extra).
- Take a pause on the padded stool area on the street entrance level to finish any outside food, then check your coat and bag for free.
- The 2nd floor has the ticket booth, STEPS cafe, plus most of the free art on the walls, ceilings, and floor below. View it on the way out if you have a timed special exhibit ticket to tend to first.

SoMa

South of Market saw redevelopment from the 1950s to the 1990s – Moscone Center, Yerba Buena Gardens, plus the 2016 SFMOMA expansion. SoMa is SF's clubbing district, and comprises the Leather & LGBTQ, SOMA Pilipinas, and Transgender districts.

AN ART SPACE MOVES DOWNTOWN

Originally established in the Dogpatch neighborhood in 2022, colorful nonprofit **Institute of Contemporary Art San Francisco** (ICA SF; Map p99) moved to what's known as The Cube on FiDi's Montgomery St in fall of 2024. Unlike other museums, ICA SF doesn't have an art collection, and instead focuses on experimental art on urgent topics from artists from all over the world. This noncommercial, non-celebrity model might seem strange in SF, where artists and techies have competed for space and attention since the gold rush – but they're co-conspirators at ICA SF, where major funders include Instagram cofounders.

Serenity in the City Center

Chill out in a green space

Intended as a green oasis and cultural center for Downtown, the three-block radius of **Yerba Buena Gardens** *(yerba buenagardens.org)* and the connecting **Yerba Buena Center for the Arts** *(ybca.org)* debuted in the 1990s as an area to organically meander through when doing the greatest hits of Downtown such as SFMOMA (p86). YBG is also aimed at visitors such as convention goers from the attached Moscone Center and IMAX movie-lovers at the connected **AMC Metreon 16**. Across a verdant lawn is the glass-paneled Martin Luther King, Jr Memorial waterfall where you can walk around both sides to contemplate his etched quotes on peace.

On the Upper Terrace sits one of San Francisco's first roof top parks, containing the Sister City Garden with 19 types of plants from each respective country. The Upper Terrace also has the Fun Zone, with a children's playground, Children's Creativity Museum, and 1906 LeRoy King Carousel. The Ice Skating & Bowling Center are open to all.

YBCA's **art gallery** *(entry $10, free Wed & 2nd Sun of the month)* is also a must-visit. It usually houses a major exhibit plus smaller ones throughout the venue. *The Only Door I Can Open: Women Exposing Prison through Art and Poetry* was curated and featured artwork by currently and formerly incarcerated women in California. In conjunction with replicas of prison living arrangements, the exhibit painted a realistic view of prison life. YBCA also features a variety of programming in its theaters – notably home to **Alonzo King LINES Ballet**, a pioneering majority-Black ballet company. From the spring through the fall is the annual **YBG Festival** *(ybgfestival.org)*, which presents free programming from concerts on the lawn and poetry events.

Culture in a Time of Change

Explore Downtown museums

One of the many strengths of Downtown is that it's a cultural center, home to some of the city's most significant museums, especially around Union Square and SoMa. Currently, that scene is anchored by SFMOMA (p86), in addition to Yerba Buena Center for the Arts (p88). At the time of writing, post-pandemic effects and unsteady federal funding made it confusing for visitors wanting to visit the museums. Is museum X closed for good or just temporarily? Virtual now or in the long-term? Moving? Current circumstances warrant the information below.

Just north of YBCA, the **Contemporary Jewish Museum** *(thecjm.org)* may reopen at the end of 2025. Wise Sons Deli closed its CJM operation in 2024. Past CJM exhibits ranged from ones on singer Amy Winehouse to those on Muppets' master Jim Henson. In the meantime, you can admire the exterior cube-shaped sculptural extension of the museum, covered in luminous blue steel panels that change color depending on the time of day and perspective. Next to SFMOMA is the **Museum of the African Diaspora** *(moadsf.org)*, which closed temporarily for remodeling and is scheduled to reopen in fall 2025, aligning with its 20th anniversary. Curator Key Jo Lee recently presented *Liberatory Living: Protective Interiors and Radical Black Joy*, examining and creating domestic interiors through a feminist framework. Just across from MoAd, the **California Historical Society** *(californiahistoricalsociety.org)* headquarters and museum has closed permanently, but its collection – known for historical documents related to the 1849 gold rush and statehood– is being moved to Stanford University. The **Mexican Museum** *(mexicanmuseum.org)*, with art ranging from pre-Columbian days to contemporary Latino art, has been moving to Yerba Buena Gardens from its previous Fort Mason (p65) home, with the goal of opening by the end of 2025. The **California Migration Museum** *(calmigration.org)* HQ is downtown, but it's actually fully virtual for accessibility purposes. Of note is its Melting Spots map and podcast of 38 immigrant-owned restaurants.

YBG GEMS

Trisha Lagaso Goldberg (@tza_lagoldberg) is Director of Programming and Engagement at the Anderson Collection at Stanford University & Curator at The Fine Arts Gallery at SFSU. These are some of her favorite spots in YBG.

YBCA: Yerba Buena Gardens came to life in the '90s. I had just graduated from the San Francisco Art Institute – an emerging artist finding my way. YBCA opened its doors to artists-as-curators, which was radical at the time. It became a site of possibility – where we could shape exhibitions and imagine futures. YBCA is always shifting. Go if you're curious about contemporary art, about this city.

Take a pause at YBG: Sit by the waterfall at YBG, eat lunch by the chess tables where Filipino elders gather, and let the day unfold from there.

EATING NEAR YBG: OUR PICKS

Dabao Singapore: Fine-dining chef Emily Lim's Singapore-style hawker stall, serving favorites like seafood laksa. *11am-3:30pm Tue-Thu, to 7pm Fri-Sun* $$

Delarosa Downtown: Longtime tenant of Yerba Buena Lane executes consistently excellent Roman-style pizzas. *11:30am-9:30pm Sun-Thu, to 10:30pm Fri & Sat* $

Ippudo San Francisco: The ramen chain's first full-dining West Coast location. Slurp *hakata*-style noodles in 18-hour *tonkotsu* broth. *11am-10pm* $$

Sana'a Cafe: A Yemeni coffee house whose flaky savory pastries and fragrant pistachio cakes are made in-house. *6:30am-10pm Mon-Fri, from 8am Sat & Sun* $

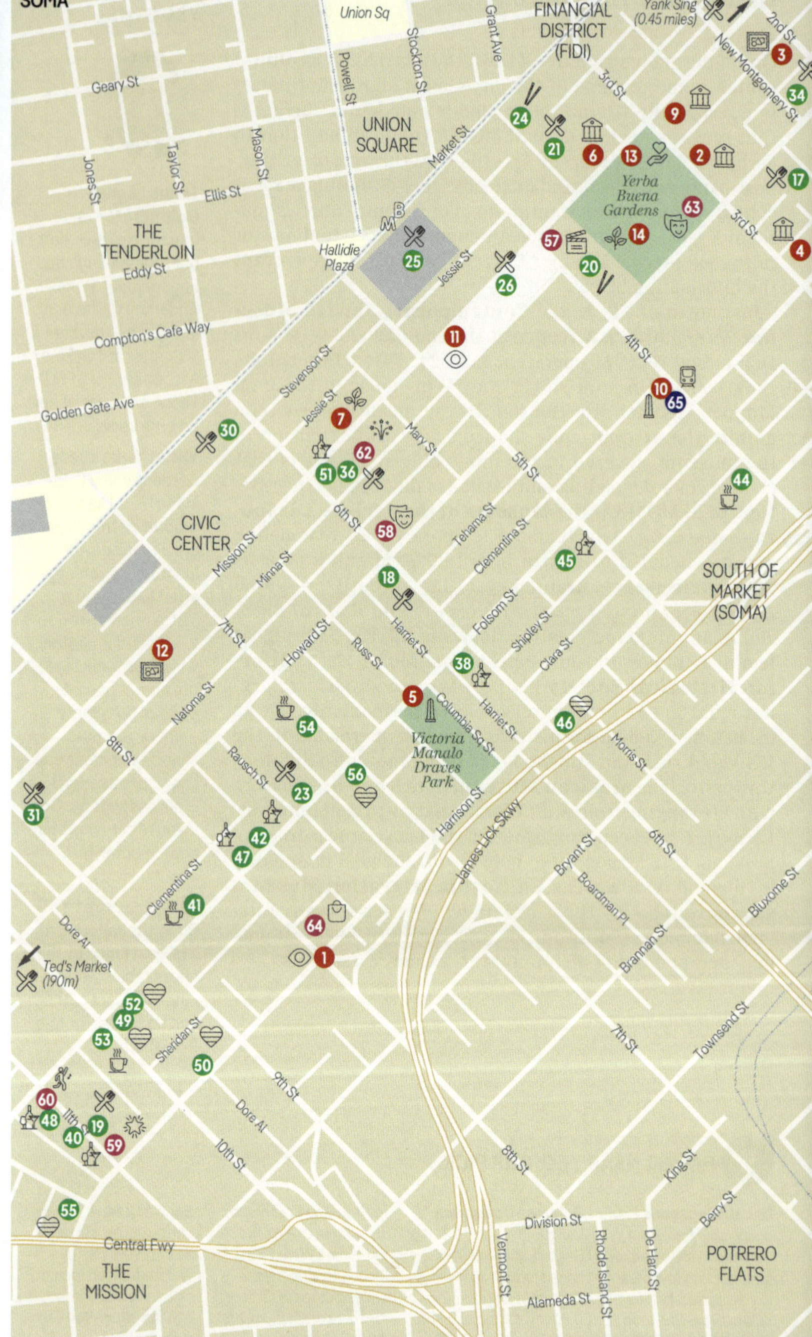
SOMA
Union Sq
Powell St
Stockton St
Grant Ave
FINANCIAL DISTRICT (FIDI)
Yank Sing (0.45 miles)
2nd St
New Montgomery St
3rd St
Geary St
Jones St
Taylor St
Mason St
UNION SQUARE
Market St
Ellis St
Yerba Buena Gardens
THE TENDERLOIN
Eddy St
Hallidie Plaza
Jessie St
Compton's Cafe Way
Stevenson St
4th St
Golden Gate Ave
Jessie St
Mary St
5th St
6th St
CIVIC CENTER
Mission St
Minna St
Tehama St
Clementina St
SOUTH OF MARKET (SOMA)
Folsom St
Shipley St
Clara St
7th St
Howard St
Russ St
Harriet St
Natoma St
Columbia Sq St
Harriet St
8th St
Rausch St
Victoria Manalo Draves Park
Morris St
Harrison St
James Lick Skwy
Bryant St
6th St
Boardman Pl
Clementina St
Bluxome St
Dore Al
Brannan St
Ted's Market (190m)
Sheridan St
7th St
Townsend St
11th St
9th St
Dore Al
10th St
8th St
King St
Berry St
Division St
Central Fwy
Vermont St
Rhode Island St
De Haro St
POTRERO FLATS
THE MISSION
Alameda St

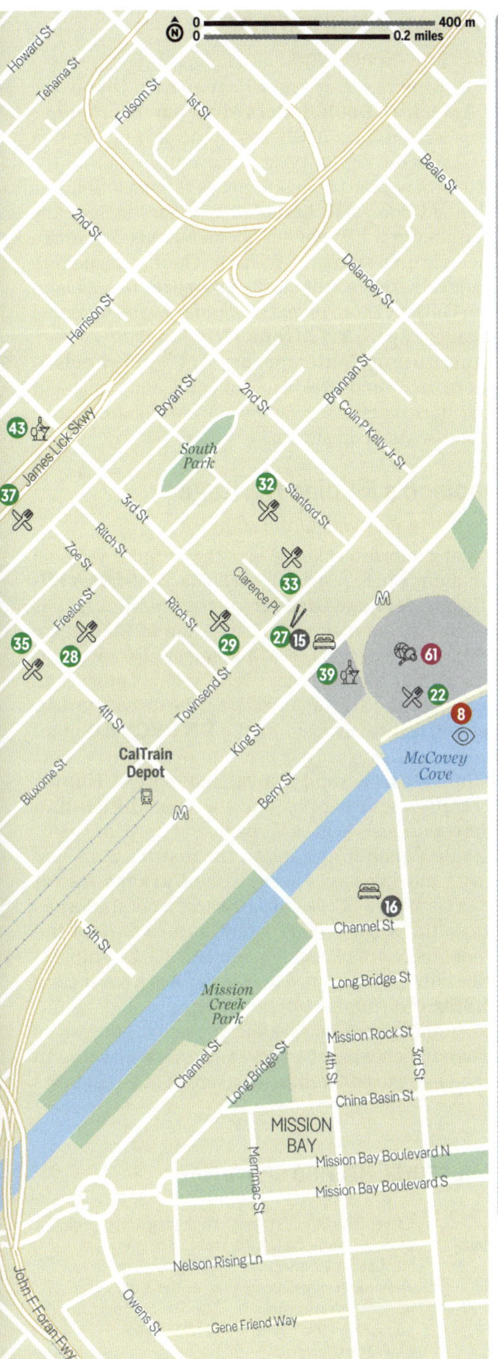

HIGHLIGHTS

1 Leather & LGBTQ Cultural District
2 San Francisco Museum of Modern Art (SFMOMA)

SIGHTS

3 111 Minna
4 American Bookbinders Museum
5 Carabao Mural
6 Contemporary Jewish Museum
7 Kapwa Gardens
8 McCovey Cove
9 Museum of the African Diaspora
10 Node by Roxy Paine
11 Oracle Park
12 Republika
13 SOMA Pilipinas Filipino Heritage District
14 Yerba Buena Gardens

SLEEPING

15 Hyatt Place
16 LUMA Hotel

EATING

17 Benu
18 Bini's Kitchen
19 Californios
20 Dabao Singapore
21 Delarosa Downtown
22 Gotham Club
23 HK Lounge Bistro
24 Ippudo San Francisco
25 Izzy & Wooks
26 JT Restaurant
27 Kaiyō Restaurant
28 Marlowe
29 Mestiza
30 Montesacro Pinseria
31 Moya
32 Rooh
33 Saison
34 Sana'a Cafe
35 Taksim
36 The Pawn Shop
37 The Sarap Shop

DRINKING & NIGHTLIFE

38 1015 Folsom
39 58 Social
40 Butter
41 Cafe Suspiro
42 Cat Club
43 City Nights
44 Delah Coffee
45 Dragon Horse
46 EndUp
47 F8
48 Halcyon
49 Hole in the Wall
50 Lone Star Saloon
51 Monarch
52 Powerhouse
53 Sextant Coffee Roasters
54 Sightglass Coffee
55 The SF Eagle
56 The Stud

ENTERTAINMENT

57 AMC Metreon 16
58 Bindlestiff Studio
59 DNA Lounge
60 Oasis
61 Oracle Park
62 UNDSCVRD
63 Yerba Buena Center for the Arts

SHOPPING

64 Mr S Leather

TRANSPORTATION

65 Central Subway System

THE SHIFT FROM MANILATOWN TO SOMA

Manilatown was once a Filipino American neighborhood that took up a 10-block radius around Kearny and Jackson Sts.

Home to 10,000 Filipinos, it was active from the 1920s to the late 1970s, with low-cost housing and family-owned businesses. With urban renewal looming, activists like Al Robles and Bill Sorro helped to organize tenants, activists, and artists to save Manilatown on the heels of the Civil Rights Movement.

In 1977, 400 riot police confronted 3000 protesters protecting the International Hotel ('I-Hotel'), an affordable housing and cultural hub. This fight contributed to the nationwide tenants' rights movement. The fall of the I-Hotel signaled the shift of the Filipino community to SoMa, where many Filipinos still live today.

Lesser-Known Downtown Art

Explore quirky niche museums

Take time to explore lesser-known art spaces. One is the non-profit **American Bookbinders Museum** *(bookbindersmuseum.org, adult/under-10 $15/free)* – the only museum in North America dedicated to preserving and promoting the art and history of western bookbinding. A recent exhibit was a timely Banned Book Jail. Recorded webinars include the dark and fascinating, like one on books bounds by human skin. While longtime street-art-friendly The Luggage Store Gallery is gone, there are still quirky art spaces like its non-profit **Swim Gallery** *(Map p106; swimgallery.com, free)*, and multi-use gallery space **111 Minna** *(111minnagallery.com, free)*. The **Institute of Contemporary Art San Francisco** *(p88; icasf.org, free)* funds free, experimental, nonpermanent exhibits that start timely conversations, from climate change to reparations, with an on-site maker space.

San Francisco's Filipino Heritage

Explore the SOMA Pilipinas Cultural District

After years-long effort to acknowledge the 100-plus-year-old Filipino community in SF, especially in SoMa, the **SOMA Pilipinas Filipino Heritage District** *(somapilipinas.org)* has become as vibrant and distinct a destination as Chinatown (p118) and North Beach (p127). SOMA Pilipinas also advocates for social justice and housing access. With a slew of other community nonprofits and arts organizations, the district throws epic parties and festivals, including the **UNDSCVRD** night market, more recently turned day party *(undiscoveredsf.com)*, the *ube* (Filipino purple yam) festival and more at **Kapwa Gardens** *(kapwagardens.com)*, and the annual **Pistahan Festival** *(pistahan.net)* held at Yerba Buena Gardens (p88).

More than 30 public works splash the district walls and windows with moving pieces such as the **Carabao Mural** by Franceska Gámez and Cece Carpio, where a floral adorned buffalo pulls a traditional village along, located at Russ and Folsom, where there are plans for an arched SOMA Pilipinas gateway to be built (also designed by Gámez). Black box theater **Bindlestiff Studio** *(bindlestiffstudio.org)* presents haunting, genre-bending pieces, such as the immersive ghost story *Mumoh*, where audience members share whiskey with actors in character, and move together through rooms of different times

EATING NEAR DOWNTOWN MUSEUMS: MELTING SPOTS MAP MAPS P90, P99

Bini's Kitchen: Chef Bini Pradhan was the first in SF to serve Nepalese *momos* (dumplings). The turkey ones pop with a tomato-cilantro sauce. *11am-3pm* $$

Moya: This unassuming SoMa corner Ethiopian spot is known for mushroom and tofu *tib* (stew). *11am-2pm & 5:30-8:30pm Mon-Fri, 5:30-8:30pm Sat* $$

Estrellita's Snacks (Map p106): A favorite La Cocina incubator alum brick-and-mortar spot dishing up huge Salvadorean *pupusas* (griddle cakes). *10am-8pm Mon-Fri* $

Yank Sing: Upscale dim sum place with daily rolling cart service – a rarity these days. *11am-3pm Tue-Fri, from 10am Sat & Sun* $$$

Pistahan Festival

and dimensions. The year 2026 is scheduled to see the debut of **Republika** *(kultivatelabs.org)*, a permanent commercial and cultural corridor on the ground floor of 5th & Mission Garage. A 2025 to 2026 exhibit at YBCA (p88), *Makibaka: A Living Legacy*, pays homage to previous generations that forged the Filipino community's *bayanihan* spirit, with a focus on SoMa and the future in the rapidly changing neighborhood.

With food being so central to Filipino culture, young food entrepreneurs who have launched in or with the help of the district include the plant-forward **The Sarap Shop** *(thesarapshop.com)*.

Safe Spaces to Play

Paint the Leather & LGBTQ Cultural District red

Come out to play in the landmark **Leather & LGBTQ Cultural District** *(sfleatherdistrict.org)*, the world's first and currently only city-recognized kink-positive leather district in the United States. District boundaries include Howard St (northwest), 6th

ORIGINS OF THE LEATHER DISTRICT

Polk Gulch in Nob Hill is often cited as SF's first 'gayborhood,' but the Castro (p192) became the epicenter of SF gay culture in the 1960s and 1970s, when suburban flight left the beautiful Victorian houses open for a new community that became mostly white-collar gay white men.

As they shaped gay Castro culture, what's now the Leather and LGBTQ Cultural District became a hub for those who favored the leather subculture and sex positivity that differed from the Castro.

Once with more than 30 bathhouses, bars, bookstores and other leather/gay spaces, the redevelopment of SoMa in the past few decades, combined with the AIDS epidemic, has reduced its cultural footprint. The district was created to preserve the history and present-day businesses – the first in the world.

EATING IN SOMA PILIPINAS: OUR PICKS

MAPS P90, P106

JT Restaurant: Inside the Mint Mall, chef-owner Tita (auntie) Tess scoops up hearty stews like chicken adobo. Cash only. *9am-7:30pm Mon-Sat* $

Kusina Ni Tess: Tiny restaurant with all-day *silog* (garlic rice and egg with protein) menu, including *pares* (braised beef stew). *8am-2pm Mon-Fri* $

Izzy & Wooks: Filipino American stall in the SF Centre food court. Try a tamarind hot chicken sandwich. *11am-3pm Mon-Thu, to 7pm Fri & Sat, to 6pm Sun* $

Mestiza: Plant-forward Filipino Mexican SoMa spot. The sweet potato *lumpia* (fried spring roll) is 11 inches long. *11am-8pm Tue-Sat* $$

St (northeast), I-80 (east) and Hwy 101 (south), plus a smaller leather district between 5th and 6th St, Harrison St and Bryant St. It's been SF's day and night party hub since the 1970s, and home to the largest concentration of gay bars and nightclubs outside of the Castro District. It overlaps with the SOMA Pilipinas (p92) cultural district and newer, more expensive housing elements, making for a diverse neighborhood.

The district has leather bars, drag cabarets and full-time LGBTQ clubs, all of which are lively, edgy, and historic. While dating app cruising has thinned the herd, many women prefer Bernal Heights dives, and some nights are slow starters, the following fixtures pack at weekends. **Oasis** *(sfoasis.com)* is SF's dedicated drag cabaret that mounts outrageous shows, sometimes literally. The title of original bear bar goes to **Lone Star Saloon** *(lonestarsf.com)*, which makes manly men warm and fuzzy at happy hour. **Hole in the Wall** *(blackwolfmetal.com)* provides a spiritual home to gay bikers and loudmouth punks. **The Stud** *(studsf.com)*, the US's first worker-owned co-op club, rose from the ashes of a pandemic shutdown, re-opening in a different SoMa location. While hosting nights of Dirty Talk game shows and Black house music and and ballroom beats, The Stud is continuously fundraising to build a stage for its drag shows. The historic **Eagle** *(sf-eagle.com)* has its line-inducing all-you-can-drink beer busts ($15) from 3pm to 7pm. Wear leather or very little. Thursdays through Sundays are best at **Powerhouse** *(powerhousebar.com)*, a sweaty bar for leathermen, shirtless gym queens and the occasional porn star – no gawkers allowed.

40 YEARS OF FOLSOM STREET

Around since 1984, the Folsom Street Fair is backed by the Folsom Street nonprofit, whose roots lie in fighting gentrification and displacement and advocating for liberation as a whole – sexual liberation plays a part.

While the fair is free, a $10 donation is suggested, which goes toward nonprofit LGBTQ+ causes such as the AIDS Emergency Fund and legal services. Folsom Street centers works with the Leather & LGBTQ Cultural District in keeping SoMa 'kinky and queer,' in their own words.

The district had gone through a lot during the AIDS crisis, losing community members and many of its businesses, yet still remained (and remains) a mutual aid and resource hub. This district shows resiliency to this day, and San Francisco wouldn't be San Francisco without it.

Let Your Freak Flag Fly

The wildest Leather District festivals

Besides **Pride** *(sfpride.org)*, the Leather & LGBTQ Cultural District's (p93) signature events include the world's biggest leather street party at **Folsom Street Fair** *(folsomstreet.org)*, where public spankings and cheap beer get the adults-only party started. More than 500,000 BDSM enthusiasts emerge from dungeons worldwide on the last Sunday of September on Folsom St between 8th and 13th Sts. As Folsom has grown in mainstream acceptance, vendors include not just BDSM goods, but also artisan high-quality wallets and belts, plus plenty of food trucks. Folsom is the culmination of **Leather Week** *(sfleatherweek.com)*, with preceding events that include the Mr SF Eagle Leather Contest and LeatherWalk.

EATING IN SOMA: OUR PICKS

HK Lounge Bistro: Top-notch, Michelin-recommended dim sum in a smallish space. Book ahead. *11am-2:30pm & 5-8:30pm Mon & Wed-Fri, from 10am Sat & Sun* $$$

Ted's Market: Family-owned since 1967 and beloved for sandwiches made of house-roasted tri-tip and steamed pastrami. *7am-7pm Mon-Fri, 9am-5pm Sat* $

Californios: Michelin-starred Cal-Mex fine dining from chef Val M. Cantú. Enjoy wild-caught *hamachi* with rhubarb and blood orange *aguachile*. *5-10pm Tue-Sat* $$$

Montesacro Pinseria: The country's first outlet serving *pinseria romana*: pizza's thin and crispy cousin. *11:30am-2:30pm & 4-9pm Tue-Thu & Sun, to 9:30pm Fri & Sat* $$

Folsom Street Fair

At summer spinoff **Up Your Alley Fair** *(folsomstreet.org)*, sun shines where it usually doesn't in Dore Alley, which is smaller and considered even more sex-positive than Folsom. Both fairs are 18-plus only; request consent and play safe. Both also have a focus on health resources and services, such as Mpox vaccination booths and free HIV testing.

If you want to prep sartorially before the fairs, go to **Mr S Leather** *(mr-s-leather.com)*, a gay-centric sex shop that is one of the most renowned of its kind of the west coast, whether it's for a leather sailor-front apron or a neoprene puppy hood.

Bring on the Night

Go clubbing in SoMa

Most nightclubs are in SoMa, but they're spread across a large area – don't walk in heels. The highest concentration of bars and clubs is around 11th and Folsom Sts. The SoMa scene, which largely favors EDM and house music these days, pops

PROTECTING LOCAL NIGHTLIFE CULTURE

With rising rents and the pandemic-era urban exodus, cities lost nightlife venues. In 2019, city supervisors introduced legislation to make it harder to convert clubs into office spaces, but couldn't save popular venues like Mezzanine – SF's largest woman-owned club. Amsterdam, New York and London instituted nightlife posts to protect these scenes.

In SF, former mayor London Breed introduced a program to help Downtown businesses produce events like drag shows and street festivals. Elected in 2024, mayor Daniel Lurie introduced new Entertainment Zones in 2025, including part of SoMa, which allow businesses to sell to-go alcohol for patios and street parties. Another small yet meaningful way to protect institutions has been to grant Legacy Business status to SoMa nightclubs such as **Butter** (p96) and **EndUp** (p96).

DRINKING IN SOMA: CAFFEINE KICKS

Sightglass Coffee: Flagship SoMa coffee roaster, serving creative drinks like orange marmalade espresso tonics. *6:30am-5pm Mon-Fri, from 7am Sat & Sun*

Sextant Coffee Roasters: Specializing in Ethiopian coffee, this flagship offers signature Wired Ghandis (spicy dirty chai). *7:30am-4pm Mon-Fri, from 8:30am Sat & Sun*

Cafe Suspiro: Coffee, records, books and art attract repeat customers to this Latino-owned joint. *8am-4pm Mon-Thu, to 3pm Fri & Sat*

Delah Coffee: Part of SF's cardamom-infused Yemeni coffee wave. Try the pistachio baklava. *6am-10pm Mon-Fri, 7am-11pm Sat & Sun*

Oracle Park

on weekends and shrivels on weekdays. From big name DJs to industrial goth nights, you have your pick of the dance party.

Cat Club *(sfcatclub.com)* is known for its New Wave and goth/industrial nights, plus a welcoming crowd. **Butter** is lowbrow and lovely – everyone's wailing to rock anthems and swilling 100% artificially flavored soda-pop cocktails here. Going hard into after hours, **EndUp**'s *(@endupsf)* Saturday nights have a way of turning into Sunday mornings. Straight people EndUp here too – but gay Sunday tea dances are SF staples since 1973. The multi-room, 250 person-capacity provides a relatively intimate club experience at **F8** *(feightsf.com)* with music ranging from house to hip-hop to dubstep. Among the city's biggest clubs, **1015 Folsom** *(1015.com)* packs for marquee EDM DJs and hip-hop acts, and has seen performances from the likes of LCD Soundsystem, with five dance floors and bars. **Monarch** *(monarchsf.com)* has a great sound system, multiple rooms with different vibes and DJs, and sometimes aerial dancers above the bar. **Halcyon**'s *(halcyon-sf.com)* LED

EATING IN SOMA: OFFBEAT GEMS

MAPS P85, P90

The Pawn Shop: Enter the speakeasy-like tapas bar through a pawn shop. Price of admission is an object to trade. *5-9pm Tue-Sat* **$$**

House of Shields: Old-school (opened 1908) SF bar. Catch chicken parm sandwich pop-up Bette's some nights. *2pm-2am Mon-Fri, from 5pm Sat & Sun* **$$**

Taksim: Modern Turkish food in a loft-like space; poached shrimp wrapped in delicate phyllo dough stand out. *5-8:45pm Mon-Thu, to 9:30pm Fri & Sat* **$$$**

Benu: Chef Corey Lee's three-Michelin star contemporary Korean cuisine has become synonymous with SF fine dining. *5:30-8:30pm Tue-Sat* **$$$**

lights in the single-room club complement its techno-heavy sets perfectly.

Younger international travelers may appreciate the 18+ clubs. While locals have a derisive rhyming nickname for **City Nights** *(sfclubs.com)*, it's one of the few 18+ clubs in the Bay Area and has been around since 1985. **DNA Lounge** *(dnalounge.com)* has 18-plus and all-ages shows and dance parties, along with an adjacent late-night pizza spot. There is something for everyone.

Root, Root, Root for the Home Team

Catch an SF Giants game

Having been a baseball team since 1883 (originally as the New York Gothams), the **San Francisco Giants** have called this city home since 1958, and are based in Mission Bay's **Oracle Park stadium** *(mlb.com/giants/tickets, $15–170)*. Baseball season runs roughly March through September, with other events like major concerts at the stadium year-round.

Preview virtual views from seats when purchasing tickets online. Book parking in advance for about $20 on an app like SpotHero – or pay up to $100! Public transit to 2nd and King Sts is cheap and easy. The park opens 90 to 120 minutes before games; inside, you can admire six bronze statues of greats like Willie Mays and Juan Marichal. Use one of the multiple stadium entrances, including one through adjoining bar **58 Social** (formerly Public House). Bring sun protection and a light jacket. Definitely read the rules of the stadium before going, and carve out three hours for games. Families can go to the iconic Coca-Cola bottle sculpture at the Fan Lot, which houses slides that kids can use.

Food lovers can map out stalls of interest online, or do a giant lap around each level. SF institution **Doggie Diner** has locations throughout with staples like hotdogs. Signature park garlic fries are true vampire repellent. **Crazy Crab'z** crab sandwiches and **Tony's Pizza** might sell out. **The Lumpia Company's** dole whip, chef **David Chang's Fuku restaurant's** fried chicken sandwiches, and **Rah Rah Ramen** are winning new fans.

HOW TO SEE A GAME FOR FREE

Along the walkway by **McCovey Cove** (back of Oracle Park), find the sign for **Triples Alley** just past the private **Gotham Club**. Space permitting, anyone can enter through the metal detectors to a shaded, caged area, which some call The Viewing Point, to view up to three innings of Giants games for free, albeit from a far outfield view. If it's not crowded, you may stay for longer.

Those with access to kayaks can also hang out in the McCovey Cove waters to watch the giant stadium screens. The new **China Basin Park** across from the cove comes to life before the games with food and drink vendors, plus plenty of seating to watch the big screens and hear the game action.

EATING NEAR ORACLE PARK: FINE DINING

Saison: Michelin-starred New American hearth cooking with seasonal dishes. Book bar seats for the $78 tasting menu. *5-9:30pm Tue-Sat* $$$

Marlowe: A local pioneer of the fancy burger movement of the 2010s continues to be an SF staple. *11am-9pm, to 10pm Fri & Sat* $$$

Kaiyō Restaurant: Nikkei (Japanese Peruvian) cuisine: opt for matcha fettuccine or a rooftop bar pisco miso cocktail. *5-10pm Sun & Tue-Sat* $$$

Rooh: 'Progressive Indian' establishment incorporates California ingredients in *dahi puri* semolina puffs with avocado. *5-9:30pm Sun-Thu, to 10pm Fri & Sat* $$$

Jackson Square & the Financial District

You'll hit Jackson Square and the iconic Transamerica Pyramid on your way from Union Square to North Beach and Chinatown. It borders the Financial District (FiDi), with its historic architecture and art.

JACKSON SQUARE AS THE WILD WEST

Before the gold rush of 1848, this was a notorious waterfront dock area. Behind the iron shutters of these Italianate brick buildings, whiskey dealers, loan sharks, brothel owners, lawyers and assorted hustlers plied their trades. Notorious gold-rush-era saloon owner Shanghai Kelly and brothel proprietor Miss Piggott made an almost literal killing, knocking out new arrivals with blows to the head and delivering them to ships in need of crew to be forcibly pressed into service. Today, Jackson Square's tenants are antique dealers, clothing retailers and interior designers.

A Unique Skyscraper

Explore iconic architecture and its surrounds

Framed by Washington, Columbus, Pacific and Sansome Sts, Jackson Square has changed much since its days as the former coastline of SF. This was a notorious waterfront dock area before the 1848 gold rush filled in the area with abandoned ships (see left). Most recently, the area has become a refuge for retailers and offices that have left the more southern parts of Downtown since the pandemic. **Hotaling Place** holds the title as oldest alleyway in San Francisco, dating back to at least 1866, and is lined with designer and boutique shops.

Anchoring the square is the **Transamerica Pyramid**, built in 1972 and SF's most distinctive skyline feature before the construction of the Salesforce Tower (p102). The half-acre redwood park that boasts 50 trees was expanded and revitalized post-pandemic. There is plenty of seating, foosball tables, a stage and rotating art in the form of woodland creature sculptures. Conceived by chef Brad Kilgore, a slew of eateries have opened or are planning to open.

The building lobby itself has stunning sculpture-like floral arrangements that get refreshed weekly, plus a small coffee bar. Adjacent to the lobby is a free exhibit space (with amazing bathrooms), recently featuring models of Norman Foster's world-renowned architectural work in *The Vertical City*, including the Gherkin in London (Foster led the revitalization of the Transamerica).

EATING IN JACKSON SQUARE: OUR PICKS

Cassava: Cute Japanese-Californian eatery specializes in Spam *onigirazu* (onigiri sandwich) and Sonoma duck confit bento. *8am-3:30pm Mon-Fri* $

Cafe Sebastian: Bistro dishes run the gamut from n'duja-stuffed medjool dates to an excellent tuna nicoise salad. *8am-4pm Mon-Fri, from 9am Sat & Sun* $$

Verjus: Bouillabaisse-like Dungeness crab soup and rare sparkling wines star at this hip wine bar and French restaurant. *4-10pm Tue-Fri, to 11pm Sat & Sun* $$$

Cotogna: Casual sister restaurant to fine-dining neighbor Quince, famous for its giant raviolo oozing egg yolk. *4:30pm-9pm Tue-Thu, 11:30am-9:30pm Fri & Sat* $$$

JACKSON SQUARE & THE FINANCIAL DISTRICT

HIGHLIGHTS
1 Ferry Building Market & Justin Herman Plaza

SIGHTS
2 140 Montgomery Street
3 Hotaling Place
4 Institute of Contemporary Art San Francisco
5 Rincon Center
6 Salesforce Park
7 Salesforce Tower
8 Transamerica Pyramid

EATING
9 Acme Bread Company
10 Barebottle Beer Garden at Salesforce Park
11 Cafe Sebastian
12 Cassava
13 Cholita Linda
14 Cotogna
15 Crustacean
16 Da Afghanan Kabob House
17 Far West Fungi
18 Ginger's
19 Hog Island Oyster Company
20 Humphry Slocombe
21 Lunette
22 Ocean Malasada Company
23 Peaches Patties
24 Señor Sisig (SF Ferry Building)
25 Turtle Tower
26 Verjus
27 Yank Sing

DRINKING & NIGHTLIFE
28 Blue Bottle Coffee
29 Red Bay Coffee (Ferry Building)
30 Rickhouse

ENTERTAINMENT
31 Punch Line

SHOPPING
32 Bernal Cutlery
33 Book Passage
34 Fog City Flea Trading Post
35 Heath Ceramics

TRANSPORTATION
36 California St Cable Car Turnaround
37 Salesforce Transit Center

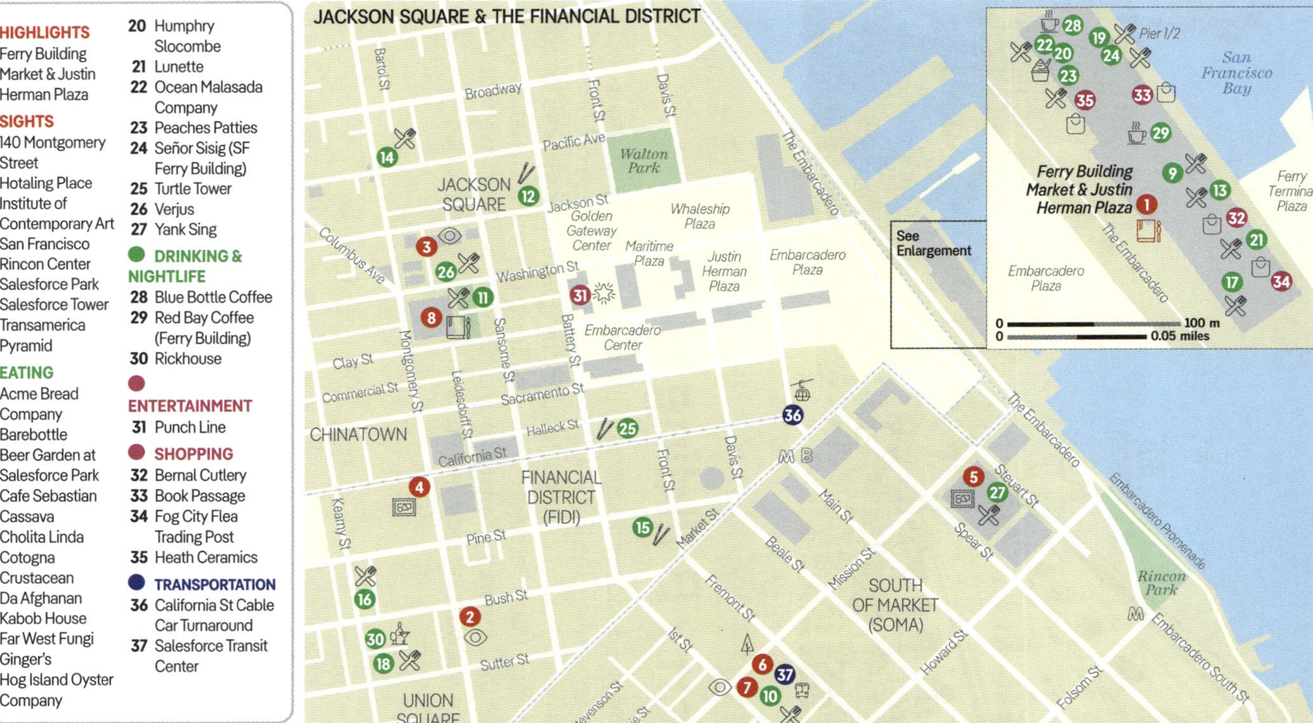

PHOTO.UA/SHUTTERSTOCK

TOP EXPERIENCE

Ferry Building

Reimagined and reintroduced to the public in 2003 after a four-year restoration, the 1898-built Ferry Building has since become a destination hub for artisanal food hopping, with bonus points for going on a Ferry Plaza Farmers Market day. Triple points if it's a Saturday, when the farmers market hosts over 100 vendors. Don't overlook the shops showcasing local makers or the actual ferries, either.

DON'T MISS

- Ferry Building Marketplace
- Ferry Plaza Farmers Market
- Retailers featuring local makers
- The actual ferries
- Views of the waterfront and Bay Bridge

Ferry Building Marketplace

The stately 240-ft-tall clock tower of the Ferry Building had been overshadowed by a freeway overpass from the 1950s until the damage from the 1989 Loma Prieta earthquake necessitated a reimagining of the Embarcadero as a pedestrian hub, all accessible by Muni, BART, bicycle, and car. The 2003 debut of the Ferry Building Marketplace welcomed artisanal food shops in the Grand Hall. While vendors do change, staples like **Humphry Slocombe** ice cream, **Blue Bottle Coffee**, **Acme Bread**

PRACTICALITIES

● ferrybuildingmarketplace.com ● 7am-8pm; farmers market 10am-2pm Tue & Thu, 8am-2pm Sat ● ferry schedules: sanfranciscobayferry.com & goldengate.org

Company, and **Far West Fungi** have held steady. Currently, marketplace favorites include Hawai'i-style *malasadas* (fried dough pastries) at **Ocean Malasada Company**, an outpost of the Filipino Mexican **Señor Sisig**, **Red Bay Coffee**, **Hog island Oyster Co.**, and **Peaches Patties**. A La Cocina food entrepreneur incubator alum includes Cambodian eatery **Lunette**.

Ferry Plaza Farmers Market

In addition to the dizzying array of joy-inducing food inside the Marketplace, the **Ferry Plaza Farmers Market** also takes place outside three times a week. About 10 to 15 vendors line the front on Tuesdays and Thursdays. The Saturday market is the beacon of California's bounty. More than 100 vendors wrap around the building, attracting 25,000 visitors weekly. Like the Marketplace, vendors change, but there's never a shortage of super fresh local produce, coffee, baked goods, hot food, and pantry staples. Current favorites include **Primavera's** egg-laden, crunchy *chilaquiles* (fried corn tacos) with salsa verde, **Dirty Girl Produce**, **Nusa's** pandan-inflected Indonesian sweets, **Delightful Foods's** creamy bean pies, and **Hodo's** organic tofu.

Retailers Featuring Local Makers

Don't overlook the non-food spaces that highlight local makers. See why **Heath Ceramics** has had an impact on mid-century design. Marvel at the expertise of the **Bernal Cutlery** staff, plus the well-curated section of pantry staples. Grab a book for your travels at the indie **Book Passage**. The huge 5000-sq-ft corner retailer **Fog City Flea Trading Post** is a bright space featuring wares of local artists, from Jenny Lemons's Swiss chard-shaped hair claw clips and Shaghayegh Tafreshi's bubble-sleeved dress-coats to Gravel & Gold's well-curated collections of vintage, deadstock, and other conscientious goods.

The Actual Ferries

The Ferry Building houses ports for ferries going all over the Bay Area. With the exception of Alcatraz ferries (p238) that launch from Pier 33, one mile north, here are ferries bound for Treasure Island (p243), Angel Island/Tiburon (p240), Sausalito, Larkspur, Vallejo, Oakland (p247), and Alameda. Some ferry lines require a round-trip ticket purchase in advance. Load up your Clipper Card beforehand, consider the SF Bay Ferry app, or else purchase paper tickets.

Views of the Waterfront & Bay Bridge

Consider taking the Embarcadero Stroll (p103) southward toward Oracle Park (p97) to enjoy the waterfront breezes and scenes. If you're around the area at nightfall, the sparkling **Bay Lights** on the Bay Bridge may be illuminated. The 250,000 lights first ran 2013-2023, with a break to install double the number of LED lights. They were turned on briefly in March 2025, and as of writing, have been turned off again for maintenance. Reopening date is scheduled for fall 2025.

FOODWISE & ITS FARMERS MARKET MISSION

Foodwise *(foodwise.org)*, the nonprofit that runs the Ferry Plaza Farmers Market, focuses on food access and education. In addition to its youth programs, its market tents provide cooking demos by local chefs, and free samples made from market finds spark healthy inspiration. A spring dish might be an herbaceous pesto made from green garlic, lemon, parmesan, garlic, walnuts, spinach, and parsley served atop a baguette.

TOP TIPS

- Wear sun protection and layers. The lines for popular vendors can be a 10- to 30-minute wait.
- Cash is the preferred payment method for many farmers market vendors. Most accept cards, but some are cash-only (ATMs inside).
- At the Saturday farmers market, store your haul for free at the Veggie Valet during market hours.
- For waterside dining at the Ferry Building, snag a table at Hog Island Oyster Co., Cholita Linda, or get takeout from any vendor for open public seating behind the building.
- Cafes on the ferries may or may not be open during your ride. Check beforehand and get (superior) food at the Ferry Building.

FIDI GEMS

Elaine Chu & Marina Perez-Wong (@twinwallsmuralcompany) are muralists. These are some of their favorite places in FiDi.

Rincon Center: The history in the financial district is fascinating – many buildings have hidden treasures inside, like the WPA murals inside Rincon Center's former post office. Panels along the upper lobby walls, by painter Anton Refregier, illustrate the **History of California**, from the Spanish conquest of California to the founding of the United Nations in SF at the end of WWII.

140 Montgomery St: The beautiful marble in the old buildings includes architect Timothy Pflueger's work, like the dark marble interior of 140 Montgomery that was inspired by Chinese brocade. Marina's great-grandfather laid a lot of the marble into the old FiDi buildings, and perhaps this was one of them.

Reimagining the Skyline

Carving out new urban spaces

Iconic skyscrapers make up SF's postcard-worthy skyline, with the Transamerica Pyramid (p98) long taking top prize. However, the 2018 opening of the 1070-ft-tall **Salesforce Tower** led the locals to accept the city's newest tallest building. The changing art projection on the top of the tower is admittedly cool, with 11,000 LED lights making up the highest public art installation in the US, titled *Day for Night* by local artist Jim Campbell. Adjacent to the tower is the **Salesforce Transit Center**, a major FiDi transit hub that houses the long 5.4-acre **Salesforce Park** on its roof, which is free and open to the public. There's even a (very short) gondola ride that goes the four stories up. In the spirit of New York City's High Line, rethinking transit spaces as green oasis opportunities complements a downtown concrete jungle. The park has 13 gardens along the perimeter representing different countries, plus a motion-activated Bus Fountain. Take a lap, bring kids to the playground, enjoy the view or a concert, or grab a tap beer and Detroit-style Joyride Pizza at the **Barebottle Beer Garden** on the roof.

Another new, creative urban space is the **Central Subway System**, debuted in 2023, where the T Muni metro line runs from 4th and Brannan Sts through Yerba Buena (p88), Union Square (p84), and Chinatown (p118). Aside from getting from one stop to the next in 1-2 minutes, 10 works of striking public art are reason to hop on for a quick ride to each. Outside the **Yerba Buena/Moscone station**, **Node by Roxy Paine** (Map p90) is a spindly 102-ft-tall stainless sculpture (the tallest freestanding one in SF) that is at once ominous and cartoonish. At the **Chinatown-Rose Pak Station**, Yumei Hou created two floor-to-ceiling laser-cut works on bold red sheet metal, mimicking traditional Chinese paper art.

EATING IN FIDI: RESURRECTED LOCAL FAVORITES

Turtle Tower: The first Northern Vietnamese-style pho outlet, serving clear broth and wide rice noodles. Gateway dish: *pho gà* (chicken pho). *11am-9pm* $$

Crustacean: The family gets credit for inventing Vietnamese American garlic noodles with roast Dungeness crab. *4:45-8:15pm Sun & Tue-Thu, to 8:45pm Fri & Sat* $$$

Ginger's: This gay bar reopened next door to its old location with a Drag-o-Licious show and food pop-ups. *5pm-midnight Wed-Thu, to 2am Fri* $$

Da Afghanan Kabob House: Rare Afghan restaurant from Fremont's 'Little Kabul.' Now a FiDi takeout spot for *qabili* (rice pilaf) with tender lamb. *11am-8pm Mon-Fri* $$

EMBARCADERO STROLL

Amble along the waterfront for bay views, public art, and historic watering holes.

START	END	LENGTH
Vaillancourt Fountain	Oracle Park	2km; 1½ hrs

At the Embarcadero (the eastern gateway to San Francisco), take a stroll along the paved waterfront – part of the San Francisco Bay Trail – to take in the bustling city, its historic places and experimental ones, starting from the brutalist 1 **Vaillancourt Fountain** in 2 **Embarcadero Plaza,** with striking concrete angles.

Pass by pickleball courts, then art vendors lining Market St. A 45-ft-tall, nude (and controversial) steel woman sculpture that 'breathes' every hour called 3 **R-Evolution** is on view until October 2025.

Turn south at the 4 **Ferry Building** (p100) and stroll along the promenade, sparkling bay waters to your left, weaving past joggers and dog walkers. The towering 5 **San Francisco-Oakland Bay Bridge** makes you appreciate more than the Golden Gate, especially if the Bay Lights turn on. Just north will be the bow and arrow of Claes Oldenberg and Coosje van Bruggen's 6 **Cupid's Span** in **Rincon Park**. Grab a burger or beer at a trio of historic waterside dive bar shacks – all with patio seating. 7 **Hi Dive** has a sea-blue exterior and $3 canned PBR. 8 **Red's Java House's** walls are plastered with sports memorabilia; it's known for its sourdough cheeseburger. 9 **Frankie's Java House** has got a modern facelift. There are also SF Giants pre-game options near 10 **Oracle Park** (p97).

Vaillancourt Fountain may or may not be filled with water during your visit, depending on maintenance and drought status.

The 70ft-tall **Cupid's Span**'s curved bow echoes the shape of the Bay Bridge.

Red's Java House and **Hi Dive** have been featured on TV and film – the *Goliath* series with Billy Bob Thornton and the *Nash Bridges* movie starring Don Johnson, respectively.

Civic Center & the Tenderloin

Civic Center is where majestic City Hall stands, the main library awes, and the Theater District houses world-class culture. North is the gritty Tenderloin, for street-smart travelers who love regional history and diverse food.

ON HOMLESSNESS

While homelessness is not new to SF, its proliferation is entwined with the pandemic-spurred 'doom loop' SF narrative: a combination of empty offices, gentrification, fentanyl crisis and inadequate homeless services creating a crime-ridden city. There is evidence that this view is exaggerated (SF is a liberal symbol, prone to both attacks and praise): return-to-office mandates are slowly repopulating Downtown – but homelessness is an ongoing issue.

Former mayor London Breed increased access to housing and mental health resources, but ordered encampment sweeps. Current mayor Daniel Lurie promises to continue addressing these issues, but the long-term effects remain to be seen.

Use your gut to decide whether to visit certain neighborhoods or give money or food.

Welcome to the Tenderloin

Touring a storied neighborhood

The Tenderloin's notoriety as a red light district keeps tourists from witnessing historic sites where Muhammad Ali boxed, Billie Holiday sang, and LGBTQ+ activists fought for their right to be served in cafeterias – and established America's first Transgender Cultural District (p284). Resident **Tenderloin Museum** *(tenderloinmuseum.org, adult/under-12 $10/free)* historians lead intrepid visitors past these and other groundbreaking Tenderloin locales; walking shoes and city smarts are essential. TLM walking tours visit the lobby of the historic **Cadillac Hotel SRO** (home of the museum), **Boeddeker Park**, **GLIDE Memorial Church**, the site of the Compton's Cafeteria Riot, past and present labor union locales. Tours also highlight some of the Tenderloin's most iconic murals and public artworks. The museum also features robust programming, such as the past production of a Compton's Cafeteria Riot play in the annex space at 835 Larkin St.

The museum itself takes about 45 minutes to peruse, showing visitors through photographs and other ephemera of the Tenderloin's long history, from the hopping nightclubs and brothels, and an immigrant hub with affordable housing, to the fact that present-day Tenderloin has around 3500 children – the highest density of kids in the city. It's a neighborhood rich in history and culture, and the museum is an essential way to learn about it.

The World on a Plate

The Tenderloin's global dining

The Tenderloin is one of the most diverse neighborhoods in San Francisco – often a landing point for new immigrants needing affordable housing. That translates to a wide variety of some of the tastiest food in the city. Local customers are a mixture of neighborhood families, Single Room Occupancy residents, UC Law San Francisco students, City Hall employees, and the remaining tech workers from the Mid-Market area. The main food drag runs north-south on Larkin Street, mostly between Golden Gate Avenue to Post St before turning into Lower Nob Hill ('Tendernob'), and east-west roughly between Polk and Jones Sts. First things first: bring cash. Some places accept cards, but some do not. Of note – La Cocina, kitchen incubator for food entrepreneurs, opened a Municipal Marketplace on Hyde that unfortunately did not last, but the space remains a second incubator kitchen for its program participants.

Little Saigon & Beyond

The Tenderloin's Vietnamese food

Officially designated in 2003, Little Saigon is marked by two marble lions atop 8ft-tall pylons that flank Larkin Street between Eddy and O'Farrell. After the Fall of Saigon in 1975, displaced Vietnamese and other Southeast Asian refugees found affordable housing in the Tenderloin. In addition to businesses and nonprofits serving the Vietnamese community, some of the city's best Vietnamese restaurants also took root here. Today, lines form out the door for **Saigon Sandwich**'s super fresh *bánh mì* sandwiches, **Hai Ký Mì Gia's** Chinese-Vietnamese Teochew duck leg noodle soup, **Pho 2000**'s spice-heavy beef *pho*, **Golden Lotus**'s soft rice rolls stuffed with crisp greens and marinated meat, and **Mong Thu**'s peppery duck and bamboo shoot noodle soup, just a block east on Hyde. Also of note is **Battambang Market** on Eddy near the police station, which opened in 1984 as SF's first Cambodian market – and still operates today, mostly with Thai offerings and an assortment of canvas paintings of a Cambodian skyline for sale.

From Yemen to Sudan

Middle Eastern, Halal & North African dining

At least since the 1970s, Yemeni and other Arab families have come to the states, including Northern California and the Tenderloin, largely due to political upheaval at home. The largest mosque in Downtown SF is on Jones St, run by the Islamic Society of San Francisco, and draws more of the community to the Tenderloin. **Yemen Kitchen**, owned by former Yemeni soccer star Abdul Al Rammah, dishes up comforting lentil soup and cardamom lamb; Al Rammah has also recently opened **Yemeni Kabab & Mediterranean**, where the super spicy lamb *saltah* stew is a specialty. **Red Chilli Halal** offers exquisite handmade *momos*. **Kinara Fusion** has a signature spicy Chicken 69. **Z Soul** is perhaps the only SF restaurant of its kind, and its Sudanese and Middle Eastern offerings include a tasty eggplant salad and daily Sudanese stew specials.

Chefs Embrace the Tenderloin

Upscale & fine dining

A recent wave of fine-dining-ish chefs have opened their own ventures in the Tenderloin. **Bodega** is an upscale Vietnamese food tribute by chef Matthew Ho to his family's previous

Continues on p110

WHAT'S SPECIAL ABOUT THE TENDERLOIN

Eric Ehler (@intheweedz), chef, pizza shop owner, skater, self-described local foodie and art lover, has been visiting and working in the Tenderloin for years. Here's what he considers special.

That Eclectic Urban Feel: It makes you feel like you're in a city. Even though the area has changed, what has stayed certain are great restaurants, galleries and people. It's home to the most diverse population in the city that keeps the city going.

United Nations Plaza: That's where the world-class **UN Skate Plaza** is now located. You can watch a local pro skate like they're in the X Games.

Heart of the City Farmers Market (p115): Truly a special experience. Truly San Francisco.

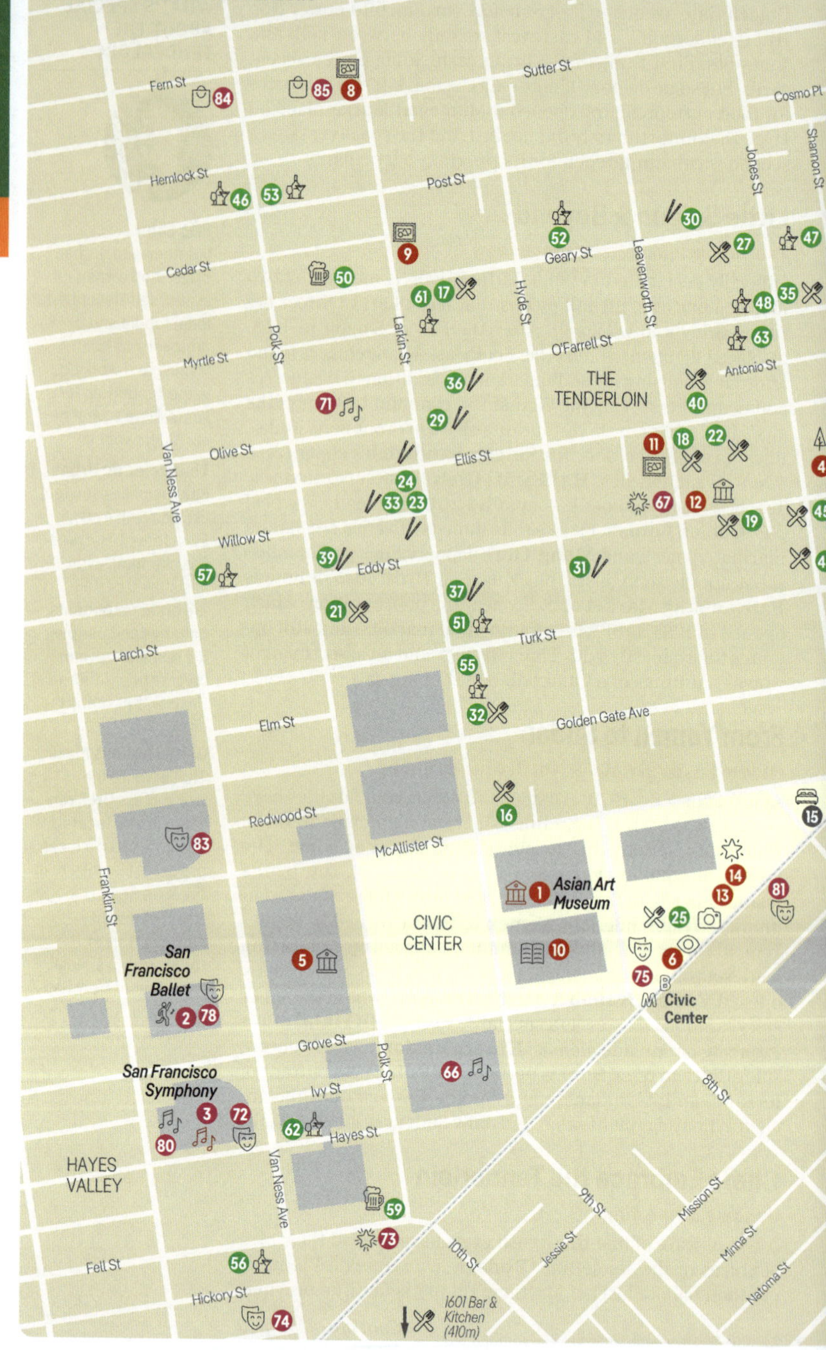
CIVIC CENTER & THE TENDERLOIN
Fern St
Sutter St
Cosmo Pl
Hemlock St
Post St
Jones St
Shannon St
Cedar St
Geary St
Leavenworth St
Hyde St
Larkin St
Polk St
O'Farrell St
Myrtle St
Antonio St
THE TENDERLOIN
Olive St
Ellis St
Van Ness Ave
Willow St
Eddy St
Turk St
Larch St
Golden Gate Ave
Elm St
Redwood St
McAllister St
Franklin St
Asian Art Museum
CIVIC CENTER
San Francisco Ballet
Civic Center
Grove St
Ivy St
8th St
San Francisco Symphony
Hayes St
HAYES VALLEY
Mission St
9th St
Minna St
10th St
Jessie St
Natoma St
Fell St
Hickory St
1601 Bar & Kitchen (410m)

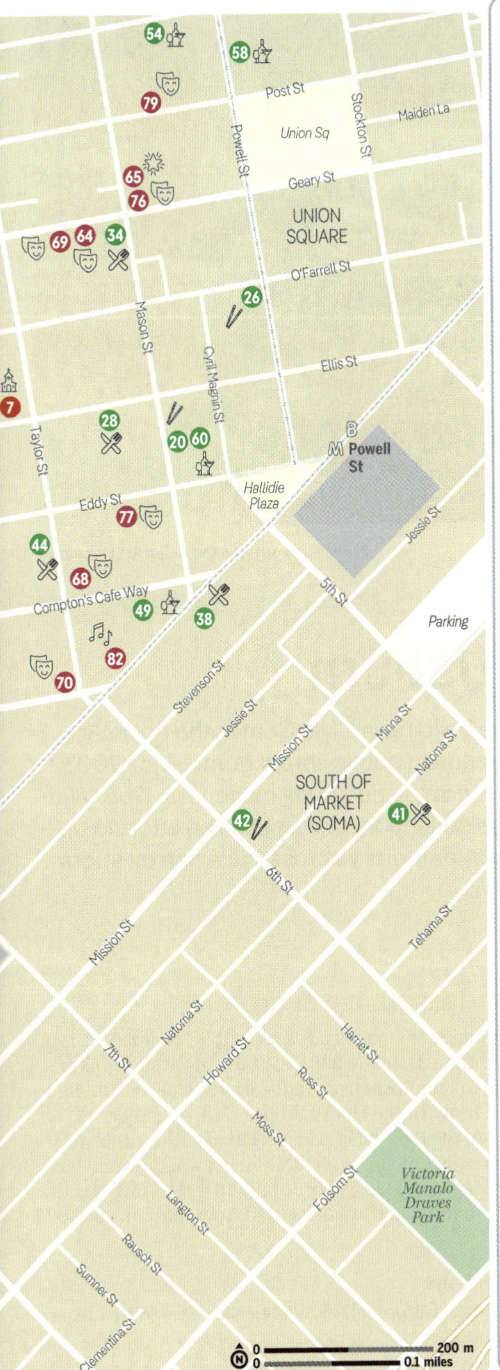

HIGHLIGHTS
1 Asian Art Museum
2 San Francisco Ballet
3 San Francisco Symphony

SIGHTS
4 Boeddeker Park
5 City Hall
6 Civic Center
7 GLIDE Memorial Church
8 Modern Eden
9 Moth Belly Gallery
10 San Francisco Main Library
11 Swim Gallery
12 Tenderloin Museum
13 United Nations Plaza

ACTIVITIES
14 UN Skate Plaza

SLEEPING
15 Proper Hotel

EATING
16 ¡Chao Pescao!
17 A La Turca
18 Azalina's
19 Battambang Market
20 Bodega
21 Brenda's French Soul Food
22 Estrellita's Snacks
23 Golden Lotus
24 Hai Ký Mì Gia
25 Heart of the City Farmers Market
26 Hinodeya Ramen Union Square
27 Kinara Fusion
28 Kusina Ni Tess
29 Lers Ros
30 Mensho Tokyo SF
31 Mong Thu
32 Outta Sight Pizza
33 Pho 2000
34 Pinecrest Diner
35 Red Chilli Halal
36 Sai Jai Thai
37 Saigon Sandwich
38 Saluhall
39 Son & Garden
40 Tadu Ethiopian Kitchen
41 Tempest Bar & Box Kitchen
42 Tú Lan
43 Yemen Kitchen
44 Yemeni Kabab & Mediterranean
45 Z Soul

DRINKING & NIGHTLIFE
46 Blind Pig Speakeasy
47 Bottle Club Pub
48 Bourbon & Branch
49 Dark Bar
50 Edinburgh Castle
51 Emperor Norton's Boozeland
52 Geary Club
53 Jackalope
54 Pacific Cocktail Haven
55 Pomeroy Bar & Grill
56 Rickshaw Stop
57 Secret Bar at Son & Garden
58 Starlite
59 The Beer Hall
60 The Felix
61 The HA-RA Club
62 Uccello Lounge
63 Zombie Village

ENTERTAINMENT
64 American Conservatory Theater
65 August Hall
66 Bill Graham Civic Auditorium
67 Black Cat
68 CounterPulse
69 Curran Theatre
70 Golden Gate Theatre
71 Great American Music Hall
72 Herbst Theater
73 Mr Tipple's Recording Studio
74 New Conservatory Theatre Center
75 Orpheum Theatre
76 Phoenix Theatre
77 SAFEhouseARTS
78 San Francisco Opera
79 San Francisco Playhouse
80 SoundBox
81 Strand Theater
82 The Warfield
83 War Memorial Opera House

SHOPPING
84 Midnite Theories
85 Punk Majesty

CLAUDINE VAN MASSENHOVE/SHUTTERSTOCK

Bronze lion outside the Asian Art Museum

TOP EXPERIENCE

Asian Art Museum

In a towering beaux arts-style building in Civic Center, the Asian Art Museum has called this former main public library home since 2003, but had its beginnings as a wing in the de Young museum in 1966. With more than 18,000 works in the collection, AAM makes an effort to bridge the ancient with the contemporary across the Asian diaspora in exciting and expansive ways.

DON'T MISS

- China's oldest dated Buddha
- Indonesian rod puppets
- Contemporary art
- East West Art Terrace
- Special Exhibits

China's Oldest Dated Buddha

One of the museum's masterpieces is a gilded bronze statue of a sitting Buddha. Dated to 338 CE, 400 years after China was introduced to Buddhism from India, it's the oldest dated Buddha from China. In the Henry R Luce Gallery (gallery 15) on the 2nd floor, the Buddha is also presented with a supplemental digital projection on the wall, showing what it could have looked like in its full glory. While only 16 inches tall, it is the largest surviving sculpture of its kind from that time period.

PRACTICALITIES

● asianart.org ● adult/under-12s $20/free ● 10am-5pm Fri-Mon, 1-8pm Thu, closed Tue & Wed

Indonesian Rod Puppets

Colorful three-dimensional rod puppets *(wayang golek)* with their large eyes and wide mouths – fine examples of Indonesian puppetry, or *wayang* – are a refreshing break from the numerous bronze vessels displayed in the museum. In the Southeast Asian galleries on the 3rd floor, see the puppets in vibrant, flowing dresses with their gracefully spindly arms, and expressions piercing enough to make one wonder if they are alive. The AAM has a large collection and rotates them on a regular basis.

Contemporary Art

Placed throughout the museum, contemporary art is concentrated in the Contemporary Gallery on the first floor. The impossibly intricate Japanese baskets in funky designs are a favorite. However, modern pieces are also in strategic places on the second and third floors, in conversation with ancient art in order to draw the connections between past and present. This could be seen in past exhibit *Divine Bodies* that placed historical Buddhist and Hindu paintings and sculptures next to video art and present-day photography.

East West Art Terrace

Completed in 2023, the 7500-sq-ft East West Art Terrace on the 2nd floor is the largest rooftop art terrace in the US. It houses large-scale sculptures such as Thai artist Pinaree Sanpitak's *Breast Stupa Topiary* that explores the Buddhist dome morphology invoking the female breast, reinforcing the coexistence of body and soul. Konkee's 'Taotie' from the past exhibit *Warring States Cyberpunk* shocks with its electric pink neon, with contemporary words woven into pictographic messages often inscribed on ancient Chinese bronze vessels. Also on the terrace is a cafe that serves beer and wine.

Special Exhibits

Many of AAM's special exhibits focus on Asian American and Pacific Islander (AAPI) artists from across the Asian diaspora. Recent ones include Taiwanese video artist Yuan Goang-Ming's *Everyday War*, a jarring immersive exhibit about the pervasiveness of violence in our culture, and Sparsh Ahuja's and Sam Dalrymple's *Project Dastaan*, a collection of personal narratives about the impact of the 1947 Partition of India and Pakistan. AAM has also recently hosted the exclusive West Coast debut of Korean pop culture exhibit *Hallyu! The Korean Wave*, as well as the *I Was, I Am, I Will Be* mural of line-drawn figures by writer, artist, Bay Area local, and sexual assault survivor advocate Chanel Miller.

FREE MUSEUM TOURS

Docent-led tours of the museum are free of charge with museum admission, and don't require advance reservations. There are one to three 45-minute tours per day, ranging from a general collection tour to the themed What's New, Family Storytelling, Museum Architecture, and a special exhibit tour (ticket to special exhibit required first). Free self-guided audio tours are also available on the Asian Art Museum app for smartphones.

TOP TIPS

- Free entry first Sunday of the month; special exhibits cost an extra $10.
- Start from the top floor, tracing the birth and path of Buddhism through Asia and time.
- The Cha May Ching Museum Boutique gift shop is worth a visit, offering everything from museum-exclusive prints to a large children's section.
- Asian Box runs the current cafe on the museum's ground floor, serving Vietnamese-influenced casual food and boba. Gluten-free and locally sourced. No ticket required for entry.
- The outdoor Sun Family Art Terrace Cafe on the 2nd floor also serves wine and beer, but requires an entry ticket.

SYMPHONY EXTRAS

Score $25 terrace seats, and you can sit right behind the musicians at the **San Francisco Symphony**. If you're from the Greater Bay Area – check to see what the latest discounts are.

Ready for an encore? Hidden behind Davies Symphony Hall is **SoundBox**, an intimate backstage space where symphony musicians and guest artists riff and experiment, backed by video projections and fueled by craft cocktails and bar bites. It was launched by legendary former conductor Michael Tilson Thomas, and the space has a Meyer Constellation Sound System that can alter the acoustics. Sit in bar seats, ottomans, or at high-top tables for an unforgettable symphony experience.

Continued from p105

Tenderloin restaurant Bodega Bistro. The James-Beard-nominated **Azalina's** went from a Malaysian food stall in the former Twitter building to its fine-dining brick-and-mortar in the Tenderloin, and offers a relatively affordable $89 five-course tasting menu. The outstanding **Outta Sight Pizza** comes from the mind of chef Eric Ehler, who has worked at Michelin-starred restaurants. **Mensho Tokyo's** creamy *paitan* chicken ramen still induces lines years after its opening in 2016.

While there are many more worthy eating spots, also of note are Turkish restaurant **A La Turca** with fluffy filled *pides* (flatbreads), upscale Thai eatery **Lers Ros**, featuring crispy pork belly with basil, and **Tadu Ethiopian Kitchen** with their spicy *misir wot* (lentil stew).

Soothing the Savage Beast

A night at the Symphony

The Grammy-winning **San Francisco Symphony** carries on the legacy of former conductor Michael Tilson Thomas's (locals lovingly refer to him as 'MTT') 25-year career at the **Louise M Davies Symphony Hall**. With the recent departure of Thomas's successor, Esa Pekka-Salonen, though, the symphony pivoted to an interesting interim solution — welcoming two dozen guest conductors in the 2025-2026 season during the search for the next music director.

Since then, German conductor David Afkham has made his San Francisco Symphony debut by conducting *The Violin Concerto in D major, Op 35*, Tchaikovsky's only violin concerto. Karina Canellakis, who has been the first female principal guest conductor for several European orchestras, including the Berlin Radio Symphony Orchestra, has conducted French pianist Alexandre Kantorow's SF Symphony debut with Prokofiev's notoriously difficult *Piano Concerto No 3 in C major, Op 26*. Given its constant innovation, it's always exciting to see what surprises the symphony presents next, whether it's the classics or screenings of *The Lord of the Rings: The Two Towers* or *Black Panther*, accompanied by a live orchestra.

DRINKING IN THE TENDERLOIN: DIVES & CRAFT COCKTAILS

Emperor Norton's Boozeland: The two-floor dive entices with a back patio, half-pint beers and an inclusive culture. *1pm-2am*

The HA-RA Club: Dive bar since 1947 with iconic neon sign and original deco door. *3pm-2am Mon, Tue & Sat, from noon Wed-Fri & Sun*

Edinburgh Castle: This flag-waving bastion of drink comes with Guinness on tap, dartboard, pool tables, and vinegary fish and chips. *6pm-2am*

Geary Club: There's no signage (and no frills) at this tiny dive – possibly SF's second smallest bar, open since 1942. *4pm-2am*

Bourbon & Branch: A speakeasy: password needed. Book for Wilson & Wilson Detective Agency. *6pm-midnight Sun-Wed, to 2am Thu-Sat*

Zombie Village: Fun tiki bar. Drinks inspired by historic Bay Area shipping-routes. *5pm-midnight Wed & Thu, to 2am Fri & Sat*

Dark Bar: Asian spirits and ingredients focus on seasonality and fermentation. Small bites are also creative. *6-11pm Thu-Sat*

Bottle Club Pub: Ode to 1950s-1970s drinking culture with floor-to-ceiling whiskey library and food menu. *5pm-midnight Sun, Tue-Sat*

JAY YUAN/SHUTTERSTOCK

Louise M Davies Symphony Hall

Arias for the New Millennium

A night at the opera

Cheer for **San Francisco Opera** *(sfopera.com)* premieres of original works, including Margaret Atwood's gripping *The Handmaid's Tale*, Grammy-winning *The (R)Evolution of Steve Jobs*, Pulitzer-Prize-winner Nilo Cruz's *El Último Sueño de Frida y Diego* (Frida and Diego's Last Dream) and Tony-Award-winner David Henry Hwang's *The Monkey King*. While inimitable painter David Hockney no longer actively works for the opera, his radical sets and haute-couture costumes are still utilized, and complement Eun Sung Kim's bold musical direction – you can appreciate both with $28 balcony seats (though you might need the $5 rental opera glasses from the north coat check). SF Opera also introduces timeless works to new audiences, such as Puccini's much-adored *La Bohème*.

For those feeling a little out of depth, pre-opera talks are a great way to get acquainted with the performance beforehand.

RUSH & STANDING ROOM OPERA TICKETS

Yes, super cheap tickets for the **San Francisco Opera** still exist!

For certain performances, they're available to everyone who creates an SF Opera account online and registers. The tickets are usually available from 11am to midnight the day before a performance, or until they're sold out. Check your email for notifications about ticket availability.

There are also 200 standing room tickets for most main stage opera performances, which are for the rear orchestra or rear balcony. Tickets are only $10 each, but are cash only. They go on sale on the day of each performance, with a limit of two per person. Starting from 10am on the day, 150 tickets become available, whereas the remaining 50 are released two hours prior to the performance.

DRINKING IN DOWNTOWN: POST-PERFORMANCE DRINKS — MAPS P99, P106

The Felix: Push a framed photo to reveal this drinking den, tucked away beneath the upscale Bodega (p105). *6pm-midnight Thu, 8pm-1am Fri & Sat*

Starlite: Beacon Grand rooftop bar. Reopened with cocktails from the Trick Dog team. *4pm-1am Thu, to 2am Fri-Sat, to midnight Sun*

Pacific Cocktail Haven: Ace bar with libations like Leeward Negroni – Sipsmith VJOP Gin, coconut-washed Campari, pandan cordial, bitters. *5pm-midnight Mon-Sat*

Rickhouse: Imbibe an impressive international whiskey collection and boozy punchbowls among old whiskey barrels. *4:30pm-midnight Mon- & Tue to 2am Wed-Sat*

Learn about the composer, the opera's music, characters, and the historical background of the piece – all from a music expert. The 20-minute talks begin an hour before the performance time. After the opening week, pre-recorded talks are usually available online for those who don't have time to get to the opera house that early.

MORE OPERA HOUSE FOOD OPTIONS

For more walkable pre-show meals near both the War Memorial Opera House and Louise M Davies Symphony Hall, peep at the eating recommendations for **Hayes Valley** (p206) or the **Tenderloin** (p104).

Shaping the Future of Dance

Mesmerizing ballet performances

The USA's oldest ballet company, whose school was founded in 1933 originally to train dancers for opera productions, is looking sharp in more than 100 shows annually. The repertoire of **San Francisco Ballet** *(sfballet.org)* runs the gamut from the classic *The Nutcracker*, whose US premiere was here in 1944, to modern originals. Performances share the **War Memorial Opera House** *(sfwarmemorial.org)* with the SF Opera, and typically run from December through May. The ballet puts together international collaborations at the intersection of visual art, fashion, and music. Examples include Gap Inc creative director Zac Posen creating gossamer pink and yellow costumes for a recent season's revitalized version of Christopher Wheeldon's 2008 *Within the Golden Hour,* and Bay area-based artist Ranu Mukherjee creating a curtain drop as part of the Fine Arts Museum of SF annual curtain commission.

You can score $15 to $20 same-day standing-room tickets at the box office, which opens four hours before showtime on performance days. Rush tickets are posted on the website 48 hours in advance and go on sale the day of the performance starting at 10am (sales stop an hour before showtime). The discounted prices range from $35 to $79, with a limit of two per person.

SO MANY BARS...

For more pre- and post-performance drink options, look at recommendations in the neighboring **Tenderloin** (p104), **Nob Hill** (p140), and **Hayes Valley** (p206).

Hitting the High Note

Get cultured in the Theater District

Nestled between and overlapping with Union Square, the Tenderloin, Mid-Market, and Civic Center, SF's **Theater District** is bursting with culture, from majestic old theaters to big concert venues to hoppin' new jazz clubs. Sample the venues to determine the flavor of your evening entertainment.

EATING IN THE THEATER DISTRICT: PRE-SHOW MEALS

¡Chao Pescao!: Cuban-Colombian restaurant spotlights deep-fried *masa* empanadas and salty-sour Tajín-fried chicken. *11:30am-8:30pm Tue-Sat* **$$**

Brenda's French Soul Food: Gumbo and *ube* (purple yam) beignets by gay Filipina-Creole chef Brenda Buenviaje. *8am-8pm Wed-Mon, to 3pm Tue* **$$**

Sai Jai Thai: Family-run restaurant beloved for its barbecued pork shoulder-fried rice, Lao-style papaya salad and extreme spice levels. *11am-9pm Thu-Tue* **$**

1601 Bar & Kitchen: A rare find in SF fine dining: Sri Lankan ingredients combined with French cooking techniques. *6-10:30pm Tue-Sat* **$$$**

JAMES_ED280/SHUTTERSTOCK

Strand Theater

For nationally touring smash-hit musicals like *Wicked* and *Hamilton*, look at the grand old **Curran** *(broadwaysf.com)*, **Golden Gate** *(goldengatetheatresf.com)*, and **Orpheum** *(orpheumsanfrancisco.com)* theaters. **Herbst Theater** *(sfwarmemorial.org/herbst-theatre)* is a smaller, 900-seat venue inside the War Memorial Opera House (p112) that hosts performances such as string quartets and solo guitarists.

Go to the **American Conservatory Theater** *(act-sf.org)* for breakthrough shows that launch at this turn-of-the-century landmark. ACT's smaller **Strand Theater** *(act-sf.org/strand)*, presents a wider range of experimental shows, such as Kristina Wong's Pulitzer Prize–nominated *Sweatshop Overlord*. Smaller or experimental companies Downtown also include **San Francisco Playhouse** *(sfplayhouse.org)*, **New Conservatory Theatre Center** *(nctcsf.org)*, **CounterPulse** *(counterpulse.org)*, **SAFEhouseARTS** *(safehousearts.org)* and **Phoenix Theatre** *(phoenixtheatresf.org)*.

HELGI TOMASSON'S THE NUTCRACKER

The Christmas season production of *The Nutcracker* is beloved worldwide, but SF's version is truly special.

Former SF Ballet artistic director and dancer Helgi Tomasson, at the helm for 37 years, created a San Francisco-specific version in 2004 – taking place in early 20th-century SF and inspired by the 1915 Panama-Pacific International Exposition – that has been performed annually ever since. Set and costume designers Michael Yeargan and Martin Pakledinaz matched colors and fashions to the time period – muted grays and blacks suggesting city fog, for instance. More than 150 dancers bring Tomasson's vision to life, complete with 150 pounds of paper snowflakes that fall during a now-iconic 4½-minute scene.

If you're here in December, don't miss the SF Ballet's take on Tchaikovsky's classic.

DRINKING IN THE THEATER DISTRICT: FUN WATERING HOLES

Uccello Lounge: Bar attached to the SF Conservatory of Music, with live performances by students and faculty. *5-9pm Thu, to 11pm Fri & Sat*

The Beer Hall: Enjoy offerings like Terpene Station IPA from the local brewer Cellarmaker, plus natural wines. *3-9:30pm Mon-Wed, to 11pm Thu-Sat*

Secret Bar at Son & Garden: This maximalist bar delights with smoke-bubble-topped cocktails. Reservations recommended. *5-9pm Thu-Sun*

Pomeroy Bar & Grill: Comfy couches make this a great burger and beer stop. Whiskey-tasting on Wednesdays. *11:30am-10pm Mon-Fri, from noon Sat-Sun*

FROM BAWDY TO BROADWAY

While the historic theaters of San Francisco all have rich history, the **Golden Gate Theatre** (p113) may have the most fun origins.

Built as a vaudeville house in 1922, as the theater evolved into a concert hall, stars like Frank Sinatra, Judy Garland, and Nat King Cole graced its stage.

During its lifetime, much of the gorgeous interior was replaced by more modern decor. However, the late 1970s saw the Golden Gate restored to its original art deco glory and it was reopened as a performing arts venue by SHN (now BroadwaySF), a major theater production company founded by the well-known San Francisco Shorenstein family. The Golden Gate was added to the National Register of Historic Places in 1986.

NICKOLAY STANEV/SHUTTERSTOCK

City Hall during Pride Month

Several jazz clubs pay tribute to past venues, where Miles Davis, Billie Holiday, and Charlie Parker had played underground. **Black Cat** *(blackcatsf.com)* is out to restore the laid-back, lowdown glory of the capital of West Coast cool with both a basement club and street-level bar. **Mr Tipple's Recording Studio** *(mrtipplessf.com)* hosts top local talent, plus a decent dumpling menu. The newest **Dawn Club** *(Map p85; dawnclub.com)* revives a 1946 jazz venue, with top-rated cocktails to boot.

Rickshaw Stop *(rickshawstop.com)* is a great small club for live indie and underground acts. Larger concert halls like **Great American Music Hall** *(gamh.com)*, **Bill Graham Civic Auditorium** *(billgrahamcivic.com)*, **The Warfield** *(thewarfieldtheatre.com)*, and **August Hall** *(augusthallsf.com)* bring big touring acts like K-pop group LE SSERAFIM and English punk band The Sex Pistols. Don't forget the long-standing **Punch Line** *(Map p99; punchlinecomedyclub.com)* comedy club in the Embarcadero, which local comedian Ali Wong graced during her rise to fame.

EATING IN DOWNTOWN: LATE-NIGHT EATS

MAPS P90, P106

Hinodeya Ramen Union Square: Inhale wholegrain ramen in a *dashi*-style broth, topped with *chashu* (braised pork belly) and soft egg. *10:00am-1:30am* **$$**

Tempest Bar & Box Kitchen: Graffiti-scrawled shot-and-beers with pool table and food like pizza pockets. *11am-2am Mon-Fri, from 12pm Sat & Sun* **$**

Pinecrest Diner: Dig into eggy breakfasts and big burgers at this family-owned diner, going strong since 1969. *7am-11pm Sun-Tue, 24 hours Wed-Sat* **$**

Dragon Horse: Cocktails, sushi, karaoke. Say no more. *4-11pm Sun-Wed, to midnight Thu-Sat* **$$**

Municipal Magic

Astounding edifices

Anchored by the gold-accented dome of the beaux arts **City Hall**, the **Civic Center** has been the site of historic happenings, from the assassination of supervisor Harvey Milk and mayor George Moscone, to the first same-sex marriages. Inside, the stunning rotunda rises for several stories, and is a popular photo shoot spot for City Hall newlyweds. Free guided tours of the building are available on Fridays at 1pm, but feel free to tour the wings of the lobby level on your own to see galleries of City Hall's past, featuring a 700lb head of the 'Goddess of Liberty' that once topped the pre-1906 City Hall, portraits of political figures, models of the building, plus community photo exhibits throughout.

Neighboring City Hall is the **San Francisco Main Library**, whose Larkin St entrance features the *Portrait of a Phenomenal Woman* – a sculpture depicting Maya Angelou – by Berkeley artist Lava Thomas. The 9-ft-tall book-shaped bronze piece weighs 6900lb, and is first monument to commemorate a Black woman in the city's Civic Art Collection. Inside, art exhibits span the entire six floors, many related to each other, an example being a recent exhibit documenting skateboarding culture in SF. The 5th floor is a treat, with artist Alice Aycock's *Functional and Fantasy Stair and Cyclone Fragment* spiral stairway projecting into the library's atrium space from the suspended, glass-enclosed reading room. The staircase wraps around a cone tipped at an angle, and as the two-story cone appears to unravel, it sheds fragments of false or imaginary stairs.

HANGING OUT AT THE CIVIC CENTER'S UN PLAZA

Connecting the main library and City Hall is the **UN Plaza**, a pedestrian mall where the **Heart of the City Farmers Market** (p115) takes place, having gone through a $2 million remodel in 2023 to attract more visitors.

Since then, the city has created a concert series, outdoor fitness stations, daily free exercise classes, and tables for ping pong, chess and mahjong instruction.

Spectra by Illuminate (nonprofit behind Bay Bridge Bay Lights, p101) consists of audio-sensitive light strings, connecting the main library to the **Asian Art Museum** (p108). The **UN Skate Plaza** (p105) has been expanded to include three skateable geometric art pieces, designed by Olympic skateboarders; legend Tony Hawk himself skated there during the opening.

EATING NEAR CITY HALL: OUR PICKS

Heart of the City Farmers Market: Stars include fresh *ube* loaves from the Rize Up Bakery. *7am-4pm Sun & Wed* $

Saluhall: Food hall at the IKEA, featuring local vendors such as Smish Smash (smash burgers). *9am-8pm Mon-Thu, to 9pm Fri & Sat, to 7pm Sun* $

Tú Lan: Longtime Vietnamese spot on a gritty corner. Chef/author Julia Child once had the Imperial rolls and fried fish in ginger sauce here. *11am-8pm Mon-Fri* $$

Son & Garden: A wild amount of fake flowers adorns this whimsical, trendy Thai brunch spot. *10am-2pm Mon-Fri, 9am-3pm Sat & Sun, 5-9pm Thu-Sun* $$

Researched by
Alison Bing

CHINATOWN & NORTH BEACH

COME FOR DINNER, STAY FOR STORIES

Grant St connects San Francisco's historic Chinese and Italian neighborhoods – and over 175 years, these neighbors have swapped epic stories of immigrant ingenuity, radical ideas, daring art and resilience against all odds.

Under Chinatown's pagoda roofs, you'll find noodles, rare teas, temples and Chinese orchestras, just like in the gold rush days – but you'll also find the future in progress, with cutting-edge contemporary art, trend-setting restaurants and a packed calendar of cultural events. Wild parrots in North Beach treetops mimic the chatter at local bohemian bars and Italian cafes, serving enough espresso to fuel the next major poetry movement at free-speech landmark City Lights. Whether you're craving Peking duck, pizza, or Peking duck pizza, you're definitely in the right place – stick around afterwards for breakthrough comedy, raucous punk shows, Chinese opera and West Coast's cool jazz at its origins.

INCLUDES

FROM LEFT: BENJAMIN HEATH FOR LONELY PLANET, ZRFPHOTO/GETTY IMAGES

Above: Chinatown (p118); Right: Coit Tower (p136)

See page 261 for places to stay in Chinatown & North Beach.

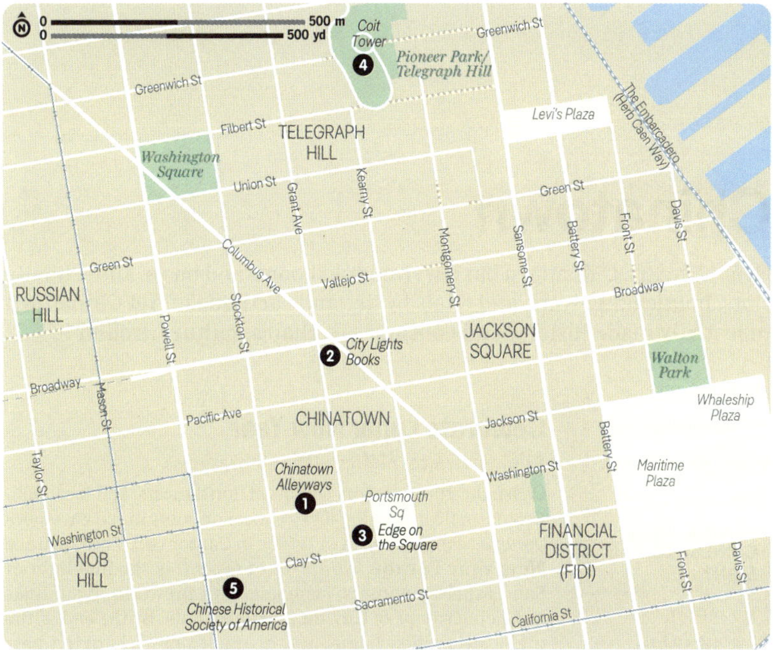

Highlights

❶ Chinatown Alleyways
Hear mah-jongg tiles, temple gongs and Chinese orchestras in story-filled SF backstreets. **p124**

❷ City Lights Books
Reflect in the Poet's Chair and celebrate free speech. **p130**

❸ Edge on the Square
Glimpse the future in the making at Chinatown's arts hub. **p118**

❹ Coit Tower
Climb Filbert Street Steps past parrots and fragrant gardens to this panoramic, mural-lined tower. **p136**

❺ Chinese Historical Society of America
Time-travel through history exhibits in the Julia Morgan–designed Chinatown YWCA. **p119**

Getting Around

Cable Car
From Downtown or Fisherman's Wharf, take the Powell-Mason or the Powell-Hyde line through Chinatown and North Beach. The California St cable car passes through the southern end of Chinatown.

Muni Streetcar
The extended T line streetcar service links Chinatown and North Beach to Downtown and Dogpatch.

Bus
Key routes passing through Chinatown and North Beach are 1, 12, 30, 39 and 45.

Chinatown

Over 175 years, Chinatown has survived gold booms and busts, anti-Chinese riots, bootlegging wars, and trials by fire and earthquake. Yet Chinatown repeatedly made history, and continues to change culture around it.

WHAT'S YOUR CHINESE ZODIAC SIGN?

According to the Chinese Zodiac, each lunar year is represented by one of 12 animal zodiac signs and five natural elements – 2026 is the year of the fire horse, 2027 is the fire goat, 2028 is the earth monkey. You'll spot zodiac figurines at night market kiosks and Grant Ave souvenir shops. Any International Orange-blooded San Franciscan knows their Chinese zodiac sign, and may well ask you about yours – and that's not some cheesy pickup line or sneaky attempt to guess your age. It's an opening to swap stories and make predictions for the year ahead – a true SF bonding moment.

Celebrate Lunar New Year

Brighten winter nights with celebrations

Chase the 200ft dragon, legions of lion dancers, and local politicians on floats tossing lucky chocolate coins in red envelopes (*hong bao* in Mandarin or *lai see* in Cantonese). The **Chinese New Year Parade** *(chineseparade.com)* is the highlight of San Francisco winters, complete with fireworks, drumlines and fierce troops of tiny-tot martial artists. By the end of the night, everyone's happy and hoarse from exchanging best wishes for prosperity – *'Gung hay fat choy!'* (Cantonese) or *'Gōng xǐ fā cái!'* (Mandarin) .

Every 12 years or so, the lunar year's animal zodiac sign coincides with the animal zodiac sign of your birth year – which means you have an extra excuse to party. If you're not sure what your sign is, the red-envelope-covered **Chinese Zodiac Wall** on **Jack Kerouac Alley** provides a handy summary of the animals, elements and character traits associated with your birth year. But Lunar New Year festivities don't begin or end with the parade. Chinatown celebrates for a month, with special **night markets** *(bechinatown.weebly.com)* on lantern-lit **Grant Avenue** supplying essential goods for an auspicious year ahead – including lucky bamboo, red envelopes and miniature mandarin trees. Calligraphers ink *fook* (good luck) wishes on paper banners, everyone joins community games of mah-jongg, and DJs get aunties dancing in the streets.

Change Your Outlook in Chinatown Galleries

Glimpse the future in the making

Just up the block from historic Portsmouth Sq is **Edge on the Square** *(edgeonthesquare.org; free)*, Chinatown's cutting-edge cultural hub and arts center. Drop in for fresh takes on current topics with impactful themed art shows like *All Eyes On Us: Invention & Ingenuity During Artistic Diasporas*. No one is a stranger or spectator at the Edge – the art invites you to leave your mark, and music and dance performances pull you into the groove. Events here blend art, community and joy, from

Chinatown Pride celebrations to live chef demos exploring Asian American identity through food.

As the exact point where east meets west is in San Francisco, atop the pedestrian bridge spanning Kearney St, a mosaic sun is perpetually rising on the steps to the **Chinese Culture Center** *(cccsf.us; free)*. This landmark art center on the Hilton's 3rd floor has expanded artistic horizons since 1965, and keeps sparking conversations through bold collaborations with contemporary Chinese artists from the mainland and across the diaspora. Major shows include *Present Tense Biennial*, where 30-plus Bay Area artists present personal takes on Chinese culture.

Visit the Center's satellite gallery at **41 Ross Alley** *(41ross.org; free)* for contemporary art collaborations, design pop-ups and creative community events, from zine festivals to drag story hours with author and drag star Panda Dulce. If you're curious about murals you've glimpsed around Chinatown, gain a deeper understanding of the local art scene on the Center's **Chinatown History and Art Walking Tours** *(1½-2hrs, four-person minimum, $45/person)*.

Between international art fairs, contemporary art stars from near and far converge at **Jessica Silverman Gallery** *(jessicasilvermangallery.com; free)*. Push the buzzer and pull Gaudi-designed bronze handles, and the frosted glass door opens to reveal stunning parallel universes, featuring Rupy Tut's cosmic gardeners, Clare Rojas' spellbinding black swans, Judy Chicago's world-birthing quilts, and David Huffman's time-traveling, history-repairing *Traumanauts*.

Time-Travel at Chinese Historical Society of America

Follow epic tales inside a living landmark

Picture what it was like to be Chinese in America during California's gold rush, the Cold War and SF's hippie heyday at this 1932 landmark, built as Chinatown's YWCA by Hearst Castle architect Julia Morgan. At the **Chinese Historical Society of America** *(chsa.org; adult/student/child $12/10/5)*, historians unearth fascinating artifacts: WWII Chinatown nightclub posters, Frank Wong's Chinatown miniatures, and Bruce Lee's martial arts costumes and extensive philosophy library. Exhibits highlight Chinese American perspectives on US history, tracing anti-Asian hate speech from the Chinese Exclusion Act (1882–1943) to today, alongside 175-plus years of history-changing civil-rights activism.

CHINATOWN'S CONTEMPORARY ARTS SCENE

Candace Huey is Head Curator at **Edge on the Square** and co-chair of **SFMOMA**'s SECA prize council.

At **Edge on the Square**, we celebrate Chinatown as an immigrant gateway and a touchstone for Asian American experience – my grandparents settled here. Our programs are free and family-friendly, expanding what it means to be American. **Chinese Historical Society of America** bridges past and present, and the **Center for Asian American Media Film Festival** launches new stories, new voices. **Great Star Theater** (p121) introduces younger audiences to Cantonese opera, and **On Waverly** (p122) beautifully curates Asian American authors and artists. Independent arts nonprofits include **Southern Exposure** (p181), **Gray Area** (p173) and **Root Division** (Map p90).

EATING IN CHINATOWN: CLASSIC DIM SUM

Good Mong Kok: Join excited eaters waiting at Chinatown's busiest counter, with shrimp dumplings, pork *siu mai* and other classics. *7am-6pm* $

Hang Ah Tea Room: The area's original dim sum. Timeless classics include spicy purse dumplings, pork buns, and thousand-year-egg-custard *bao*. *10:30am-8pm* $

Dim Sum Bistro: Don't be fooled by the bargain prices: this is high-quality takeout, from tender shrimp and chive dumplings to toasted sesame balls. *8am-3pm* $

Today Food: Witness dumpling mastery: loaded with veggies, shrimp and organic chicken, pan-fried or steamed to enjoy with aged soy, vinegar, chili and awe. *8am-8pm* $

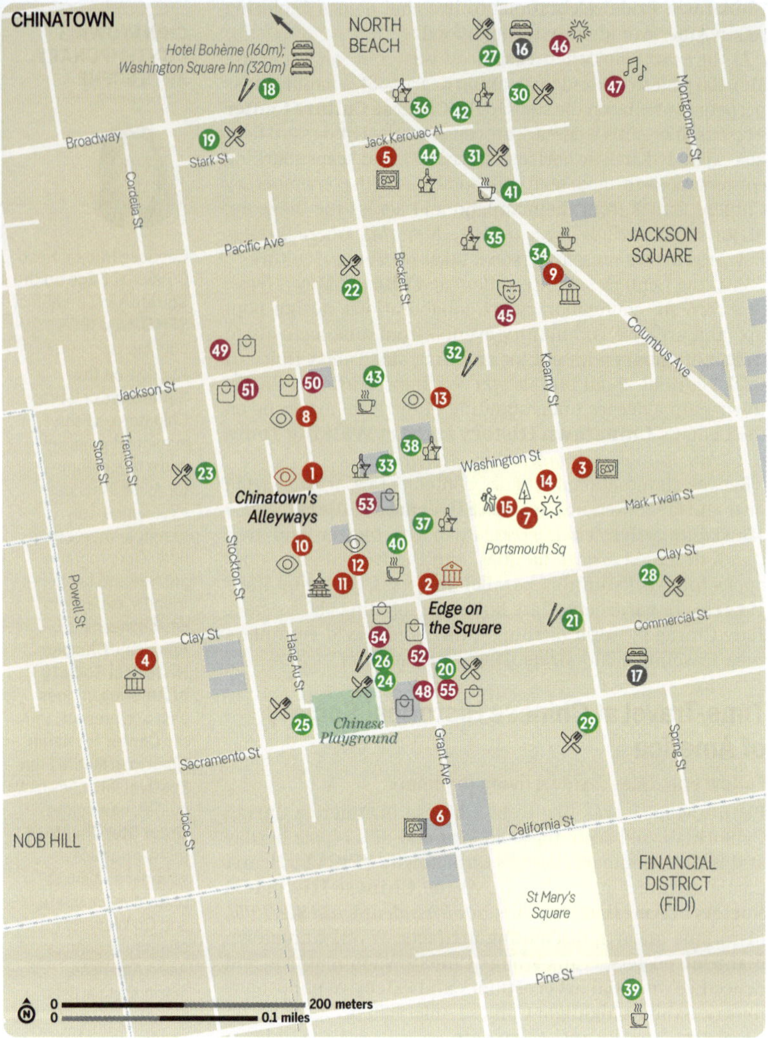

CHINATOWN

EATING IN CHINATOWN: SWEET TREATS

Grand Opening: SF star pastry chef Melissa Chou serves baking breakthroughs at Mister Jiu's takeout window – mortadella scallion *bao* and black sesame almond cake, yes please. *11am-2pm Sat & Sun* $

Golden Gate Bakery: To answer the obvious questions: the line is for egg-custard tarts, it's cash only, and yes it's worth it for flaky-crust, gooey-center eggstraordinary treats. Call ahead. *hours vary* $

Golden Gate Fortune Cookies: Write your own fortunes for custom cookies, or get cookies with fortunes labeled 'regular' or 'X-rated' (actually just cheesy relationship jokes). Cash only. *9am-6pm* $

Eastern Bakery: Seasons don't change in SF without Eastern's mooncakes, filled with lotus-seed or sweet-bean paste – Autumn Moon Festival staples for 100-plus years. Call ahead. *hours vary* $

HIGHLIGHTS
1 Chinatown's Alleyways
2 Edge on the Square

SIGHTS
3 Chinese Culture Center
4 Chinese Historical Society of America
5 Chinese Zodiac Wall
6 Jessica Silverman Gallery
7 Portsmouth Square
8 Ross Alley
9 Sentinel Building
10 Spofford Alley
11 Tin How Temple
12 Waverly Place
13 Wentworth Place

ACTIVITIES
14 Chinatown Alleyway Tours
15 Drag Me Along Tours

SLEEPING
16 Green Tortoise Hostel
17 Pacific Tradewinds Hostel

EATING
18 China Live
19 Dim Sum Bistro
20 Eastern Bakery
21 Four Kings
22 Golden Gate Bakery
23 Good Mong Kok
24 Grand Opening
25 Hang Ah Tea Room
26 Mister Jiu's
27 Osmanthus Dim Sum Lounge
28 Outta Sight Pizza
29 Today Food
30 Tommaso's
31 Tosca Cafe
32 Z & Y

DRINKING & NIGHTLIFE
33 Buddha Lounge
34 Cafe Zoetrope
35 Comstock Saloon
36 Devil's Acre
37 Empress at Boon Lounge
38 Li Po
39 PlenTea
40 Red Blossom Tea Company
41 Réveille
42 Specs
43 Ten Ren Tea
44 Vesuvio

ENTERTAINMENT
45 Great Star Theater
46 Keys Jazz Bistro
47 Mabuhay Gardens

SHOPPING
48 Chinatown Kite Shop
49 Dong Hing Supermarket
50 Golden Gate Fortune Cookies
51 Jumbo Mart
52 KIM + ONO
53 On Waverly
54 Unbound
55 Wok Shop

Find Non-Touristy SF Souvenirs

Score SF signatures

Happens to everyone: SF fog catches you unprepared, and suddenly you're in the market for an 'I escaped Alcatraz' sweatshirt. Grant Ave souvenir shops have you covered there – but while you're in the neighborhood, you'll also find some truly unique boutiques that make SF memories. **Chinatown Kite Shop** has been making windy SF days worthwhile since 1971, brightening gray skies with colorful kites: fierce 9ft-long flying dragons, pirate-worthy wild parrots (SF's city birds), surreal floating legs, and flying pandas that look understandably stunned.

Hollywood pinups were heavily inspired by the sassy, slinky silk-robe style of 1930s to '50s Chinatown burlesque stars – Anna May Wong, Rita Hayworth, Lena Horne, Judy Garland and Ronald Reagan all frequented nightclubs here, and you can still catch legendary Grant Ave Follies senior showgirls in action at **Great Star Theater** *(greatstartheater.org)*. Today Chinatown sister-duo designers Renee and Tiffany Tam are bringing boudoir-as-streetwear back to its origins at **Kim + Ono** *(kimandono.com)*. Kimonos range from satin poly to silk charmeuse ($55 to $150-plus for custom and bridal designs), splashed with bodacious blossoms and the occasional peacock peeking over a shoulder.

TECH TRAILBLAZERS

California's earliest high-tech adopters were switchboard operators c 1887 at the **Chinese Telephone Exchange** at Grant and Washington Sts. Operators spoke six languages and memorized thousands of Chinatown residents by name, residence and occupation. For decades, women operators worked the switchboard seven days a week, without holidays – until they unionized in 1943. After WWII ended, private phone lines were installed citywide, and the exchange quietly closed.

EATING IN CHINATOWN: FAMILY-STYLE FEASTS

Mister Jiu's: Globally acclaimed, Californian Chinese banquets with lamb with plum sauce, scallion milk-bread with caviar, and roast Sonoma duck. *5-9pm Tue & Wed, to 10pm Thu-Sat* $$$

Z&Y: Sumptuous banquets guaranteed to make faces shine – spicy Sichuan pork dumplings, flaming cauliflower, and chili-oil-poached fish leave lips buzzing. *11:30am-3pm & 4:30-9pm Wed-Sun* $$

Osmanthus Dim Sum Lounge: Rule-breaker Osmanthus puts XO sauce on string beans, spinach wrappers around shitake dumplings, and pu-erh tea into Old Fashioneds. *10:30am-8pm* $$

China Live: Chef Chen creates modern Chinese dishes with Californian flair – *kurobuta* pork-soup dumplings, kumquat-glazed Peking duck – plus top-notch tea and cocktails. *4-9pm Sun* $$

GET STEEPED IN CHINATOWN'S TEA CULTURE

Since its first appearance 4000 years ago in China, tea drinking has become an art form – and in Chinatown, you get to benefit from millennia of expertise plus two centuries of direct trade with Chinese farmers.

Grant Ave tea importers let you sample tea, but the hard sell may begin before you finish sipping. For a more relaxing teatime, head to dim-sum restaurants known for their selections.

Chinatown's latest, greatest import is Taiwanese bubble tea: milky iced tea polka-dotted with boba (chewy, gently sweet tapioca pearls). You'll find bubble tea advertised with brightly colored photos at corner kiosks, often made with pre-mixed powdered tea that can leave an artificial aftertaste. Stick to tea kiosks that brew fresh daily, with menus of specialty regional teas and informative descriptions.

Other shops sell generic SF memorabilia, but **On Waverly** *(onwaverly.com)* showcases delightful locally designed, culturally iconic reminders of your time in Chinatown: smiling bok choy patches, mah-jongg-tile guest soap sets, risograph prints of Chinatown neon signs, bamboo steamers brimming with dim-sum plushies. On Waverly's brilliantly curated book and zine section makes Asian American culture accessible to all ages: Angel Halo Chang's *Asian Market Shopping Spree* teaches toddlers counting in a tasty way; bilingual Chinese folktales broaden bedtime-story options; Karen Fang's biography of legendary Disney artist Tyrus Wong reveals the brilliant mind behind *Bambi*; and Helen Zia's *Asian American Dreams: The Emergence of a People* updates America's immigrant narratives for the 21st century.

Go Gourmet in Chinatown

Collect secret ingredients, tools and tips

Amid the bustling groceries and Chinese apothecaries of Stockton St, you might spot a well-fed watch cat curled up in a sunny doorway, snoozing on the job. That's one lucky cat – Stockton St is a gourmet dream, lined with fresh ingredients and dim-sum takeout joints. Before joining the inevitable line for the shrimp *har gow* at **Good Mong Kok** (p119), savvy regulars make pitstops to pick up gourmet condiments like aged black vinegar and fermented chili sauce at **Dong Hing Supermarket** (7:30am-6pm), plus fresh fruit for dessert. Staff are scrupulous about freshness (no squeezing please!), make fresh noodles in-house (going fast!), and know who's next even when the checkout line seems chaotic (cash only please!).

Once you browse seasonal produce, you'll recognize seasonal signatures on Chinatown menus – and you'll be good and hungry for dinner. If you've miraculously managed to score reservations for a counter table at wildly popular **Four Kings** (itsfourkings.com; book exactly 29 days in advance, and expect to eat around 9pm), you can observe how the pros at SF's buzziest bistro ingeniously reinvent Chinatown's Cantonese classics with hints of North Beach: popcorn chicken with basil aoli, Sichuan-peppercorn-spiked *ma po* spaghetti. escargot in XO sauce sopped up with milk bread. If your party is bigger than two and you don't have reservations, join the waitlist at **China Live** *(p121; chinalivesf.com)* for regional Chinese cuisine with California-fresh ingredients. While you wait, you can browse chef/owner George Chen's well-curated selection of key ingredients, cookbooks and fancy kitchenware in the adjoining shop.

If you want to cook your own five-star meal, you'll need to get equipped. You may think you know your way around pots and pans, but you're about to get schooled at the **Wok Shop** *(wokshop.com)*. Octogenarian owner Tane Chan likes to joke that she's sold 'woks for all woks of life' since the 1970s – tell her what you like to cook and she'll put a carbon-steel wok in your hand to see how it suits you. She's found the right fit for

ELENA GRAHAM/SHUTTERSTOCK

Wok Shop and Chinatown Kite Shop

cooks ranging from politician Nancy Pelosi to award-winning *Breath of a Wok* author Grace Young, and she'll set you up with all the tools too – just don't get her started on nonstick. For recipes and tips, join the free Wok Wednesdays online cooking group.

When it's time to head to San Francisco International Airport, a world of plane snacks awaits at **Jumbo Mart**. This aptly named basement bodega stocks lifetime supplies of flavored sunflower seeds (get the black garlic) plus eight more aisles of packaged snacks, many worth trying for the name alone (report: Lonely God potato twists taste like truffles). The rear section sells sauces from across Asia that could change your life, or at least your lunch – pass the Guilin fermented chili sauce, please.

LIONS ROAMING CHINATOWN

Year-round, anytime you spot lion dancers and fire crackers erupt into action in Chinatown, you'll know a business is launching or celebrating an anniversary. Show your support with a purchase and/or a wish: *Saang yi hing lung* (Cantonese) or *Shēng yì xīng lóng* (Mandarin), meaning 'May business flourish!' You may find lions roving Grant Ave night markets (held the second Friday of the month from May to October, 5pm to 9pm), which feature free entertainment from Chinatown to North Beach all the way from California St to Filbert St – plus local vendors doing brisk trade in dumplings, boba tea and pizza. To take the festive spirit home with you, Chinatown Kite Shop (p121) sells two-person, papier-mâché lion-dance costumes and lion-headed kites.

DRINKING IN CHINATOWN: TEA

Red Blossom Tea Company: Second-generation tea merchants feature 100-plus specialty teas at their showroom, where staff share tea-prep tips and recommend samplers. *11am-5pm Wed-Sat*

Hang Ah Tea Room (p119): Chinatown's go-to hangout for over 100 years for specialty teas – try rare Taiwan High Mountain or delicate chrysanthemum – with classic savory and sweet dim sum. *10:30am-8pm*

PlenTea: Tea-ristas fill mini-milk bottles with just-brewed, certified-organic bubble tea – classic green or black, seasonal fruit, or original SF flavors like sea-salt cream oolong. *11am-11pm*

Ten Ren Tea: A Chinatown institution since 1953, with specialty teas to sample, iced fruit tea flavors like kumquat lemon, and classic King's oolong milk boba tea. *10:30am-6pm*

SANTI RODRIGUEZ/SHUTTERSTOCK

Waverly Place

TOP EXPERIENCE

Chinatown Alleyways

Chinatown's 41 historic alleyways have seen it all: gold rushes and revolution, incense and opium, fire and icy receptions. Brick temple balconies jut out over storefronts just as they have since 1870, when exclusion laws restricted Chinese immigration, employment and housing. Today Chinatown's alleyways are cultural touchstones and places of possibility with community art, mutual aid and shared celebrations.

DON'T MISS

- Waverly Place
- Tin How Temple
- On Waverly
- Ross Alley
- Golden Gate Fortune Cookies
- Spofford Alley
- Wentworth Place

Waverly Place

Through earthquakes, world wars and Prohibition gunfights, **Waverly Place** changed the culture around it. There was no place to go but up in Chinatown in the 19th century, when racist laws restricted where Chinese San Franciscans could live and work – so the community built temples and mutual-aid associations atop Waverly Place barber shops, laundries and restaurants. You'll spot the flag-festooned balcony of **Tin How Temple** *(9:30am-3pm Fri-Wed)*, where services have been held since 1852 – even after SF's 1906 earthquake and fire, when altars were still smoldering. To pay your respects,

PRACTICALITIES

● free ● btwn Grant Ave, Stockton St, California St & Broadway follow sandalwood-incense aromas upstairs. Entry is free but offerings customary; no photography inside, please.

Readers may remember Waverly as a heroine's namesake in Amy Tan's novel *The Joy Luck Club* – and bilingual booklovers may find new Chinese-language favorites at **Unbound** *(unboundsf.co)*, Chinatown's independent bookstore. The first US Chinese restaurant to earn a Michelin star, **Mister Jiu's** *(p121; misterjius.com)* brings new life to Waverly Place's 130-year-old clinker-brick banquet hall. **On Waverly** *(p122; onwaverly.com)* celebrates Chinatown's boundless creativity and deep generosity with gifts, books, art and design featuring Asian American makers.

Ross Alley

You might recognize **Ross Alley** from its cameos in ho-hum Hollywood blockbusters – *The Karate Kid, Part II*, *The Pursuit of Happyness*, *Big Trouble in Little China* – and its star turns in indie gems like *Chan Is Missing* and art-doc *Who Is Michael Jang?* Find inspiration at contemporary art gallery shows at the **Chinese Culture Center** (p119) and design popups at **41 Ross** *(41ross.org; free)*, then seek your fortune at **Golden Gate Fortune Cookies** *(p120; goldengatefortunecookies.com)*. Here cookies are stamped from vintage presses – just as they were in 1909, when fortune cookies were invented in Chinatown for SF's Japanese Tea Garden.

Spofford Alley

Sun Yat-sen once plotted the overthrow of China's last dynasty here at number 36, and during Prohibition, this was the site of turf battles over local bootlegging and protection rackets. **Spofford Alley** has mellowed with age – but the quiet alley livens up around sundown, when a Chinese orchestra may strike up a tune, mah-jongg games start with a cascade of clicking tiles, and local barbers and florists trade the day's best gossip.

Wentworth Place

This restored cobblestoned lane was formerly known as Salty Fish Alley, since this was where fisherfolk sold the day's catch. Today you might catch new murals in progress – follow Jeremy Novy's signature koi fish stenciled on the pavement into **Wentworth Pl**.

Some Wentworth murals are created by local students with artist-mentors – '**Love Our People Like You Love Our Food**,' requests one mural created by students with Chinese Culture Center director Vida Kuang. '**Dragon Boats Chasing Moonlight**' commemorates the Autumn Moon Festival in mosaics by Chinatown Community Development Center's youth program with mentor Margarita Soyfertis. Artist Justin Hoover and Gold Mountain Calligraphy painted a poignant *duai lien* (14-character) poem capturing Chinatown's history: 'Digging for gold, (we) experience bitterness and tears. Building the railway, (we) are credited for its success.'

CLINKER BRICKS

Notice twisted, blackened clinker bricks in Chinatown alley walls. Chinatown was originally built by non-Chinese landlords with unreinforced bricks – so during SF's 1906 earthquake, Chinatown toppled and burned. Survivors rebuilt it using repurposed bricks. Chinatown's architecture of survival became a California Arts and Crafts signature, gracing buildings statewide.

TOP TIPS

- Teenage Chinatown historians guide you on two-hour **Chinatown Alleyway Tours** *(chinatownalleywaytours.org; adult/student/child $50/20/10)*, a nonprofit program of the Chinatown Community Development Center. Youth leaders share epic true stories – from Sun Yat-sen plotting China's revolution to martial-artist Bruce Lee breaking down racial barriers – and share their perspectives on the challenges and prospects ahead.
- Chinatown is more than a tourist attraction – it's America's most densely populated neighborhood west of Manhattan, home to more than 15,000 San Franciscans. Be mindful to respect people's privacy in their homes and businesses when taking photographs.

GRANT AVENUE'S BRILLIANT NEON

Grant Ave, with its vintage neon signs, became one of America's brightest streets 100 years ago, as part of Chinatown's brilliant redesign.

After the 1906 earthquake, developers tried to push Chinatown outside San Francisco, on the pretext that this thoroughfare was a red-light strip. Savvy Chinatown leaders led by Bank of Canton founder Look Tin Eli lobbied to rename Chinatown's shady DuPont St 'Grant Ave', and consulted architects to design its modern, pagoda-roofed Chinatown deco style. Dim red lanterns were replaced with dazzling neon and dragon-wrapped street lamps.

The image overhaul worked like a charm: photographers, partiers and celebrities flocked here, establishing neon-lit Li Po and Buddha Lounge as signature SF attractions.

Play in Portsmouth Square

Come out to play

Tai chi practitioners greet the dawn, picnickers assemble lunch banquets, toddlers rush the playground in the afternoon, and chess players plot moves well into the night. Welcome to **Portsmouth Sq**, Chinatown's unofficial living room.

This hillside plaza has been action-packed since 1846, when Captain John B Montgomery pulled up his 20-gun ship the *Portsmouth* nearby to stake the US claim on Yerba Beuna, an unceded Ohlone pueblo loosely governed by Mexico that the church dubbed San Francisco. An uneasy peace was reached – until gold was found in the hills across the Bay, and chaos ensued. In those Wild West days, Portsmouth Sq was where everything happened in San Francisco: burlesque Jenny Lind Theater doubled as SF's first City Hall, conveniently located across from the brothels of euphemistically named Commercial St, alongside San Francisco's first newspaper offices, public school and vigilante headquarters.

The Victorian madams and vigilantes are long gone, and Portsmouth Sq has mellowed with age – but as you see, this park is still full of life and open to ideas. Presiding over the plaza is the **Goddess of Democracy**, a bronze replica of the plaster statue that Tiananmen Sq protesters made in 1989. Portsmouth Sq's pedestrian bridge is a magnet for arts and events – including **Chinatown Pride** *(cccsf.us)*, the outdoor-and-proud festival celebrating the neighborhood's LGBTQ+ community with Pride poster-printing, an all-ages disco and amazing drag runway walks. To glimpse what's ahead for the city and the world beyond its shores, watch this space – and bring a picnic.

DRINKING IN CHINATOWN: ICONIC SF BARS

Li Po: Enter the faux-grotto doorway for *baijiu* (rice-liquor)-spiked Chinese mai tais under the golden Buddha. Brusque bartenders, cellar bathrooms, random dance-offs: a world-class dive bar. *2pm-1:30am*

Comstock Saloon (p129): Wild West saloon, complete with trough where cowboys relieved themselves. The cocktails are potent as ever, but ragtime-jazz bands entertain bathroom lines. *4pm-midnight Tue-Sat*

Buddha Lounge: The vintage red-neon Buddha sign promises dangerously enlightening nights featuring an eclectic jukebox, cheap well drinks and beer straight from a laughing-Buddha bottle. *1pm-2am*

Empress at Boon Lounge: Chinatown's 1966 landmark is crowned by this swanky octagonal lounge, featuring inventive top-shelf cocktails and inspired Cantonese bites by chef/owner Ho Chee Boon. *5-10pm Mon-Sat*

North Beach

Standing atop the Filbert St Steps, you can understand what Italian fishermen, Beat poets and wild parrots saw in North Beach: there's more sky than ground here, and it's sociable but never entirely tamed.

Rock Out in North Beach

Catch live shows at iconic underground venues

You're right on time to catch the revival of legendary North Beach underground clubs, bringing West Coast jazz, punk and indie bands roaring back to life. North Beach launched West Coast jazz from the 1930s to '70s at Broadway venues such as El Matador, featuring talents like Oscar Peterson, the Modern Jazz Quartet, Sergio Mendes and SF's own Vince Guaraldi – before he found fame with the holiday classic *A Charlie Brown Christmas*. Now **Keys Jazz Bistro** (Map p120) is bringing next-generation jazz talents back to this iconic North Beach venue, with raucous reinventions of classics by SF's Jazz Mafia, guaranteed good times with Lavay Smith and Her Red-Hot Skillet-Lickers, and rotating residencies by international jazz talents *(keysjazzbistro.com; shows $15–50)*.

Across Broadway is another sensational comeback story: the **Mabuhay Gardens** (Map p120) is back. In the 1970s to '80s, this former Filipino supper club took a chance on local acts, introducing then-unknown comics (including Whoopi Goldberg and Robin Williams) and releasing a sonic boom into the stratosphere with The Dead Kennedys (fronted by trickster-prophet and SF mayoral candidate Jello Biafra), The Avengers (featuring the defiant brilliance of Penelope Houston), and an unsigned but impressively loud band called Metallica.

During peak Covid, music fans worried about the future of independent live music venues – but one staunch survivor is **Bimbo's 365 Club** *(bimbos365club.com)*. Agostino Giuntoli came to SF as a Palace Hotel janitor in 1922, and by 1931 opened this speakeasy with stiff drinks, burlesque bar murals, and parquet dance floors for high-stepping like Rita Hayworth (she led the chorus line here). His grandsons are in charge now, booking intimate showcases with major marquee talent (Adele, Van Morrison, Lizzo, Brandi Carlile, Bebel Gilberto) plus indie bands that get the dance floor bumping (Zap Mama, Dandy Warhols, The Walkmen). This is a classy joint: dress snazzy and bring cash to tip coat-check and powder-room attendants. Most shows are 21-plus, with a two-drink minimum; no recording.

PUNK'S NOT DEAD

In the 1970s, the North Beach club scene that defied obscenity laws, musical genres and dress codes launched West Coast punk. Rock-radio was dude-centric, but bands fronted by women regularly rocked the **Mabuhay Gardens** – including Blondie, Patti Smith, The Runaways, Pearl Harbor and the Explosions. The Mab attracted acts from LA (X, Black Flag, Go-Gos, Germs) to the UK (The Clash, Damned, Police, Sex Pistols). Its impossible run of 3600 bombastic live shows ended in 1987, when the venue changed ownership – but one person never gave up the punk-rock vision. When Francesca Valdez was hired to clean the building, she vowed to revive the Mab's punk heyday, and in 2022, when it went up for sale, Valdez crowdfunded the down payment from punk fans. Now the Mab's roaring back – watch out, punks.

HIGHLIGHTS
1 City Lights Books
2 Coit Tower

SIGHTS
3 Beat Museum
4 Filbert Street Steps

SLEEPING
5 Hotel Bohème
6 Washington Square Inn

EATING
7 Cafe Jacqueline
8 Da Flora
9 Fairuz Eatery
10 Golden Boy
11 Liguria Bakery
12 Mario's Bohemian Cigar Store Cafe
13 Molinari
14 Palermo II Delicatessen
15 Ristorante Ideale
16 Sotto Mare
17 Tony's Pizza Napoletana

DRINKING & NIGHTLIFE
18 Belle Cora
19 Cafe Angolo
20 Caffe Trieste
21 Golden Sardine
22 Graffeo Coffee
23 Red Window
24 Tony Nik's

ENTERTAINMENT
25 Savoy Tivoli

SHOPPING
26 101 Music
27 Friend of a Friend
28 Little Vine
29 San Francisco Rock Posters & Collectibles
30 Vacation

Another new/old space to watch is the **Savoy Tivoli** *(savoy tivoli.com)*, a seemingly quaint 1907 club with vintage Italian murals and a tiny stage that somehow survived decades of earth-shaking shows by The Ramones, Muddy Waters and SF drag phenomenon Beach Blanket Babylon. Today the bar is restored, the stage reinforced, and the calendar packed with local bands and comedians – ready when you are.

Dare to Drink in Devil's Acre Saloons

Party like it's 1899

Hope you're thirsty. San Francisco's swaggering Western saloons have survived brawls and busts, fires and earthquakes – and today they're roaring back to life with historically accurate gin cocktails and whiskey concoctions. Start happy hour at the crossroads of Chinatown and North Beach at **Comstock Saloon** *(comstocksaloon.com)*, and you may never make it to your next stop – the live music (Wednesday through Saturday), gourmet bar menu, and potent, historically accurate cocktails fill many happy hours.

Back in the 19th century, San Francisco had some 3000 saloons plus 2000 'blind pigs' (speakeasies), all vying for attention with signature cocktails like the 1862 liquid-fire Blue Blazer, which required whiskey, sugar, fire and nerve. But cocktails were risky propositions in North Beach's notorious **Devil's Acre saloon district**, where lightweight gold-rush miners were literally shaken down for gold dust. Happy hours that started with smiles and shots could end days later, when bar patrons awoke to find they'd been drugged and indentured as sailors on ships bound for faraway ports, like Patagonia or Shanghai – hence the expression 'got shanghaied.' To this day, North Beach regulars prefer bars with well-lit bottles and brusque barkeeps.

On **Drag Me Along Tours** *(dragmealongtours.com)*, you can explore the Devil's Acre with a bona-fide legend: gold rush burlesque star Countess Lola Montez, reincarnated in drag by SF historian Rick Shelton. In two action-packed hours, her Highness leads you past saloons where sailors were shanghaied, into alleys where Victorian ladies made and lost reputations. San Francisco's most memorable gold-rush characters gambled, loved and lived dangerously – expect adult content (reservations required; $120 for up to four people).

Despite their dangerous reputations, Devil's Acre saloons may actually have saved some sailors' lives with their

SF'S MULTICULTI PIZZA CRAVINGS

San Francisco loves all flavorful flatbreads – so if you're ready to explore the world beyond pepperoni, you're in the right place.

Outta Sight Pizza (Map p120): At the edge of Chinatown and North Beach, Outta Sight serves slices with Peking duck, caramelized onions and a dash of hoisin.

Fairuz Eatery (p137): Brings bright, mouthwatering Lebanese flavors to crispy thin-crust *sfeeha* (flatbread with beef, pine nuts and pomegranate molasses) and *manaeesh* (za'atar-topped flabread) with creamy labneh.

Zante: In the Mission, Zante is credited with inventing Indian pizza 30-plus years ago – the paneer tikka pizza loaded with masala-spiced eggplant, cauliflower and spinach tastes fresh as ever.

EATING IN NORTH BEACH: PIZZA & FOCACCIA

MAPS P120, P128

Liguria Bakery: All sorts line up before 8am for cinnamon-raisin focaccia hot from the 100-year-old oven, leaving dawdlers a choice of rosemary-garlic or tomato. Takeout only. *7am-noon Tue-Sat* $

Tony's Pizza Napoletana: Pizza world-champion Tony Gemignani offers legit Jersey tomato pies, prosciutto-fig Cal Italia pizza, even coal-fired NY slices. *noon-9:30pm Mon-Thu, to 11pm Fri-Sun* $$

Golden Boy: Punks and tattoo artists have politely queued since 1978 for the foccacia-crust pizza – get pesto/veggie and clam-and-garlic slices. Takeout only. *11:30am-9pm Sun-Thu, to 11pm Fri & Sat* $

Tommaso's: Charming North Beach Italian since 1935, with wood-fired brick-oven Neapolitan pizza, well-priced wine, booths and communal tables. *5-10:30pm Tue-Sat, 4-9:30pm Sun* $$

TOP EXPERIENCE

City Lights Books

Free spirits and free speech have found refuge at **City Lights Books** *(citylights.com)* since 1957. Words were dangerous business back in the '50s, when library books were often banned, Hollywood screenwriters were blacklisted and comedians got arrested for swearing in North Beach nightclubs – but poet Lawrence Ferlinghetti founded City Lights Books anyway.

'A Kind of Library Where Books Are Sold'

As Ferlinghetti's sign suggests, browsing is encouraged here. City Lights publications include titles by Angela Davis, Diane di Prima and Noam Chomsky, proving the point on another of Ferlinghetti's signs: 'Printer's Ink Is the Greater Explosive.'

Poetry Room

City Lights' affordable Pocket Poets series brought poetry to the people – including Allen Ginsberg's *Howl and Other Poems* (1956), a sensation that got Ferlinghetti and City Lights manager Shigeyoshi Murao arrested for publishing poetry with homoerotic content. They fought obscenity charges not on technicalities but on artistic merits, winning a landmark free-speech victory. Celebrate your freedom to read freely in the upstairs **Poetry Room**'s designated **Poet's Chair**, with 60 Pocket Poets titles – including *Howl*, available in 24 languages.

Nonfiction Cellar

The nonfiction cellar is unconventionally organized by countercultural themes, including Stolen Continents, Muckraking and Pedagogies of Resistance. This cellar once housed the paper dragon for Chinese New Year (p118) celebrations, and enigmatic wall slogans were left by a 1930s cult. Visitors to this literary-underground landmark will recognize truth in the cult sign declaring 'I am the door': City Lights is the door to new ideas and nonstop revelations.

TOP TIPS

- Duck into **Jack Kerouac Alley** (p118), a poetry-paved shortcut between Chinatown and North Beach.
- Visit Kerouac's favorite haunts: **City Lights Books**, **Vesuvio** (see right) and a stool by the golden Buddha at **Li Po** (p126) – Kerouac was a true believer in literature, Buddhism and beer.

PRACTICALITIES

- citylights.com
- free
- 10am-10pm

STEVE WOOD/SHUTTERSTOCK

LIZ HAFALIA/THE SAN FRANCISCO CHRONICLE VIA GETTY IMAGES

Comstock Saloon (p126)

citrusy, scurvy-curing cocktails. Today, potent potions and lip-smacking quack cures are proudly served at the neighborhood's Victorian apothecary-style bar, the **Devil's Acre** *(Map p120; thedevilsacre.com)*. Here sworn enemies Call a 'Treuse – their signature cocktail, featuring chartreuse, vermouth, egg white and mysterious 'gold rush bitters.' Tartly quaffable Lavender 75 (lemon, lavender, gin, bubbly) is a surefire cure for scurvy and/or sobriety. Reserve online for parties of four-plus; no food.

For long pours and tall tales, seek out the alley speakeasy known as **Specs** (Twelve Adler Museum Cafe if you're fancy, which no one here is; specsbarsf.com; Map p120). The walls here are plastered with merchant-marine memorabilia, and you'll be plastered too if you try to keep up with the salty characters holding court in the back over pitchers of beer and the sailor's special: cheese, saltine crackers and hot sauce. Surrounded by seafaring mementos – including a massive walrus organ over the bar – landlubbers find their sea legs with navy-strength gin drinks. Cash only.

Across the street, a guy walks into a bar, roars and leaves. Without missing a beat, the bartender says to the next customer, 'Welcome to **Vesuvio**, honey – what can I get you?' Jack Kerouac blew off Henry Miller to go on a bender here – and after you've joined neighborhood characters for microbrews on the stained-glass mezzanine you'll see why *(vesuvio.com)*. If you're here for just one drink, make it the di Prima, named for legendary Beat poet Diane di Prima. Once when di Prima was leaving an Allen Ginsberg party to get home and relieve her babysitter, Kerouac quipped that if she wanted to write,

BEST HISTORIC COCKTAILS

Martinez: SF's martini precursor was invented to tide over a Victorian boozehound on the ferry. **Comstock Saloon** (p126; Map p120) serves it with gin, vermouth, bitters, maraschino liqueur and wild abandon. *4pm-midnight Tue-Thu & Sat, from noon Fri*

'Cappuccino': Tosca Cafe (Map p120) served brandy-spiked hot cocoa through Prohibition, and you can still order their air-quote special at the vintage bar. *5-11pm Tue-Sat*

Dirty martini: North Beach celebrated Prohibition's 1933 end at **Tony Nik's** (Map p128) tiny 'cafe' – an original deco bar with a vintage martini that's salty and a touch pickled. *4pm-1am Mon-Fri, 2pm-2am Sat, 2pm-1am Sun*

di Prima: the literary-legendary cocktail (rye/Aperol/bitters) at **Vesuvio** (Map p120) recalls Diane di Prima's maxim: 'to remind us all/to celebrate/ there is no time too desperate/no season that is not a Season of Song.' *11am-1am Sun-Thu, to 2am Fri & Sat*

THE OTHER BROADWAY

When San Franciscans reminisce about Broadway shows, they're not talking about Disney musicals. North Beach's Broadway strip has seen it all since the 1930s: the nation's first openly lesbian bar (Mona's, in 1936), dedicated drag venue (Finocchio's, 1936), uncensored comedy acts (Lenny Bruce at the Jazz Workshop, 1961), topless strip club (Condor Club, 1964), and unionized strip club (Lusty Lady, 1997).

Not all SF Broadway shows were well received. Carol Doda was arrested for going topless but won her case, and reportedly got her breasts insured for $1.5 million. Lenny Bruce was arrested and acquitted of obscenity charges, but hounded by law enforcement until his untimely death. Yet night after night, SF Broadway shows continue to push buttons and boundaries, honoring almost a century of fearless performers.

she should forget her babysitter – but she ditched him instead, made it home to relieve her babysitter, and went on to publish 50 acclaimed poetry books and host her own parties as San Francisco Poet Laureate.

If you're planning a night out to remember tomorrow, roll up Columbus to the **Red Window** *(theredwindow.com)*. Low-proof and nonalcoholic cocktails are the breakout stars of the creative bar menu here – the nonalcoholic spritz and deceptively decadent espresso martini (low-proof rum, espresso, cocoa nibs and walnut bitters) are true North Beach sensations.

Hang with Poets at the Beat Museum

Free your mind, feel the Beats

Dylan jam sessions erupt in the bookshop, Allen Ginsberg spouts poetry nude in documentary footage, and stoned visitors grin beatifically at it all. Welcome to the **Beat Museum** *(kerouac.com; adult/student $8/5)*, spiritual home to all 'angel-headed hipsters burning for the ancient heavenly connection' (to quote Ginsberg's *Howl*).

This is the closest you can get to the complete Beat experience without breaking a law. The 1000-plus artifacts in the museum's literary ephemera collection include the sublime (the banned edition of Ginsberg's *Howl*, with the author's own annotations) and the ridiculous (Kerouac bobblehead dolls are definite head-shakers). Highlights include overdue tributes to Diane di Prima and other women Beats, and the writing desk of City Lights founder and SF's original Poet Laureate, Lawrence Ferlinghetti. Enter the museum through the adjoining museum store, stocked with poetry chapbooks and obscure Beat titles you won't find elsewhere; bookstore entry and poetry readings are free.

North Beach Comedy Nights

Catch bold, breakthrough stand-up acts

On good nights in North Beach comedy clubs, wildly unpredictable routines have been known to break laws, free minds and leave audiences gasping for breath between laughs. Comedy and drag cabaret acts have been packing clubs along Broadway since the 1930s, and comedian Lenny Bruce got arrested here for cursing in 1961. In a hard-won legal victory for free speech, Bruce was acquitted – establishing North Beach as a proving ground for bold, original comics. Tiny but fearless clubs here helped launch huge careers – Ali Wong, Anjelah Johnson, Ellen DeGeneres, Dana Carvey, Robin Williams, Whoopi Goldberg and Woody Allen, to name a few – and major stars return to North Beach to test out risky new material and film comedy specials.

Comedy stars regularly sell out downtown SF venues like **Masonic Auditorium** (p43), **Bill Graham Civic Auditorium** (p114) and **Punch Line** (p114) – but they play faster and looser at intimate North Beach venues like **Bimbo's** (p127) and **Cobb's Comedy Club**. Bumper-to-bumper tables at Cobb's pull you into the action, and keep you on the edge of your

SEYHAN AHEN/SHUTTERSTOCK

Beat Museum

seat as the test audience for new comics as well as big-name acts (Mo Amer, John Oliver, Michelle Wolf, Paul Reiser) – fair warning that anyone sitting close to the stage may become part of the act. Check Cobb's website for shows (most are 18-plus with a two-beverage minimum; tickets from $25). **The Lost Church** is a newer nonprofit performance space that feels like a neighborhood institution, because this is exactly the kind of 50-person-max basement theater that built North Beach's reputation for underground comedy and indie artists – recent acts range from monthly comedy speakeasy The Setup to mind-reading magicians and furious flamenco *(thelost church.org; doors open 7:30pm; shows $15–50)*. Comics work up material year-round for **SF Sketchfest** *(sfsketchfest.com)* spotlights here and Chinatown's **Great Star Theater** (p121) – and when everyone else watches their comedy special, you can say you saw it here first.

DRINKING IN NORTH BEACH: ESPRESSO CULTURE

MAPS P120, P128

Caffe Trieste: Espresso fuels conversation and fills notebooks at mosaic tables thronged by artists, writers and filmmakers. Cell phones are discouraged, and food irrelevant. Cash only. *7am-10pm*

Cafe Angolo: Linger over espresso at sunny bistro tables – this isn't your average American office-cafe, but a true North Beach social hub. *8am-5pm*

Graffeo Coffee: Luciano Repetto is the North Beach legend behind light roasts that are darker than most, and dark roasts that are deliciously diabolical. No drinks here, just top-quality beans. *9am-5pm Mon-Sat*

Réveille: If this sunny flat-iron storefront doesn't lighten your mood, cappuccino with a foam-art heart will – and with just-baked chocolate-chip cookies and sticky buns, life is grand. *7:30am-4pm*

SEYHAN AHEN/SHUTTERSTOCK

Caffe Trieste (p133)

Score Rock-Star Vintage

Free your inner San Franciscan

Ever suspect you were an SF rock star in a previous life or parallel universe? Bring that inner rocker to life in North Beach vintage shops, where a day's haul might include stage-worthy platform shoes, psychedelic show posters, and rare vinyl. Escape from the tyranny of beige and find your signature SF style in the colorful, well-curated racks at **Vacation** *(vacation-sf.com)*. The key to timeless SF rocker style is mixing and matching decades – and Vacation has you covered with glam-rock metallic platforms, inexplicably well-preserved punk concert tees, mint dead-stock denim, psychedelic shifts, and Victorian tasseled handbags. Upbeat staff stylists make it their mission to find fits for every gender, size and SF occasion. To cash in on your castoffs, call ahead to check buying hours.

EATING IN NORTH BEACH: SIGNATURE SEAFOOD

Ristorante Ideale: Roman chef-owner Bruschi makes his pasta by hand ('of course!') and prepares today's catch simply, perfectly paired with North Beach's top-value Italian wine list. *5-10pm Tue-Sun* **$$**

Cafe Jacqueline: Dinner can hardly get more romantic than seafood soufflé floating across your tongue like fog over the Golden Gate Bridge...until you order the chocolate soufflé. *5:30-10pm Tue-Sat* **$$**

Da Flora: Get cozy in this candle-lit *osteria* over chef Jen McMahon's market-fresh menus – buttery, pan-kissed Pacific halibut, plump poached in saffron risotto. *5-9pm Wed-Sat* **$$**

Sotto Mare: From tonight on, the clatter of bowls will make you remember seafood *cioppino* (stew) so fresh, it's practically swimming in rich tomato broth. *11:30am-9pm* **$$**

You'll notice that many North Beach storefronts proudly feature screen-printed posters and handbills advertising local shows – and **San Francisco Rock Posters & Collectibles** *(rockposters.com)* has an unbelievable stash of them in mint condition from decades of legendary local shows. At this trippy temple to the rock gods, you'll still find first-run psychedelic Fillmore concert posters featuring the Grateful Dead, for a price – but you might find some bargains among the hand-printed handbills for San Francisco acts like Santana, the Dead Kennedys, and Sly and the Family Stone.

Now that you've found your SF rock-star style and poster art, you're practically a poster-child for San Francisco – all you need is your personal SF anthem. Odds are you'll find one in the 'Local Musicians' record bin at **101 Music**, the second home of local DJs and hard-core collectors – Tom Waits and Carlos Santana have been spotted here. Duck so you don't knock your head on vintage Les Pauls, and flip through crates of $10 to $30 vinyl – you might score rare recordings by Nina Simone, Janis Joplin, Alice Coltrane and San Francisco's own Dead Kennedys.

On Location in North Beach

Capture SF movie magic

Movie-star sightings aren't unusual in North Beach, but one filmmaker is a fixture here: Francis Ford Coppola, who drafted the script for *The Godfather* at **Caffe Trieste** *(p133; caffetrieste.com)*, and transformed a local landmark into a movie monument. If the copper-clad walls of the **Sentinel Building** (Map p120) could talk, they'd name-drop shamelessly. The Sentinel's original occupant was notorious political boss Abe Ruef, ousted in 1907 and sent to San Quentin for bribing city supervisors. The basement became a speakeasy during Prohibition, then a comedy club where Lenny Bruce performed – and when Grammy-winning folk group the Kingston Trio took over the tower in the 1960s, it became a recording studio where the Grateful Dead recorded. Coppola bought it in 1972, and over the years shared offices here with Wayne Wang and Oscar-winning actor-director Sean Penn.

Today, the ground floor is open to the public as **Cafe Zoetrope** *(Map p120; cafecoppola.com/cafezoetrope)*, a prime spot for character studies or sketching plotlines while sipping

THE TATTOOED LADIES OF NORTH BEACH

Back in the 1950s, Ringling Brothers Circus drew crowds just to see a 'tattooed lady' – meanwhile in San Francisco, Lyle Tuttle quietly opened a tattoo parlor that would inspire women worldwide to get tattoos. Over his 60-year career, Tuttle inked women across six continents and attracted celebrities to his shop – including Jane Fonda, Joan Baez, Janis Joplin and Cher.

Tuttle credited his success to women's liberation, and was proud to assist women taking control over their own bodies and self-expression at his North Beach shop – and he made the process safer for everyone, championing sanitary tattooing practices with SF's health department. Tuttle has gone on to that great ink cloud in the sky, but you'll spot his Western Traditional designs around North Beach.

DRINKING IN NORTH BEACH: WINE

Friend of a Friend: Farmer and winemaker Christopher Renfro pours rare finds from independent wineries and Black winemakers – including his own SF-grown Teroldego. *noon-7pm Wed-Sun*

Golden Sardine: The next Renaissance is underway with Beat poetry readings, winemaker tastings, and free-flowing creativity fed with sardines and cheese. *4-10pm Tue-Fri, 2-11pm Sat, 2-9pm Sun*

Little Vine: Consult cheesemonger Melissa Gugni to pair California wine with artisan cheese and charcuterie or today's panini – and return for $5 Thursday tastings with winemakers. *11am-7pm Tue-Sun*

Belle Cora: Join the sidewalk-cafe block party with affordable Italian wines and upbeat live music, from ragtime Parlor Tricks to Danny Herrera's Salsita Brass. *3pm-midnight Sun-Thu, to 2am Fri, 1pm-2am Sat*

TOP EXPERIENCE

Coit Tower

The exclamation mark atop Telegraph Hill is Coit Tower, dedicated to first responders by firefighting millionaire Lillie Hitchcock Coit, who raised eyebrows in 1860s SF for smoking cigars, gambling and wearing men's clothes like her crew at Knickerbocker Engine Company #5. Coit Tower's 1930s lobby murals celebrating SF workers were initially denounced as communist, but are now landmarked.

JUDD IRISH BRADLEY/SHUTTERSTOCK

TOP TIPS

- For a parrot's-eye panoramic view of San Francisco 210ft above the city, take the creaky 1930s elevator to the tower's open-air **viewing platform**.
- For a challenge, hike up 13 flights of stairs to the viewing platform.

Secret Treasures in the Stairwell

Book a tour up the narrow 2nd floor **stairwell**, where recently revealed stairwell murals were hidden for 80 years. The seven murals show San Francisco in the 1930s – the showstopper is Jane Berlandina's strikingly modern egg-tempera mural **Home Life**, showing San Franciscans baking pies and kicking back.

Lobby Murals

Publicly funded **1930s lobby murals** show what daily life was like here during the Depression: San Franciscans organized dockworkers' unions, lined up at soup kitchens, partied despite Prohibition and read books – including Marxist manifestos – in Chinese, Italian and English. When they were completed in 1934, the artworks were so controversial, the opening of the tower was delayed by censors. Authorities called the 26 artists that painted them communists, and demanded that radical elements be removed. The artists refused, and in a last-minute compromise, park employees painted over a hammer-and-sickle symbol. Public opinion overruled the censors: San Franciscans embraced the murals as symbols of the city's openness. In 2012 voters passed a measure to preserve them as historic landmarks, and today the murals are freshly restored – and as bold as ever.

PRACTICALITIES

● sfrecpark.org ● nonresident elevator adult/student/child $10/7/3, mural tour full/2nd fl $10/5 ● 10am-6pm Apr-Oct, to 5pm Nov-Mar

Coppola's signature Napa wines, either at sidewalk tables or indoors, surrounded by *Godfather* movie memorabilia. Order the classic movie-star lunch: Caesar salad, first served on these premises in 1924, a decade before it made its Hollywood debut.

Telegraph Hill Stairway Hikes

Earn panoramic, romantic city views

In the 19th century, a ruthless entrepreneur began quarrying and blasting away roads on the side of **Telegraph Hill**. City Hall eventually stopped the quarrying, but the view of the bay from the **Filbert Street Steps** is still (wait for it) dynamite. Halfway through the steep climb up the Filbert Street Steps to **Coit Tower**, you might wonder if it's all worth the trouble. Take a breather and notice the scenery you're passing: sweeping **Bay Bridge** vistas, hidden cottages along **Napier Lane**'s wooden boardwalk, and sculpture-dotted gardens in bloom year-round. If you need further encouragement, the colorful wild parrots in the trees have been known to interject a few choice words.

For more well-earned views, find the urban trailhead between 150 and 155 Francisco St to **Francisco Street Steps**. Cross the courtyard, ascend to Grant Ave, and turn left to reach **Jack Early Park**, where you'll find scenic seats for two – a popular spot for marriage proposals, despite the ominous view of Alcatraz from here. Climb higher for Golden-Gate-to-Bay-Bridge panoramas, then descend via Grant Ave for a well-earned slice at **Golden Boy** (p129).

SF'S SCENE-STEALING CAMEOS

San Francisco is a filmmakers' dream, with consistent light, moody fog and iconic buildings. But as you may notice from movies set in San Francisco, there's a trick to shooting here: this city tends to pull focus from the stars.

Local stars know how to strike the right balance – no one romps through the city quite like Robin Williams *(Mrs Doubtfire)*, or shoots Chinatown shadows like Wayne Wang *(Chan Is Missing, Joy Luck Club)*, or wisecracks her way around town like Ali Wong *(Always Be My Maybe)*.

Yet even Marilyn Monroe and North Beach's own baseball star Joe DiMaggio appeared to be swallowed up by the scenery when they posed for their wedding photos in front of Sts Peter and Paul Church on Washington Sq (p139).

EATING IN NORTH BEACH: PANINI

Molinari: Grab a number and sing along to Sinatra while wisecracking staff prepare massive panini to order – get the house-cured salami. *9am-5:30pm Mon-Fri, to 9pm Sat, 11am-3:30pm Sun* $

Palermo II Delicatessen: Lucrezia is the second-generation Sicilian deli boss behind *Godfather*-themed panini, crispy arancini (risotto balls), and eggplant parmigiana with her secret-recipe marinara. *10am-5pm Tue-Sun* $

Fairuz Eatery (p129): North Beach *nonnas* line up for falafel perfected over 20 years: crunchy yet fluffy, with nutty tahini and citrusy sumac in warm pita. *11am-8pm Sun-Thu, to 10pm Fri & Sat* $

Mario's Bohemian Cigar Store Cafe: Mario's gave up smoking in the 1970s and turned to piping-hot panini – enjoy onion focaccia with meatballs, eggplant or grilled chicken, plus Chianti and people-watching. *11am-9pm* $

WALKING TOUR

North Beach Beat

Find inspiration for your own creative pursuits in the literary stomping grounds of North Beach, where poets, writers, and San Francisco's cast of original characters Kerouac called 'the mad ones' still roam free. In streets named for spoken-word legends, you can get moved to poetry and debate philosophy without missing a Beat.

1 City Lights Books

At **City Lights Books** (p130), home of Beat poetry and free speech, find a few choice words to inspire your journey into literary North Beach – Ferlinghetti's San Francisco Poems make excellent companions.

The Walk Head up and across Columbus to the block of Vallejo St Ferlinghetti called 'Poet's Piazza.'

2 Caffe Trieste

Duck into **Caffe Trieste** (p133) for opera on the jukebox and potent espresso in the back booth, where Francis Ford Coppola drafted *The Godfather* screenplay.

The Walk Walk up Grant Ave to Filbert St, then hang a right to duck into the quiet, hidden alleyway honoring Beat poet Bob Kaufman for a moment of quiet reflection.

3 Bob Kaufman Alley

Observe a moment of silence in **Bob Kaufman Alley**, honoring the legendary Black Jewish Buddhist spoken-word poet and co-founder of *Beatitude* magazine. Frequently jailed for 'resisting arrest' in verse, Kaufman was never at a loss for

KIRKIKIS / GETTY IMAGES

Vesuvio (p131) and City Lights Books (p130)

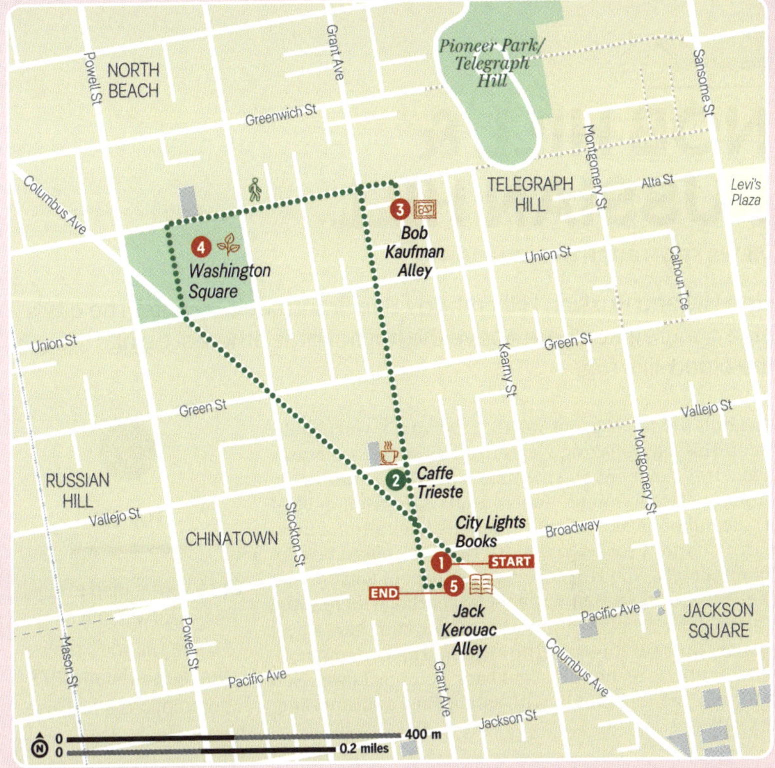

words – until Kennedy's assassination, when he took a vow of silence that lasted 12 years, until the Vietnam War ended. Then he walked into a North Beach cafe and recited his ode to peace, 'All Those Ships That Never Sailed.'

The Walk Back on Filbert St, turn your back on Coit Tower and walk downhill to Washingtown Sq.

❹ Washington Square

SF's first official park was built in 1850 on the ranchland of city founder Juana Briones – rest awhile on the bench dedicated to her. Notice **Washington Sq**'s odd statue of Ben Franklin – a replacement for the original statue of eccentric dentist Henry D Cogswell, who believed water cured alcoholism and plunked a statue of himself here. Neighbors deemed Cogswell too homely for public view, and toppled his statue. The time capsule Cogswell buried here was opened in 1979 to reveal a 19th-century feminist manifesto, SF Chinese-language newspaper, and antique dental tools. Another time capsule was buried in its stead, containing a Lawrence Ferlinghetti poem, Levi's jeans and NorCal wine (sorry, Henry).

The Walk Walk down Columbus past City Lights, and swing into mural-covered, poetry-paved Jack Kerouac Alley.

❺ Jack Kerouac Alley

On the Road author Jack Kerouac once blew off Henry Miller to go on a bender at **Vesuvio** (p131), until bartenders ejected him into the backstreet now named for him: **Jack Kerouac Alley** (p118). Vesuvio's signature cocktail is named for Beat poet Diane di Prima – she published 50 books in her lifetime, including her epic *Revolutionary Letters*. After today, you'll have enough material to write revolutionary letters of your own.

Researched by
Margot Seeto

NOB HILL & RUSSIAN HILL

VIEWS FROM SUCH GREAT HEIGHTS

Nob Hill and Russian Hill embody San Francisco's heights. The city's elite congregated here above the hoi polloi as ethereal beings living in the cloud-like fog.

The hills are no joke, but worth traversing if you're able. 'Snob Hill' has amazing views from its parks, staircases and curvy Lombard St, spanning from Coit Tower to the Transamerica Pyramid. Robert Louis Stevenson dubbed it 'the hill of palaces' due to residents like railroad magnates Charles Crocker and Mark Hopkins, plus a bevy of luxury hotels. Nob Hill encompasses part of Polk St, and the Polk Gulch section was SF's 'gayborhood' before the Castro. Polk remains a nightlife street with bars of all genres. North is Russian Hill – less quirk, more money – with boutique restaurants and bars. South is Lower Nob Hill, aka 'the Tendernob', with established and emerging art galleries.

TOP TIP

Once you've tried to climb these hills with the help of a cable car, you'll realize that those vintage 1873 contraptions aren't just here for looks. The Powell-Hyde and Powell-Mason lines cover these hills, but fair warning: both lines start at Powell St terminus, where waits are notoriously long. If the cars are packed, they might not stop at all marked stops – but it's worth a shot if you're tired and quick to hop on board. Alternatively, take the California St line, which rarely has queues.

FROM LEFT: NICHOLAS J KLEIN/SHUTTERSTOCK, KIT LEONG/SHUTTERSTOCK

Above: Lombard St (p144); Right: Grace Cathedral (p145)

See page 261 for places to stay in Nob Hill & Russian Hill

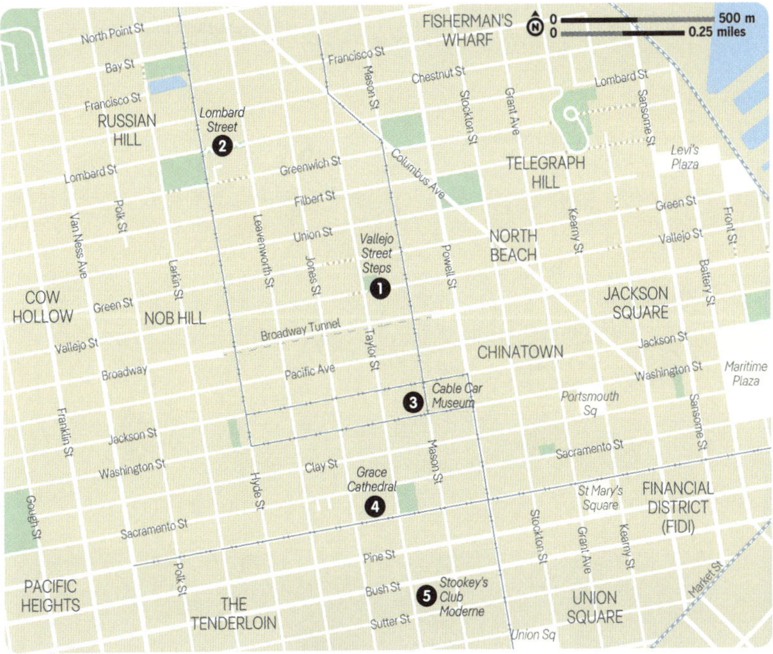

FISHERMAN'S WHARF
0
500 m
0
0.25 miles
North Point St
Bay St
Francisco St
RUSSIAN HILL
Lombard Street
2
Lombard St
Greenwich St
Filbert St
Union St
Vallejo Street Steps
1
Francisco St
Mason St
Chestnut St
Stockton St
Grant Ave
Lombard St
Sansome St
Columbus Ave
TELEGRAPH HILL
Levi's Plaza
Green St
Vallejo St
Front St
Van Ness Ave
Polk St
Larkin St
Leavenworth St
Jones St
Powell St
NORTH BEACH
Kearny St
Battery St
COW HOLLOW
Green St
NOB HILL
Broadway Tunnel
Taylor St
JACKSON SQUARE
Jackson St
Vallejo St
Broadway
Pacific Ave
CHINATOWN
Washington St
Maritime Plaza
Cable Car Museum
3
Portsmouth Sq
Sansome St
Franklin St
Jackson St
Washington St
Clay St
Sacramento St
Hyde St
Grace Cathedral
4
Mason St
St Mary's Square
FINANCIAL DISTRICT (FIDI)
Gough St
Sacramento St
Stockton St
Grant Ave
Kearny St
Pine St
Market St
Polk St
PACIFIC HEIGHTS
THE TENDERLOIN
Bush St
Sutter St
Stookey's Club Moderne
5
Union Sq
UNION SQUARE

Highlights

❶ Vallejo Street Steps
See North Beach unfurl below like a magic carpet, hovering between the Bay Bridge and Downtown skyscrapers. **p147**

❷ Lombard Street
Photograph the famous switchbacks, then discover views at George Sterling Park and Lombard Financial Center Mosaics. **p144**

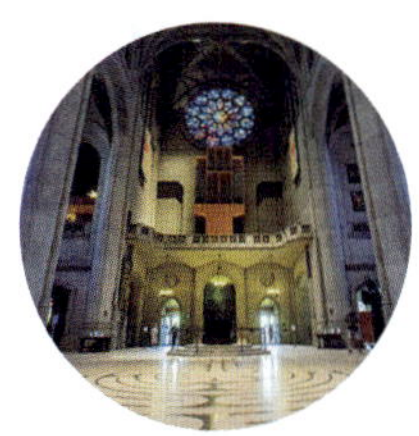

❸ Cable Car Museum
Witness San Francisco's original 1873 steampunk technology in action. **p144**

❹ Grace Cathedral
The stunning sights include 'Human Endeavor' stained-glass windows and the Interfaith AIDS Memorial Chapel. **p145**

❺ Stookey's Club Moderne
Enjoy live jazz and historically inspired cocktails at this swell art deco bar. **p146**

Getting Around

Bus

Buses 10 and 12 link downtown with Russian and Nob Hills. Bus 27 connects the Mission, SoMa and Downtown to Nob Hill. Buses 41 and 45 connect downtown to Russian Hill and Cow Hollow.

Cable car

The Powell-Hyde line serves Russian and Nob Hills; Powell-Mason serves Nob Hill; and California runs from Downtown through Chinatown and over Nob Hill to Van Ness Ave.

Car

Don't drive if you can avoid it. With gradients from 24% to 31.5%, Nob Hill and Russian Hill are not good for your brakes. Leave driving to pro taxi drivers.

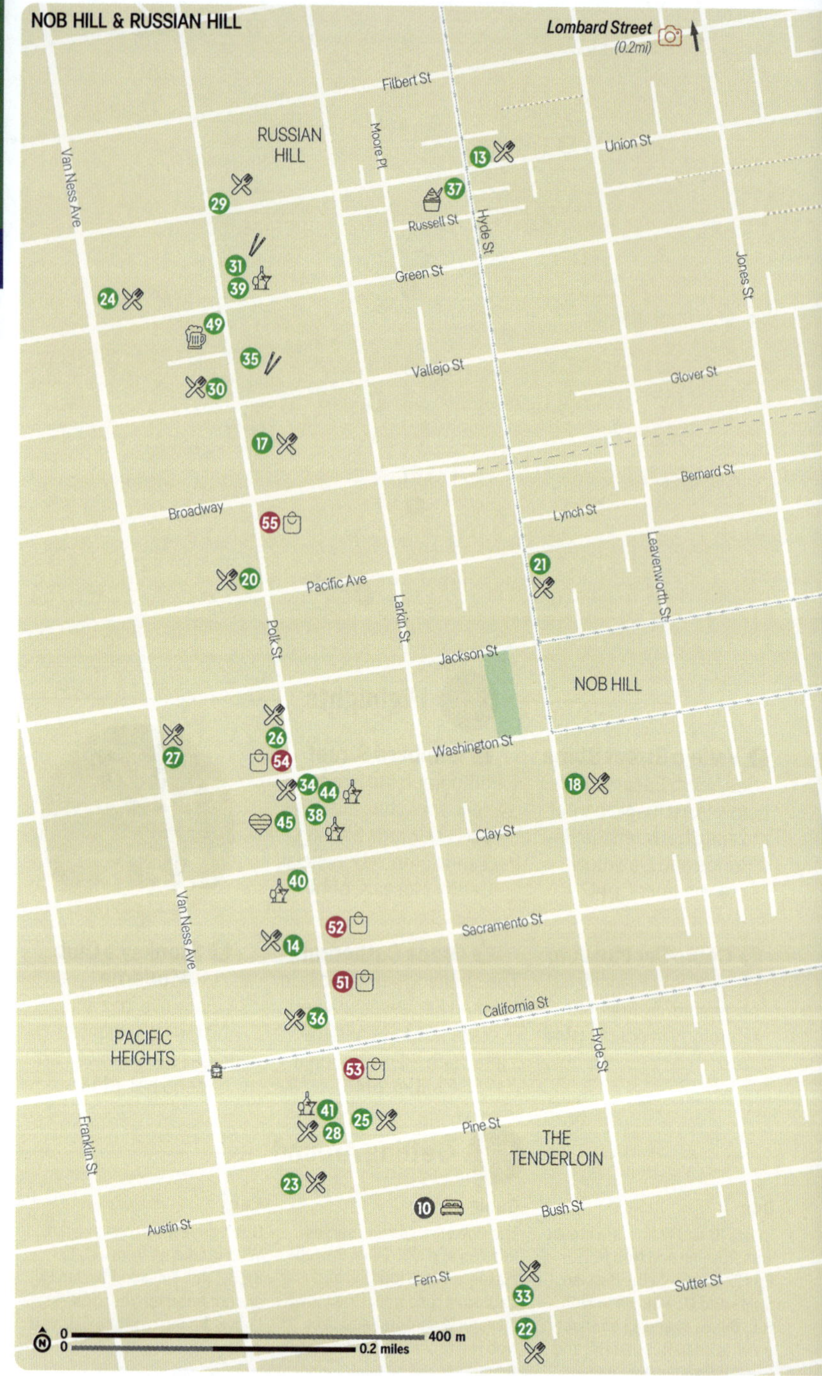
NOB HILL & RUSSIAN HILL
Lombard Street
(0.2mi)
Filbert St
RUSSIAN
HILL
Moore Pl
Union St
Van Ness Ave
Russell St
Hyde St
Green St
Jones St
Vallejo St
Glover St
Bernard St
Broadway
Lynch St
Pacific Ave
Leavenworth St
Larkin St
Polk St
Jackson St
NOB HILL
Washington St
Clay St
Sacramento St
Van Ness Ave
California St
PACIFIC
HEIGHTS
Hyde St
Pine St
THE
TENDERLOIN
Franklin St
Bush St
Austin St
Fern St
Sutter St
0
0
400 m
0.2 miles

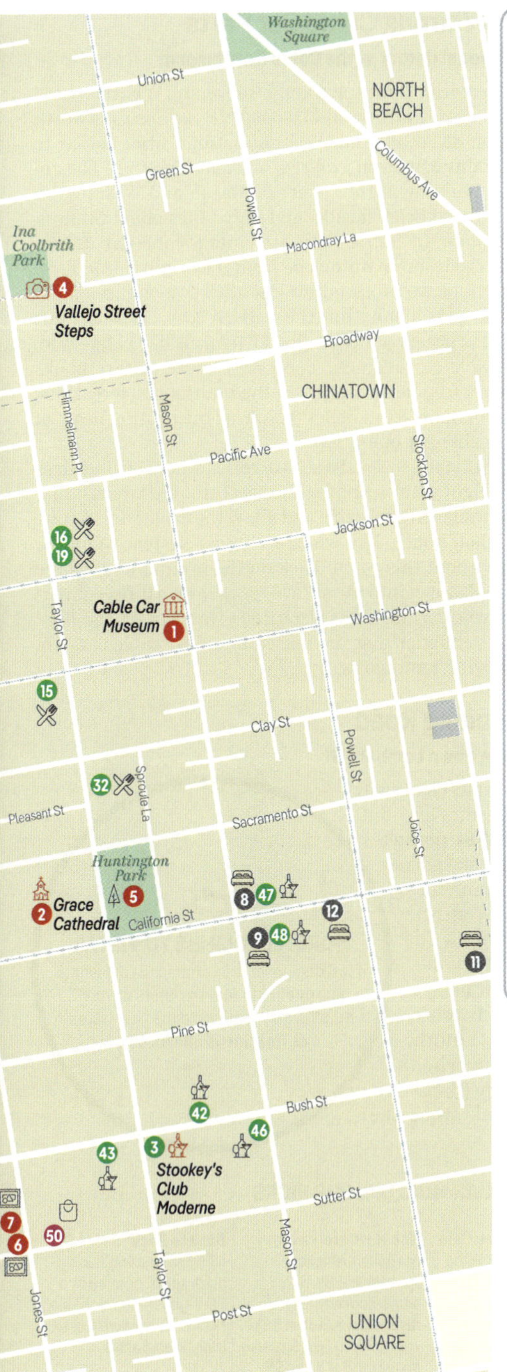

HIGHLIGHTS
1 Cable Car Museum
2 Grace Cathedral
3 Stookey's Club Moderne
4 Vallejo Street Steps

SIGHTS
5 Huntington Park
6 Ryan Graff Contemporary
7 The Birdcage

SLEEPING
8 Fairmont San Francisco
9 InterContinental Mark Hopkins
10 Music City Hotel & Hostel
11 Ritz-Carlton
12 Stanford Court Hotel

EATING
13 Abrazo
14 Acquerello
15 Back to Back
16 Better Than Sweet
17 Bi-Rite Market (Polk St)
18 Bob's Donuts
19 Cafe Isabella
20 Cheese Plus
21 Collina
22 DACHA Kitchen & Bar
23 Grubstake Diner
24 Helmand Palace
25 Himalayan Cuisine
26 Hot Cookie
27 House of Prime Rib
28 Juniper
29 Leopold's
30 Macondray
31 Nisei
32 Nob Hill Cafe
33 Sofiya
34 Sorella
35 SSAL
36 Swan Oyster Depot
37 Swensen's

DRINKING & NIGHTLIFE
38 Amélie
39 Bar Iris
40 Harper & Rye
41 Hi-Lo Club
42 Key Klub
43 Peacekeeper
44 Polkcha
45 The Cinch Saloon
46 The Summer Place
47 Tonga Room & Hurricane Bar
48 Top of the Mark
49 Woods Polk Station

SHOPPING
50 Argonaut Book Shop
51 Fashion Exchange
52 Good Vibrations
53 Out of the Closet
54 ReLove
55 Russian Hill Bookstore

THE 2025 CABLE CAR SHEAVES UPGRADE PROJECT

In early 2025, Muni completed a project to refurbish and reinstall all 21 street sheaves along the Powell-Hyde, Powell-Mason and California cable-car lines. The process involved each sheave being removed from its respective vault beneath the street, and then taken to the cable-car barn at the Cable Car Museum. There, the shaft bearings and related hardware were rebuilt. Since sheave replacement parts are no longer manufactured, staff needed to rebuild each part in order to extend the life of each sheave.

The last major cable-car-system maintenance project was the Cable Car Barn Propulsion Gearbox Rehabilitation Project in 2017, which overhauled and refurbished five gearboxes that had been in service since 1984.

Watch Whirring Cable Car Parts

An educational detour at the Cable Car Museum

Halfway between Downtown and Fisherman's Wharf on both the Powell-Hyde and Powell-Mason cable-car lines, it's worth hopping off at Powell and Washington for a brief detour to the **Cable Car Museum** *(cablecarmuseum.org; free)*. The unassuming building at the corner of Mason and Washington has a faded red-brick facade, and only takes about 30 minutes to explore. Of course there are vintage cable cars to see, including the last remaining one from the original 1873 fleet. Photographs of inventor Andrew Hallidie's system throughout its 150-year-plus history line the walls. A cozy, cash-only gift shop is full of cheesy-yet-charming SF trinkets like palm-sized, sparkly, cable-car magnets, and essential SF history books (don't forget to take advantage of the bathrooms, too). However, the small museum belies its role as the beating heart of the city's cable-car operation.

Walk downstairs to see the sheave room, where behind glass walls are eight giant spinning sheaves (grooved wheels) that guide the underground cable and allow the cable cars to travel along their route. The whole cable-car system would be nothing without this room. Back on the ground level where you can look down into the sheave room from a different perspective, you may also see mechanics working on the floor – another reminder that the museum and its cable cars are living, moving landmarks.

The Winding Road

Zigzagging down Lombard St

You've seen its eight switchbacks in movies, but **Lombard St** doesn't deserve its nickname as 'San Francisco's crookedest street' – Vermont St in Potrero Hill deserves that honor. Lombard is more scenic, though, with flowerbeds lining its brick-paved 1000 block since the

MORE HILL CLIMBS TO VISTAS

If walking down the Lombard St hill whets an appetite to test the limits of your quadriceps, connect to the hilly vistas of Treasure Island (p243).

EATING NEAR THE CABLE CAR MUSEUM: OUR PICKS

Cafe Isabella: Tiny neighborhood gem known for breakfast burritos and coffee, with a few small tables. *8:30am-3pm Tue-Sun* $

Better Than Sweet: Cafe Isabella's neighbor is the owner's sister's. Go for jackfruit smoothies and kimchi grilled cheese. *9am-2:30pm Tue-Sun* $

Nob Hill Cafe: Family-run Italian-American spot since 1989, with home-cooked vibes. No reservations. *5-9pm Sun-Thu, to 10pm Fri & Sat, also 11am-3pm Sat & Sun* $$

Back to Back: One of SF's many natural wine-and-pizza spots, opened by a third-generation Nob Hill family. *5-9pm Sun-Tue, to 10pm Wed-Sat* $$

TOP EXPERIENCE

Grace Cathedral

San Francisco's reinforced-concrete Gothic hilltop Grace Cathedral took 40 years to complete, with commanding, sculpted, bronze front doors that are a post-WWII mold of the original in the Battistero di San Giovanni in Florence, Italy. Inside, spectacular stained-glass windows celebrate science. The Interfaith AIDS Memorial Chapel features artist-activist Keith Haring's final work.

DALTON JOHNSON/SHUTTERSTOCK

Yoga, Grace Cathedral

Science in Stained Glass

The 68 stained-glass windows are pleasantly overwhelming. Look up the high walls for the 'Human Endeavor' series by Gabriel Loire, celebrating science and social progress. See Albert Einstein amid swirling nuclear particles, activist and Nobel Peace Prize–winner Jane Addams, and Justice Thurgood Marshall.

Interfaith AIDS Memorial Chapel

Upon entering the cathedral, a small room to the right is the Interfaith AIDS Memorial Chapel that features artist-activist Keith Haring's last work before his death from AIDS in 1990. On a bronze triptych in the style of a Russian altar, Haring's *Life of Christ* features a signature thick-lined, multi-armed figure representing compassion cradling a baby, surrounded by angels. On the opposite wall hangs a section of the AIDS Memorial Quilt, and beneath it is a Book of Remembrance.

Yoga, Sound Baths, Concerts and More

Being a progressive, inclusive church that's also a stunning venue, public programming occurs with regular frequency. Twice-weekly yoga sessions ($20 to $30, book online) are taught on the interior labyrinth, set to live music from local musicians. Also on offer are sounds baths, dance performances, organ recitals and art installations.

TOP TIPS

- Even if not religious, attend a service like Thursday Choral Evensong for ethereal singing.
- Outside Grace Cathedral, **Huntington Park**'s centerpiece is Fountain of the Tortoises, a recreation of a 400-year-old limestone fountain in Rome.
- Meditation labyrinths exist on the cathedral floor and front courtyard.

PRACTICALITIES

- gracecathedral.org
- adult/senior/12-22 years/under-12s $14/12/10/free (no charge if attending services or praying/lighting a candle)
- 10am-5pm Mon-Sat, from 1pm Sun

LAST HOUSE ON THE LEFT

The last building on the left when going downhill – the **1000 Lombard** building – is a calming cream color with sea-blue trimming. Its history, however, is hauntingly tragic.

In the 1960s, socialite, TV personality and writer Pat Montandon threw an occult-themed party. The tarot reader, whose request for a drink was forgotten, cursed Montandon and the house. A series of physical illnesses, vandalism, strange smells and noises, and deaths in the following years were believed by some to be a result of the curse. The last fatality involved a fire that mysteriously couldn't be linked to the cause of death.

The apartment has since been exorcised and sold. Respect the property as one would for any private residence.

1960s. The street wasn't always so bent: it plunged straight downhill until too many joyriders crashed in the 1920s. Today traffic is slow and skating is banned – so Lombard St thrills featured in Tony Hawk's Pro Skater video game are strictly virtual.

For drivers, Lombard traffic flows one way – downhill from Hyde to Leavenworth. More than one million people make this drive annually. No right turns from the northbound Hyde (it's a one-way street in this area) onto Lombard are allowed between 11am and 8pm except for residents of the 1000 block. At the mandated 5mph, the drive only takes about five minutes. During peak tourist season, the wait to drive down can take up to 20 minutes. Patience is a virtue both in the line and cruising down the street, with smart phones poised to record the ride.

The Powell-Hyde cable-car line stops directly at Lombard St, so walking down (or up) Lombard is another popular option. You can also get there on foot as an extension of the walking tour (see right). If you're planning to park by Lombard to walk it, don't leave valuables or anything visible in the car.

Historic Hotel Hop

Opulent, architectural time travel

Nob Hill has the nickname 'Snob Hill' for a reason. Since the gold rush and the subsequent railroad boom that followed, movers and shakers of San Francisco like the Big Four (magnates Leland Stanford, Mark Hopkins, Charles Crocker and Collis P Huntington) have called this high and hilly neighborhood home, building lavish gilded-age mansions. Naturally, luxury hotels were also built to serve the elite. Wander into three of them to bask in old-time opulence in each grand lobby.

Walk north of Union Sq, take the bus, or hop on the California St cable-car line to first stop off at the **Ritz-Carlton** *(ritzcarlton.com)* on the Stockton St border between Nob Hill and Chinatown. The exterior of the 1909 neoclassical building, dubbed the 'Temple of Commerce' originally for the Met Life Insurance Co, stands Greek godly with 17 Ionic columns, plus Haig Patigian's terra-cotta figurines above depicting an American family, protected by a winged figuring representing insurance. The grand lobby has crystal chandeliers above and 19th-century art on the walls. Reserve a classy afternoon tea slot.

Next, travel 0.25 miles west on California St to stop off at **Fairmont San Francisco** *(fairmont-san-francisco.com)*, the original Fairmont, easily spotted by international flags

DRINKING IN NOB HILL: OUR PICKS

Key Klub: Natural wine bar that's quiet at dinner and more dance party on the weekends. *5-11pm Tue-Wed, to midnight Thu-Sat*

Stookey's Club Moderne: Chrome-lined 1930s decor with white-jacketed bartenders shaking stiff drinks. Enjoy live jazz in the neighboring Stookey's Blue Room. *5pm-2am*

Peacekeeper: Tequila-centric, light-filled cocktail bar with a chill ambiance. *3pm-2am Mon-Fri, from 1pm Sat & Sun*

The Summer Place: Dive bar that's been given a facelift, with a giant rock facade, windowless interior and welcoming vibe. *2pm-2am Mon-Fri, from noon Sat & Sun*

TRAVERSE HILLY STAIRWAYS & PARKS

Work those quads to be rewarded with views (on views on views) of and from iconic landmarks.

START	END	LENGTH
Vallejo Street Steps	Lombard Financial Center	3.9km; 2½ hrs

Reach staggering heights with spectacular views along the ❶ **Vallejo Street Steps** connecting North Beach with Russian Hill. Ascend Vallejo toward Mason St, where stairs rise toward Jones St, passing ❷ **Ina Coolbrith Park**, named after California's first poet laureate. Pause for nighttime views of the Bay Bridge lights (if they're on). Take the scenic route down to ❸ **Macondray Lane** via steep stairs and past gravity-defying wooden cottages, and have an ice cream at ❹ **Swensen's** (p148) on Hyde and Union. Nearby ❺ **Filbert Street Hill** awaits with a 31.5% grade, and the honor of SF's steepest street (shared with 22nd St in the Castro). Look over the North Beach churches to see Coit Tower (p136). One block north on Hyde is ❻ **George Sterling Park** – from here enjoy ace sunset views over the Golden Gate Bridge and understand why the poet namesake called SF 'the cool grey city of love.' Head a block east to walk down the stairs of ❼ **Lombard Street** (p144), next to the curvy red-brick road and its eight switchbacks. It won't take long, so climb back up, then go west on Lombard to the ❽ **Lombard Financial Center Mosaics** at Chase Bank. California modernist Millard Sheets designed mosaics highlighting SF history.

No photos are allowed inside Chase Bank (2750 Van Ness Ave). However, plenty of **mosaics** cover the building exterior. Snap away.

Armistead Maupin used **Macondray Lane** as the model for Barbary Lane in his *Tales of the City* series.

Ina Coolbrith was also in Mark Twain's literary circle. A surprising additional celebrity connection: her uncle was Mormon prophet Joseph Smith.

BEST NOB HILL SPOTS

Matthew Charnock (@underscore_sf), writer, editor, owner of Underscore_SF.

Nob Hill is the quintessential San Francisco neighborhood. the Manhattan of the West Coast, due to the area's density and walkability, from SF's world-renowned **Cable Car Museum** (p144) to a litany of coffee-shop choices – so long as you're OK with climbing some of the city's steepest street sections.

Polk St hosted San Francisco's first-ever Pride Parade in 1970. Twice a year, the sun perfectly aligns with California St during an event called 'San Francisco Henge' and makes for jaw-dropping pictures. Even if your trip doesn't align with this celestial anomaly, I promise that sipping a coffee from atop Huntington Park while watching the sunrise wash over downtown won't disappoint.

NOAH SAUVE/SHUTTERSTOCK

Fairmont San Francisco (p146)

hanging outside and a smiling 8ft-tall bronze **Tony Bennett statue** on the grounds along Tony Bennett Way. The crooner first sang 'I Left My Heart in San Francisco' at this hotel in 1961. Enter the magnificent marble lobby of the building, which had been scheduled to open in 1906 when the earthquake hit, but survived and opened in 1907. Inside the beaux-arts lobby, butter-yellow marble columns hold up gold-paneled ceilings, oozing opulence. Downstairs is the iconic tiki bar, the **Tonga Room & Hurricane Bar** – the concept may be outdated, but it's still an experience. While sipping rum-heavy tiki drinks like mai tais, watch a cover band play on a floating island in the middle of the room, with rain showers sprinkling down every 30 minutes.

Just south on Mason is the 1926 **InterContinental Mark Hopkins** *(ihg.com)* hotel, built on the former grounds of the Hopkins family mansion that burned down in the 1906 earthquake fires. The Renaissance Revival architecture incorporates French château style with Spanish ornamentation, including intricate terra-cotta flowers in the lobby archways – bask in the light of the crystal lobby chandeliers. Visit the famous **Top of the Mark** rooftop bar for end-of-the-world views,

EATING IN NOB HILL: OUR PICKS

Helmand Palace: An Afghan staple since 1971. Try lamb dwopiaza served with black-eyed peas and mushrooms. *5:30-10pm* $$

Leopold's: Austrian-German specialties include schnitzel. *5:30-9pm Wed & Thu, to 10pm Fri & Sat, to 9:30pm Sun, also 11:30am-2:30pm Sat & Sun* $$

Collina: Casual, cozy sister restaurant to the lauded Seven Hills with stunners like giant raviolo and 48-layer lasagnette. *5-9pm Sun-Thu, to 9:30pm Fri & Sat* $$

Swensen's: The original Swensen's ice-cream shop, opened in 1948 with throwback flavors like peppermint stick. *noon-10pm Tue-Sun* $

while feeling like a 1980s Wall Street investor talking shop over old-fashioneds and martinis in the wood-paneled bar.

Polk Street by Day

Eating, shopping, quirky art-hopping

Usually known for its nightlife (p151), Polk St, which runs north–south from Civic Center (p104) all the way up to Ghirardelli Sq, has a strip called **Polk Gulch**, spanning from Pine to Union Sts. With numerous restaurants, cafes, shops, galleries and a surprising museum, it's a worthwhile place to explore in the daytime.

Clothing shopping, especially thrift/vintage, is a hallmark of Polk St, with the well-curated **ReLove** *(shoprelove.com)* as a top choice, including designer labels. The Polk St location of national chain **Out of the Closet** *(outofthecloset.org)* donates proceeds toward HIV care, and has a consistently large selection of clothing. Neighboring **Fashion Exchange** is less dynamic, but has a wall of sequined showgirl outfits. **Punk Majesty** *(Mp p106; punkmajesty.com)*, the city's only punk showroom, creates one-off and custom upcycled leather vests and more, in addition to being the exclusive carrier of punk-scene and drag-queen photographer Leee Black Childers' photos. Visit **Midnite Theories** *(Map p106; midnitetheories.com)* skate shop for the commissioned bathroom mural and cool goods even non-skaters will like. Going into tonier Russian Hill is **Russian Hill Bookstore** *(russianhillbookstore.com)*, one of the few indie new-and-used bookstores in SF that includes 1980s copies of *The Baker Street Journal* – a quarterly dedicated to the study of Sherlock Holmes and all things 'Sherlockiana.'

A very San Francisco entity is the free **Antique Vibrator Museum** *(antiquevibratormuseum.com, 18-plus only)* in the back of the Polk St outpost of sex-positive shop **Good Vibrations** *(goodvibes.com)*, where vintage versions of 'personal massagers' from household brands like Hamilton Beach are neatly displayed in an exhibit room that takes about 30 minutes to see.

Small but Mighty Creative Spaces

Art galleries of the 'Tendernob'

The quirky neighborhood art galleries and small businesses that span the Tenderloin to Lower Nob Hill (Tendernob), mostly along Larkin just one block east of Polk, give a sense

NURTURING THE ARTS SCENE

John Vochatzer *(@calamityfair)*, artist, co-owner of Moth Belly Gallery, and SF First Thursday Art Walk organizer

Many of our galleries, venues and creative hubs were lost to the pandemic and the rising cost of living.

Moth Belly Gallery (p150) was born in late 2020 out of a need for new spaces.

In 2021, I took on stewardship of the **Tenderloin/Lower Polk First Thursday Art Walk**, which dates back to 2011. At the time, only a few spaces participated monthly; it has now grown to 20 to 25 venues and draws hundreds of visitors each month.

As a Tenderloin resident for over two decades, I've seen a lot of change that has brought many challenges – but the neighborhood remains one of the most diverse areas in San Francisco.

EATING ON POLK STREET: OUR PICKS

Swan Oyster Depot: Fresh seafood since 1912. Oysters and off-menu 'Sicilian sashimi.' Cash only. *8am-2:30pm Mon-Sat* $$$

Bob's Donuts: Opened in 1960 at a premises down the street. Eat apple fritters and giant donuts used in lieu of birthday cakes. *24hr* $

Bi-Rite Market: This branch of the Mission District-based darling is the biggest location yet, with house-made grab-n-go foods like quinoa bowls. *8am-9pm* $

Cheese Plus: Get grilled cheese made with *fromage du jour* at this 20-year-old grocer. *10am-7:30pm Mon-Fri, from 9am Sat & Sun, to 7pm Sun* $

BEFORE THE CASTRO, THERE WAS POLK GULCH

Comedian **Margaret Cho** grew up around her parents' now-shuttered Polk St bookstore – iconic gay bookshop Paperback Traffic – in the 1970s. Steeped in queer and drag culture, Cho recalled that the smell of her childhood was 'pantyhose and balls.' Polk Gulch was SF's 'gayborhood' before the Castro was, adjacent to the queer-friendly Tenderloin, and SoMa (see **Valley of the Queens walking tour**, p286). The 1962 formation of Polk St LGBTQ+ business owners as The Tavern Guild helped support more queer businesses and culture, seeing the first Pride parade in the early 1970s, and going strong through the 1980s. Sadly, the owners and patrons aged out, succumbed to the devastating AIDS epidemic, or were priced out. Today, **The Cinch Saloon** (see right) remains the last queer bar of the era on Polk.

PAULAAH293/SHUTTERSTOCK

Grubstake Diner

of the current city and neighborhood culture. **Moth Belly Gallery** *(Map p106; mothbelly.org; free)* is an anchor of the scene, with 'The Green Show' featuring 50 Bay Area artists like Mariana Varela's *Headfirst for Chaos* oil and acrylic quadriptych with surrealist-like images of an anthropomorphized sun and storm. **Modern Eden** *(Map p106; moderneden.com; free)* skews toward fantasy, like Sandra Yagi's Faerie Realm oil paintings of skeletons frolicking in nighttime forests with giant snails and lizards. On the corner of Sutter and Bush is a trio of artsy spots: cafe-gallery **The Birdcage** (*thebirdcagesf.com; free*), closed Mondays, hosts both exhibitions and art markets; **Ryan Graff Contemporary** *(ryangraffcontemporary.com; free)*, which has featured Ukrainian artist Kateryna Reznichenko's oil and acrylic portraits exploring transformation and chaos; and rare bookstore **Argonaut Book Shop** *(argonautbookshop.com)*. Many are part of the SF First Thursday Art Walk (p149), but if you're not around for that, it's easy to visit during some galleries' weekend hours, and many can quickly accommodate appointment requests – even same-day or the day before.

EATING IN NOB HILL: OFF POLK STREET

Sofiya: SF's only Uzbek restaurant fills comfort cravings with palm-sized *manti* dumplings stuffed with beef and onions. *11am-10pm* $$

DACHA Kitchen & Bar: Californian Eastern European cuisine and a queer-friendly environment. *5-10pm Wed-Sat, to 9pm Sun, also 11am-3pm Sat & Sun* $$$

Acquerello: Chef Suzette Gresham's Cal-Italian cuisine features seasonal signatures like rabbit-mortadella-filled *cappellacci* pasta. *5:30-9:30pm Tue-Sat* $$$

Abrazo: Spanish-Californian food at a cozy neighborhood gem. Get the paella and charred octopus, plus choose from the extensive wine list. *5:30-9pm Tue-Sun* $$$

Nightlife on Polk Street

Trailblazing queer bars to couture cocktail

For decades, Polk St in Polk Gulch had a reputation for hopping nightlife, from queer bar Suzy-Q to the punk bar and concert venue Hemlock Tavern – both figments of yesteryear, unfortunately. The pandemic's effect on the area was harsh, and the nightlife strip is still recovering and rediscovering its identity. That said, there are still plenty of places for a decent bar hop, and the eclectic variety of watering holes means there is something for everyone, with plenty of good eats for beforehand or afterward.

The Cinch Saloon, opened in 1974, deserves the Polk St crown, as the last holdover from Polk Gulch's prime 'gayborhood' days from the 1960s to 1980s. The cash-only Western-ish bar offers fruity cocktails and no-nonsense beer, with handcuffs dangling from the bar and a back pool room that doubles as a *Star Wars* tribute. A couple of supporting players pay homage to Polk's LGBTQ+ history, like the late-night **Grubstake Diner** *(grubstakesf.com)* and a second location of the racy, Castro-famous **Hot Cookie** *(hotcookie.com)*.

The rest of the Gulch's nightlife offers an impressive spread. On the Tenderloin border, divey **Jackalope** *(Map p106; jackalope-sf.com)* offers a $10 Plinko game to win a variety of drinks, plus video games upstairs. Get the **Blind Pig Speakeasy** *(Map p106; blindpigspeakeasy.com)* password on Instagram for pan-Asian cocktails inspired by the Monkey King legend, or go for a Korean-night-market-inspired Melona ice-cream-bar cocktail at **Polkcha** *(polkcha.com)*. Sip on a mezcal, carrot and lime cocktail at **Harper & Rye** if you're waiting for a reservation at **House of Prime Rib** *(houseofprimerib.net)*, or a brandy and benedictine number at **Hi-Lo Club** (*hilosf.com*). For a cozy glass of wine, try **Amélie** *(sfamelie.com)* or **Woods Polk Station** *(woodsbeer.com)*. Up in Russian Hill, try a Tsukemono Martini garnished with pickled cauliflower at **Bar Iris** *(bar-iris.com)*.

A few eating spots worthy of mention include the fine dining Japanese **Nisei** *(restaurantnisei.com)* and fine dining Korean **SSAL** *(ssalsf.com)*. More casual, delicious eats include **Himalayan Cuisine** *(himalayancuisinesf.square.site)*, **Macondray** *(macondraysf.com)* for lobster rolls, **Juniper** *(juniper.cafe)* bakery and **Sorella** *(sorellasf.com)*, the more casual Cal-Italian sister restaurant of **Acquerello** *(see left; acquerellosf.com)*.

TONGA ROOM'S LIVING LEGACY

Modern tiki bars like **Zombie Village** (p110; *thezombievillage.com)* aim to be less stereotypical than amalgamations of Polynesian, East Asian, and Caribbean cultures; nostalgia lends a glow to old-school ones.

Tonga Room & Hurricane Bar (p148) inside The Fairmont is 80 years old, and is SF's second-oldest tiki bar (the first being Trad'r Sam). The 1907 hotel pool was transformed into a bar in 1945, keeping the pool for the band's floating stage. While signature rain storms sprinkle down every 30 minutes, patrons don't get wet. Getting wet – by jumping into the pool – earns a $1000 fine.

Researched by
Alison Bing

JAPANTOWN, FILLMORE & PACIFIC HEIGHTS

POSTCARD-PERFECT VICTORIANS, WAVING KITTIES & MUSIC LEGENDS

Fillmore St leads from Pacific Heights' swanky boutiques, through Japantown's cultural and culinary hotspots, to buzzworthy Fillmore music venues, towards Alamo Sq's iconic Postcard Row.

Don't let the quaint Victorians and upscale boutiques fool you: this neighborhood totally rocks. Japanese Americans have called this area home for over a century and today, Japantown is where J-pop stars and cosplay TikTokkers shoot music videos in Peace Plaza. The Fillmore has been a nightlife hub since the jazzy 1930s and turned totally trippy in the psychedelic 1960s – and music legends are still made at live shows here. Hilltop Pacific Heights is ringed with mansions, many owned or once-owned by powerful women – including nude model turned museum founder Alma Spreckles, 19th-century Black billionaire and Underground Railroad pioneer Mary Ellen Pleasant, and former US House Speaker Nancy Pelosi.

TOP TIP

Every San Franciscan has a favorite Victorian. To find yours, head to prime Victorian zones around Alamo Sq (from Golden Gate to Fell St, between Divisadero and Webster), and from Japantown's Sutter St up to Jackson St in Pacific Heights. Multicolor 'Painted Lady' Victorians are irresistible photo-ops – but respect residents' privacy when taking photos.

FROM LEFT: SVETLANASF/SHUTTERSTOCK, HAYK_SHALUNTS/SHUTTERSTOCK

Above: Peace Pagoda (p160), Peace Plaza; Right: Painted Ladies (p162)

See page 262 for places to stay in Japantown, Fillmore & Pacific Heights

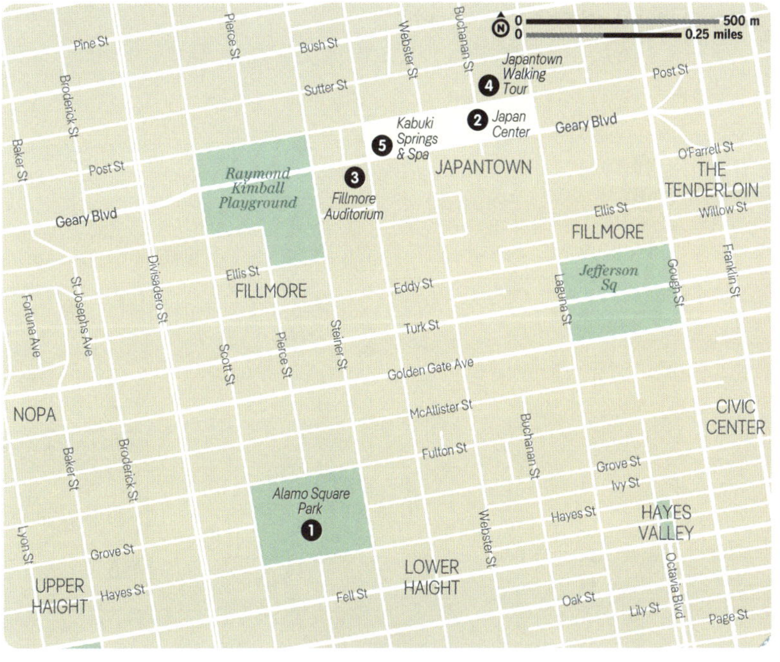

Highlights

❶ Alamo Square Park
Admire Victorian mansions that have hosted earthquake refugees, hippie communes, speakeasies and satanic rites. **p162**

❷ Japan Center
Slurp ramen, read manga, play anime arcade games, and cultivate bonsai gardens – all inside a midcentury mall. **p158**

❸ Fillmore Auditorium
Rock out with music legends in San Francisco's shrine to the psychedelic '60s. **p157**

❹ Japantown Walking Tour
Follow in the footsteps of culture heroes and civil rights trailblazers. **p160**

❺ Kabuki Springs & Spa
Unwind in communal Japanese baths to take the edge off foggy SF days. **p161**

Getting Around

Bus
The 38 Geary bus will pick you up downtown and drop you right at Geary and Fillmore. Lines 1, 2 and 22 also serve this area.

Cable Car
Hop the California line west from the foot of Market St to Van Ness Ave, then walk to Pacific Heights or Japantown.

Walk
From Van Ness, walk along Sacramento St (a block north of California), detouring through Lafayette Park. Go south along Fillmore. At Post St, head east to Japan Center, or west to to Pierce St, then south to Alamo Sq.

JAPANTOWN, FILLMORE & PACIFIC HEIGHTS
PACIFIC HEIGHTS
Nest (80m)
Freda Salvador (193m)
Sacramento St
Perine Pl
California St
Orben Pl
Pine St
Wilmot St
Bush St
Webster St
Monte Christo (354m)
Broderick St
Divisadero St
Scott St
Pierce St
Steiner St
Sutter St
Japan Center
See Fillmore Enlargement
FILLMORE
Post St
Hamilton Recreation Center
Geary Blvd
O'Farrell St
Byington St
Fillmore
Fillmore St
Kabuki Springs & Spa
Japan Center
Fillmore Auditorium
FILLMORE
0
100 m
Eddy St
Turk St
Fillmore St
Golden Gate Ave
Pierce St
Scott St
Broderick St
McAllister St
Steiner St
Divisadero St
NOPA
Baker St
UPPER HAIGHT
Fulton St
LOWER HAIGHT
Alamo Square Park
Hayes St
Fell St
0
400 m
0
0.2 miles
41
37
22
6
13
48
60
52
54
25
28
36
47
31
30
45
33
11
53
29
39
4
44
42
51
20
2
15
16
24
12
38
56
8
1
49
23
46
57

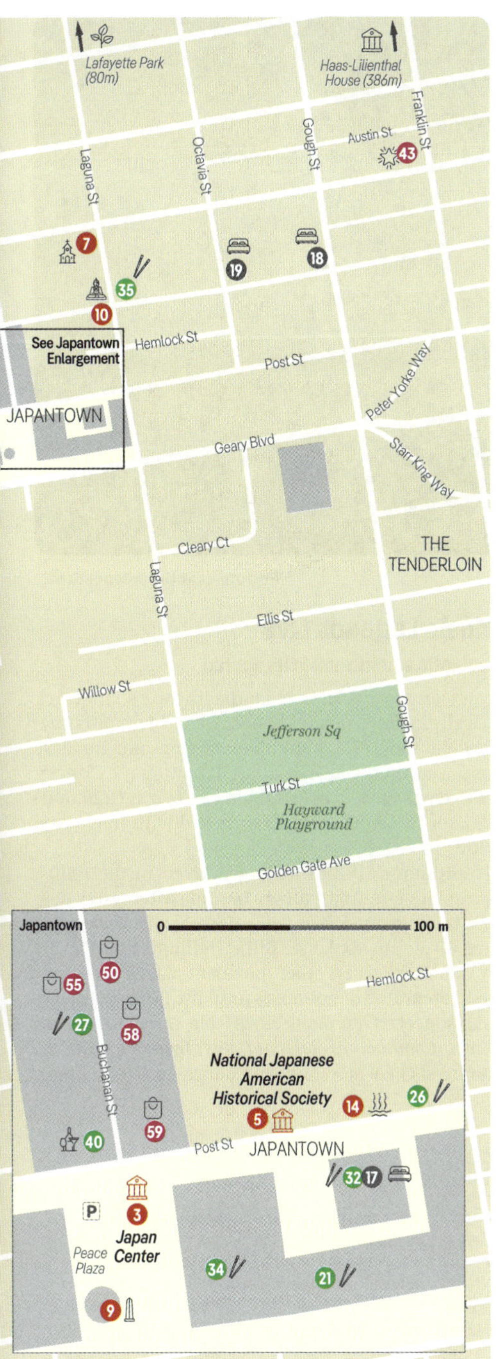

HIGHLIGHTS
1 Alamo Square Park
2 Fillmore Auditorium
3 Japan Center
4 Kabuki Springs & Spa
5 National Japanese American Historical Society

SIGHTS
6 Cottage Row
7 Konko Church
8 Painted Ladies
9 Peace Pagoda
10 Sokoji – Soto Zen Mission of San Francisco
11 Tokaido Arts
12 Westerfeld House

ACTIVITIES
13 Japanese Cultural & Community Center of Northern California (JCCCNC)
14 Pearl Spa
15 Westside Cuts & Style

SLEEPING
16 Chateau Tivoli
17 Hotel Kabuki
18 Hotel Majestic
19 Queen Anne Hotel

EATING
20 Aji Kiji
21 An Japanese Restaurant
22 b. patisserie
23 Bar Crudo
24 Brenda's Meat & Three
25 Copra
26 Daeho Kalbijjim
27 Hinodeya Ramen Bar
28 Jane the Bakery
29 Jina Bakes
30 Marufuku Ramen
31 Minnie Bell's Soul Movement
32 Nari
33 On the Bridge
34 Sasa
35 Sobakatsu
36 State Bird Provisions
37 Tataki
38 The Mill
39 Yakitori Edomasa

DRINKING & NIGHTLIFE
40 Fermentation Lab
41 Scopo Divino
42 Social Study

ENTERTAINMENT
43 Audium
44 Boom Boom Room
45 Festa
46 Independent
47 Sheba Piano Lounge

SHOPPING
see 54 Baby, the Stars Shine Bright
48 Crossroads Trading
see 15 Effin Relax
49 Fibers of Being
50 Forest Books
51 In the Black
52 Jonathan Adler
53 Kinokuniya Books
54 New People
55 Paper Tree
56 Perish Trust
57 Rare Device
58 SF76
59 Soko Hardware
see 54 Sou Sou
60 Zuri

FILLMORE POSTERS

When San Francisco's hippie scene exploded, psychedelic sounds rocked the Fillmore Auditorium with era-defining acts – including Sly and the Family Stone, Jefferson Airplane and of course the Grateful Dead, who played the Fillmore 51 times between 1965 and 1969.

San Francisco psychedelic artists like Wes Wilson, Bonnie MacLean, Stanley Mouse Miller and Victor Moscoco silkscreened promotional posters in Day-Glo colors and fonts so trippy, they were nearly impossible to read. Soon every rock star wanted their illegible name on a Fillmore poster.

Today the Fillmore's hallways and bars are lined with iconic posters, while artists from Snoop Dogg to Green Day play the intimate hall for the thrill of it – and for the collectible posters.

DANA JACOBS/GETTY IMAGES

Performer at the Independent

Catch Music Legends Live

Hear SF's eclectic soundtrack at its source

Playlists can't get more eclectic than the historic soundtrack of this musically inclined neighborhood: 1930s blues, '50s jazz, '60s psychedelic rock, '70s punk, '90s hiphop and timeless taiko drums. You might hear it all at Japantown's **Cherry Blossom Festival** *(sfcherryblossom.org)*, drawing 220,000-plus people over two April weekends packed with free music and festivities.

This extraordinary SF music scene started in the 1930s, when Japantown's late-night diners became after-party destinations for touring musicians tired of playing at segregated auditoriums for polite applause. Billie Holliday, Ella Fizgerald, Dinah Washington and other top talent played tiny clubs with packed, integrated dance floors until the 1960s, when redevelopment squeezed out many clubs – but the 1930s **Boom Boom Room** *(boomboomroom.com)* still brings crowds to the well-stomped checkered linoleum dance floor with blues, soul and funk.

DRINKING: BARS WITH MUSIC

Social Study: Observe San Franciscan dating rituals, while DJs spin soul and bartenders pair local wine and beer with gourmet 'study snacks.' *5-10pm Mon, from 1pm Tue-Sun*

Sheba Piano Lounge: The Alamayehu sisters host Fillmore's jazz supper club with spicy Ethiopian platters, NorCal wines and beer, plus *tej* (honey wine) cocktails. *5-11pm Wed-Sun*

Fermentation Lab: Sip successful experiments – yuzu margaritas with fermented-chili bitters, or the Nihonmachi (Toki whisky with cherry-infused vermouth). *3:30-11pm Tue-Thu, from 9am Fri-Sun*

Scopo Divino: Wine and music blend brunch into happy hour (3pm to 6pm) – and jazz combos regularly swing 5pm to 8pm. *3-8:30pm Sun-Tue, to 11pm Wed-Sat, brunch 11am-2:30pm Sat & Sun*

When you see lines down the block, it's showtime at the legendary **Fillmore Auditorium** *(thefillmore.com)*. Jimi Hendrix, Janis Joplin, Aretha Franklin and the Grateful Dead all played the Fillmore multiple times, and the upstairs bar is lined with '60s psychedelic posters to prove it. Bands that sell out stadiums keep rocking this 1250-capacity dance hall, and for sold-out shows, free posters are still handed out.

Bragging rights are also earned with breakthrough shows at the small but mighty **Independent** *(theindependentsf.com)*, featuring indie dreamers (Magnetic Fields, Death Cab for Cutie), music legends (George Clinton, Metallica), alterna-stars (Superchunk, Tokimonsta) and international bands (Tokyo Chaotic, L'Impératrice). Ventilation is poor in this max-capacity-800 venue, but the sound is stellar, drinks reasonable (ID required) and bathrooms improbably clean.

Pick up genre-defying, mind-altering vibes at the **Audium** *(audium.org; tickets adult/student $30/20)*, a sound sculpture lined floor to ceiling with 176 speakers that surround you with sound as you sit in darkness. Since 1967, Stan Shaff and his son Dave have blended found audio into meditative, 90-minute 'room compositions', with tones ranging from muscle-car hums and sci-fi sound effects to oddly endearing foghorn wheezes.

SF Signature Style

Try on global trends and SF styles

You've come to the right place to update your look with only-in-SF fits and jet-set style. Those fabulous, colorful printed tunics and dresses you've admired around town probably come from **Zuri** *(shopzuri.com)* design collaborative's flagship Fillmore store. Zuri's easy, upbeat styles are ethically and sustainably made in Kenya by women entrepreneurs in all sizes, with limited-edition prints inspired by everyday joys: stained glass, chickens, pretzels, fireworks... **New People** *(newpeopleworld.com)* brings Tokyo style to SF, with Lolita Goth mini-pinafores at **Baby the Stars Shine Bright** *(shop.baby-aatp.com)* and mod graphic shifts inspired by *kantoui* (tunics) worn circa 500 BCE at **Sou Sou** *(sousouus.com)*. **Fibers of Being** *(shopfibersofbeing.com)* offers modern one-stop shopping for all genders, with SF rodeo tees, suede bomber jackets, and black denim long shorts – plus nonbinary bling, from chainmail earrings to turquoise beads. Pro tip: upscale design boutiques line upper Fillmore St, but you can score those looks for less at at **Crossroads Trading**

SHARP CUTS & BIG NIGHTS

Nate Thorner *(@natethebarber)* owns legacy SF barbershop **Westside Cuts & Style** (p159).

My pops started this barbershop with a partner, Jordan – they called it Hair Jordans. Pops told me don't rush – you'll find a clientele because you take your time. People with notoriety come through – I accompanied my counterpart Brandon to cut hair at Chase Center for a Warriors player. People come here for consistency, a good cut and fade, and because it feels like home.

Historically this was a thriving African American neighborhood, and I'm doing my part to keep that alive. Next door, **Effin Relax** *(effinrelax.com)* makes natural products. I also like Brenda's Meat & Three (p160), Bar Crudo and Minnie Bell's (p160), plus shows at the Independent and the Fillmore.

EATING: DATEWORTHY SHARED PLATES

Nari: Bright, lush Thai-California dishes including cured kampachi with pear and chili jam, and caramelized fish-sauce cabbage. *5:30-9pm* $$

Copra: Indian flavors and SF flair: Kerala shrimp mango curry, passionfruit *poori*, an array of chutneys, and cocktails with Indian rum. *5-10pm Mon-Sun, 11:30am-2pm Sat & Sun* $$

State Bird Provisions: Mini-plates with mega-flavors – ricotta-sourdough pancakes, pickled-lime albacore toast, and quail in slow-cooked onions. *5:30-10pm* $$

Bar Crudo: Pair craft beer with local oysters and seasonal dishes, plus happy-hour (5-6:30pm) fish tacos and seafood chowder. *5-9pm Mon-Sat* $$

TOP EXPERIENCE

Japan Center

Time-travel to 1968 as you cross Japan Center's indoor footbridges, with *noren* (curtains) and *maneki-neko* (cat figurines) waving welcomes – yet this kawaii-cute mall started with a knock-down fight. After WWII, 1500 Japantown residents were displaced to build a generic mall. Japantown residents rallied, stopping evictions and converting the mall into a community hub with culturally relevant arts, restaurants and entertainment.

KIT LEONG/SHUTTERSTOCK

East Mall, Japan Center

TOP TIPS

- West Mall has fun boutiques, arcades, sweet treats and noodles galore. But wait, there's more: across Peace Plaza in Japan Center's East Mall, you'll find cozy date-night restaurants and cultural programs.
- Top dining choices in Japan Center include Sasa (p161), Marufuku Ramen (see right), Jina Bakes (p164), Yakitori Edomasa (p160) and An Japanese Restaurant (p161).

PRACTICALITIES

- sfjapantown.org
- 8:30am-10pm
- free

From Manga to Ukiyo-e

Entire afternoons disappear at **Kinokuniya Books** *(usa.kinokuniya.com)*, between stunning art books (ooh, Daido Moriyama photography books), tempting cookbooks (mmm, bento-box lunches), and toys (aww, smiling sushi plushies) – plus manga comics and Tokyo street-fashion mags. Across the hall, Kinokuniya's office and school supplies promise to make work and studying more fun – slow down with sloth-themed to-do lists and reward homework with panda-donut stickers. On Japan Center's indoor pedestrian bridge, stop at **Tokaido Arts** *(tokaidoarts.com; free)* to see a major collection of original *ukiyo-e* (Japanese woodblock prints), in mint condition – including Hokusai's sublime views of Mt Fuji, still vibrant at 200-plus years old.

All-Ages Entertainment

Vampire kittens and Alice in Wonderland characters occasionally roam the halls of Japan Center, queuing politely for anime-themed photo booths and arcade games. Cosplay costumes could signal a festival, anime event or pop-up art mart – or just a typical Japan Center Saturday. Follow sounds of familiar tunes into **Festa** *(festalounge.com; age 21-plus)* karaoke lounge, where you too can rock the miniature stage for $2 per song plus *yuzu shochu* cocktails.

(*crossroadstrading.com*), thanks to PacHeights socialites who ditch last season's wardrobe here.

To go the distance from Alamo Sq to Japantown dining, you might want to invest in sturdy yet stylish shoes – and sleek, comfortable shoes with low stacked heels from **Freda Salvador** (*fredasalvador.com*) are designed in Sausalito and handcrafted in Spain to last. Complete your look with sharp cuts and clean fades from **Westside Cuts & Style** and accessories from **In the Black** (*intheblackshop.com*), Fillmore's Black design showcase for all occasions – bucket hats for sunny days, 'The City' hoodies for fog, hand fans for hot shows at the Fillmore.

Discover Hidden Talents

Learn Japanese art forms from seasoned pros

Japantown has inspiration to spare – so nonprofit **Japanese Cultural & Community Center of Northern California** (JCCCNC) generously offers affordable workshops with acclaimed local artisans, chefs, artists and performers. Get hands-on experience in person and online with *kaiseki* (seasonal meal) cooking, ikebana flower-arranging, *washi ningyo* (paper dolls), *doburoku* (home-brew sake) and *magawappa* bento-box woodcraft. Check the calendar for upcoming events, including dance and taiko drumming workshops, and performances from **GenRyu Arts** (*genryuarts.org*).

Endless possibilities unfold at **Paper Tree** (*paper-tree.com*), the paper-craft emporium located on Pedestrian Osaka Way behind Ruth Asawa's bronze *Origami Fountains*. Paper Tree has inspired original origami since 1968, filling display cases with astounding creations: cocoon dresses, minuscule frogs and vast coral reefs made entirely of paper. Beginners can fold their own Death Star with *Star Wars* kits, while decoupage pros get creative with handmade washi paper.

Japantown keeps a busy schedule of festivals and creative workshops year-round – between the **Nihonmachi Street Fair** (*nihonmachistreetfair.org*) and **Cherry Blossom Festival** (p156), GenRyu also organizes arts programs to celebrate Hina Matsuri (Girls' Day), Keiro no Hi (Respect for the Aged) and Midori no Hi (Greenery Day). Since 1925, four generations of the Ashizawa family have made it their mission to source ikebana, bonsai, tea-ceremony and Zen rock-garden supplies at **Soko Hardware** (*sokohardware.com*), so you can take the inspiration home.

JAPANESE ARTS & CULTURE IN ACTION

Sensei Melody Takata is the founder of GenRyu arts and a renowned taiko drummer, shamisen player and arts educator.

I first came to San Francisco with my taiko group – now I'm raising my two kids, and teaching and performing in Japantown.

The Cherry Blossom Festival (p156) is Japantown's biggest event, **Nihonmachi Street Fair** is going strong after 50 years, and **Japan Day** (*japanweeksf.com*) is a mini Cherry Blossom Festival. There are arts events and workshops year-round at the JCCCNC, Japan Center pop-ups, and weekly free Paper Tree origami classes. We're staging shows in the Julia Morgan–designed **Issei Women's Building**, where Civil Rights movement leaders worked – bringing those stories forward is an honor.

EATING: NOODLES

Sobakatsu: Few seats, no reservations or takeout, soba only: no problem with organic, handmade soba noodles this tasty. Come around 2pm to dodge rushes. *noon-7pm* $

Marufuku Ramen: Slurp-worthy ramen with 20-hour *tonkotsu* broth, handcut ultra-thin noodles, creamy seasoned eggs. *11am-10pm* $

Hinodeya Ramen Bar: Dashi broth perfected since 1885 is graced with ramen, Kurobota pork, black garlic and jammy eggs. *10am-10pm Sun-Thu, to midnight Fri & Sat* $

On the Bridge: Nakamura family specialties since 1979: curries made from scratch, vast Japanese beer menus, and *mentaiko* spaghetti with cured cod roe. *12:30-8pm* $

NIHONMACHI

Nihonmachi (Japantown) started in the 1880s, when Japanese American farmers settled Cottage Row. Savvy builders applied swanky Pacific Heights style, attracting middle-class Filipino, Jewish and Black entrepreneurs to Japantown.

WWII changed everything. In 1942, President Roosevelt issued Executive Order 9066, imprisoning Japanese Americans in camps as 'enemy aliens.' Meanwhile, thousands of Black workers were settled in areas where Japanese Americans had been forced out.

After WWII, many Japanese Americans returned, only to discover that real-estate speculators had earmarked 60 blocks in and around Japantown for demolition. Japanese American and Black neighbors worked together to demand fair housing – sparking SF's Civil Rights movement.

Take a Deeper Look at Japantown

Witness epic stories spanning eight generations

There's more to Japantown than meets the eye. The **National Japanese American Historical Society** (NJAHS) shares insider perspectives on events that have unfolded here over eight generations, with compelling **Peace Gallery** exhibits covering marathon baseball games, art in desert incarceration camps, and origami to promote world peace. NJAHS also organizes insightful, docent-led **Japantown walking tours** *(tour adult/student $20/15 by prior booking, 10am-5pm Mon-Fri)* and fascinating tours of the **Presidio's Army Intelligence School** *(p61; tours $20 per person by prior booking, 10am-5pm Wed-Fri)*, where Japanese American soldiers were trained for top-secret missions in WWII and for postwar US occupation of Japan.

Meditate in Japantown

Pause for reflection at Japantown landmarks

When travel schedules or news headlines get you stressed, take a breather in Japantown. Yoshiro Taniguchi's **Peace Pagoda** is a striking modernist landmark that invites reflection, donated by San Francisco's sister city of Osaka, Japan in 1968. Sit on boulder benches in the renovated **Peace Plaza**, and notice how the concrete stupa provides a steady focal point for life unfolding around it: cherry trees bloom, kids chase seagulls, Tiktokkers shoot dance videos. For a more secluded spot, detour to **Cottage Row**, where serene 1860–70s clapboard cottages from the early days of Nihonmachi (Japantown) line a brick-paved pedestrian promenade. The bonsai grove on the Sutter St entry honors Issei (first-gen) gardeners who held their ground here through war and peace – and made it bloom. Homes are private, but the blooming mini-park is ideal for meditation.

Two of Japantown's longest-established spiritual centers graciously open their doors for meditation practice. Founded in 1934, **Sokoji – Soto Zen Mission of San Francisco** *(sokoji.org)* welcomes newcomers to Wednesday evening zazen sitting meditation – if you're new to zazen, contact Reverend Kurotaki, who offers helpful introductions. Inside the low-roofed, high-modernist **Konko Church** *(konkofaith.org)*, you'll find a community that has welcomed all faiths since 1931. On weekdays, Reverend Joanne Tolosa kindly answers any questions about spirituality, the church and its Shinto-

EATING: COMFORT FOOD

Brenda's Meat & Three: Only superheroes finish chef/owner Brenda Buenviaje's fried chicken or shrimp and grits, plus biscuits and red beans and rice. *8am-9pm* $

Daeho Kalbijjim: Go early or late for shareable platters of *kalbijjim* beef with bonus *banchan* (sides). *11am-2:30pm & 4:30-9pm Mon-Fri, 10:30am-9pm Sat & Sun* $$

Minnie Bell's Soul Movement: Enjoy NorCal bubbly, with rosemary fried chicken, mac-n-cheese and braised greens. *4-9pm Tue-Thu, 11am-2pm & 4-10pm Fri & Sat* $$

Yakitori Edomasa: Edomasa makes yakitori skewers to order – chicken thighs, miso-glazed pork, *harami* skirt steak, shiitake mushrooms. *11am-2:30pm & 5-9:30pm Tue-Sun* $

ELAN FLEISHER/SHUTTERSTOCK

Kabuki Springs & Spa

inspired beliefs, then leaves you to quiet contemplation in the blond-wood sanctuary.

For more context on meditation and spiritual practices, Japantown's **Forest Books** *(instagram.com/forestbookssf)* offers a thoughtful selection of new and used books to accompany you on your quest for inner peace. As the storefront sign says: 'Work quietly and diligently for peace. Begin within.'

Relax in Japantown Spas

Glow up and mellow out in Jtown spas

Gooong! At **Kabuki Springs & Spa**, that subtle hint shushes chatty spa-goers, restoring meditative silence to Japantown's communal, clothing-optional bathhouse. Over a couple of restorative hours, you can salt-scrub in the steam room, soak in the hot pool, take a cold plunge, reheat in the sauna, rinse and repeat. Men and women alternate days (cisgender and transgender alike); on all-gender Mondays and Tuesdays, bathing suits are required and nonbinary changing rooms available. Book bath access *($49, or $20 with spa treatment)* and/or

Continues on p164

DIY JAPANTOWN HISTORY TOUR

'What happened here?' asks an intriguing sign in Peace Pagoda Plaza, on the outside wall of Japan Center. This sign marks the beginning of JCCCNC's self-guided 10-block **Japantown History Walk**, following the footsteps of Japantown's trailblazers.

Along the way, you'll read how President Roosevelt's 1942 Executive Order 9066 imprisoned Japanese Americans in camps as 'enemy aliens' – and how Japantown leaders fought this civil rights violation, winning reparations and an official apology in 1988. Take a picture of this sign as a map reference and handy timeline of key events in 150 years of Japantown history – then follow your map to explore the origins of San Francisco sushi, Japanese baseball, civil rights movements, the psychedelic music scene, and Japantown's enduring community.

EATING: SUSHI

Sasa: Settle in for a seasonal menu, or order *kanpachi nigiri* sushi and scallop-salmon '49er rolls. *5:30-9pm Mon, noon-2pm & 5:30-9pm Tue-Sun* $$$

Tataki: Satiny, sustainable seafood lures sushi savants away from Japantown to this cozy spot for brilliant happy hours (to 6:30pm). *4:30-8:30pm* $$

Aji Kiji: Impress picnic dates by preordering Aji's jewel-box *moriawase* bento boxes – meticulously prepared and packaged sashimi, *nigiri* and *maki*. *11am-4pm Tue-Sat* $$

An Japanese Restaurant: Book via text to enter this sushi speakeasy, serving 20 diners eight-course *omakase* ($135) or seafood à la carte. *5:30-9:30pm Tue-Sat* $$$

CANADASTOCK/SHUTTERSTOCK

Painted Ladies

TOP EXPERIENCE

Alamo Square

The graceful 'Painted Lady' Victorian mansions around **Alamo Sq** have housed bordellos, jazz speakeasies and hippie communes, and survived elegantly intact – including east-end Postcard Row (aka the *Full House* backdrop) and northwest-corner Westerfeld House, once home to SF's biggest hippie commune. Earthquakes and fire couldn't destroy these Victorians, yet redevelopment almost did – but neighbors banded together and saved this diverse, historic district that graces countless San Francisco postcards.

DON'T MISS

- Postcard Row
- Westerfeld House
- Colorist Movement color schemes
- Theater mask embellishments
- Hilltop park picnics
- Mini-mansion playground

Meet Painted Ladies

San Franciscans seldom miss an opportunity to show off, as you can see from the opulent Victorian homes ringing hilltop Alamo Square Park. When prospectors struck it rich in the gold rush, they upgraded from downtown tenements to these pastel 'Painted Lady' Victorians, embellished to the eaves with gilded woodwork and look-at-me bay windows. These ornaments served a practical purpose: rows of Victorian flats were hastily constructed using a similar template,

PRACTICALITIES

● sfrecpark.org ● free ● 5am-midnight

and residents needed to know which stairs to stumble up after wild Barbary Coast nights.

The 1906 quake and fire destroyed many historic buildings east of Van Ness Ave – and much of San Francisco's kitschy, colorful charm went up in smoke. Since Alamo Sq mansions were built on bedrock away from downtown, many Painted Ladies were spared. But in the 1950s, developers earmarked 60 blocks of this ethnically diverse neighborhood for demolition to clear the way for luxury high-rise condos. Some 38 blocks of affordable Victorian homes and small businesses were destroyed before public outcry halted the destruction of the neighborhood – a landmark win against discriminatory housing policies, in favor of San Francisco's diverse, characterful neighborhoods.

Colorful Comebacks

The pale Painted Ladies of famed **Postcard Row** on Alamo Sq's eastern side pale in comparison with the vibrant Victorians along the northern side of the park and along parallel McAllister St and Golden Gate Ave. You'll spot wild 6-10 color schemes that are a tribute to the 1970s Colorist Movement, when San Franciscans set out to restore Painted Ladies to their full glory. When the San Francisco tech economy boomed in the 1990s, these colorful characters weren't as appealing to newly minted millionaires as they had been a century earlier – and many Painted Ladies were painted historically incorrect but marketable shades of white or gray. During the Covid lockdown, local homeowners realized the Colorists had a point: color can change the mood of the entire neighborhood. Now you'll spot fresh, bright color schemes around Alamo Sq – mansions currently go for $3 million to $8 million, in case you're in the market.

Westerfeld House

On the northwestern corner of Alamo Square Park, you can't miss the **Westerfeld House**, a gilded green Stick Italianate Victorian capped by a spooky watchtower. This confectionary 28-room mansion was built by candy baron William Westerfeld in 1889, and survived subsequent incarnations as a jazz speakeasy and home to the 50-person hippie commune described in Tom Wolfe's psychedelic '60s chronicle *The Electric Kool-Aid Acid Test*. Filmmaker Kenneth Anger filmed satanic rituals in the tower with Church of Satan founder Anton LaVey, involving hundreds of candles and one grumpy lion, coaxed up four flights of stairs. Today the mansion has been painstakingly restored to Victorian glory by Jim Siegel, the former Haight teenage runaway turned Burning Man steampunk outfitter – somehow that makes perfect sense here.

VICTORIAN, BUT MAKE IT FUN

The city's signature architectural style was labeled 'Victorian,' but demure Queen Victoria would surely blush to see the eccentric architecture perpetrated in her name here. Few of SF's older buildings were actually built during Victoria's 1837–1901 reign, except for some stern, gabled Gothic Revivals. Most SF 'Victorians' are cheerfully inauthentic Californian takes on vaguely Anglo-Continental styles, with rococo flourishes, stucco garlands and gingerbread trim along peaked roofs. Local legends claim that a carved theater mask signalled a bordello – and you'll spot many masks grinning above doorways and windows near Alamo Sq.

TOP TIPS

- On sunny days, claim a hilltop picnic table and see the city skyline framed by gabled Victorian rooflines and wind-sculpted pines.
- 'Dog-o'clock' occurs daily around sunset, when pups frolic freely on the grassy west side of Alamo Square Park.
- At the hilltop park playground, kids climb up and slide down Victorian mansion playhouses like giants on holiday.

ROBERT HOLMES/GETTY IMAGES

Haas-Lilienthal House

Continued from p161

treatments like herbal shiatsu massage online *(from $135)*. Wish you could relax like this at home? **Soko Hardware** (p159) supplies accessories for an authentic Japanese home spa, from fragrant salts to *hinoki* (cypress-wood) buckets.

For a skincare glow-up, K-beauty fans head to **Pearl Spa**, Jtown's women-only, clothing-free, fastidiously clean Korean spa. Recover from jet lag and late Fillmore nights in the cedar sauna, hot tub, cool pool, warming clay-ball pit and Himalayan-pink-salt room – maybe it won't cure anything, but it leaves your outlook decidedly rosier. Get access with appointment-only treatments, including deliciously slurpy seaweed massages *($200 per 90 minutes)*.

Peak Moments in PacHeights

Reach giddy heights at hilltop parks

To see how the city looks from above – and glimpse how the leisure class has lived since the gold rush – head up to Pacific Heights, nicknamed PacHeights or 'Specific Whites' for its target demographic. Window-shop your way up boutique-lined

EATING: BAKED GOODS

b. patisserie: Try *kouign-amann* in sensational flavors – get the black sesame – plus tartines for lunch and pistachio-raspberry cake anytime. *8am-4pm Wed-Sun* $

Jane the Bakery: Expect a seratonin glow from Jane's chocolate hazelnut babka, hearty California multigrain bread, and cookies big enough to share...maybe. *7am-5pm* $

Jina Bakes: Matcha butter mochi, *hojicha* cream puffs, and croissants filled with Daeho's *kaljibim* beef – don't miss Jina Kim's latest crossover sensation. *10am-4pm Wed-Mon* $

The Mill: Baked with organic whole-grain flour, the bread becomes brunch with California-grown almond butter, or lunch with smoked trout and crème fraîche. *7am-5pm* $

Fillmore St to Clay St, then head west to **Alta Plaza Park** for giddy hilltop city-view picnics. Here you'll find puppies in sweaters on parade and kids racing around well-kept playground while their parents day-trade on smartphones.

Along Washington St at terraced hilltop **Lafayette Park**, sprawling mansions vie for attention like socialites at a ball. Just off the parks's northeast corner is a Victorian showstopper: the 1886 **Haas-Lilienthal House** *(haas-lilienthalhouse.org; house tour $10/person)*, a Queen Anne–style Victorian mansion with nonstop gilded-age swagger, from the sweeping staircase entry to the tip of the turret. Docents from architectural conservation nonprofit **SF Heritage** invite you inside this turreted PacHeights mansion on one-hour tours, ushering you from the parlor to the ballroom like an honored guest of the prominent Jewish refugee Haas family – then taking you behind the scenes to reveal how staff kept the household going. If these red-velvet walls could talk, they'd tell you about earthquakes, booms, busts and untimely deaths – check the website for upcoming fancy-dress Victorian balls and eerie haunted-house tours.

Go Maximalist in Home Design Boutiques

Take decor hints from Painted Ladies

Once you've glimpsed the wildly colorful interiors of Alamo Sq Victorians or the gilded Haas-Lilienthal House, there's no going back to safe beige minimalism. Home-decor boutiques along Fillmore, in Japantown, and along Divisadero make it their mission to introduce eclectic, colorful, joyous maximalism into spare modern homes. Fillmore St window displays brim with inspiration – especially at **Jonathan Adler** *(jonathanadler.com)* where cookie jars labeled 'LSD' and mirrored Lucite bar carts bring swinging '70s vibes to any home. As California pop-art potter Jonathan Adler says, 'Minimalism is a bummer.' **Nest** *(nestsf.com)* is another installation artwork that doubles as a store, where bird baths overflow with hand-dyed textiles, ladders are laden with cocktail cookbooks and dessert plates, and toys peek out from antique French millinery cabinets. In Japantown, **SF76** *(sf-76.com)* upgrades ho-hum housewares to joyous modern Japanese designs, creating stunning tablescapes with hand-forged knives and stoneware bowls by San Francisco potters. Rainbows of colorfully glazed cups and vases brighten even the foggiest days at **Rare Device** *(raredevice.net)*, a showcase for local artists and clever designers on Divisadero. Up the block, **Perish Trust** *(theperishtrust.com)* makes fingertips tingle with earthy textures: sleek brass barware, raw terracotta candelabras, creamy SF-made Heavenly sake soaps, and wind-sculpted driftwood brushes by SF's Erin Irber. Maximalism has never felt better.

WHERE DID THE VICTORIANS GO?

If you're wondering why there are no Victorians around Geary Blvd, that's the result of 1950s US urban redevelopment policies targeting Black and brown communities.

Declaring this historic multiethnic, interfaith, middle-class neighborhood to be 'urban blight,' developers demolished 38 square blocks of affordable Victorian flats and family businesses to make way for high-rise condos. With wrecking balls swinging around Alamo Sq's iconic Postcard Row, Japanese American, Filipino, Latino, Black and white neighbors banded together to stop the luxury-condo takeover.

On Fillmore St sidewalks, bricks mark spots where local luminaries once lived and worked – from jazz greats to Civil Rights movement leaders. Today, this neighborhood remains a vibrant patchwork of eclectic architecture, resilient small businesses, and welcoming cultural venues.

Researched by
Alison Bing

THE MISSION, DOGPATCH & POTRERO

SUNSHINE, MURALS, BOOKS AND FLAVORS GALORE

Enjoy the district's sunny microclimates with a burrito in one hand and a book in the other, surrounded by a local crowd of filmmakers, grocers, techies, skaters and novelists.

Calle 24 (24th St) is SF's designated Latino Cultural District, and the Mission is also a magnet for lesbians, Southeast Asian Americans, and Arab Americans. Valencia St may be hipster central, but you'll be won over by their excellent coffee, baked goods, vintage shops and maker spaces. By the waterfront in Dogpatch, you can brunch like a champion, unwind with wine, and mingle with innovators and artists creating in revamped waterfront warehouses. Potrero Hill has become a bedroom community for Silicon Valley, but just downhill, art and culinary venues have creatively repurposed warehouses in Potrero Flats.

INCLUDES

FROM LEFT: LARRY ZHOU/SHUTTERSTOCK, CLYDE CHARLES BROWN, CC BY-SA 4.0, VIA WIKIMEDIA COMMONS

Above: Dolores Park (p168); Right: Roxie Cinema (p175)

Highlights

❶ Mission murals
See more than 500 murals on garage doors and storefronts, and in alleyways. **p180**

❷ Calle 24 Latino Cultural District
Share local passions for murals, books, mosaics and food. **p176**

❸ Dolores Park
Play, picnic and people-watch entire days away, while avoiding any form of adult responsibility. **p168**

❹ Minnesota Street Project
Enjoy local art, design, wine- and chocolate-making. **p184**

❺ Roxie Cinema
See cutting-edge film in the nonprofit 1909 theater that launches Oscar winners. **p175**

Getting Around

BART
Hop off at 24th St Mission for Calle 24. 16th St Mission is sketchy, but gets you near the bustling Valencia/16th hub.

Bus
Lines 12, 14, 48 and 49 go near Calle 24. The 48 runs from Dogpatch to Ocean Beach; 14 connects Mission to Downtown and the Embarcadero; 49 travels Van Ness Ave to the Wharf, and bus 22 connects Dogpatch, the Mission, Haight, Fillmore and Pacific Heights.

Walk
The Mission is flat and walkable, though you may want to hop a bus to Potrero and Dogpatch.

The Mission

Mission Street's art deco storefronts house discount stores and trend-setting restaurants, while Valencia St is lined with indie boutiques and bars. Calle 24 (24th St) is SF's Latino Cultural District, featuring mural-swathed bookstores and taquerias.

ENGAGE YOUR SENSES IN THE MISSION

The Mission is packed with restaurants, bars, boutiques, galleries and clubs you'll want to explore. While you'll feel at ease in the daytime, it's not always the safest area to walk alone in at night, especially around 16th St BART station. Keep your city smarts sharp in the Mission east of Valencia, in Potrero Hill below 18th St, and around deserted Dogpatch warehouses. Don't flash fancy technology on the street (this isn't San Jose) and don't bring the bling (this isn't LA). Take out your earbuds, so you can hear oncoming cars and bikes – plus ice-cream vendors.

Join Mission Cultural Festivals

Celebrate life to the fullest

No place celebrates life and death quite like the Mission, from Carnaval conga lines to Día de los Muertos altars. SF is far from Rio, but you'd never know it during **Carnaval** *(carnavalsanfrancisco.org; free)*, when everyone shakes their tail feathers in Mission streets. On **Día de los Muertos** *(dayofthedeadsf.org; free)*, brass bands, lowriders, Aztec dancers in feather regalia, dancing skeletons and Fridas galore meet in the Mission to honor the dead. Offerings line the processional route along Calle 24, culminating in moving outdoor community altars at **Potrero del Sol/La Raza Skatepark** (p181). This is a true community gathering – grassroots and family-friendly, with zero corporate sponsorship. Don't miss Día de los Muertos altar displays and epic mole tastings at **Mission Cultural Center for Latino Arts** *(MCCLA; missionculturalcenter.org)*, where year-round celebrations of Latin culture range from gallery openings to documentary screenings. Strike a tango pose, take up the conga, or silk-screen a protest poster at MCCLA, all with the kindly guidance of accomplished artists offering hands-on workshops for neighbors, fellow artists and visitors of all ages.

See SF's Sunny Side at Dolores Park

Loll the day away

Welcome to San Francisco's sunny side, the land of street ball and Mayan-pyramid playgrounds, semiprofessional tanning and glorious taco picnics. At **Dolores Park** *(sfrecpark.org; free)*, grassy slopes are dedicated to the fine art of lolling, while lowlands host soccer, frisbee, political protests and other local sports. Good weather brings cultural events, including Easter's **Hunky Jesus** drag contest *(thesisters.org; free)*, free summer movie nights and fall performances by **San Francisco Mime Troupe** *(sfmt.org; free)*. Fair warning: secondhand highs from smokers outside the bathroom may have you chasing the *helados* (ice-cream) cart.

Dolores Park was built on the site of a former Jewish cemetery that was used as a staging ground by Barnum & Bailey Circus, then sold to the city in 1905 – but it remained bumpy, squishy and poorly drained until its regrading. Climb to the upper southwestern corner for superb downtown views framed by palm trees.

THE GOLDEN FIRE HYDRANT

Across from Dolores Park at the corner of 20th and Church Sts, note the fire hydrant painted gold. This was the Mission's main water source during the 1906 quake, and stopped the fire from spreading south of 20th St. Neighbors with long memories and infinite gratitude repaint it regularly.

Toast Herstory at Lesbian Landmarks

Welcome home to the Mission's legacy lesbian bars

Women have been making herstory in the Mission since the 1970s, running women-centered nonprofits at the **Women's Building** (p180), staging groundbreaking theater at **Brava** (p173), organizing the annual **Dyke March**, and providing sliding-scale, whole-person healthcare for women and LGBTQ+ folks at **Lyon-Martin Community Health Clinic** (p271). After all that work, lesbians deserve somewhere to unwind – and the Mission provides options.

According to the Lesbian Bar Project, the US has fewer than three dozen lesbian bars nationwide – but SF has the most of any city, and the Mission is home to Sapphic strongholds plus newer lesbian-identified venues. Lesbian-owned since 1962, **Wild Side West** *(wildsidewest.com)* has stayed busy making herstory in the beer garden and making out on the pool table (Janis Joplin started it). The sculpture garden began in the 1970s, when killjoy neighbors chucked junk over the fence to protest against women enjoying themselves – but cast-off toilets upcycled into planters became the pride of the Wild Side.

When the Mission's landmark Latin trans/gay bar El Noche closed after 35 years in business, the community mourned – until **Mother** *(mothersf.com)* stepped in. You'll recognize this femme-forward, cash-only corner bar by its purple exterior and punk vibes. Pint-sized margaritas keep nights unpredictable, but if you're feeling brave, get the Ex – a tart gingery gin cocktail that's slightly bitter. Afterward, you may want to switch to the nonalcoholic BFF – just like the Ex, 'but without the drama.'

At women's watering hole **Jolene's** *(jolenessf.com)*, the neon sign announcing 'you are safe here'

Continues on p172

FRIDA KAHLO'S FIRST COMMISSION

Frida Kahlo kicked off her professional art career at age 24 with a portrait commission from a doctor at **San Francisco General Hospital**. The portrait still hangs in the lobby of the Mission hospital, near the painting *La Tortillera* by her partner Diego Rivera.

EATING: CLASSIC MISSION BURRITOS

La Taqueria: Miguel Jara's James Beard Award–winning burrito has hardly changed since 1972: grilled meats, slow-cooked beans, flour tortillas, just-made salsa, period. *11am-8:45pm Wed-Sun* $

La Corneta Taqueria: Roving mariachis serenade Mission families feasting on extra-special burritos with plump prawns, velvety pinto beans, and ultrafresh salsas. *10am-9pm* $

Pancho Villa: Meal-sized 'baby burritos' are not to be confused with baby-sized 'regular' – choose veg or meat and slather with salsas. *10am-10pm* $

Taqueria El Farolito: Follow late-night lines into this no-frills, cash-only taqueria for meat-packed, avocado-studded, tinfoil-wrapped, forearm-sized burritos. *10am-1:45am Sun-Thu, to 2:45am Fri & Sat* $

HIGHLIGHTS
1 Calle 24 Latino Cultural District
2 Dolores Park
3 Mission murals
4 Roxie Cinema

SIGHTS
5 500 Capp St
6 826 Valencia
7 Balmy Alley
8 Catharine Clark Gallery
9 Clarion Alley
10 Creativity Explored
11 Drawing Room Annex
12 Et al.
13 Hosfelt Gallery
14 House of Seiko
15 Incline Gallery
16 Jack Fischer Gallery
17 Precita Eyes mural
18 Southern Exposure
19 Women's Building

ACTIVITIES
20 Mission Cultural Center for Latino Arts
21 Potrero del Sol/La Raza Skatepark
22 SoMa West Skatepark

EATING
23 Bi-Rite Creamery
24 Burma Love
25 Craftsman & Wolves
26 Donaji
27 Farmhouse Kitchen Thai Cuisine
28 Flour + Water
29 Foreign Cinema
30 Freekeh
31 Garden Creamery
32 Humphry Slocombe
33 Komaaj Mazze & Wine Bar
34 La Corneta Taqueria
35 La Palma Mexicatessen
36 La Taqueria
37 Mitchell's Ice Cream
38 Old Jerusalem
39 Pancho Villa
40 Reem's
41 San Ho Won
42 Shizen
43 Stonemill Matcha
44 Taqueria El Farolito

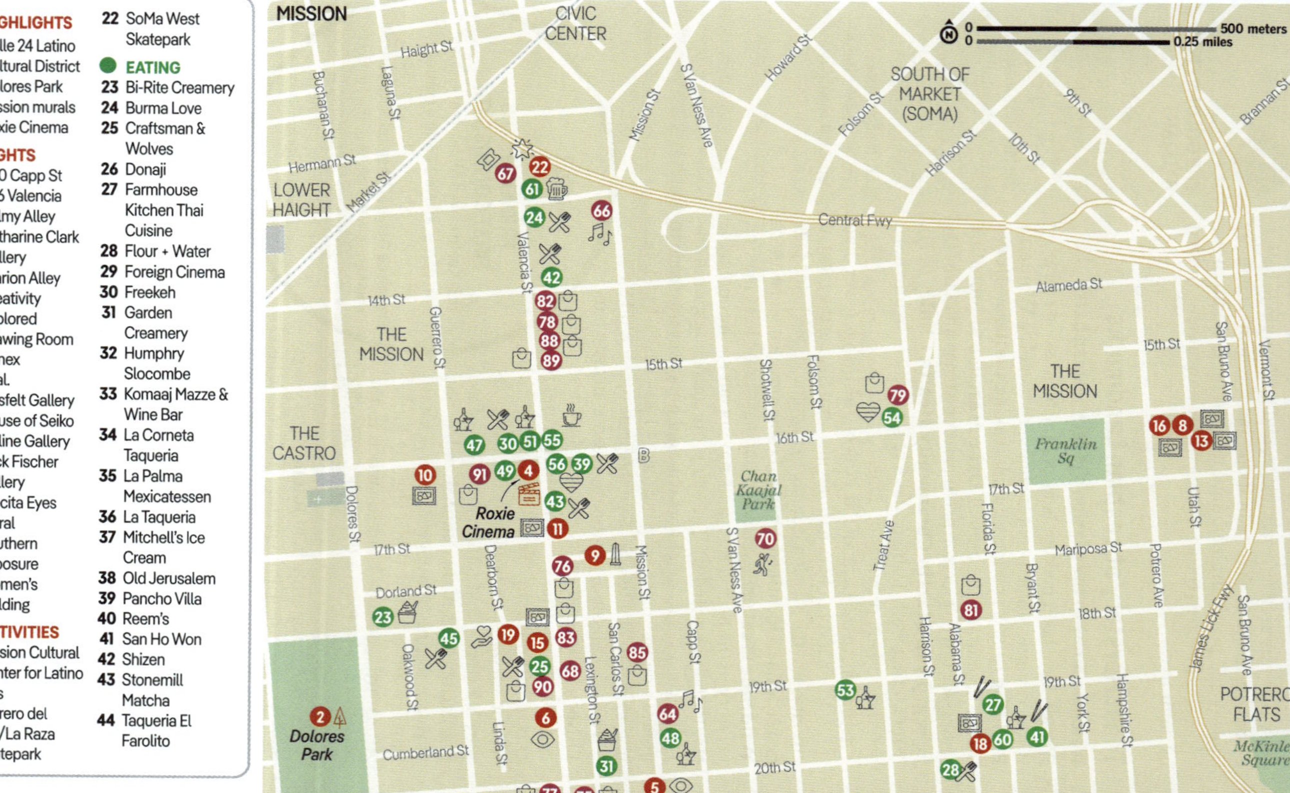

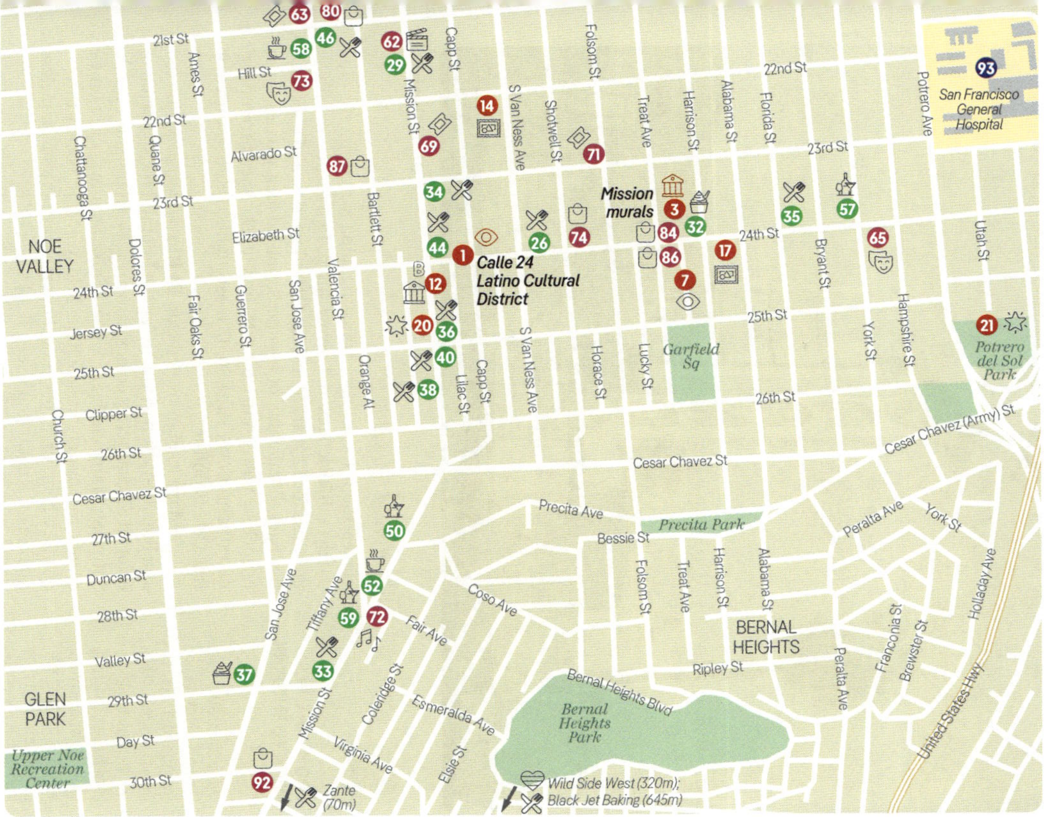

45 Tartine
46 Udupi Palace

DRINKING & NIGHTLIFE
47 %ABV
48 Casements Bar
49 Dalva & Hideout
50 El Rio
51 Elixir
52 Finjan Qahwa
see 88 Four Barrel Coffee
53 Homestead
54 Jolene's
55 Manny's
56 Mother
57 Pop's Bar
58 Ritual Coffee Roasters
59 Royal Cuckoo Organ Lounge
60 Trick Dog
61 Zeitgeist

ENTERTAINMENT
62 Alamo Drafthouse Cinema
63 Artists' Television Access
64 Bissap Baobab
65 Brava Theater
66 Brick & Mortar
67 Chan National Queer Arts Center
68 Chapel
69 Gray Area
70 ODC Theater
71 Red Poppy Art House
72 The Knockout
73 The Marsh

SHOPPING
74 Adobe Books & Arts Coop
75 Baggu
76 Community Thrift
77 Dog Eared Books
78 Double Down
79 Empress Vintage
80 Gravel & Gold
81 Heath Ceramics & Newsstand
82 Ian James
83 Landline
84 Medicine for Nightmares
85 Mission Comics & Art
86 Mission Skateboards
87 Needles & Pens
88 No
89 Nooworks
90 Open Editions
91 Sour Cherry Comics
92 Thrillhouse Records

INFORMATION
93 San Francisco General Hospital

Grand Theater

FROM DOLORES PARK TO THE PINK PARTY

Up to 100,000 lesbian, bisexual and transgender women rally in Dolores Park for SF's annual Dyke March (last Saturday in June) when Dykes on Bikes motorcycle contingent leads the way to Castro's Pink Party.

Continued from p169

makes room for lesbian, trans, nonbinary and questioning partiers to kick back and throw down. Join scenes already in progress for 12 years at lesbian UHaul parties, and check out the packed calendar of events: Sapphic block parties, drag brunches, power-suit contests, and 'queer speed-friending' marathons. Cover runs $0–15 most nights; get discounted or free tickets online.

Legendary lesbian-owned club **El Rio** *(elriosf.com)* started as a Brazilian gay bar, and today the full rainbow spectrum of colorful SF characters comes here to party. Highlights include Saturday Mango lesbian parties, Salsa Sundays, drag bingo events, free oysters from 5:30pm Friday, and air hockey throw-downs whenever. Expect knockout margaritas and shameless flirting on a patio that's seen it all since 1978.

Irish pubs and lesbian bars have historically attracted different clienteles in the Mission – but Irish lesbian-owned

EATING: VEGETARIAN

Shizen: Think vegan sushi is boring? Think again: eggplant *nigiri*, marinated mushroom rolls, and the 'prime suspect' (tempura asparagus with egg-free gochujang aioli). *5-9pm Sun-Thu, 4-9:30 Fri & Sat* $$

La Palma Mexicatessen: Loads of tamales, *huaraches* (stuffed corn patties), and *pupusas* (tortilla pockets) with vegan masa, vegetarian (or meat) fillings, and tangy tomatillo sauce. *8am-5pm Wed-Mon* $

Udupi Palace: Hot dates start by sharing 2ft-long paper *dosa* (lentil-flour pancakes) and satisfying *idli* (fluffy lentil-rice cakes), dipped in *sambar* (vegetable stew) and coconut chutney. *noon-8:30pm* $

Burma Love: Flavors here hug your tongue, then deliver a swift kick – get fermented tea-leaf salad, caramelized eggplant, coconut sticky rice, and top-notch cocktails. *11:30am-3pm & 5-10pm* $$

Casements Bar (named for Irish poet, independence leader and human rights advocate Roger Casement) brings everyone together on the mural-lined patio for proper pints of Guinness, whiskeys from 50 Irish distilleries, 'Irish coffee without the Irish' (ie booze-free) and Irish pub grub made with California-fresh ingredients.

Showtime in the Mission

Hang onto the edge of your seat

Choose your seat wisely: you may spend the evening on the edge of it at the Mission's cutting-edge performance spaces. Think you can tell the differences between art and science, culture and technology? **Gray Area** *(grayarea.org; events sliding scale $0–50)* blurs the boundaries with mind-expanding, 'antidisciplinary' programs – immersive electronica shows, workshops on personal digital security and 3D art, psychedelic cyberpunk festivals, and other events you just have to experience in the historic **Grand Theater**.

With risky, raw performances and the sheer joy of movement, **ODC** has been redefining dance for more than 50 years at shows featuring ODC company dancers from September to December, plus touring and international artists year-round. When (not if) you feel moved to dance, ODC Dance Commons offers 200-plus classes a week from flamenco to vogue for all dance levels.

LGBTQ+ performers have a new space to call home here: the **Chan National Queer Arts Center** *(sfgmc.org/chan-national-queer-arts-center)*, named for San Francisco Gay Men's Chorus leader Terrence Chan and his mom Pansy. Home to the crowd-pleasing Chorus – as seen in the award-winning documentary *Gay Chorus Deep South* – the center also stages boundary-pushing Q-lab immersive theater, experimental drag-art cabaret, and raucous events like Punk Pride.

Brava Theater *(brava.org)* has been producing women-run theater for 40-plus years, hosting acts from V-day monologist Eve Ensler to Culture Clash comedy troupe – all inside a landmark building covered with a stunning wraparound mural by Agana and her crew. The nation's first company committed to producing original works by women of color and LGBTQ+ playwrights stays busy year-round with more than 200 events, hosting theater, dance, community fiestas, holiday shows and emerging-talent showcases in a fabulous 1926 deco theater.

One-acts and monologues at the **Marsh** *(themarsh.org)* involve the audience in the creative process to launch new works, from comedian Marga Gomez' *Swimming with Lesbians* to Monday local storytelller showcases. Sliding-scale pricing allows everyone to participate; reserved seats occasionally available *(tickets from $50)*.

Load Up on Comics & Zines

Spend action-packed afternoons in the Mission

Book-club selections seem tame compared to the indie comics and freshly photocopied zines lining Mission shelves. Heads will roll, fists will fly and furious vengeance will be wreaked

ALEJANDRO MURGUIA'S POETIC MISSION

Alejandro Murguía is SF's Poet Laureate, American Book Award winner, MCCLA co-founder, and Professor of Latino Studies at San Francisco State University.

Poetry is all around us. You'll hear Mayan blessings in Balmy Alley for **Flor y Canto Literary Festival** *(sfpl.org)*, Brazilian samba songs at **Carnaval** (p168) and multilingual poetry in *panaderías* and at **Brava Theater** (see left). Mission Cultural Center's **Dia de los Muertos** (p168) Aztec dances aren't performances – they're prayers. **Medicine for Nightmares** (p175) and **Adobe Books** (p174) host multilingual readings, and the **Precita Eyes** (p180) mural at 24th and Folsom honors Alfonso Texidor, *El Tecalote*'s poetry editor. Juana Alicia's mural is a flowering nopal (cactus) – a symbol of resistance on a library built by capitalist Andrew Carnegie. What could be more poetic?

BEST MISSION LIVE MUSIC VENUES

Chapel: Musical prayers are answered in a 1914 California arts-and-crafts landmark with heavenly acoustics for folkYEAH! indie artists and performance-art mayhem by the likes of Robyn Hitchcock and the Residents.

Brick & Mortar: Break out of radio ruts and playlist loops with outlandish bands rocking the mortar loose, from breakthrough Popscene shows to NPR Tiny Desk artist showcases.

Bissap Baobab: Come for shareable Senegalese food, stick around for live acts and DJs after 9pm – bachata, Cuban jazz, Afrobeats, flamenco and breakout jam sessions.

Red Poppy Art House: A snug Mission storefront doubles as a concert hall for international artists-in-residence, from Armenian duduk virtuosos to Argentine tango quartets – plus roving local artists at Mission Stoop Fest.

inside **Mission Comics & Art** *(missioncomicsandart.com)*, with shelves of indie comics (*Snotgirl*, *Head Lopper*) alongside new and used marquee titles (*Walking Dead*, *Star Wars*). Signings and events showcase local comic-book heroes, from *Poison Ivy* cover artist Jessica Fong to *Raised by Ghosts* graphic novelist Briana Loewinsohn – and comic fans come correct at trivia nights and dog-costume contests. **Sour Cherry Comics** *(sourcherrycomics.com)* earns dedicated fan followings for its vast selection of queer comics, monthly manga club, regular community fundraisers, and DIY zines covering top-of-mind-topics from affordable housing to how to say no to working overtime.

Fill your head and home with more wild ideas at **Needles & Pens** *(needles-pens.com)*, a zine newsstand/indie gift shop/design emporium. Pick up gifts your hosts will actually keep – fancy houseplants, cards by local artists, *Crap Hound* collage zines– and some treats for yourself, including H Finn Cunningham's *Mental Health Cookbook*. The shelves at **Dog Eared Books** *(dogearedbooks.com)* are action-packed with new and used graphic novels, trusty staff picks and small-press titles by local authors – including Paul Madonna's *All Over Coffee* and Jordan Karnes' *It Hasn't Stopped Being California Here*. **Double Down** (p181) is a zine that emerged from SF's women and nonbinary street-skater scene, and now its Valencia St HQ is the low-key epicenter of a global movement – load up here on back issues and inspiration to start your own zine.

Dream on in Mission Bookstores

Get lit in the Mission

The Mission never runs out of ideas, thanks to local literary festivals, member-supported bookstores, and the many authors that call this creative neighborhood home. Stranger-than-fiction events unfold each October during **Litquake** *(litquake.org)*, the nation's biggest and most outlandish literary festival, with authors leading Mission story sessions and spilling trade secrets over drinks at the legendary **Lit Crawl**. Poetry fills Calle 24 with shimmering words in multiple languages each June for **Flor y Canto** *(Flower and Song; sfpl.org)*, the Mission's celebration of spoken word and song led by SF Poet Laureate Alejandro Murguía.

Adobe Books & Arts Coop *(adobebooks.com)* delivers year-round, wall-to-wall inspiration – just-released fiction, limited-edition art books, rare cookbooks, well-thumbed poetry

DRINKING: MISSION COFFEE

Finjan Qahwa: Conversation flows easily over shared baklava and Yemeni coffee, served in brass teapots with sweets – or nontraditionally, in iced lattes. *7am-10pm Sun-Thu, to 11pm Fri & Sat*

Ritual Coffee Roasters: Devotees queue for house-roasted coffee with distinctive flavor profiles – descriptions comparing roasts to grapefruit peel or toasted hazelnut aren't exaggerating. *6:30am-7pm*

Four Barrel Coffee: SF's hippest *and* friendliest cafe, with upbeat baristas handling pour-overs, a sunny parklet, gallery-worthy art, and no wi-fi to hinder conversation. *7am-5pm*

Manny's: Manny's serves community as well as coffee, with comedy shows and forums on SF hot topics from climate to cannabis – plus tasty cortados. *8am-8pm Mon-Fri, from 9am Sat & Sun*

– plus zine-launch parties, comedy nights and art openings. Mingle with Mission characters debating all-time-greatest pulp-fiction covers and San Francisco history (founder Andrew is a whiz), and see San Francisco artists in the gallery before they hit Whitney Biennials. Adobe is a nonprofit, volunteer-run cooperative; purchases underwrite community events and prison library programs.

When news headlines loom large, **Medicine for Nightmares** *(medicinefornightmares.com)* puts them back into perspective. Part bilingual bookstore, part community center, Medicine for Nightmares stocks bookshelves with new and used bilingual titles in the front, and hosts local art shows and events in the back – the neighborhood converges here for free live jazz, multilingual poetry readings and Howard Zinn history talks.

When you're running low on pirate supplies and/or freshly published ideas, nonprofit **826 Valencia** *(826valencia.org)* stocks eye patches, spyglasses and McSweeney's literary magazines to support on-site writing workshops and tutoring for youth. Before you leave, step behind the velvet curtain into the Fish Theater, where tropical fish are immersed in Method acting. The ichthyoid antics may not always be up to Broadway standards, but, as the sign says, 'Please don't judge the fish.'

Looking for something specific? The Mission has you covered: **Et al.** (p179) stocks rare art books and **Dog Eared Books** *(dogearedbooks.com)* proudly stocks local authors among its new and used titles.

See Something New in Old Mission Cinemas

Catch eye-opening Mission movies

When you're bored of standard streaming options, watch something completely new in historic, independent Mission cinemas – with zero ads and personal introductions to many films. If artists programmed TV instead of profiteers, the result would be nonprofit **Artists' Television Access** *(atasite.org)*, showing mesmerizing art video, local filmmaker showcases, and global underground films since 1984.

The Mission's vintage 1909 **Roxie Cinema** is a neighborhood nonprofit with an international reputation for distributing documentaries and showing controversial films banned elsewhere, from Oscar-winning *No Other Land* to IndieFest's *Resistance Revival Chorus*. The Roxie screens movies for film festivals year-round, including Center for Asian American Media's

Continues on p178

MISSION SCHOOL COOL

In the 1990s, indie skate culture, underground comics, and graffiti art met in Mission alleys – and the art world hasn't been the same since. Art critic Glen Helfand dubbed the movement 'Mission School,' noting that Mission alleys provided outlets for artists who drew outside the lines of MFA programs and commercial-gallery ambitions.

SF graffiti/mural/zine skater-artists Margaret Kilgallen, Barry McGee, Ruby Neri and Chris Johanson drew inspiration from Mission murals and hand-painted signage. SF's indie art spaces invited Mission School artists indoors, launching a group show dubbed 'Beautiful Losers' – outsider slang from Leonard Cohen's 1966 counterculture novel – with a global tour and 2008 documentary that made Mission School artists mainstays at museum shows and art fairs.

What's next? Find out in Mission alleys.

EATING: SPECIAL OCCASION DINING

San Ho Won: Opulent Korean flavors with fresh ingredients. Try the *jebi churi* filet flavor bomb and the mouthwatering *banchan* (sides). *5-9:30pm Thu-Sun, to 10pm Fri & Sat* $$$

Flour + Water: Rustic yet elegant Italian dishes, from classic (mortadella-stuffed tortellini) to creative (duck and butternut garganelli, honey-drizzled *matsutake* mushroom pizza). *5-9:30pm* $$

Farmhouse Kitchen Thai: Californian meets Thai, with turmeric Sonoma fried chicken, spicy eggplant with blue rice, and cocktails. *11:30am-2pm & 5-8:30pm Sun-Thu, 4:30-9:30pm Fri & Sat* $$

Donaji: Organic Oaxacan-Californian food: red-mole-braised short ribs, black-mole chicken tinga enchiladas, Oaxacan chocolate-churro s'mores. *5-10pm Wed-Thu, to 10:30pm Fri & Sat* $

WALKING TOUR

Calle 24

Turn onto Calle 24 (24th St) and monumental murals unfold around you, reaching around Victorian bay windows. Aromas beckon: flowering trees, fresh coffee, pan dulce at historic *panaderías* (bakeries). Storefronts bedecked with *papel picado* (cut-paper streamers) set a fiesta mood, year-round. Now you understand why 4000-plus people stroll this street every day, and why it's known as *el corazón de la Misión* (the beating heart of the Mission).

1 Medicine for Nightmares

Before there were street signs in the Mission, native Ohlone, Spanish friars and Mexican ranchers found their way around by memory, sharing landmark stories and collective wisdom. Calle 24's bookstores keep those memories alive, and find new words to point the way forward. When bookstores nationwide began losing business to online megastores, Mission readers rallied, turning this bilingual bookstore into a community-supported collective with a new name capturing its purpose: Medicina para Pesadillas (Medicine for Nightmares, p175).

The Walk Cross Calle 24 to the colorful byway that's inspired generations of Mission *muralistas*.

2 Balmy Alley

To see where the Mission mural movement took off, duck into **Balmy Alley** (p180), where Mujeres Muralistas (Women Muralists) began transforming garage doors into artistic statements in 1973. You may recognize beatified activist Archbishop Romero and surrealist painter Frida Kahlo among

LIZ HAFALIA/THE SAN FRANCISCO CHRONICLE VIA GETTY IMAGES

La Palma Mexicatessen (p172)

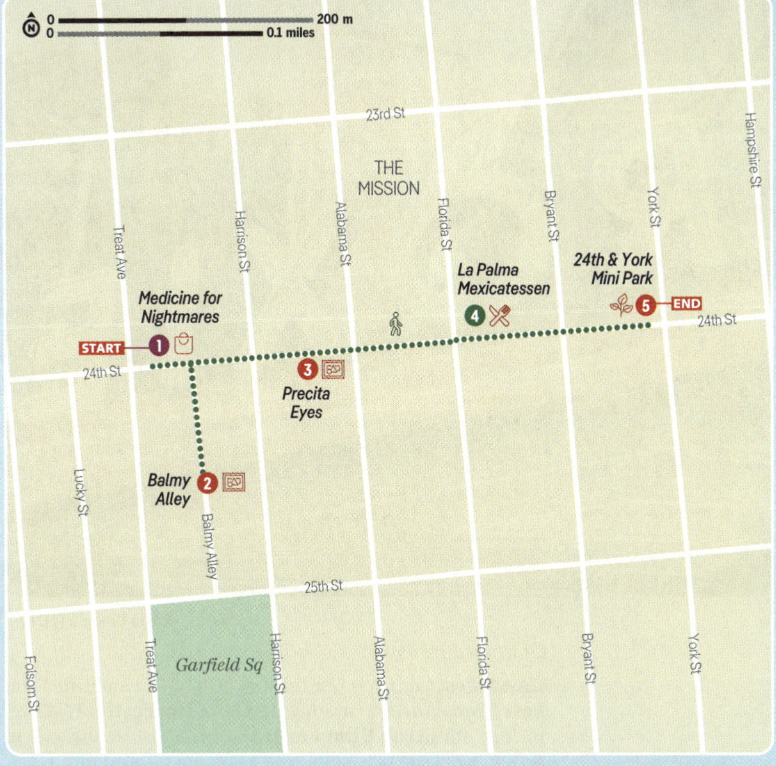

the colorful characters illuminating this mural-covered backstreet.

The Walk Walk a block and a half east along Calle 24 to the nonprofit behind Mission murals.

3 Precita Eyes

Calle 24 murals always look fresh thanks to **Precita Eyes** (p180), the mural arts nonprofit that restores historic murals, organizes new commissions and leads Balmy Alley mural walking tours. You can't miss Precita Eyes' Calle 24 storefront, graced by a stunning mosaic of flower goddess Xochiquetzal by muralist and founder Susan Cervantes.

The Walk One and a half blocks east along Calle 24, lunch awaits on the northeast corner.

4 La Palma Mexicatessen

Follow the sound of applause to **La Palma Mexicatessen** (p172), where that clapping means *tortilleras* are busy making organic tortillas by hand. Enjoy tacos, tamales and *huaraches* (stuffed masa) made to order at a sunny sidewalk table under the mural honoring Centeōtl, the Aztec god of corn.

The Walk Walk another block east to an art-lined green space, with a gate that opens by day.

5 24th & York Mini Park

Dazzling mosaic serpent-god Quetzalcoatl raises his fierce head from the rubberized ground of the idyllic **24th & York Mini Park**. Quetzalcoatl first appeared in murals here in 1972, when neighbors rallied to transform a derelict lot into a point of Mission pride. Today his mosaic sculpture is irresistible to toddlers, and his transformative powers are irrefutable – since Quetzalcoatl first appeared here, San Franciscans have created 40 more mini-parks citywide. As you leave Calle 24, may the spirit of Quetzalcoatl guide your onward journey.

PHOTO:JOHNB30/SHUTTERSTOCK

Roxie Cinema (p175)

Continued from p175

CAAMFest *(caamfest.com)* in May, LGBTQ+ **Frameline Film Fest** *(frameline.org)* in June, **Jewish Film Festival** *(jfi.org)* in July, and **Arab Film Festival** *(arabfilminstitute.org)* in November. Tickets to film-festival premieres and rare revivals often sell out - buy tickets online - but if the main show's packed, discover riveting documentaries in teensy next-door Little Roxy instead *(roxie.com; tickets adult/child $14–15/11)*.

Landmark 1932 New Mission cinema is restored to its original Timothy Pfleuger-designed art deco glory as the SF home of independent **Alamo Drafthouse Cinema**, screening blockbusters, cult revivals, horror flicks, and art-house premieres - sometimes followed by filmmaker Q&As *(drafthouse.com; tickets $13.75–17.75)*. Dinner-and-a-movie dates are better with

EATING IN THE MISSION: ICE-CREAM OBSESSIONS

Mitchell's Ice Cream: Causing happy dances on Mission sidewalks since 1953, with crowd-favorite tropical flavors like Kahlua mocha cream, *macapuno* (young coconut), and *ube* (purple yam). *11:30am-11pm* $

Humphry Slocombe: Treat your tastebuds to original flavors like Vietnamese coffee, 'Secret Breakfast' (bourbon and cornflakes) and 'Here we GOAT again' (goat cheesecake) - ideally with hot fudge, California olive oil and sea salt. *1-10pm* $

Bi-Rite Creamery: Even VIPs humbly queue behind velvet ropes for Sonoma honey-lavender or salted-caramel ice cream with housemade hot fudge, or seasonal balsamic strawberry buffalo-milk soft-serve. *noon-9pm* $

Garden Creamery: Luxurious textures and intense flavors like black sesame and 'strawberry on steroids' come from slow-churning local organic cream with hand-picked California fruit and SF-favorite Asian ingredients. *6-10:30pm Wed-Fri, noon-9:30pm Sat & Sun* $

movie-themed cocktails and mocktails, beer and burgers, and all-day brunch – delivered to your plush banquette seats.

If you prefer dinner with a side of cinema, head to **Foreign Cinema** *(foreigncinema.com)*. Like the timeless films screened in the courtyard, award-winning chef Gayle Pirie's California signature dishes are critically acclaimed – her sesame-fried chicken and seasonal, sustainable seafood dishes are SF classics.

MORE FILM-FEST FAVORITES

Catch award contenders and hear live directors' commentary every April at the **San Francisco Film Festival** *(SFFILM.org)*, which screens major features at George Lucas' own *Star Wars* screening room at **Letterman Campus** (p62) in the Presidio.

Explore the Mission's Alternative Art Spaces

See breakthrough art in unusual spaces

Whether you're looking for fresh creative inspiration or a change of scenery, the Mission's indie art scene has you and your walls covered. Be the first to glimpse artworks destined for museum retrospectives, international art fairs and Marc Jacobs handbags, all by local artists with developmental disabilities at nonprofit arts center **Creativity Explored** *(creativityexplored.org)*. Openings of themed gallery exhibitions are joyous occasions, where you can meet artists and their families and pick up original artwork plus limited-edition T-shirts, notecards and prints – proceeds directly support the artists and their families. Inspired? Join the artists and get creative in the studio at **Imaginate Saturdays** *(noon-3pm Sat; free, all ages welcome)*.

Mission storefronts emptied by Covid and economic shifts are filling in with artists collectives. 'Free ideas' says the sign outside **Et al.** *(etaletc.com; free)* – that's both a manifesto and an invitation to enter this low-key arts bookstore/high-profile gallery and multimedia events space, previously featuring Whitney Biennale art-star animator Kota Ezawa, SF's Venice Biennale multimedia trailblazer Lynn Hershman Leeson, and local Pulitzer Prize–winning poet Forrest Gander. Meanwhile in a former furniture store, the **Drawing Room Annex** *(drawingroominc.org; entry free, events sliding scale)* hosts

EATING: MISSION MEZZE

Komaaj Mazze & Wine Bar: Bold, brilliant flavors from Northern Iran shine with local ingredients – pomegranate-glazed smoked trout, Persian cucumbers with fermented dalar dressing – paired with Armenian wines made from Iranian grapes. *5:30-9pm Tue-Thu, noon-3pm & 5:30-10pm Fri-Sun* $$

Reem's: Acclaimed Syrian-Palestinian chef/owner Reem Assil serves sensational, sustainable Palestinian Californian comfort food hot from the oven, including *mana'eesh* flatbread – get 'Pali-Cali' sumac-laced chicken with caramelized onions. *11am-3pm & 5-9pm Tue-Sat* $

Freekeh: Share classic mezze dips and tangy *musakhan* (sumac chicken or slow-cooked mushrooms rolled into lavash bread) with *arak limonada* (mint lemonade spiked with Gray Goose and Lebanese arak). *5:30-9pm Tue-Sun, brunch 10am-2:30pm Sat & Sun* $

Old Jerusalem: Bond over generous portions of Palestinian and Syrian classics: shawarma, *mansaf* (pine-nut-studded lamb pilaf), mezze (starring falafel, fava bean stew and roast cauliflower) and *kenafeh* (cheese pastry) hot from the family-heirloom griddle. *11am-10pm Wed-Mon* $

TOP EXPERIENCE

Mission Murals

Frida Kahlo and Diego Rivera have no idea what they started. Since the Mexican painting power couple came to SF for a working honeymoon in the 1930s, they've inspired generations of muralists to create 500-plus Mission murals – a splendid show of political dissent, community pride and street-art bravado. Today multistory murals cover Calle 24, SF's Latino Cultural District.

FEDERICA GRASSI/GETTY IMAGES

Clarion Alley

TOP TIPS

- If you're posting pics on social media, credit the muralist – Mission muralists know their copyright law, and allow noncommercial use only.
- Muralists lead nonprofit **Precita Eyes** *(precitaeyes.org)* two-hour weekend walking tours, covering 50 to 70 Mission murals; check availability online.

PRACTICALITIES

Bus Buses 12, 14, 48 and 49 drop off near Balmy Alley and mural-lined 24th St. **BART** 24th St Mission stop is blocks from Balmy Alley.

Balmy Alley

Inspired by Mexican mega-artists Frida Kahlo and Diego Rivera, Mujeres Muralistas ('Women Muralists') began painting garage doors here in 1973, turning a neglected backstreet into a neighborhood landmark. Today **Balmy Alley** murals are maintained by nonprofit **Precita Eyes**, including early Frida Kahlo homages, Placa artists' 1985 memorial for El Salvador activist Archbishop Óscar Romero, and Lucía González Ippolito's homage to 'Women of the Resistance.'

Clarion Alley

Most graffiti artists shun broad daylight – but not in **Clarion Alley**, SF's street-art showcase maintained by neighbors and Clarion Alley Collective. Over 900 murals have been created by Clarion artists, but few survive the tests of time and tagging – survivors include Megan Wilson's daisy-covered *Tax the Rich* and Jet Martinez' glimpse of Clarion Alley inside a forest spirit.

Women's Building

America's first women-owned-and-operated community center has housed 150 women's organizations since 1979 – and the 1994 *MaestraPeace* mural celebrates the **Women's Building** as a herstory landmark. Mission muralistas worked with 100 volunteers to cover the building with goddesses and women trailblazers, including poet Audre Lorde, artist Georgia O'Keeffe, Palestinian human-rights leader Hanan Ashrawi and Nobel Prize–winner Rigoberta Menchú.

themed group shows of emerging artists, Saturday local maker pop-ups, and Friday night communal table drawing events.

White-box galleries aren't the Mission's style – new arts spaces keep the quirky character of bygone businesses. Lose track of time in the repurposed watch-repair shop that's now **House of Seiko** gallery *(houseofseiko.info; free)*, a showcase of think-pieces by California artists – from Nik Gelormino's hand-carved, enigmatic zodiac signs to Quintessa Matranga's blurry, luminous remembered California landscapes. Ramp up your art collection at **Incline Gallery** *(inclinegallerysf.com; free)*, a sloping gallery at the rear of an ex-mortuary where bodies were once transported for embalming. Today this is where San Francisco's emerging talents begin upward career trajectories with wall installations along the skylit ramp, from Jose Arias' iconic Mexican Americana photographs to Gary Miller's rhinestone-studded glitter-drag portraits.

Even without federal funding, Mission arts nonprofits provide backing and space for new artists and ideas. Art really ties the room together at nonprofit arts center **Southern Exposure** *(soex.org; free, donations welcome)*, where works are carefully crafted not just with paint and canvas, but a sense of community – from fundraising drawing rallies to Resist and Rejoice art-parties. At **500 Capp St** *(500cappstreet.org; free)*, the Mission District home of late conceptual sculptor David Ireland now serves as an arts nonprofit and environmental artwork, filled with experimental art installations – be part of the ongoing social sculpture with free self-guided Saturday visits.

Skate the Mission

Shred with Mission skate legends

Street skating is the chosen sport, art and commuting method of the Mission's cool kids – and their parents. Women and nonbinary street skaters get their due at **Double Down** *(double downzine.com)*, SF's women and nonbinary street-skater zine, with its own eye-popping Valencia storefront brimming with back issues, merch, free stickers and general mayhem. SF street-skate legend Scot Thompson owns **Mission Skateboards** *(missionsk8shop.com)*, which supplies instant street cred with locally designed Mission decks, custom tees to kick-flip over, cult skate shoes, and stacks of San Francisco's own *Thrasher* magazine. Around the corner at **Potrero del Sol/La Raza Skatepark** *(sfrecpark.org)*, you can grab air with pro skaters blasting ollies off SF's best concrete bowls – though graffiti on the concrete can make for a slippery ride. Wait for a clean area of the bowl to bust big moves, and leave room for kiddo skaters in kneepads. Shredders brave **SoMa West Skatepark** *(sfrecpark.org)*, the urban-legendary skatepark under San Francisco's freeway – regulars can get territorial and the scene turns sketchy at sunset, but there's no place better to earn respect with big, bold moves.

BEST MISSION DEEP DIVES

Royal Cuckoo Organ Lounge: DJ jams on organ, regular plays trumpet, lucha-libre-masked customer yells, 'Yesss, Chet Baker is my jam!' – just another epic, Cuckoo night. *6pm-midnight Mon, 4pm-2am Tue-Thu, from 3pm Fri-Sun*

Pop's Bar: Approach the 1937 bar for cocktails named after lowrider cars – get the classy Cutlass (rye, Avena, Aztec chocolate bitters) – that kick into overdrive when DJs spin. *6am-2am*

Zeitgeist: At this biker beer garden, you've got two seconds to choose a craft beer from 64 on tap – tough but fair. *2-11pm Mon-Wed, to midnight Thu, to 1am Fri & Sat, noon-9:30pm Sun*

Homestead: Your friendly Victorian dive, with carved-wood bar, cast-iron fireplace, and Mission characters galore – when Iggy Pop hits the jukebox, stand back. *3-11pm Sun-Thu, to 2am Fri & Sat*

OHAD BEN-YOSEPH/GETTY IMAGES

Skateboarding (p181), 24th St

Rock Original Mission Designs

Raise your street fashion game on Valencia St

To blend in on Mission sidewalks, bland beige won't cut it – have you seen the murals here? Add Mission edge to your style with local-artist-designed, limited-edition, women-owned, California-made gear at **Nooworks** *(nooworks.com)*. You've probably seen Nooworks' graphic-print jumpsuits, tops and sundresses on socials – maybe covered in rainbows and tigers, or mystical Tarot symbols – but art-teacher tunics sell out here before they hit Insta, and the back-room sales rack holds scores galore.

To signal to Valencia St passersby what team you're playing for – Team Art, of course – get **Open Editions** *(open-editions.com)* not-sports apparel designed by local artists: Stephanie

EATING IN THE MISSION: GREAT BAKED GOODS

Craftsman & Wolves: Break breakfast rules with the Rebel Within cheesy muffin with a soft-boiled egg baked inside – and/or seasonal mini-cakes, like yuzu coconut or cassis-champagne mousse. *7:30am-3:30pm Mon-Fri, 8am-4pm Sat & Sun* $

Tartine: Riches beyond your wildest dreams: butter-golden pain au chocolat, creamy cappuccinos, gooey ham-and-cheese croque monsieurs with béchamel. *7:30am-6pm* $

Stonemill Matcha: Teatime here means dreamy baked goods with SF-favorite Asian flavors: black-sesame cream puffs, flaky *matcha* croissants, chicken *katsu* milk-bread sandwiches. *10am-4pm Mon-Fri, 9am-5pm Sat & Sun* $

Black Jet Baking: Artisan bakers reinvent nostalgic packaged treats with California-fresh ingredients – get the flaky toaster pastries with housemade jam – and serve seasonal pizza slices. *8am-2pm Tue-Wed, to 4pm Thu-Sun* $

Syjuco's battleship-dazzle-pattern hoodies, Mitsu Okubo's *Sigh* Twombly caps, and bandanas patterned with Bob Aufuldish's original 1996 dingbat typeface.

You can get back in touch with nature and California's hippie roots without leaving sight of a Mission sidewalk at **Gravel & Gold** *(gravelandgold.com)*. This woman-owned design company makes Cali clothing that's wild and free, but also smart, sustainable and impressively durable – breezy smock-dresses, hand-printed cotton tops, raffia bucket hats, train-conductor-striped denim chore jackets.

By now you'll need a carryall for your haul. SF's own **Baggu** *(baggu.com)* supplies colorful, lightweight, durable nylon totes to help you avoid the city-mandated 25¢ bag fee, and earn compliments besides. **Ian James** *(ianjamesmade.com)* handcrafts stylish leather satchels in his storefront studio with his signature X pattern and subtle contrasting outstitching – plus clever cardholders for Mission nights out.

Go on a Vintage Mission

Score unique finds in deep-cut vintage stores

Elsewhere, vintage is a trend – in the Mission, it's a way of life. Fashionistas everywhere are realizing that vintage can save money and spare the planet from fast fashion – but Missionistas know it's also a bonding experience, where total strangers exchange arcane denim knowledge and share unbridled enthusiasm for equestrian prints. **Empress Vintage** *(empressvintage.com)* does the deep digging to surface iconic designs - '70s YSL, '80s Betsey Johnson, '90s Miu Miu – including originals by legendary SF designers like mod Joseph Magnin and boho Gunne Sax. In-house stylists will outfit you for any themed occasion, and arrange tarot readings besides.

No *(ohnonotno.com)* takes a gleefully contrarian approach to vintage – here you'll find no current trends, no global brands, no prized concert tees. Instead you'll score one-off finds: suede patchwork jackets, hand-knit punk mohair sweaters, an avocado-green 1970s record-producer pantsuit, a medical-convention tote advertising gynecological gel.

Landline *(landlinehome.com)* is your connection for vintage housewares, including novelty cookie jars, complete sets of printed Pyrex mixing bowls, and bar carts laden with crystal stemware and smoky gray '70s goblets. As the shopkeeper notes: 'Those highballs were free with fill-ups at SoCal gas stations – like, they were encouraging people to drink and drive? But these survived.'

When local collectors and retailers have too much of a good thing, they donate it to nonprofit **Community Thrift** *(communitythriftsf.org)*, where proceeds go to 200-plus local charities – all the more reason to gloat over your $3 porcelain teacup and $12 vintage platform heels, and donate your own cast-offs here, until 5pm daily.

BEST COCKTAILS

Trick Dog: Each new menu captures an SF obsession – Whole Earth Catalog, Mission muralists, death-defying circus acts – proof that the bar often called America's best never runs out of tricks. *4pm-midnight Sun-Thu, to 2am Fri & Sat*

Dalva & Hideout: Discuss Roxie movies over Altered States (mezcal, vermouth, gentian) or hit backroom Hideout to dish Dolores Park gossip with Friend of the Devil (rye, stout, amaro). *5pm-midnight Sun-Tue, to 2am Wed-Sat, Hideout from 7pm*

%ABV: Discerning drinkers recognize the name ('percent alcohol by volume') and appreciate the craft – tangerine oil in martinis, hand-cut ice cubes in Japanese malt whiskey. *4pm-2am*

Elixir: SF's first certified-green bar is an 1858 Wild West saloon with organic whiskey cocktails that inspire air-guitar-rocking to the killer jukebox. *4pm-midnight Sun-Wed, to 2am Thu & Fri. noon-2am Sat*

Dogpatch

Waves of creativity are filling industrial shipping warehouses with art galleries, maker spaces, scrappy startups, and massive raves. Wander new trails along the sunny waterfront, with pitstops for food and wine.

Look ahead at Minnesota St Projects

See gallery shows that launch art movements

Art took root amid the concrete warehouses of Dogpatch in 2016, when venture-capitalist arts patrons Deborah and Andy Rappaport decided to convert an old factory into low-cost art studios, nonprofit art centers and rent-subsidized showcases for SF talents at the **Minnesota Street Project** *(minnesotastreetproject.com)*. Shows here are free and fearless, from meticulously crafted dreamscapes at **Eleanor Harwood Gallery** *(eleanorharwood.com)* to multimedia think-pieces at **Jack Fischer Gallery** *(Map p170; jackfischergallery.com)*. **Casemore Gallery** *(casemoregallery.com)* features renowned photographers who find the sublime in the ordinary – Jim Jocoy's club-kid portraits, Todd Hido's eerie suburban subdivisions, Larry Sultan's revealing family photos. For 30-plus years, **Anglim/Trimble Gallery** *(anglimtrimble.com)* has been a launching pad for Bay Area art movements, from Beat assemblage to Bay Area conceptualists. Yet shows here maintain the element of surprise, from political provocateur Enrique Chagoya's immigration-themed Mayan codexes to Grace Munakata's abstract urban-bird sanctuaries, poignantly patched with *boro* (fabric scraps).

Galleries stay open until 8pm for **First Saturdays**, when SF artists give free talks and workshops, dress up for each other's art openings, and toast artistic freedom with free drinks. Make a night of it at on-site **Besharam** *(besharamrestaurant.com)*,

DRINKING: WINE

MAPS P185, P189

Ungrafted: Trust master sommelier Rebecca Fineman's inspired pairings for za'atar flatbread and caviar-topped arepas – plus Thursday blind tastings and Saturday classes. *noon-8pm Tue & Wed, to 9pm Thu-Sat*

Domaine SF: Organic and biodynamic wines at their natural best – ethically farmed, crisp and refreshing – including alcohol-free options, plus gorgeous gourmet platters for Crane Cove Park picnics. *noon-4pm Sun & Mon, to 7pm Tue-Sat*

Dig: Discover hard-to-find wines under $50 at weekend wine tastings – for more deep cuts, visit the vinyl and sake annex. *noon-6pm Wed-Fri, to 5pm Sat*

Ruby Wine: Brilliant pairings reward hikes up Potrero Hill, where this natural wine specialist partners with next-door Alimentari Aurora on wine-and-cheese combos and Friday tastings. *3-9pm Sun-Thu, 11am-11pm Fri & Sat*

HIGHLIGHTS
1 Minnesota Street Project

SIGHTS
2 Anglim/Trimble Gallery
3 Casemore Gallery
4 Crane Cove Park
5 Eleanor Harwood Gallery
6 hugomento
7 Letterform Archive
8 Museum of Craft & Design

EATING
9 Bandit
10 Besharam
11 Neighbor Bakehouse
12 Ramp

DRINKING & NIGHTLIFE
13 Dig
14 Ungrafted

SHOPPING
15 Domaine SF

where openings are celebrated with Gujarati-Californian cocktails and clever *chaat*: paratha with Point Reyes blue cheese, drunken *pani-puri* with gin-spiked tamarind water, and show-stopping blueberry saffron cheesecake.

Cheer on the Warriors

Catch the game at Chase Center

The sing-song chant 'Warr-i-ors!' is both a San Francisco game-day greeting and a taunt to fans of visiting teams, taking on San Francisco's frequent NBA champions (four times since 2014) with a home-court advantage. Single-game tickets are sold via **Chase Center**'s website *(nba.com)*, with prices rising steeply from $40 nosebleed bleachers to high triple digits for grudge matches against LA Lakers. Between the October and May seasons, Chase Center hosts marquee headliners from pop (Paramore, Drake) to comedy (Jerry Seinfeld–Jim Gaffigan double bill), plus monster-truck rallies and community events.

CALLING ALL SPORTS FANS

San Francisco has two other championship-level teams: the SF Giants play baseball at Giants Stadium, aka **Oracle Park** (p97) and the 49ers compete in American football at **Levi's Stadium** (located in suburban Santa Clara).

Go Handmade in Dogpatch

Celebrate handicrafts in AI-obsessed SF

Self-driving cars roam waterfront streets and conceptual carpets cover warehouse floors in Dogpatch, where high tech and high craft might seem odd – but they're not necessarily at odds. Big-tech angel investors back radical poster art here at nonprofit **Letterform Archive** *(letterformarchive.org; adult/student $10/5)*, where punk zine publishers and Adobe software designers converge to see iconic, wordy works on paper, from 1960s Black Panther newspapers to 1980s AIDS awareness posters.

One sensory delight to offset screen time is **hugomento** *(hugomento.com; free)*, a wonderfully cozy showcase for lushly textured, handmade, 'storied art and objects.' Fascinating, meticulous abstract works by local artists bring SF innovation to deeply rooted NorCal crafts – from Carrie Crawford's delicately webbed, hand-dyed textiles to George William Bell's glowing burl sculptures made of sand-carved, mirrored glass.

One-off original works not meant for mass production reignite wonder at the **Museum of Craft & Design** *(sfmcd.*

EATING: MVP GAME-DAY FOOD

Spark Social: This sociable park hosts dozens of food trucks, wine and beer vendors, covered dining areas with couches, and SF-themed mini-golf. *11am-3pm & 5-9pm Mon-Fri, 11am-9pm Sat & Sun* $

Old Skool Cafe: At SF's nonprofit jazz speakeasy, at-risk youth who are restaurateurs-in-training serve soulful comfort food. Locations: Chase Center's portal 44, 1429 Mendell St. *5-9pm Wed-Sat* $

Che Fico Pizzeria: On the stadium balcony, catch games on mega-TVs with bayfront views, blistered pizza, craft beer and NorCal wine. *11:30am-2pm Mon, 11:30am-2pm & 5-9pm Tue-Fri, 4-9pm Sat & Sun* $$

Ramp: Laze days away at waterfront umbrella tables with tall Bloody Marys, games on big-screen TVs, peak people-watching and dancing at Salsa Saturdays. *11am-8:30pm Sun-Thu, 10am-10pm Fri & Sat* $$

SUNDRY PHOTOGRAPHY/SHUTTERSTOCK

Chase Center

org; adult/student $10/8). Traditional crafts find fresh purpose here: high-concept carpets capture the topography of climate-changed wetlands, an entire cosmos is collaged from fossils, and durags completely covered in buttons become contemporary crowns. Shows often include a hands-on maker space equipped with supplies so that you can capture inspiration while it's fresh.

If you'd rather leave craft to the pros, the museum's shop features works by accomplished local artisans, from printed pearl necklaces to Mi Cocina's denim chef's knife carry cases. For more collectable crafts, head to **Heath Ceramics & Newsstand** *(Map p170; heathceramics.com)* for signature stoneware with ceramist Edith Heath's midcentury lines and new colors – plus local artisan pop-ups.

Escape to the Waterfront

Check out Crane Cove Park

Dogpatch hums with stealth-mode start-ups and cottage industries – which makes this industrial waterfront an especially delightful place to explore. Dogpatch piers are dotted with rusted equipment leftover from San Francisco's industrial past and WWII shipbuilding era – poignant reminders that every boom/bust cycle is bound to pass. San Franciscans look fondly on the massive industrial cranes – nicknamed **Nick** and **Nora** – framing San Francisco's central Bay port for more than a century, and insisted on preserving them as features of the new 7-acre **Crane Cove Park** *(sfport.com; free).* Nora

EXTROSPECTIVELY/SHUTTERSTOCK

Crane Cove Park (p187)

overlooks San Francisco's most scenic dog run, while Nick watches over paddleboarders braving chilly Bay waters and kiddos playing on the rocky beach (there's no lifeguard here). Bayside picnic tables are thoughtfully provided to enjoy sensational savory pastries from **Neighbor Bakehouse** *(instagram.com/neighborbakehouse)* – the curry pocket is a winner – and breakfast sandwiches from **Bandit** *(banditsf.com)* – get the Deviant with fluffy eggs, housemade chicken sausage, gooey cheese and creamy avocado. Afterwards, you can wander the **Bay Trail** all the way to the Embarcadero, or head down to the **Midway** to catch a show.

Feel the Beat at Pier 80

Rave on at epic music events

Once Dogpatch was a working port, but now these docks are ready to party. Down by Pier 80, **The Midway** *(themidwaysf.com)* comes roaring to life with indoor and outdoor events, including DJ day parties with touring acts and electronica mega-raves like the '90s never ended. Deep inside the Midway is **Envelop,** a nonprofit immersive audio venue lined with 32 speakers and interactive lights where you take off your shoes to feel, hear and see epic albums played in their entirety – *Purple Rain*, *Dark Side of the Moon*, *Sgt. Pepper*, *Kid A*. Crowds thoroughly pound Pier 80 during the **Portola Festival** *(portolamusicfestival.com)*, squeezing three decades of electronic and power-pop music mayhem into two days – headliners have included the Chemical Brothers, The Prodigy, Christina Aguilera and LCD Soundsystem. Go wild and wear sunscreen.

Potrero

Below residential Potrero Hill, the warehouses and design district showrooms of Potrero Flats keep a low profile – but look closer and you'll discover avant-garde galleries and punk-rock venues.

Catch Art Stars in Potrero Flats

Look ahead at cutting-edge galleries

Art fans don't head to Potrero Flats to find art to match the couch in Design District showrooms – they come here to change their worldview. Art revolutions are instigated at **Catharine Clark Gallery** *(Map p170; cclarkgallery.com)*, a showcase for such gorgeous provocations as Masami Teraoka's paintings of geishas and samurai battling the AIDS epidemic, and Zeina Barakeh's entrancing videos of ancient Egyptian guardians evolving to defend cyberspace. The gallery's on-site **EXiT shop** is what a museum shop should be, with rare art books and original, affordable editioned works by gallery artists. Next door at **Hosfelt Gallery** *(Map p170; hosfeltgallery.com)*, trancelike states are induced by dreamy, finely detailed interior worlds: ultra-slow, extra-pixellated images artistically engineered by

SF'S ALTERNATIVE ART SCENE

Erik Scollon is an artist represented by Romer Young Gallery (p190), and California College of the Arts (p190) Core Studio Program chair.

Minnesota Street Project (p184) packs a lot of art in a tight space, so you can see what's going on creatively. We have great museums, like the **de Young** (p224) and **SFMOMA** (p86), but what really makes SF are the alternative arts spaces like **Southern Exposure** (p181), **500 Capp St** (p181) and **Gray Area** (p173). I'm curious to see how SF artists collectively respond to current challenges to art and culture – being under threat is never good, but I've seen how we can coalesce and flourish in times like these. You can already see the DIY, punk, queer aesthetic bubbling up.

INSTALLATION VIEW, MASAMI TERAOKA: WAVES AND PLAGUES REDUX, CATHARINE CLARK GALLERY, SAN FRANCISCO, CA/JOHN JANCA

Jim Campbell (of Salesforce Tower fame), and Marco Maggi's meticulously cut paper curls covering vast surfaces. On the flip-side of Potrero Hill at **Romer Young Gallery**, artists perform mysterious alchemy: Erik Scollon weaves all-seeing eyes and erotica into talismanic textiles, and Leah Rosenberg evokes cake and community in vast, vivid dot paintings.

Brave new visions have emerged for more than a century from **California College of the Arts** *(cca.edu)*, the Bay Area's top art and design school. Stop by the converted Greyhound bus station that now serves as CCA's main campus to catch **PLAySPACE**'s themed group shows and public arts events at the **Wattis Institute**, or wander past the storefront **Campus Gallery** (1480 17th St) to check out experimental new work. Hitting the books takes on another meaning entirely at nearby **San Francisco Center for the Book** *(sfcb.org)*, San Francisco's nonprofit community press – a booklover's dream for classic binding and letterpress workshops, plus exhibits of unique art books that fit into matchboxes, pop up into theaters, and stash secret treasures.

Punk Rock Around Potrero

Roar for more live punk shows

'Go ahead, punk: make my day,' snarled Clint Eastwood as a San Francisco cop in *Dirty Harry* – but SF punks kept rocking anyway. **Bottom of the Hill** *(bottomofthehill.com)* still tops the list for rocking with punk legends like the Avengers, Pansy Division and Dead Boys – fair warning, the handbill-covered patio here may induce FOMO – plus newcomers worth

Catharine Clark Gallery (p189)

checking out for their names alone (Junior Painkillers, The Hot Takes, Buzzed Lightbeer).

Down the block is **Thee Parkside** *(theeparkside.com)*, where the punk-band stickers plastering courtyard walls may actually be holding the place together – local bands have rocked hard here every weekend for decades, ever since Malia Spanyol (who also owns Mission lesbian bar **Mother**, p169) took charge. Mondays and Tuesdays mellow out with movies and board games, and anytime's good for tater-tot nachos and legit margaritas on the sunny, dog-friendly back patio *(cover free to $15)*. Live dangerously: take shots with total strangers in the vintage photo booth.

For more punk action, head over Potrero Hill to volunteer-run, nonprofit **Thrillhouse Records** *(Map p170; thrillhouse records.com)*, well-stocked with punk on vinyl and (because this is SF, punk) original jazz pressings. Thrillhouse throws free weekend shows, and its outdoor billboard is a snapshot of SF's punk scene: photocopied flyers for bands with intriguingly offputting names (Curb Creeps, Guilty Strangers, Braintooth), bands recruiting new members ('death/doom/goth sound... some experience preferred, all welcome'), Gaza fundraiser announcements, street-philosophy zines, and punk recipes for cheap tasty eats ('because SF is so goddamn expensive'). Up the block is **The Knockout** *(Map p170; theknockoutsf.com)*, which books fun, loud bands – plus chill reggae, danceable darkwave, and punk drag shows – and serves craft beer, PBR with JD shots, and a memorable cocktail called the Off-Kilter: St George Botanist gin, St Germain and tonic, stirred with rosemary and attitude. Go ahead, punk: enjoy your night.

Researched by
Dylan Lalanne-Perkins

THE CASTRO

WELCOME TO THE GAYBORHOOD!

Rainbow flags gaily wave hello at the world's premier LGBTQ+ culture destination, spiritual home to club kids, career activists, leather daddies and drag stars alike.

After the 1967 Summer of Love brought thousands of hippies to the Haight, the LGBTQ+ community there embarked on an exodus south to this working-class neighborhood in Eureka Valley. The Castro became a queer hub, made famous in the 1970s by Harvey Milk, the first openly gay man elected to public office in California, representing the Castro as a member of the SF Board of Supervisors. Castro nightlife is legendary, but when the sun comes out, the neighborhood really shines – being out in broad daylight is a freedom this community fought for, and thoroughly enjoys – especially on weekends, when crowds come to people-watch, shop and drink. Today the little neighborhood under the giant rainbow flag is a global symbol of freedom.

TOP TIP

Historic streetcars that look like toy trains run to the Castro from Fisherman's Wharf, covering Market St through downtown. Trouble is, they sometimes get stuck in traffic and you can wait for what feels like forever. If the service is slow, take underground-metro K, L or M trains, which move (much) faster beneath Market St – same ticket, same price.

FROM LEFT: PHOTOJOHN830/SHUTTERSTOCK, ELENA GRAHAM/SHUTTERSTOCK

Above: Castro St; Right: Rainbow crosswalk

See page 262 for places to stay in the Castro

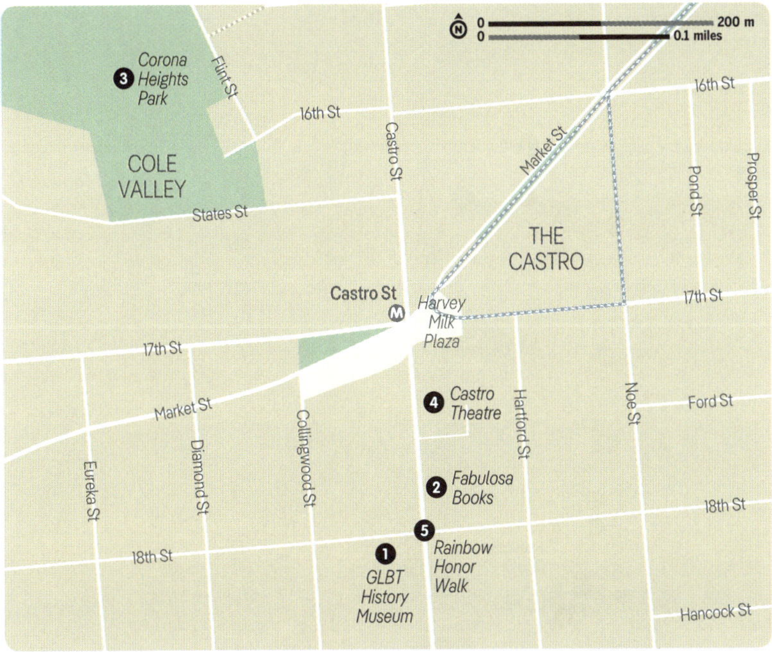

0 200 m
0 0.1 miles
Corona Heights Park
COLE VALLEY
THE CASTRO
Castro St
Harvey Milk Plaza
Flint St
16th St
Castro St
Market St
Pond St
Prosper St
States St
17th St
Market St
Eureka St
Diamond St
Collingwood St
Hartford St
Noe St
Ford St
18th St
Hancock St
Castro Theatre
Fabulosa Books
Rainbow Honor Walk
GLBT History Museum

Highlights

1 GLBT Historical Society Museum
Time travel through decades of LGBTQ+ history at America's first gay museum. **p201**

2 Fabulosa Books
Read the rainbow at this neighborhood bookshop, featuring an expansive inventory of work by LGBTQ+ authors. **p197**

3 Corona Heights Park
Climb to the summit at sunset and watch Market St light up below, then make scientific discoveries at the Randall Museum. **p201**

4 Castro Theatre
Catch a movie premiere, or drag show – or, soon, live concerts – and hear the Mighty Wurlitzer's pipes roar before showtime. **p196**

5 Rainbow Honor Walk
See how far we've come along Castro sidewalks honoring LGBTQ+ pioneers. **p196**

Getting Around

Metro
K, L and M trains run beneath Market St to Castro Station. J trains travel from downtown along Church St to 18th St and beyond.

Streetcar
Vintage streetcars operate on the F-Market line, from Fisherman's Wharf to Castro St.

Bus
The 24 connects the Castro to bustling Divisadero St, and the 33 goes to the Haight and the Mission.

THE CASTRO
COLE VALLEY
Market St
Harvey Milk Plaza
17th St
Castro St
Hartford St
Castro Theatre
THE CASTRO
Fabulosa Books
Rainbow Honor Walk
18th St
GLBT Historical Society Museum
19th St
0
100 m
Page St
Haight St
Waller St
Lloyd St
Buena Vista Ave E
Buena Vista Park
Duboce Ave
Alpine Tce
Divisadero St
Buena Vista Tce
Park Hill Ave
14th St
COLE VALLEY
Henry St
15th St
Roosevelt Way
Corona Heights Park
Beaver St
Flint St
16th St
States St
Ord St
Douglass St
Corbett Ave
Diamond St
Eureka St
Eureka Valley Recreation Center
Caselli Ave
Thorp La
Clayton St
Eagle St
Iron Al
Yukon St
Seward St
20th St
Collingwood St

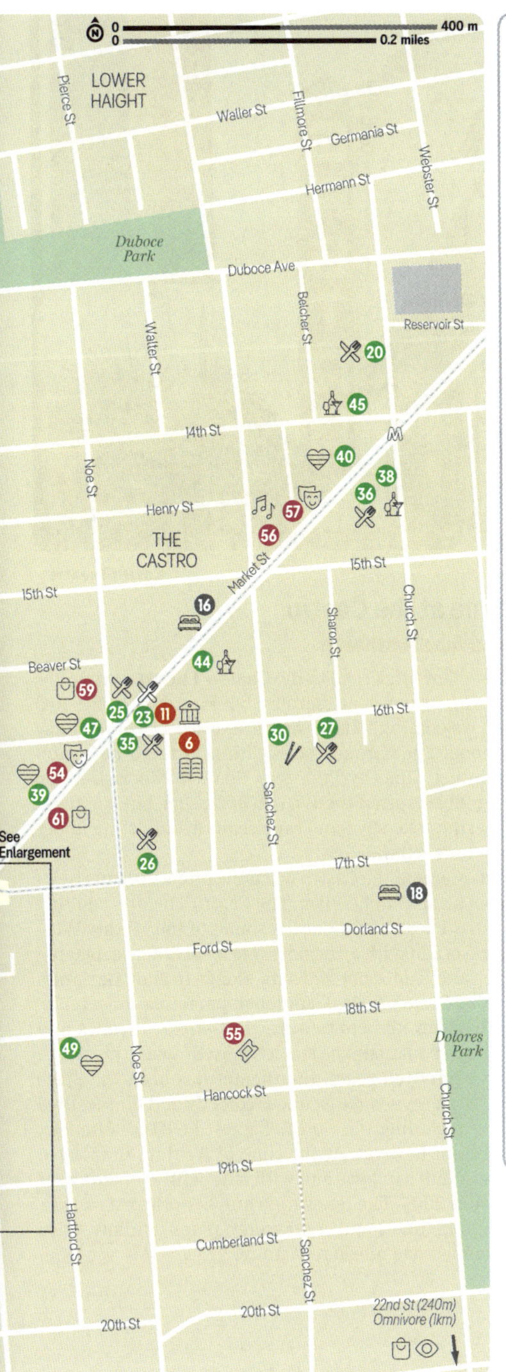

HIGHLIGHTS
1 Castro Theatre
2 Corona Heights Park
3 Fabulosa Books
4 GLBT Historical Society Museum
5 Rainbow Honor Walk

SIGHTS
6 Eureka Valley Library
7 Harvey Milk Plaza
8 Jane Warner Plaza
9 Kite Hill
10 Nobby Clarke Mansion
11 Photo Booth Museum by Photomatica
12 Queer Arts Featured
13 Randall Museum
14 Strut

ACTIVITIES
15 Seward Street Slides

SLEEPING
16 Beck's Motor Lodge
17 Hotel Castro
18 Parker Guest House

EATING
19 Anchor Oyster Bar
20 Beit Rima
21 Blind Butcher
22 Cafe de Casa
23 Dinosaurs Sandwiches
24 Fable
25 Fisch & Flore
26 Frances
27 Gai Chicken Rice
28 Hot Cookie
29 Hot Johnnie's Smokehouse
30 Kitchen Story
31 Orphan Andy's
32 Poesia
33 Poesia Cafe
34 Spike's Coffees and Teas
35 Starbelly
36 Thoroughbread & Pastry

DRINKING & NIGHTLIFE
37 440 Castro
38 Aquitaine Wine Bar and Bistro
39 Beaux
40 Blackbird
41 Blush!
42 Castro Village Wine Co.
43 Copper Bar
44 HiTops
45 Last Rites
46 Lobby Bar
47 Lookout
48 Midnight Sun
49 Moby Dick
50 QBar
51 Swirl
52 The Cafe
53 Twin Peaks Tavern

ENTERTAINMENT
54 Art House SF
55 MAG Galleries
56 Swedish American Hall & Cafe du Nord
57 The Academy SF

SHOPPING
58 Cliff's Variety
59 Flore Dispensary
60 Local Take
61 Stag & Manor

RAINBOW HONOR WALK

Cruising around the Castro, you're always in good company. The **Rainbow Honor Walk,** running along Market and Castro Sts, is composed of a series of gold sidewalk plaques honoring LGBTQ+ heroes.

In 2014, following a lengthy public forum process to choose honorees, installation began with 20 initial plaques of figures lesser known to the general public, who were self-expressed LGBTQ+ individuals who made significant contributions in their fields.

Today, a total of 68 trailblazers are pointing the way forward. So watch your step, don't tread on literary giant James Baldwin, Nobel Laureate Jane Addams, civil-rights activist Bayard Rustin, or local icons like trans activist and GLBT Historical Society founder Lou Sullivan and San Francisco's Absolute Empress José Sarria, founder of the Imperial Court System.

Castro Theatre

Showtime at the Castro

A 1922 deco-fabulous theater

Follow the yellow brick road to the **Castro Theatre** *(castrotheatre.com)* with its towering marquee blinking out C-A-S-T-R-O in the sky, welcoming folks to San Francisco's legendary gay neighborhood. The baroque facade hints at the ornate interior – architect Timothy Pflueger's Spanish-Moorish-Asian decor allegedly inspired the *Wizard of Oz* sets, but you'll notice that earthquake-shy San Franciscans avoid sitting under his pointy metal chandelier.

Showtime starts at the Castro when the mighty organ rises – and no, that's not a euphemism. The Castro Theatre wouldn't be the Castro Theatre without the sound of the Mighty Wurlitzer, a pipe organ with a considerable local fanbase, playing show tunes and leading crowd sing-alongs to Judy Garland's anthem 'San Francisco.' At audience-participation events, everyone is given kits containing glow sticks, bubbles and noisemakers to punctuate the movie's most dramatic moments.

For over a hundred years, the theater has been the place for all-star drag revues, A-list queer comedy and film-festival premieres – including the world's biggest LGBTQ+ film fest, Frameline Film Festival. At the time of writing, the Castro Theatre was under renovation, with a hopeful reopening set due for winter 2025. The renovation and historic restoration, not without neighborhood controversy, plans to allow space for an expanded live music repertoire.

Frameline Film Festival

Here, queer and ready for premiere

Founded in 1977, **Frameline** *(frameline.org; admission $19.50–35)*, the San Francisco International LGBTQ+ Film Festival, is the oldest, biggest lesbian, gay, bisexual, transgender and queer film fest anywhere. Over the course of two weeks in June, binge-watch up to 150 films from 40 countries, screened in venues across San Francisco and Oakland. While some films are making their debut – or their 'queer premiere' if previously screened at a non-queer film fest – Frameline also makes space for retrospective titles and recently restored queer classics.

People-Watching at the Plaza

Let the gay world pass you by

Jane Warner Plaza is named for the pioneering lesbian officer who patrolled the Castro. Historic streetcars that look like colorful toy trains make their last stop here, do a perfect pivot turn, and head back to Fisherman's Wharf. Rainbow-themed seating and bizarre public art make for prime people-watching – including glimpses of Castro nudists on sunny days, legally obliged to cover up with strategically placed socks. Somewhere over the rainbow (across the street) is **Harvey Milk Plaza** – currently under construction with fundraising still underway to transform the space into an additional public gathering space for the neighborhood – where a huge rainbow flag flaps.

Oh So Fabulosa!

Read the rainbow at Fabulosa Books

True to its name – 'Fabulosa' means 'fabulous' in Polari, 19th-century gay theater slang – beloved neighborhood bookstore **Fabulosa Books** *(fabulosabooks.com)* carries a selection as colorful as the Castro's rainbow crosswalks. With an eclectic mix of genres, ranging from Lesbians!! to Gender-Funky Sci-Fi, Fabulosa Books embraces a spirit of inclusivity, carrying literature that represents all identities (including straight people). Whether you're digging through bins of vintage ephemera for a punk zine or retro skin mag, or browsing a display of forgotten literary masterpieces, you'll find something you never knew you'd love. Author readings here are magnets for local characters, and Books Not Bans,

FIND OUT WHAT'S GOING ON IN THE CASTRO

Bay Area Reporter: If you don't spot a free copy of this LGBTQ+ community newspaper with stellar event listings in Castro cafes or bookstores, find the latest issues and records since 1971 at ebar.com.

Notice board: Check out the outdoor bulletin board at 18th and Castro St to see what's happening in the Castro now: circuit parties, drag political fundraisers, bands seeking guitarists and the perennial favorite: missed connections, documenting brief, anonymous encounters of any and all kinds.

Flyers: Wrapped around every post along the main drag are colorful posters for myriad events, like a trans-temporal evening for the gender playful, cowboy vs aliens dance party, or David Lynch tribute show (Mulholland Drag).

EATING IN THE CASTRO: CALIFORNIA CUISINE

Starbelly: The sun-drenched flavors you'd expect from California, with farmer's market ingredients. *11:30am-9pm Mon-Thu, to 10pm Fri, 10am-10pm Sat, 10am-9pm Sun* **$$$**

Frances: Seasonal menus showcase handmade pastas, juicy steaks and lumberjack date cake to satisfy your discerning lumberjack date. *5:15-9:15pm Tue-Sat* **$$$**

Kitchen Story: Korean-inspired scrambles and Millionaire's Bacon make this SF's best and most popular brunch spot – go early. *9am-2pm Mon-Fri, to 2:30pm Sat & Sun* **$$**

Fable: Snag a table in the lush garden and sip on select California wines paired with local halibut or bougie burgers. *11am-9pm Mon-Fri, 10am-10pm Sat, 10am-9pm Sun* **$$$**

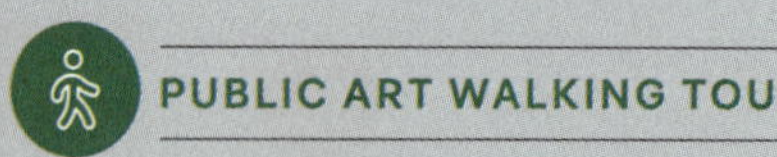

PUBLIC ART WALKING TOUR

In the Castro district, public art and murals celebrate the culture, history, and resilience of the LGBTQ+ community. This walking tour takes you through some of the neighborhood's most famous works.

START	END	LENGTH
Pink Triangle Memorial	Barbie-Doll Window	1.1 miles; 25min

Start at the 1 **Pink Triangle Memorial**, wedged between 17th and Market. Triangular granite columns sprout from the grass, dedicated to the queer lives lost during the Holocaust.

Continue along Market St under the giant 2 **Gilbert Baker Memorial Rainbow Flag**, named for the pride flag creator, to 16th St, where 3 **The Hope for the World Cure** mural tells a kaleidoscopic story about the chaos of the AIDS epidemic and the solidarity of the global queer community.

Turn right on Sanchez and walk to 18th St, a crossroads guarded by J Manuel Carmona's 4 **portrait of Juanita MORE!**, the most painted drag queen in San Francisco. Two blocks over is Serge Gay Jr's 5 **Gear Up**, symbolizing a person getting their armor ready for a march on the streets.

Strut over rainbow-pinstriped crosswalks to 6 **Queer Arts Featured** (p200), the former location of Harvey Milk's Castro Camera shop where the Mayor of Castro St continues to watch over his neighborhood from the window. And no loop through the Castro would be complete without a peek at the 7 **Barbie-Doll Window** on Castro and 19th, featuring trans Barbies and gay Kens arranged in protest lines, complete with signs. One says it best: 'It's Castro, Bitch.'

Watch your step as you walk – underfoot is the **Rainbow Honor Walk** (p196) with 68 trailblazing LGBTQ+ icons featured in sidewalk plaques.

Find local produce, baked goods and artisan foods, plus charmingly offbeat folk music, at the Wednesday **Castro Farmers Market**.

The southeast corner of **Castro and 18th** is a community hub, where altars honor bygone neighbors and street performers do their thing.

a nonprofit effort sending LGBTQ+ books to communities across the country where access is restricted, operates out of the (literal) closet in the back.

Castro Art Walk

Gallery-hop around the neighborhood

See what the Castro's creative community has been dreaming up lately at the monthly **Castro Art Walk** *(castroartwalk.com; free)*, held on the first Friday of each month from 5pm to 8pm. Stroll from **Art House SF** *(arthousesf.com)* to **MAG Galleries** *(mag-galleries.com)* to the collection of neighborhood businesses that have transformed into art exhibitions showcasing local talent. Members-only LGBTQ+ social club **The Academy SF** *(academy-sf.com)* opens its doors to the art-loving public, and **Flore Dispensary** *(floredispensary.com)* displays work in the window under the 'queer weed' sign. For the complete list of participating local businesses and artists each month, check the Castro Art Walk website.

Historic Gay Bars

Stiff drinks and drag numbers

The vintage rainbow neon arrow points the way to a local landmark: opened in 1935, **Twin Peaks Tavern** *(twinpeakstavern.com)* became the world's first gay bar with windows open to the street in 1971. Nab a window spot, or an outdoor seat on sunny afternoons, for prime people-watching, cozy up to the Victorian carved-wood bar for cocktails and conviviality, or grab a back booth to review Castro shows over wine by the glass. Come prepared, this bar holds onto its roots by remaining a cash-only institution.

You can call anyone Ishmael here, as long as you're buying. **Moby Dick**'s sign has been a Castro photo op since 1977, and the mural commemorating a century of protests is fabulous. The fish tank over the bar is mesmerizing – there's something thrusting out of the coral, and it's definitely not fishy. On weekdays, this is a mellow spot for pool and pinball with boozy slushies, plus there are Wednesday drag shows.

The most happening bar in the neighborhood, **440 Castro** *(the440.com)* – previously Daddy's, The Bear, Bear Hollow – is a magnet for bearded 30- and 40-something dudes, especially on 2-for-1 Wednesdays and Fridays, when go-go boys twirl. Monday's underwear night welcomes bears (a term that was

22ND STREET

In the city of a thousand hills, **22nd St** ranks among the steepest. With 31.5% grades – about 17-degree slopes – this Castro climb ties with Filbert Street, between Hyde and Leavenworth, in Russian Hill, but 22nd is longer and has fewer cars.

Daredevil skaters and cyclists can't resist testing their luck on the sharpest plunge between Vicksburg and Church Sts, trying not to go flying headfirst off their wheels.

Photographers snap the slope from a titled angle, making the street look level and the houses off-kilter; a classic San Francisco optical illusion.

And despite the literal uphill battle – thankfully, sidewalk stairs are there to assist – the view from the peaks of 22nd St makes it worth the climb.

EATING IN THE CASTRO: LUNCH SPOTS

Dinosaurs Sandwiches: Monster *bánh mì* stomp hunger with vegan-optional protein on crunchy bread with all the fixings – jalapeños, mayo and pickled vegetables. *10am-7pm* $

Gai Chicken Rice: The solution to cold snaps and tentative tummies: comforting, tender Hainan-style slow-poached chicken with rice. *11am-9pm* $$

Beit Rima: Palestinian lager pairs with Arabic comfort food: Gazan braised lamb shank, shakshuka, and lemony hummus. *11am-9pm Sun & Tue-Thu, to 9:30pm Fri & Sat* $$$

Fisch & Flore: Enjoy brunch staples and fresh seafood, and watch the entire gay world go by from the patio on the neighborhood's most happening corner. *11am-10pm Fri-Sun* $$$

Twin Peaks Tavern (p199)

coined in SF for good reason) and Peter Pans alike – but if you think 440's Battle of the Bulge contest has something to do with WWII, this is not your bar, honey.

While Twin Peaks was the first gay bar to get plate-glass windows, **Midnight Sun** *(midnightsunsf.com)* bookended this history in 2011 when it became the last bar in the neighborhood to install them. Today in the Castro, patrons have an abundance of bars where they can be out, proud and visible – but 'servicing the Castro for over 50 years' is no small claim to fame, and Midnight Sun lives up to its motto daily with a steady flow of good vibes and strong drinks (two for one until 9pm every day).

Queer Arts Featured

LGBTQ+ art in a historic storefront

It's no secret that the Castro is queer – after all, this neighborhood is home to artist-led gallery and retail space **Queer Arts Featured** *(queerartsfeatured.com)*. Located in the historic storefront that once housed Harvey Milk's Castro Camera, and was most recently the center for the Human Rights Campaign,

DRINKING IN THE CASTRO: WINE BARS

Blush!: Kick back on red velvet sofas and pair a glass with tarot readings and live music. *4pm-midnight Mon-Thu, to 1:30am Fri, 3pm-1:30am Sat, 3pm-midnight Sun*

Swirl: Come as you are – pinstripes or leather, gay, straight or whatever – this wine-shop bar has universal appeal and reliably delicious bottles. *11:30am-9pm*

Castro Village Wine Co.: Pop-and-pop shop where old-school locals hang at the back bar for weekend wine tastings. *noon-7pm Sun & Tue, from 3pm Mon, to 8pm Wed-Sat*

Aquitaine Wine Bar and Bistro: Vibrant interior; imported French wines pair with Gascony-inspired cuisine. *4-9pm Tue-Thu, 11:30am-9:30pm Fri & Sat, 11:30am-9pm Sun*

Queer Arts Featured upholds this legacy by celebrating and promoting local artists across the LGBTQ+ spectrum. Shop for tarot decks featuring queer icons throughout history – Oscar Wilde lounging on a marble throne is Justice, while ACT UP demonstrators marching to end the AIDS epidemic are the transformative Death card – or feed your imagination with an evening of Queer Bedtime Stories where anyone is welcome to bring a reading to share or simply listen along.

Cafe du Nord

Indie up-and-comers in an underground speakeasy

The Castro was once known as Little Scandinavia after the sailors who docked here – and the secret to their community spirit was the speakeasy running in the basement of their local meeting hall since 1907. Today the updated **Cafe du Nord** *(cafedunord.com; tickets $18–35)* speakeasy is an atmospheric singer-songwriter hot spot, hosting prolific artists like Cat Power, Bon Iver, and St Vincent, while the upstairs **Swedish American Hall** hosts folkYEAH! indie-breakthrough showcases. A few nights a month, laughter reverberates below street level as comedians take over the intimate stage for an evening of stand-up, with some all-ages shows; most are 21-plus.

Summit Corona Heights

Discover stunning views and scientific wonders

If there's one thing San Francisco has in ample supply, its jaw-dropping views – a reward for the uphill battle you must embark on to reach them. For romantic sunsets with panoramic views from the Castro to the Bay, scramble up the red rocks of the 520ft-high peak at **Corona Heights Park**. Face southeast as the sun sets, and watch rainbow lights twinkle welcomes across the Castro. Be sure to bring a jacket with you once afternoon fog blows in – you'll be glad to have it.

While adults are asleep downhill, eight-year-olds are making scientific discoveries at the **Randall Museum** *(randall museum.org; free)* atop Corona Heights Park. After Josephine Randall became a pioneering Stanford zoologist in 1910, she turned a jail into a kids' science and arts center as San Francisco's first Rec & Parks Superintendent. Highlights include state-of-the-art science and tech labs, woodworking and ceramics studios, a habitat for 100 stray and wounded animals, plus Lionel trains chugging along the expansive Golden Gate Model Railroad. Check the website for wonder-inspiring hands-on workshops, often available on a walk-in basis.

Learn from the GLBT Historical Society Museum

Explore queer public history

America's first queer history museum, the **GLBT Historical Society Museum** *(glbthistory.org; admission $10)* showcases a century of San Francisco LGBTQ+ ephemera – including Harvey Milk's campaign literature and Keith Haring's posters

CASTRO MEET-CUTES

Frederick Smith is the author of *One and Done*, a queer Black romance set in the Castro. If you're hoping for a love story of your own, here are his top spots for a meet-cute.

Beaux (p204): At Drag Brunch, Beyoncé's greatest hits and bottomless mimosas create the perfect setting for romance – lock eyes over a plate of vegan tacos and see where the rest of the weekend takes you.

Hot Johnnie's Smokehouse: The pastrami will make you swoon and the gorgeous, vine-draped back patio is perfect for date night. For dinner and a show, check the calendar for monthly drag performances.

QBar: This neighborhood bar really creates a sense of community for people of color, and women and femmes. Under rainbow lights, people from different backgrounds gather and find connection – what the Castro has always been about.

NOBBY CLARKE MANSION

The strange **Nobby Clarke Mansion**, notable for its several turrets, gables, and unique shingle pattern on the roof, was built in 1892 by Alfred E Clarke, an attorney who amassed a fortune by dubious means. Looking for sunnier weather than swanky Nob Hill afforded, he spent millions in today's money – the typical cost of housing in modern SF but an unheard-of expenditure for the time – building this baroque Queen Anne, only for it to go uninhabited after construction when his wife refused to move in. Snob Hill socialites dubbed the mansion 'Nobby Clarke's Folly.'

LYNN FRIEDMAN/SHUTTERSTOCK

Lookout

urging SF to 'Act Up, Fight AIDS' – alongside exhibits highlighting queer culture and movements throughout history. Since 1985, the GLBT Historical Society, which sponsors the museum, has worked to collect and preserve community history. Visits here are bonding experiences for the LGBTQ+ community and civil-rights allies alike, with moving multimedia stories sharing deep struggles and sheer queer joy. The shop features books researched at the museum, historic event posters – yes, SF's 1970 Gay-In was an actual event – and fridge magnets echoing Harvey Milk's words: 'You gotta give 'em hope.' Indeed.

Race Ya!

Twin concrete slides snake down a steep hill

Climb steep hills to Seward Mini Park – and ride back down on one of the city's hidden concrete slides! Designed by a local high schooler, winner of a competition put on by sculptor Ruth Asawa, these **Seward Street Slides** have been entertaining generations of San Franciscans since 1973. Cardboard is necessary for descents, and there's usually a stack by the

DRINKING IN THE CASTRO: CREATIVE COCKTAILS & MICROBREWS

Blackbird: Mysterious tinctures turn cocktails into irresistible potions in this cozy den. *5-11pm Mon, to midnight Tue-Thu, 4pm-2am Fri, 2pm-2am Sat, 2pm-11pm Sun*

Last Rites: Out of the wreckage of a deserted-island plane crash came this tiki bar with flaming rum drinks. *5-11pm Sun-Wed, to 1am Thu, 6pm-2am Fri & Sat*

Lobby Bar: Signature cocktails for out-of-towners and neighborhood regulars at Hotel Castro. *3-10pm Sun, 5-11pm Wed & Thu, to midnight Fri, 4pm-midnight Sat*

Copper Bar: Cozy spot – get a tasting flight to sample everything from Copper IPA to Castro Cream. *4-11pm Mon-Wed, from 11am Sun & Thu, to 1am Fri & Sat*

slides – BYO waxed paper for faster speeds, and be sure to wear sturdy pants. Bring kids: a park sign reads, 'No adults unless accompanied by children.' Neighbors don't love noise, but sometimes it can't be helped...wheeee!

Strut Your Stuff

Life-saving care and life-affirming art

In the 1980s and '90s, the AIDS epidemic devastated the Castro – but amid incalculable loss, the community got organized. The Castro's resurgence is a testament to groundbreaking, humane healthcare pioneered by community organizations including San Francisco AIDS Foundation, the nonprofit behind **Strut** *(sfaf.org)*. This landmark community health and wellness center offers free and low-cost services for all, including PrEP prophylaxis, health screenings, walk-in counseling, substance-abuse treatment and support groups. ID is required, and privacy assured (no photos indoors). Book appointments or expect waits for walk-in clinical services, especially on weekends.

When cheers and wolf whistles burst out of the center's giant glass doors, you know it must be that time of the month again – every third Tuesday, Strut hosts the city's most unique (and most rambunctious) open-mic night. This health organization has a rotating events calendar that rivals that of any gay bar: **Beyond Binary**, an afternoon of art and activities for intersex and non-binary community members of any age, every third Monday; art openings in the gallery space; and staged readings of plays.

Sports Fans & Jock Lovers

Catch the game at a gay bar

Soon there may be a groove worn across Market St between the Castro's biggest gym and the **Lookout** *(lookoutsf.com)*, where post-workout crowds gather. Perched about the corner of Noe and Market, this rooftop bar offers striking views of the neighborhood – herds of nudist bicyclists coast past and confused drivers make a mess of the intersection, as any bartender will attest. Grab a drink and listen to stripped-down rugby players deliver truth in advertising at Jock, the Sunday afternoon fundraising party for LGBTQ+ sports teams.

At Castro's first gay sports bar, **HiTops** *(hitopsbar.com)*,

BEST SHOPPING FOR HIM & HOME

Cliff's Variety: Hardware maestros at this 1936 general store – famous for gasp-worthy window displays – won't raise an eyebrow at your need for silver body paint and a jar of rubber nuns.

Local Take: Take in the local scenery with a Castro Theatre marquee print, F streetcar T-shirt or belt buckle featuring vintage Muni maps, and support SF's creative economy.

Omnivore Books: Salivate over signed cookbooks by chef-legend Alice Waters, satisfy insatiable appetites with ancient Filipino diets and DIY moonshine recipes, and attend events with luminaries like Michael Pollan.

Stag & Manor: Dashing decor lets you take the Castro home: brass lanterns wink welcome at guests, and fair-trade throw pillows show dates how thoughtful yet laid-back you are.

EATING IN THE CASTRO: COZY CAFES

Poesia Cafe: Local produce and Italian imports combine: buttery cornettos and killer espresso. *8am-6pm Sun, to 5pm Mon, 7:30am-5pm Tue-Thu, 7:30am-6pm Fri & Sat* $

Cafe de Casa: Dark roast Brazilian coffee balances out colorful Brazilian fare that rivals the Castro's rainbow spirit. *8am-6pm Mon-Sat, to 5pm Sun* $

Thoroughbread & Pastry: Enjoy pastries with pedigree, creations of Michelin-starred Michel Suas, founder of the SF Baking Institute. *8am-4pm Wed-Fri, to 5pm Sat & Sun* $

Spike's Coffees and Teas: Bulldog scowl from to-go cups of fair-trade joe and pink tees of locals repping this fiercely independent cafe. *7am-5pm Mon-Fri, from 7:30am Sat & Sun* $

BEST KID-FRIENDLY ACTIVITIES

Panda Dulce is a founding queen of Drag Story Hour. Here are her recommendations for family-friendly afternoons in the Castro.

Kite Hill At this rocky overlook, a favorite hiking spot for dog owners, your eyeline can follow Market St to where the wharf kisses the Pacific.

Photo Booth Museum by Photomatica I love to take visitors of all ages here. Snap some old school, four-shot strips in retro photo booths.

Eureka Valley Library Be regaled with a Drag Story Hour, where drag artists perform fun read-alouds for kids. A note on etiquette: remember to ask permission to take a photo or selfie. Cash tips are customary and appreciated because as my drag mother, Estée Longah, says, 'it takes a lot of money to look this cheap!'

you can wear rainbows and team colors (as long as they're either blue and yellow, or orange and black). Giant-screen TVs and supersized snacks set the scene for instant bonding – and Thursday Gym Class amps up locker-room antics with whiskey shots and go-go boys. For friendly competition, hit the shuffleboard table and Tuesday trivia nights.

Night Market

Peruse local wares all evening long

Every third Friday of the month from 5pm to 10pm, the neighborhood gets all dolled up for the **Castro Night Market** *(castronightmarket.com)*, a showcase of Castro-based queer-owned businesses, celebrating community and supporting the ultra-local economy. Vendor booths line 18th street between Collingwood and Hartford, selling handmade wares: ceramic vases with an ancient Greco-Roman aesthetic (phalli intact), baskets of crocheted strawberries, tote bags adorned with vintage pulp-novel covers, and small leather goods and accessories, like teddy bears in full bondage gear. Food stands fill the air with the smell of Latin-inspired gourmet burgers, Peruvian-fusion ceviche bowls, and tea-infused ice cream. On stage, DJs spin dance beats while go-go dancers in fairy wings draw a crowd.

Dance the Night Away

Hit the rainbow dance floor

With a Harvey Milk mural and rainbow light-up dance floor, **The Cafe** *(cafesf.com)* is the obvious place to throw your own coming-out party. Most nights the crowd seems recently graduated, and parties range from Latinx Picante Thursdays to lesbian Sugar Saturdays; check the calendar. Kick-ass sound and trippy light shows pack the dance floor; cruise the open-air patio between sets. Determined 20-something club kids shimmy and shout over pop remixes on the cramped dance floor at **QBar** (p201; *qbar-sf.com)*, while smokers flirt on the patio. Perpetually busy bartenders mix mean dirty martinis and lemon drops, if you ask nicely. The candy store of Castro clubs, **Beaux** *(beauxsf.com; cover $10–20)* serves every flavor, from Pan Dulce Wednesdays to Throwback Thursdays, and go-go Manimal Fridays. Weekends peak with Nitty Gritty dirty disco (find the mezzanine for floor views) and Big Top Sundays, when *RuPaul's Drag Race* stars emcee. Once a month

EATING IN THE CASTRO: COZY DINNER SPOTS

Anchor Oyster Bar: Since 1977, Anchor remains Castro's port of call for sustainably sourced local oysters and SF's famous *cioppino* (seafood stew). *2-8pm Thu-Mon* $$$

Orphan Andy's: Bask in flamboyant flair at this local haunt, serving up retro realness alongside an expansive repertoire of classic diner staples. *24hr* $$

Poesia: Get cozy at this bay-window *osteria* with feel-good handmade pastas and excellent DOC Italian wines. *5-9:30pm* $$$

Blind Butcher: Intimate seating and moody lighting make this a popular date-night spot for meatlovers and vegetarians alike. *5-10pm Mon-Fri, 11am-3pm & 5-10pm Sat & Sun* $$$

PETER HORREE/ALAMY

Hot Cookie

is LesBeaux, a sapphic dance party for women and femmes. Arrive before 9pm to beat the lines and the cover.

Hot Cookie

Put something sweet in your mouth

If the smell wafting down Castro St isn't enough to draw you into tiny **Hot Cookie** *(hotcookie.com)*, maybe this will: freshly baked phallic-shaped treats of firm macaroon cookie dough dipped in white or dark chocolate, and a wall of hot customers posing in eye-catching branded underwear. Rumor has it that adult films were shot here after-hours back in the day, making this an essential stop for modern OnlyFans influencers looking to put something sweet in their mouth.

Researched by
Dylan Lalanne-Perkins

THE HAIGHT & HAYES VALLEY

SAN FRANCISCO'S HIPPIE HOTSPOT

Hippie idealism thrives in the Haight with street musicians, anarchist comic books and psychedelic murals splashed on every available surface.

In the 1960s, thousands of young people from across the country flocked to Haight and Ashbury, drawn in by psychedelic bands, free-love communes and revolutionary politics. Counterculture kids called themselves freaks and flower children; *San Francisco Chronicle* columnist Herb Caen dubbed them 'hippies.' The Upper Haight has hung onto its roots: hippies reminisce about glory days trailed by teenage relations, and new-age practitioners load up on chakra-cleansing crystals. Down in the Lower Haight there are mellower vibes – dog walkers mosey like urban cowboys wrangling their herds and cyclists dodge steep hills. Next door in Hayes Valley, Zen monks and jazz legends drift past some of the city's best restaurants.

TOP TIP

You'll need more than fair-trade coffee or local microbrews to power through Haight St sightseeing, so veer off the main drag to Divisadero for affordable brunch and lunch spots, or head to Hayes Valley for critically acclaimed dining experiences.

FROM LEFT: WIRESTOCK, INC/ALAMY, PAULAH293/SHUTTERSTOCK

Avove: Clock at Haight and Ashbury (p210); Right: Cold Steel America (p210)

See page 263 for places to stay in the Haight & Hayes Valley

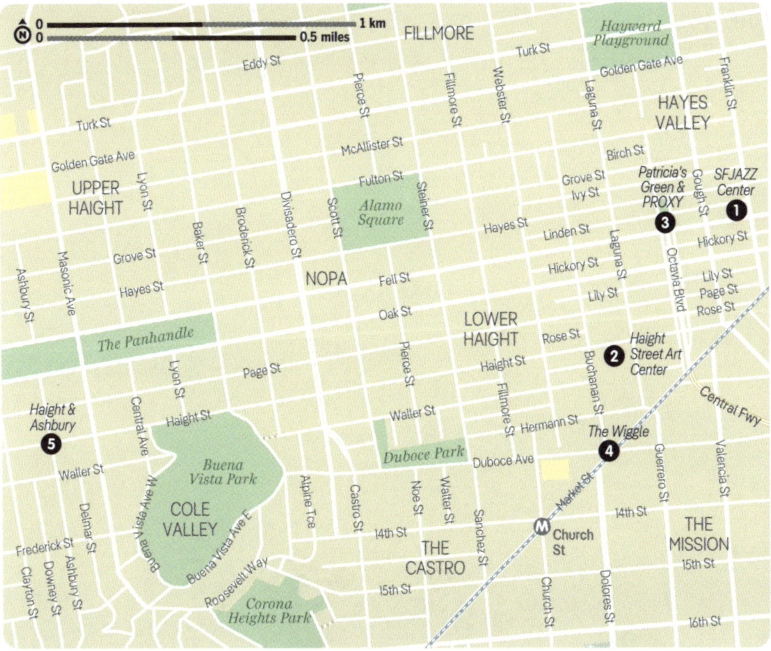

Highlights

1 SFJAZZ

Toast jazz giants with a thematic cocktail between rousing sets in front of tiled music-history murals. **p220**

2 Haight Street Art Center

View psychedelic concert posters at this gallery and screen-printing workshop. **p217**

3 Patricia's Green and PROXY

Enjoy gourmet delights and free outdoor events at this shipping container community hub. **p220**

4 The Wiggle

Cycle along the parks and past the murals of the Lower Haight, dodging steep hills on the way to Golden Gate Park. **p217**

5 Haight & Ashbury

Celebrate International Bong-Hit Time (4:20) at legendary intersection 'Hashbury.' **p210**

Getting Around

Bus

Bus lines 6 and 7 travel along Haight St, connecting Downtown to Golden Gate Park. The 22 links the Lower Haight to the Mission and the Marina, while the 43 connects the Upper Haight to the Marina.

Muni

Van Ness station is one block east of Hayes Valley, offering Muni lines across the city. The N line goes through the Lower Haight and onward to Ocean Beach.

BART

The Civic Center station is four blocks east of Hayes Valley, with trains to the Mission and the East Bay.

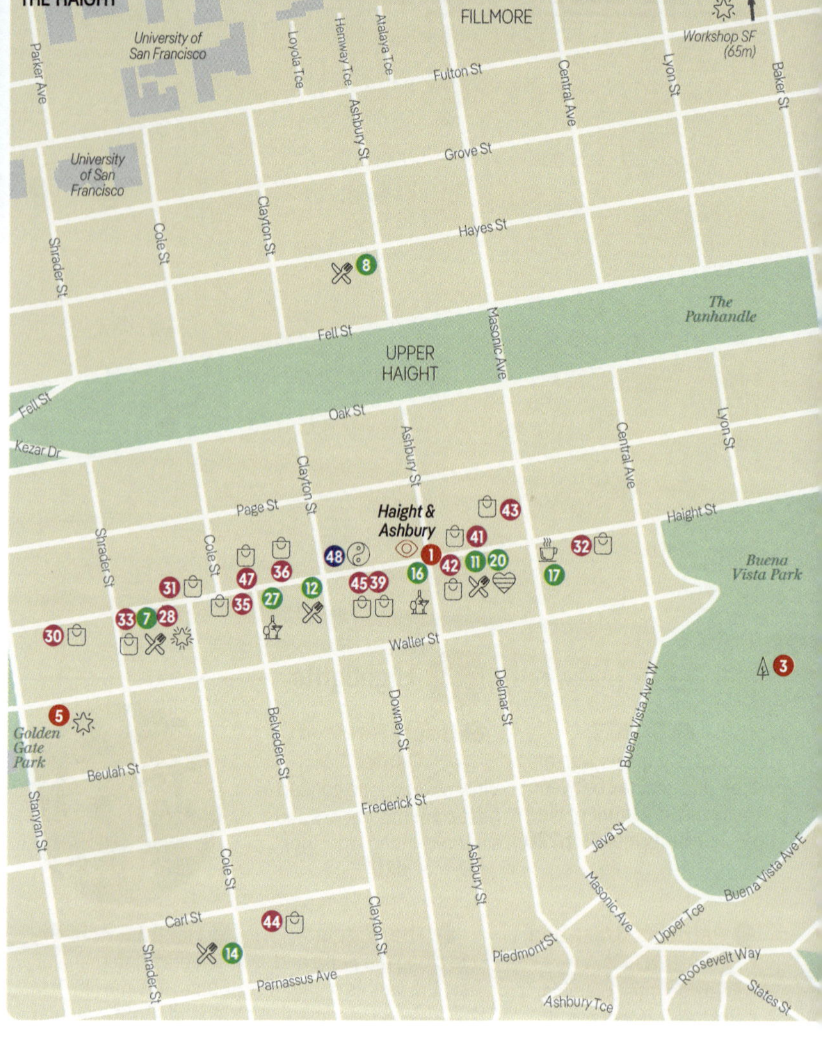

HIGHLIGHTS
1 Haight & Ashbury
2 The Wiggle

SIGHTS
3 Buena Vista Park

ACTIVITIES
4 Church of 8 Wheels
5 Free Gold Watch

SLEEPING
6 Metro Hotel

EATING
7 Escape from New York Pizza
8 Karma Cafe
9 Nopalito
10 Otra
11 Pork Store
12 Street Taco
13 That's My Jam
14 Zazie

DRINKING & NIGHTLIFE
15 Cafe International
16 Club Deluxe
17 Coffee to the People
18 Le Cafe du Soleil
19 Madrone Art Bar
20 Mary's
21 Millay
22 Noc Noc
23 Stoa
24 The Page
25 Toronado

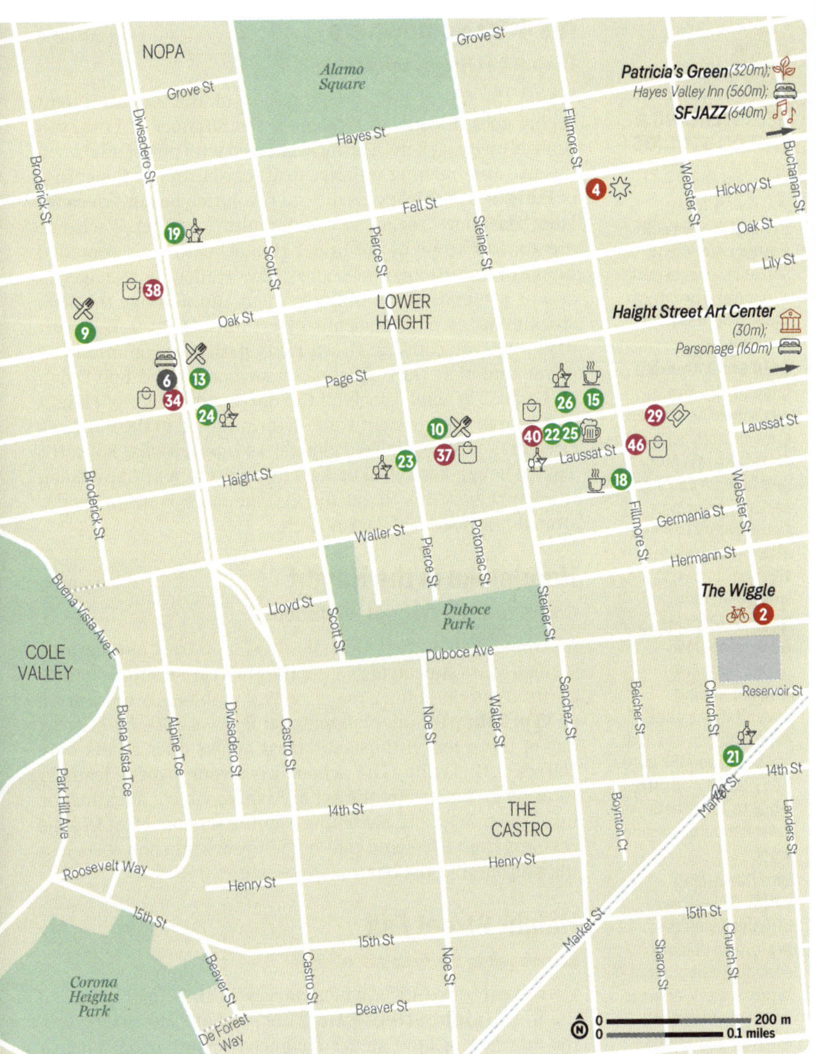

26 Uva Enoteca
27 Zam Zam

ENTERTAINMENT
28 Booksmith
29 Faight Collective

SHOPPING
30 Amoeba Music
31 Borderlands Books
32 Bound Together
33 Cold Steel America
34 Comix Experience
35 Decades of Fashion
36 FTC Skateboarding
37 Fuzz & Sway
38 Gamescape
39 Held Over
40 Idle Hand
41 Piedmont Boutique
42 Relic Vintage
43 Rose Gold's Tattoo & Piercing
44 Sword and Rose
45 The Love of Ganesha
46 Upper Playground
47 Wasteland

INFORMATION
48 Haight-Ashbury Free Clinic

BEST PIERCING & TATTOO STUDIOS

There's a chance you'll walk away from the Haight with a more permanent souvenir – get expert service and artistry at these neighborhood institutions.

Cold Steel America (Map p208): The city's most acclaimed piercing shop with an expansive inventory of rare antique earrings and a wide array of body jewelry in metal alternatives: glass, silicone, amber, stone, wood and horn.

Rose Gold's Tattoo & Piercing (Map p208): Piercers give ear-styling consultations, their expert advice as solid as the 14k and 18k gold body jewelry on offer, while tattoo artists craft intricate fine-line work.

Idle Hand (Map p208): Browse over 500 flash sheets of pre-drawn designs spanning a century of tattoo history, or make an appointment with artists constructing individualized adaptations of classic trad tats. Cash only.

It's 4:20 Somewhere

MAP P208

Drop out at Haight and Ashbury

Was it the fall of 1966 or the winter of '67? As the Haight saying goes, if you can remember the Summer of Love, you probably weren't here. The fog was laced with pot, sandalwood incense and burning military draft cards, and at the corner of **Haight & Ashbury**, a cultural revolution began – decades later, 'Hashbury' remains a counterculture magnet. Weekends are a major scene in the Upper Haight, with white-bearded hippies reminiscing about glory days trailed by teenage relations pretending not to know them and new-age thinkers stocking up on chakra-cleansing crystals. On average Saturdays here, you can sign Green Party petitions, commission a poem, and hear Hare Krishna on keyboards and Bob Dylan on banjo. The cubic clock on the northeast corner of Haight and Ashbury is frozen at 4:20 – a term coined in the Bay Area circa 1971, now recognized globally as International Bong-Hit Time. Though local clockmakers through the years have taken it upon themselves to get the vintage clock running again, stoned pranksters always reset it.

Handmake in the Haight

MAP P208

Counterculture crafts at WorkshopSF

Macrame, stoneware pottery, tie-dyes, tapestries, block prints, stained-glass suncatchers – the Haight's classic hippie handicrafts are undergoing a major revival with hands-on courses at **WorkshopSF** *(workshopsf.org; lessons $50–120)*. Every day of the week, enthusiastic local artists offer adults-only classes at this sunny DIY school. Keep your favorite jeans in rotation by mastering the art of Sashiko visible mending, or take it easy at a Chill Sketching evening session. Most lessons cost less than $75 – and that home-brew workshop costs less than a round at the bar.

Haight Street Fair

Flashback to the Summer of Love

Every year since 1977, when Harvey Milk helped organize the first **Haight Street Fair** *(haightashburystreetfair.org)*, the Summer of Love stages a comeback: free music on two stages – funk groups groove in their tie-dye jumpsuits and middle-school rockers headbang – plus vendors selling rainbow

DRINKING IN THE HAIGHT & HAYES VALLEY: DIVE BARS

MAP P208

Noc Noc: Who's there? Trance DJs, anarchist hackers, Burning Man founders, that's who, at this post-apocalyptic cave rave with local drafts. *5pm-1am Sun-Thu, to 2am Fri & Sat*

Zam Zam: Persian arches, *One Thousand and One Nights* murals, jukebox jazz and top-shelf cocktails at low-shelf prices. *3pm-2am Mon-Fri, from 1pm Sat & Sun*

Toronado: Glory hallelujah, beer-lovers: your prayers are answered. Genuflect before the chalkboard altar that lists 40-plus beers on tap. *11:30am-2am*

The Page: Dark, moody – for some reason, carpeted – spot where live bands play and old-timers swap stories of Divisadero's jazz heyday. *4pm-2am Mon-Fri, from 1pm Sat & Sun*

PAULAAH293/SHUTTERSTOCK

Wasteland

macramé and trippy tarot decks, skateboarders performing tricks for the crowd, and pot smoke wafting overhead thick enough to rival the fog.

Vintage Shopping Spree

MAP P208

Wander through wardrobes of the past

The Upper Haight is the place to rock a new old style with vintage concert tees, jumpsuits ready for the disco dance floor, and a steady supply of go-go boots – at reasonable (not bargain) prices, anyone can afford a few fashion risks. Head to **Wasteland** *(shopwasteland.com)*, a converted-cinema vintage superstore, to peruse the wall of prized vintage rock tees and the racks of high-end leather jackets plucked straight off the runway. **Decades of Fashion** *(decadesoffashionsf.com)* is a wearable museum featuring everything from frilly Gilded Age opera gloves to *Dynasty*-era shoulder pads. Travel to the early 20th century at **Relic Vintage** *(relicvintagesf.com)*, an elegant haberdashery of pinstriped suits and poodle skirts. **Held Over** is the spot for 1970s Western wear and flared denim for days,

HOMELESSNESS & THE HAIGHT

From buskers to teens scrounging for bus fare, panhandling – no judgment, no obligation – has been part of the Upper Haight since the '60s, when America's youth first fled here as a place to fit in.

But in 2010, San Francisco's controversial Sit/Lie Ordinance targeted the Haight, making 7am to 11pm sidewalk 'loitering' punishable by up to $100 fines – but with limited shelter beds to accommodate unhoused people citywide, many street kids have no place else to go.

While you're in town, volunteering at or making donations to homeless-service nonprofits, like Haight Ashbury Food Program, are thoughtful gestures to repay San Francisco hospitality, and ensure everyone has a chance to feel at home here.

EATING IN THE HAIGHT & HAYES VALLEY: BRUNCH SPOTS

– MAPS P208, P213

Pork Store: A cozy pink diner that's been servin' up pork chops and scralifornia (avocado and salsa ranchero scramble) since '79. *8am-2pm Mon-Fri, to 3pm Sat & Sun* **$$**

That's My Jam: It's breakfast time all weekend at this boutique bistro, with photo-worthy Painted Lady Lattes in pastel hues of iconic SF homes. *9am-3pm Fri-Sun* **$$**

Zazie: Hearty and wholesome – the line out the door lets you know just how good this neighborhood bistro is. Tip-free. *8am-2pm Mon-Fri, 9am-3pm Sat & Sun* **$$**

Chez Maman West: Buckwheat crepes with prosciutto béchamel, berry *pain perdu* and bubbly by the glass. *11:30am-10pm Mon-Fri, from 10:30am Sat & Sun* **$$$**

DEATH OF HIPPIE

On October 6, 1967, the Summer of Love was laid to rest. A mock funeral kicked off at Buena Vista Park with the San Francisco Diggers – a legendary community action and street theater group famous for giving out free food every day in the Panhandle – burning copies of their underground newspaper and pieces of flower power clothing, and shaving off unruly beards and long hair. Down Haight St, a procession carried a coffin bearing the inscription 'Hippie, Son of Media.' Their message: stop flocking to SF, drawn in by the media's depiction of hippies – instead, 'bring the revolution to where you live.' But Hippie's untimely demise was not enough to snuff out the '60s idealism, still alive in the Haight today.

the perfect pregame for an evening of line dancing (yeehaw). If you tumble downhill to the Lower Haight, the vintage party keeps grooving at **Fuzz & Sway**, a carefully curated spot for funky maxi skirts and mod dresses.

Wandering Buena Vista

MAP P208

Beautiful views at SF's oldest park

True to its name, hilltop **Buena Vista Park** offers splendid vistas over the city. Choose any of the secluded trails that weave around the park to enjoy spectacular views on the upper slopes, where the Golden Gate Bridge can be seen peeking through the fog.

Founded in 1867, this is one of San Francisco's oldest parks, populated by century-old coast live oak trees. A world of woodland creatures thrives in the shadows of the stately oaks. Keep an eye out for the dramatic scarlet plumage of a red-breasted sapsucker drilling for sap and tubby gophers emerging from their burrows to nosh on roots and seedlings. As you wander, peek under your feet for fragments of a forgotten last name – the engraved marble chunks bordering the park's paths are remnants of San Francisco's earliest tombstones. Take Buena Vista Ave West downhill to ogle Victorian mansions that survived the 1906 earthquake and fire, and the 1967 Summer of Love hippie commune boom. If you go on any nighttime excursions in the park, you are likely to catch a good view of something else: Buena Vista has a longstanding reputation as a gay cruising hotspot.

Drop the Needle on Amoeba Music

MAP P208

Shop deep cuts and certified bops

Enticements are hardly necessary to lure fans to the West Coast's most eclectic collection of new and used music and video, but **Amoeba Music** *(amoeba.com)* offers listening stations, free zines with uncannily accurate staff reviews, and upwards of 100,000 vinyl records, CDs, cassettes for everything from mainstream hip-hop to obscure jazz, along with DVDs and VHS for anyone looking to ditch streaming once and for all. This cavernous former bowling alley regularly transforms itself into a venue for Live at Amoeba, a free concert and album signing series. Oh, and when Amoeba's not feeding your record collection, they're running a foundation that's saved one million acres of rainforest.

EATING IN THE HAIGHT & HAYES VALLEY: PIZZA & PASTA

MAPS P208, P213

Escape from New York Pizza: Pesto with roasted garlic and potato is the necessary carb-loading to recharge you for more shopping. *10am-10pm Sun-Thurs, to 2am Fri & Sat* $

Gioia Pizzeria: *Gioia* – great pleasure and happiness in Italian – is just what this place delivers with fresh, seasonal toppings and housemade cannolis. *11am-10pm* $$

Doppio Zero: Michelin-recognized Neapolitan pizzas baked in a wood-fire oven and creative pastas. *11:30am-10pm Mon-Thurs, to 11pm Fri & Sat, to 9:30pm Sun* $$$

a Mano: Classic pizzas and show-stealing pastas tangled up in caramelized cipollini and short-rib ragu. *11:30am-9:30pm Mon-Thu, to 10:30pm Fri & Sat, to 9pm Sun* $$$

HAYES VALLEY

HIGHLIGHTS
1 Haight Street Art Center
2 Patricia's Green
3 SFJAZZ Center

SIGHTS
4 San Francisco Zen Center

SLEEPING
5 Hayes Valley Inn
6 Parsonage

EATING
7 a Mano
8 Arbor
9 Chez Maman West
10 Doppio Zero
11 DragonEats
12 Dumpling Home
13 Gioia Pizzeria
14 Na Ya Dessert Cafe
15 Nojo Ramen Tavern
16 Om Sabor
17 Papito Hayes
18 Rad Radish
19 Rich Table
20 Zuni Cafe

DRINKING & NIGHTLIFE
21 Birba
22 Hôtel Biron
23 LOQUAT
24 Martuni's

ENTERTAINMENT
25 Mint
26 San Francisco Ballet

SHOPPING
27 Isotope
28 Marine Layer

HAIGHT STREET FREE CLINIC

The original hand-carved **Haight-Ashbury Free Clinic** (Map p208)sign still hangs at the eastern corner of Haight and Cole Sts, along with a mural of its motto: 'Healthcare is a right, not a privilege – love needs care.'

After a little drug experimentation, a local doctor opened San Francisco's legendary 'hippie clinic' during the Summer of Love, providing judgment-free treatment to the neighborhood's influx of hippies. Support flooded in from SF big shots, most notably concert producer Bill Graham who staged 'Rock Medicine' benefit concerts.

Police raids frequently targeted the clinic in search of drugs and Berkeley protestors, but for over 50 years, the clinic was a safe haven running life-saving, substance-abuse treatment, mental-health and women's-health services, all free or low-cost.

Play Around at Free Gold Watch

MAP P208

Retro pinball galore

The name sounds too good to be true, but you've hit the jackpot: step inside **Free Gold Watch** *(freegoldwatch.com)* to discover a working screen-printing shop absolutely crammed with 50-plus vintage pinball games. Most cost a buck or less to play, including Elvis, Godzilla and SF-favorite Dirty Harry themed games. Regulars proceed directly to the next level of gamer heaven: Secret Juju Gallery of rare 1970s games. At the time of writing, Free Gold Watch just won big, securing a food and beverage license to be able to serve up arcade staples – pizzas, hotdogs and nachos – and craft beers and cocktails. Righteous.

Browse Book Nooks

MAP P208

Read, drink, repeat

Throw a stone in SF and you'll probably hit a writer (ouch) or reader (ouch again) headed to/from Booksmith. Literary figures organize **Booksmith** *(booksmith.com)* book signings, raucous poetry readings and politician-postcard-writing marathons. This is no library, as you'll discover at keg parties featuring zines and tarot readings. Next-door bar Alembic is co-owned by the Booksmith, so boozy book browsing is encouraged – when you wake up tomorrow amid piles of signed San Francisco novels, you'll know exactly what happened last night. Reserve seats at events for free online; book purchases are encouraged, especially at author signings.

Explore the outer realms of literature at **Borderlands Books** *(borderlands-books.com)*, a store dedicated to science fiction, fantasy, mystery and horror, with a special focus on small-press and indie publishers. Once voted the 'Best Place to Meet a Kinky Space Cadet' by the *SF Bay Guardian*, this shop is a gathering place for the city's more far-out readers.

Since 1976, **Bound Together** *(boundtogether.org)*, a volunteer-run, nonprofit anarchist bookstore, has kept free thinkers supplied with organic-permaculture manuals, social history and radical comics, all while coordinating the annual spring Anarchist Book Fair, running the Prisoners' Literature Project and retouching the Anarchists of the Americas storefront mural – makes us tools of the state look like slackers. Hours are impressively regular, but call ahead to check.

DRINKING IN HAIGHT & HAYES VALLEY: CUTE CAFES

MAPS P208, P213

Coffee to the People: Hemp-milk cappuccinos are an acquired taste and beware the quadruple fair-trade espresso shot Freak Out. *7am-5pm Sun-Fri, to 6pm Sat*

Cafe International: Fuel up with a Turkish coffee and a side of live music courtesy of the regulars performing on the colorful back patio. *7am-4:30pm*

Le Cafe du Soleil: Bright outdoor seating invites you to linger over a fresh brew, and Croque Monsieur or Croque Madame, the power couple of Saturday mornings. *7am-5pm*

LOQUAT: Coffee from local roaster Four Barrel and foods of the Jewish diaspora – don't skip cinnamon date babkas or seasonal veggie bourekas. *8am-5pm Wed-Mon*

HISTORIC HOUSES WALKING TOUR

Legendary psychedelic bands, far-left militant groups, free-love communes – the Haight's colorful Victorians have been home to a unique cast of characters.

START	END	LENGTH
Buena Vista Park	636 Cole St	1 mile; 20min

Start on the edge of Buena Vista Park between Broderick and Divisadero at 1 **Cockettes House** (944–948 Haight), the former communal home of the acid-loving drag troupe, disco legend Slyvester among their ranks. Neighborhood old-timers claim the Symbionese Liberation Army used 2 **1235 Masonic Ave** as a safe house for kidnapped-heiress-turned-revolutionary-bank-robber Patty Hearst. Right on Waller and left uphill leads to 3 **32 Delmar St**, site of the 1978 Sid Vicious overdose that broke up the Sex Pistols. Like surviving members of the Grateful Dead, the purple Victorian at 4 **710 Ashbury** sports a touch of gray. This was where Jerry Garcia and bandmates blew minds, amps and brain cells. After getting busted for drugs in 1967, they held a press conference here arguing that if everyone who smoked marijuana were arrested, San Francisco would be empty. Across the road is the former headquarters for biker gang the Hells Angels at 5 **715 Ashbury**. And 6 **635 Ashbury St**, the pink building on the corner? One of many known SF addresses for Janis Joplin, who had a hard time hanging onto leases in the 1960s – but as she sang, 'Freedom's just another word for nothin' left to lose.' 7 **636 Cole St** was the Summer of '67 pad of the world's most notorious hippie, Charles Manson, and early recruits to his 'family.'

The **John Spencer House** is a brilliant behemoth of Queen Anne architecture that has survived decades of earthquakes.

Joana Zegri's 1967 **Evolutionary Rainbow** is a Summer of Love relic and the city's first community mural.

You may recognize the faces on the **Anarchists of the Americas mural** at Bound Together – if not, staff can recommend introductory texts.

UPPER HAIGHT
The Panhandle
Buena Vista Park
COLE VALLEY
Corona Heights Park
START
END
John Spencer House
Evolution Rainbow Mural
Anarchists of the Americas Mural
Grove St
Hayes St
Fell St
Oak St
Page St
Haight St
Waller St
Duboce Ave
Frederick St
Carl St
Parnassus Ave
Grattan St
15th St
States St
Roosevelt Way
Cole St
Clayton St
Ashbury St
Masonic Ave
Central Ave
Lyon St
Baker St
Divisadero St
Shrader St
Downey St
Delmar St
Buena Vista Ave W
Buena Vista Ave E
Park Hill Ave
Buena Vista Tce
Alpine Tce
0 250 m
0 0.2 miles

BEST SPOTS TO READ A BOOK

Becka Robbins is the founder of nonprofit Books Not Bans *(@booksnotbans)*, sending LGBTQ+ literature to communities facing book bans. Here are her favorite reading spots in the Haight.

Zam Zam (p210): Bring a book light and read in the bar because books are awesome and so are Zam Zam's Manhattans. The jukebox provides the perfect reading background music.

Karma Cafe (Map p208): Think tie-dye tapestries, Tibetan prayer flags, and rainbow outdoor seating. Pull up to this cute hippie joint with a book or borrow one from the library cart.

Club Deluxe (Map p208): This place is my paradise (thankfully in the process of being resurrected). Perfect for a solitary outing where you can listen to the best local bands while enjoying a good book.

SEYHAN AHEN/SHUTTERSTOCK

The Love of Ganesha

Queer Nightlife

Party loud and proud

Mary's (Map p208) is everything a dive bar should be: dark but relatively clean, with faded red pool tables, glowing neon signs, and a rainbow flag draped behind the bar. This Upper Haight institution has been pouring barrel-aged cocktails since the 1970s, making it the longest-running and last remaining relic of the neighborhood's past as a pre-Castro LGBTQ+ enclave. Mingle with local characters – and possibly a gay ghost or two, if local legend is to be believed – and enjoy the cheapest drinks in the neighborhood.

Slip behind the velvet curtains into **Martuni's** *(Map p213; martunis.restaurants-world.com)*, the city's top piano bar on the edge of Hayes Valley, where the rainbow spectrum of regulars seems to have memorized the words to every show tune. Comedy nights are a blast and sing-alongs a given – especially after a couple of world-famous lemon drops or top-notch martinis. Enjoy the complimentary popcorn that comes with every round. Big voices at the mixed straight-gay karaoke bar **Mint** *(Map p213; themint.net)* could rattle pennies in the US mint uphill. If you can't decide what to sing from the 30,000-

EATING IN HAIGHT & HAYES VALLEY: MEXICAN FOOD

MAPS P208, P213

Otra: Start with spicy *salsa macha* on black beans, then vegetarian-friendly entrees like sweet potato tacos or cauliflower asparagus enchiladas. *5-10pm* $$

Papito Hayes: Cozy and casual spot for well-seasoned enchiladas, tortas and fajitas, and spicy hibiscus margaritas. *11am-9pm Sun-Wed, to 10pm Thu-Sat* $$

Nopalito: Fresh, organic ingredients in colorful meals that can pierce through the foggiest of days. *11:30am-9pm Sun-Tue & Thu, to 9:30pm Fri & Sat, 4:30-9pm Wed* $$$

Street Taco: Haight skateboarders swerve here for fresh salsa, handmade tortillas, and *al pastor* (grilled pork) hot off the rotisserie. *11am-10pm* $

plus playlist, know this: George Michael never fails, and the two-drink minimum practically guarantees applause. Reserve seating online, bring a posse, and tip the DJ if you want to sing any time soon.

Ride the Wiggle

MAP P208

Bike through the Lower Haight

While much of San Francisco is famous for its calf-burning climbs, thousands of cyclists coast through the Lower Haight along **The Wiggle**, a zigzagging path that dodges inclines on the way to Golden Gate Park. The 400ft *Duboce Bikeway Mural: Gateway to the Wiggle* welcomes riders to this bike highway, celebrating all of San Francisco's forms of carless transportation. Wind through the neighborhood's well-worn grooves, following green signs that guide your way to the park – from there, you can ride through the trees all the way to Ocean Beach. Rent from **Bay Wheels** (p31), San Francisco's official bike-share program with docking stations all over the city. A single ride gets you 30 minutes for $3.99, then $0.30 for every minute after; day passes are $15.

Psychedelic Poster Prints

MAP P213

SF's artistic soul at the Haight Street Art Center

Look for Jeremy Fish's bronze bunny-skull sculpture and enter a wonderland of psychedelia. The **Haight Street Art Center** *(haightstreetart.org; free)*, open from noon to 6pm Thursday through Sunday, is a nonprofit organization dedicated to silk-screened posters – San Francisco's signature art form. Visitors can glimpse posters in progress at the on-site screen-printing studio, plus jaw-dropping gallery shows: rooms plastered floor-to-ceiling in original retro-futurist glam-rock poster prints – think Bowie in metallic platforms, strutting straight out of a moon-age daydream. Gracing the stairwell is a hidden SF treasure: Reuben Kadish's 1937 WPA fresco *Dissertation on Alchemy*, surely the trippiest mural ever commissioned by the US government.

Party at Madrone Art Bar

MAP P208

Windows signs proclaim 'life without art is stupid'

San Franciscan artist Tom Marioni famously said 'drinking beer with friends is the highest form of art' – but at the Victorian parlor-art **Madrone Art Bar** *(madroneartbar.com)*,

BEST SHOPS FOR SEQUINS & STARDUST

Sword and Rose (Map p208): Candlelight glows onto tarot decks, and glass jars shimmer with ritually prepared, consecrated powder incense. Behind velvet curtains, practitioners do tarot, palmistry and astrology readings. Appointments are best, but you might snag a walk-in spot if the timing is right.

Piedmont Boutique (Map p208): The sign reads 'no playing in the boas' – gleefully ignored by drag stars, Burning Man costumers and people who take Halloween dead seriously (read: all SF). Since 1972, signature costume getups have been designed and sewn in the city.

The Love of Ganesha (Map p208): The prize jewel of crystal shops, carrying everything from amethyst to zircon. If you're lucky, the back meditation room will be open – recharge before hitting more Haight St shops.

EATING IN HAIGHT & HAYES VALLEY: VEGAN & VEGETARIAN

MAPS P208, P213

Rad Radish: A casual joint with a totally radical, plant-based menu that satisfies all munchies. *9am-8:30pm Mon-Thu, to 9pm Fri, 10am-8:30pm Sun, 10am-9pm Sat* $$

Om Sabor: Creative, eco-friendly spins on nostalgic faves for the vegetarians occasionally, secretly missing their meat-eating days. *5-10pm Wed-Sat, to 9pm Tue* $$

Stoa: Unexpected snacks at this cocktail bar – all are gluten- and dairy-free, from savory grilled mochi to strawberry empanadas. *4-10pm Mon-Thu, to midnight Fri & Sat* $$

DragonEats: The *bánh mì* at this vegan-friendly Vietnamese deli will make you roar – add jalapeños for a little fire in your breath. *11am-6pm Mon-Sat, to 5pm Sun* $

ADELE HEIDENREICH/SHUTTERSTOCK

Colorful street corner, Masonic Ave and Haight St

make it a Madroni (gin, Campari and Carpano). Enjoy boozy exhibitions of sculptures, murals and multimedia wonders, and join crowds grooving and bumping into the rotating art installations on Motown Mondays, Saturday global disco, and monthly indie-rock dance party Fringe, or Pop Life, when Prince/Michael Jackson mash-up parties bring all the freaks to the floor. Bring cash for drinks, tips and song requests.

Skate at the Church of 8 Wheels

MAP P208

Believe in the power of 'rolligion'

At the **Church of 8 Wheels** *(churchof8wheels.com; admission $18)*, worship begins with '80s music blaring from the pulpit and congregants skating backwards under a disco ball, its lights dancing across stained-glass windows. This church-turned-roller-rink is a hit for all ages, with family-friendly skate sessions from 5pm to 6:30pm on Fridays, 2:30pm to 6:30pm on Saturdays, and 6pm to 7:30pm on Sundays and Tuesdays. After that, the floor is for anyone 18 and up looking to get

EATING IN THE HAIGHT & HAYES VALLEY: UPSCALE DINING

MAP P213

Rich Table: Mind-bending dishes: porcini doughnuts, Dungeness crab latkes, and sea-urchin cacio e pepe. Book two to four weeks ahead. *5-10:30pm Tue-Sat* **$$$**

Zuni Cafe: Turning staples into gourmet go-tos since 1979: Caesar salad with house-cured anchovies, brick-oven-roasted chicken. *5-9:30pm Tue-Sun & 11am-3pm Fri-Sun* **$$$**

Nojo Ramen Tavern: Find clarity on foggy nights with eye-opening bowls of proper ramen. *5-9pm Mon-Thu, 11:30am-2:30pm & 5-9:30pm Fri & Sat, 4-8pm Sun* **$$$**

Dumpling Home: Casual, Michelin-approved spot that excels in soup dumplings – full of a variety of meats. *11:30am-2:15pm & 5-8:15pm Sun-Thu, to 8:45pm Fri & Sat* **$$$**

their skate groove on – at Goth nights, silent discos and Soul Roll Sundays. Check the calendar for theme nights and rent a pair of skates for just $5.

Hang Out at the Faight Collective

MAP P208

See what Faight has in store for you

Looking for an affordable yoga studio? A radically free craft workshop? Comedy show? Place to get a DIY thigh tat? At the crossroads of Fillmore and Haight, the aptly named **Faight Collective** *(thefaight.com)* is the ultimate third place. The street-level Upper Faight serves as a retail space, featuring work from local makers. Take home the scents of the city with hand-poured zip-code candles, or don a stenciled jean jacket that dares you to 'break fake rules.' Downstairs, Lower Faight is an events space with an unpredictable lineup. Morning Vinyasa yoga flows into afternoon 'Bad Art Club' workshops. By evening, the space transforms into a carnival of open mics, live music sets, and something called 'collective envisioning.'

Breathe In, Breathe Out

MAP P213

Meditate at the SF Zen Center

This Italianate brick landmark that rises from a sea of Victorian flats in Hayes Valley has sheltered people of all faiths. In 1922, Julia Morgan, the first woman to be licensed as an architect in California and designer of famed Hearst Castle, designed this to be the Emanu-El Sisterhood, a residence for low-income Jewish women – note the ironwork Stars of David on the 1st-floor loggia. Today, it's the **San Francisco Zen Center** *(sfzc.org; free)*, home to the largest Buddhist community outside of Asia since 1969.

Watch the sunlight fill the Zendo during free morning zazen, every day at 5:25am. Other programs are available on a semi-regular basis – check the calendar for half-day meditations in the lush garden courtyard and fun evening workshops blending the art of breathwork and beatboxing. Every other Thursday at 7pm is Trans Sangha, a meditation group by and for the trans community; beginners and newcomers are always welcome.

BEST LOCAL BRANDS

Upper Playground (Map p208): Blend into SF scenery with a locally designed 'Golden State of Mind' hoodie, tectonic-plate map tee, and snap-back cap featuring the elusive Golden Gate Park coyote by SF's own Jeremy Fish.

FTC Skateboarding (Map p208): Big air and big style at this SF skateboard outfitter – rock the SF look with 'For the City' chore jackets and caps, and show insider flair as you grab air with decks designed by local guest artists.

Marine Layer (Map p213): Get California cool without getting shivers in 'absurdly soft' tees, which this clever SF company makes by blending cotton and recycled beechwood yarn. Add a 'shacket' (heavyweight flannel overshirt) or canvas chore coat for chilly Ocean Beach bonfires.

DRINKING IN THE HAIGHT & HAYES VALLEY: WINE BARS

MAPS P208, P213

Hôtel Biron: Duck into the alley to this walk-in wine closet, with vintages, and just a few tables for two. *5pm-midnight Wed-Sat, 5pm-10pm Sun, to 11pm Mon & Tue*

Uva Enoteca: Servers dole out sound advice and top-notch Soave by the taste or carafe. *5:30-9pm Mon-Thu, to 9:30pm Fri & Sat, to 8:30pm Sun*

Birba: New and old world wines at this timeless garden spot with daily 'cheeky hour' plus aperitivos and $9 wines. *3-9pm Mon-Fri, 1-9pm Sat, 1-8pm Sun*

Millay: A vibey spot with an expansive selection of sake, organic wines and Japanese snacks. *5pm-midnight Fri, from 3pm Sat, 3-8pm Sun, 5-10pm Mon, Wed & Thu*

GEEK OUT IN SAN FRANCISCO

Shop at the neighborhood's coolest stores for geek culture.

Isotope (Map p213): At this comic-book lounge, flip through superhero serials, eye the toilet seats signed by famous illustrators, then head upstairs to relax on comfy leather sofas with local graphic novelists, some of whom lead workshops here. Don't miss signings and free-comic-book days.

Gamescape (Map p208): Since 1985, this has been the city's tabletop gaming headquarters. Find award-winning Eurogames, local-designed cooperatives and hobby gaming supplies – and hang around the back tables for indie board games nights and card tournaments.

Comix Experience (Map p208): Tiny neighborhood shop with comic book deep cuts, signed first editions and kid-friendly graphic novels. Join the club to get the best graphic novel of the month at your doorstep.

Find Bliss at SFJAZZ

MAP P213

Catch a show at the world's premier jazz venue

Jazz legends and singular talents from Argentina to Yemen are showcased at the **SFJAZZ Center** *(sfjazz.org; tickets $35–105)*, America's largest jazz center. Enjoy brilliant sound in Miner Auditorium, where the stage is regularly stormed by soul icon Mavis Staples, punk poet Laurie Anderson and Tony-winning dancer Savion Glover. Jazz-themed cocktails are served on the balcony, and you can take them with you to your seat – even upper-tier bargain seats have drink holders (and clear stage views). Hear fresh takes on classic jazz albums and poets riffing with combos in the downstairs Joe Henderson Lab. Test your knowledge of jazz history against stunning tiled murals composed of influential jazz venues across the country.

Hayes Valley Town Square

MAP P213

The utopia of Patricia's Green and PROXY

After the 1989 earthquake damaged freeway ramps, San Francisco voters nixed the cement skies of a freeway overpass in favor of a walkable community hub. At **Patricia's Green**, a hip pocket-park featuring Burning Man–inspired sculpture installations, kids scramble up the dome-shaped playground, and in the evenings after a few rounds, adventurous adults take a turn too – especially when neighbors envelop the play structure in a glowing 'sensory tent' filled with dry ice and light shows. On Hayes St, San Franciscans are envisioning

MATTHEW KIERNAN/ALAMY

SFJAZZ Center

a car-free utopia: Fridays and Saturdays until 10pm, it's a pedestrianized extension of the park – grab a partner to do-si-do at free line-dancing lessons, available some evenings.

At the eastern end is **PROXY**, a hamlet of upcycled shipping containers. Graze your way across gourmet attractions: the shipping-container outpost of Mission roastery Ritual Coffee offers creamy single-origin espresso and at San Francisco's Hometown Creamery, indecisive orderers get an ice-cream flight of five farm-to-cone seasonal flavors. Lines stretch down the block at Biergarten – wear sunblock, order two rounds of seasonal Fort Point brews at once, and get the pickled deviled eggs to share with newfound friends at communal picnic tables. Spring through fall, free Friday-night 'bike-in' movies are shown on the outdoor projector, screening recent award-winning animations and indie foreign flicks – layer up to stay warm and snag a roll of green turf to lounge on.

GIRLS' NIGHT OUT

Emely Baisa is a writer and native San Franciscan who loves a night out with friends. Here are her suggestions for places to go with your girls.

Na Ya Dessert Cafe (Map p213): Order different things and share with your friends – Mango Tango (sticky rice with milky bingsu shaved ice), Kaya Toasted (nutty pandan sauce on thick bread), and Black Thai Tea Crepe.

Arbor (Map p213): This is a great spot to chat and catch up – get yourself some seasoned curly fries and sit out on the spacious, tree-lined patio for a casual evening out. You might encounter a squirrel or two. It's a vibe.

San Francisco Ballet (Map p213): Get all dressed up and catch a show at this beautiful theater with an eclectic repertoire and a lot of history.

Researched by
Alison Bing

GOLDEN GATE PARK & THE AVENUES

WELCOME TO SF'S WILD WEST

Bison roam, penguins waddle, hippies drum and surfers rip along San Francisco's most outlandish stretch of scenery.

Hard-core surfers and gourmet adventurers meet in the foggy avenues around Golden Gate Park. Between the Richmond and Sunset districts, this is one chill global village. In the residential avenues that cover 50-odd (occasionally very odd) blocks from Stanyan St to Ocean Beach, you'll find Korean BBQ, Gaelic jam sessions, French pastries and Hong Kong movie matinees. South of Golden Gate Park are candy-colored Sunset District homes, mom-and-pop restaurants on Irving St, and surf hangouts around Judah and 45th. North of the park are indie boutiques and cinemas, plus some of SF's best bakeries, bars and affordable dining.

INCLUDES

Above: Sutro Baths (p235); Right: de Young Museum (p224)

Presidio of San Francisco
1
Pacific Ocean
Lincoln Park
SEA CLIFF
California St
Lands End 4
Point Lobos Ave
Geary Blvd
25th Ave
THE RICHMOND
Park Presidio Blvd
Geary Blvd
Sutro Heights Park
Balboa St
Fulton St
de Young Museum 2
3 California Academy of Sciences
1 Golden Gate Park
Crossover Dr
Ocean Beach 5
Great Hwy
Lincoln Way
Upper Great Hwy
Sunset Blvd
THE SUNSET
19th Ave
7th Ave
0 1 km
0 0.5 miles

Highlights

❶ Golden Gate Park

Have fun at SF's wild streak: stroll, bike, Lindy-Hop and roller-boogie through the park, and race bison. **p224**

❷ de Young Museum

Follow Andy Goldsworthy's sidewalk fault lines to discover groundbreaking global art. **p224**

❸ California Academy of Sciences

Enjoy sunsets on the roof and wild nights at kids-only sleepovers and 21-plus NightLife events. **p226**

❹ Lands End

Glimpse seals, sunsets and shipwrecks along San Francisco's wild waterfront walk. **p233**

❺ Ocean Beach & Sunset Dunes

Numb your toes in the Pacific, then warm up at bonfires in artist-designed firepits. **p234**

Getting Around

Walk & Bicycle

Paved paths and off-road trails criss-cross 48-block-long Golden Gate Park for mellow strolls and epic hikes. Hire a bike inside the park at Parkwide Bike and Surrey, near the Japanese Tea Garden.

Bus

Buses 1, 31 and 38 run from downtown through the Richmond; 7 and 6 go from Downtown to the Sunset. Buses 5 and 21 skirt the north of Golden Gate Park; buses 28, 29 and 44 cut across the park. Bus 2 covers Clement St; 33 connects to the Haight, Castro and Mission.

Streetcar

The N line runs from Downtown through the Sunset to Ocean Beach.

EDDIE-HERNANDEZ.COM/SHUTTERSTOCK

Hardly Strictly Bluegrass

TOP EXPERIENCE

Golden Gate Park

When San Franciscans refer to 'the park,' there's only one that gets the definite article: Golden Gate Park. Everything SF holds dear is here: free spirits and free music, butterfly domes and underground art, tiny, chatty penguins and hushed redwood groves, tenacious bonsai and massive, mellow bison. Landmark venues celebrating nature, music, art and science are dotted across the park's 1017 acres.

DON'T MISS

- de Young Museum
- San Francisco Botanical Garden
- California Academy of Sciences
- Conservatory of Flowers
- National AIDS Memorial Grove
- Blue Heron Lake

Art in the Park

The oxidized-copper building by Swiss architects Herzog & de Meuron (of Tate Modern fame) may keep a low profile, but there's no denying the park's all-star art attraction: the **de Young Museum** (*famsf.org; adult/youth $20/free*). The cross-cultural collection spans genres and borders: main-floor exhibits range from Inuit carvings to California prison photography; upstairs features **Oceanic collection** carvings and 11,000-plus **textile collection**; and blockbuster basement retrospectives range from surrealist Frida Kahlo to photographer Ansel Adams. Crowd-favorite events here include the

PRACTICALITIES

● sfrecpark.org ● free ● 24h

de Young Open showcase of local talent, Saturday drag story hour, and the annual Bouquets to Art, featuring art-inspired floral arrangements. For park panoramas, take the elevator up the 144ft **observation tower** – or cloudwatch in **James Turrell's Skyspace** installation, hidden under **Osher Sculpture Garden**. Access is free to the tower and store; ticket includes free same-day entry to the Legion of Honor.

Inspired? City-supported nonprofit **Sharon Art Studio** offers workshops to create your own masterpieces (ages 18-plus; one- to three-day workshops $150–350), and **Out There Watercolors** offers guided outdoor-painting expeditions to capture park scenery and SF landmarks in your own style (*outtherewatercolors.com; $120/hr up to four people, ages 12-plus*).

Park Music Events

Golden Gate Park has hosted epic festivals ever since the 1967 Human Be-In urged free spirits to 'tune in, turn on, drop out.' Dig the vibes year-round at free **Music Concourse** shows, weekend **Hippie Hill** drum circles, and free annual **420 Festival** (*420hippiehill.com*), named after International Bong Hit Time (4:20pm).

Mega-festivals are held around the **Polo Fields** – notably free **Hardly Strictly Bluegrass** (*hardlystrictlybluegrass.com; first weekend in October*) and alt-Coachella fest **Outside Lands** (*sfoutsidelands.com; one-/three-day pass $235/539; first weekend in August*). The West goes wild over three days of Hardly Strictly Bluegrass free shows by 75-plus bands across six stages – headliners have included bluegrass legends like Emmylou Harris and Tanya Tucker, singer/songwriters sich as Elvis Costello and Rickie Lee Jones, and musical rebels like Meat Puppets and Patti Smith. Score Outside Lands tickets the minute they go on sale mid-May to attend the music festival *Billboard* named America's best, featuring marquee acts that range from pop (Doja Cat, Tyler the Creator) to artsy (Lorde, Beck) to legendary (A Tribe Called Quest, Big Freedia).

Natural Wonders

SF's mile-wide, 3-mile-long wild streak starts with the elegant **Conservatory of Flowers** (*gggp.org; adult/youth/senior & child $17/7/3*), where flower power thrives in a restored 1878 greenhouse full of outer-space orchids, serene lilies and creepy carnivorous plants. Check the website for light shows, holiday and art events; combined tickets offer same-day admission to San Francisco Botanical Garden and **Japanese Tea Garden** (*p227; adult/youth/senior & child $33/21/9*). Next to the Conservatory, tiny but fierce **Dahlia Garden** (*dahliadell.org; free*) is spikier than an SF mosh pit from August to September, with in-your-face neon blooms cultivated by SF's hardcore dahlia fans.

There's always something blooming in the 55-acre **San Francisco Botanical Garden** (*gggp.org; adult/youth/senior & child $17/7/3*), which covers a world of vegetation from South African savanna to New Zealand cloud forest. The year-round

ROMANCE ALERT

Though a local newspaper once cautioned that Golden Gate Park's scenic benches led to 'excess hugging,' San Franciscans have flocked to the park since its inception. On a single sunny day in 1886, almost a fifth of the city's entire population made the trip to the park – canoodling shamelessly, no doubt.

TOP TIPS

- John F Kennedy Dr is pedestrian-only starting at 9th Ave – a weekend hotspot with roller disco and free Lindy Hop dance lessons.
- To plan a picnic, protest or concert at Golden Gate Park, check in at **McLaren Lodge** at the park's eastern entrance, under the splendid Monterey cypress that's the city's official tree.
- Volunteer docents lead free tours covering park history; for times, see sfcityguides.org.

HOW THE PARK PERSEVERED

This urban-garden dreamscape seems far-fetched now, but it was considered impossible when backed by San Franciscan voters in 1866. New York's Central Park architect Frederick Law Olmsted balked at transforming 1017 acres of dunes into the world's largest developed park – so plans fell to tenacious civil engineer William Hammond Hall. He insisted that instead of planned casinos, racetracks and a plaster igloo village, Golden Gate Park should showcase – here's a radical idea – nature.

Garden of Fragrance is designed to appeal to the visually impaired, rare Asian magnolias blossom in winter, and the California native-plant section bursts into wildflowers in spring off the redwood trail. In spring and fall, pianos pop up amid the flowers: welcome to **Flower Piano** (*gggp.org/flowerpiano*), where professional musicians serenade global flora with music from around the world. Romance awaits across the street at the secluded **Shakespeare Garden**, where sonnets dot flower beds containing 200-plus flowering plants mentioned in Shakespeare's writings – an SF favorite spot for smooches and proposals.

Just when you thought SF couldn't get any wilder, blue butterflies alight on your shoulders in the **Osher Rainforest Dome**, starfish wave hellos in **Steinhart Aquarium** and penguins waddle your way in the **African Hall**. The **California Academy of Sciences** (*calacademy.org; adult/child $49–55/45–49*) has championed weird, wild science since 1853, and acclaimed architect Renzo Piano's 2008 remodel brought thousands of live animals and 60 research scientists under a 2.5-acre **wildflower-covered roof**. Night owls party on at 21-plus Thursday **NightLife** events (*$25; 6-10pm*), featuring themed cocktails and time-traveling **Planetarium** shows. Kids may not technically sleep during **Academy Sleepovers**, but they might jump-start promising careers as scientists (see website for upcoming dates and prices).

At the park's wild western edge, the **Buffalo Paddock** has been Golden Gate Park's home where the buffalo roam since 1889 – though technically, they're bison. SF's mellow, well-fed

BENJAMIN HEATH FOR LONELY PLANET

Conservatory of Flowers (p225)

herd rarely moves – but when their tails point upward, you may be about to witness bison bucking.

Meditative Moments

Since 1894, 5-acre **Japanese Tea Garden** (*gggp.org; adult/youth/senior & child $15/7/3; first hour free*) has blushed pink with cherry blossoms in spring and turned flaming red with maple leaves in fall. Don't miss the meditative **Zen Garden** and **Tea House** fortune cookies (introduced right here). For peaceful reflection ringed by redwoods and paving-stone tributes, step into **National AIDS Memorial Grove** – founded in 1991 to commemorate millions of lives lost to the AIDS epidemic, and to strengthen national resolve for compassionate care and a lasting cure. Visits to this valley are always moving, but especially on World AIDS Day (*Dec 1*) and volunteer work days (*8:30am to 12:30pm third Saturday of the month, March to October*). At **Breast Cancer Memorial Garden** *(sfrecpark.org)* off Conservatory Drive, the secluded hilltop is ringed with benches and often strewn with flowers. Behind the park's baseball diamond in **Monarch Bear Grove**, you'll notice offerings left on Druid altars, made from the ruins of a Spanish monastery bought and abandoned by William Randolph Hearst.

Playtime in the Park

The park is packed with adventures for kids. In good weather, pedal boats and rowboats are available at restored 1946 **Blue Heron Boathouse** *(blueheronboathouse.com; row/pedal boars $26/32.50)* – or just glimpse waterfalls, picnic in pagodas and feed ducks along the shores of **Strawberry Hill**. For thrilling weekend boat races, **San Francisco Model Yacht Club** *(sfmyc.org; free)* hosts remote-controlled mini-yacht races across Spreckels Lake – turtles snoozing onshore seem unfazed by the competition. Since blockbusters like *The Avengers* and *Brave* revived San Francisco's Victorian-era archery craze, certified coaches with nonprofit **Golden Gate Junior Olympic Archery Division** *(JOAD; goldengatejoad.com)* offer traditional archery classes for adults and kids (*age 8-plus with guardian consent; lesson $35*). Over 150 years, kids have flocked to the park's lovely, historic **children's playground** to ride the vintage 1912 carousel *(ride adult/child $2.50/1)*, scoot down 1970s concrete slides and scale the climbing wall.

TINY TREES WITH DEEP ROOTS

The Japanese Tea Garden's century-old bonsai grove was cultivated for decades by landscape architect Makoto Hagiwara and his family, until they were forced to leave for WWII Japanese American incarceration camps. After the war, the Hagiwaras discovered their prized evergreens had been sold by profiteers, and they spent decades rebuilding their mighty miniature forest. Today you'll find tiny evergreens in the Tea Garden, near the road now called Hagiwara Dr.

HIGHLIGHTS
1 California Academy of Sciences
2 de Young Museum
3 Golden Gate Park
4 Lands End
5 Ocean Beach

SIGHTS
6 Buffalo Paddock
7 Conservatory of Flowers
8 Dahlia Garden
9 Japanese Tea Garden
10 Legion of Honor
11 Lincoln Park
12 National AIDS Memorial Grove
13 San Francisco Botanical Garden
14 Shakespeare Garden
15 Sutro Baths

ACTIVITIES
16 Aqua Surf Shop
17 Blue Heron Boathouse
18 Children's Playground
19 Coastal Trail
20 Golden Gate Junior Olympic Archery Division (JOAD)
21 Out There Watercolors
22 San Francisco Model Yacht Club
23 Sharon Art Studio

EATING
24 Arsicault Bakery
25 Aziza
26 Bettola
27 Breadbelly
28 Chapeau
29 Cinderella Russian Bakery
30 Day Moon Bread
31 Dragon Beaux

32 Han Il Kwan
33 Hook Fish Co
34 Mamahuhu
35 Manna
36 Mini Potstickers
37 Taqueria Los Mayas
38 Thanh Long
39 The Laundromat

DRINKING & NIGHTLIFE
40 Beach Chalet
41 High Treason
42 Judahlicious Vegan Cafe
43 Palm City Wines
44 Plough & Stars
45 Tommy's Mexican Restaurant
46 Violet's Tavern
47 Woods Outbound

ENTERTAINMENT
48 Balboa Theatre
49 Four Star Theater

SHOPPING
50 Case for Making
51 Foggy Notion
52 Green Apple Books
53 Love Street Vintage
54 Mollusk
55 Park Life

INFORMATION
56 McLaren Lodge

The Sunset

The Sunset District is mostly foggy and residential, with pockets of home-style restaurants and cafes along Irving around 9th Ave and 22nd Ave. Beachcombers hang with surfers along Judah St in the Outer Sunset (19th Ave to Sunset Dunes).

Explore the Sunset Surf Scene

Stay dry or get wet with Sunset surfers

Watching Ocean Beach surfers brave gnarly Pacific riptides may leave you with questions, namely: why do they do this, and can I? Dip your toe into SF surf culture at **Mollusk**, where a geodesic-dome tugboat marks the spot where ocean meets art. Legendary shapers (surfboard makers) create limited-edition boards for Mollusk, and the back gallery showcases Thomas Campbell ocean collages and other works by SF surfer-artists. Surfers browse wetsuits, back issues of the *Surfer's Journal*, and the latest edition of the *Surfing Guide to California* – while kooks (newbies) try on Mollusk's signature hoodies and 'kelp bed cruiser, wave peruser' T-shirts.

Ready to hit the waves? Most SF surfers get their start in protected coves, like East Beach (p60) at Crissy Field. But when you're ready to earn Sunset surf cred the hardcore way, check out the rental surf gear and surf lessons offered at **Aqua Surf Shop** *(aquasurfshop.com; lessons $120–150; rental per day bodyboard/wetsuit $10/15, surfboard $25–35)*. Ocean Beach currents are challenging even for experienced surfers, so Aqua only offers rentals when conditions are safe. For instant cool without getting wet, check out Aqua skateboards and signature merch.

DRINKING IN THE SUNSET: HOT & COLD

Andytown Coffee: Go early for a Snowy Plover – double-shot of espresso (or *matcha*) with bubbly water, ice and whipped cream – plus Irish soda bread baked on-site. *7am-5pm*

Woods Outbound: Microbrews with unexpected ingredients – hibiscus, yerba mate, cocoa nibs – and Norcal beer/wine, from Albariño blonde to Merlot red ale. *4-10pm Mon-Fri, noon-11pm Sat, 1-8pm Sun*

Palm City Wines: Sunny corner serving wine with hearty hoagies – think skin-contact Ribolla Gialla with shrimp-salad hoagies – plus hot-dish specials on corkage-free Monday/Tuesday. *4-10pm Mon & Tue, noon-9pm Wed-Sun*

Judahlicious Vegan Cafe: Made-to-order organic smoothies like the N-Line (banana, pineapple mango, coconut) plus organic fair-trade coffee, yerba mate, and vegan house chili. *9am-5pm*

SABRINA DALBESIO/LONELY PLANET

Mollusk

See Flower Power in Action at Fort Funston

Get bird's eye views at SF's peaceful coastal park

Grassy dunes up to 200ft high at **Fort Funston** *(parksconservancy.org; free)* give an idea of what the Sunset District looked like until the 20th century. Flower power is taking over this defunct military installation, now a peaceful national park – you'll notice moss growing on 146-ton WWII guns aimed seaward and wildflowers along abandoned Nike missile silos near the parking lot. Nuclear missiles were never launched from Fort Funston silos, which are now used as hang-gliding jump sites.

Today butterflies and shorebirds flock to this peaceful park, now part of the **Golden Gate National Recreation Area**. Bring binoculars to spot tiny, endangered bank swallows nesting here March to July, diligently drilling holes deep into sandstone cliffs for safety. The National Park Service is gradually replacing invasive ice plants with native vegetation, and volunteers are welcome to join habitat restoration efforts at the **Fort Funston Native Plant Nursery** (see website for details).

For an easy, scenic, one-hour hike, take **Sunset Trail** down to the beach and back (1.5 miles). Bring the family – trail and

FREE CONCERTS IN THE PARK

Hear that echo across Golden Gate Park? It's probably a concert – and quite possibly a free one. Opera divas, indie acts, bluegrass greats and hip-hop heavies take turns rocking SF gratis, from the often wintry days of June through golden November afternoons.

Most major shows and festivals are held in **Sharon Meadow** or **Polo Fields** on weekends; for upcoming events, consult the park calendar at sfrecpark.org.

Free, all-ages outdoor concerts are held three times a week from March through November at **Golden Gate Park's Music Concourse Bandshell**, located between the de Young Museum and Academy of Sciences. Fridays are musical happy hours, Sundays bring reggae acts, and Wednesdays feature singer/songwriters; for specific listings, see *sfrecpark.org/1570/Golden-Gate-Bandshell-Concerts*.

EATING IN THE SUNSET: TASTE SENSATIONS

Thanh Long: Classic crab – roasted or 'drunken' (Chardonnay-simmered) – with signature garlic noodles and An family welcomes. *4:30-8pm Sun & Wed-Thu, to 9pm Fri & Sat* $$

Hook Fish Co: Join local surfers at outdoor tables for fresh, sustainable Pacific seafood in tacos or burritos, atop salads, or fish and chips. *11:30am-9pm* $

Mini Potstickers: Dumpling experts pan-fry or steam mini-dumplings, including wagyu beef and tasty vegetarian options. *10:30am-3pm & 5-8:30pm Mon-Fri, 10:30am-8:30pm Sat & Sun* $

Manna: Home-style Korean cooking, including kimchi pancakes, *kalbi* (barbecue short ribs) and *dol-sot bibimbap* (sizzling stone-pot rice). *11am-9:30pm Tue-Sun* $

PAULAAH293/SHUTTERSTOCK

Stern Grove Festival

hang-glider launch areas are wheelchair and stroller accessible, and dogs are allowed off the leash in many areas. For a longer hike, pick up the **Coastal Trail** here and head north toward Sunset Dunes, Ocean Beach and Lands End beyond. The park entrance is on your right off Skyline Blvd, past Lake Merced.

COASTAL TRAIL SHORTCUT

When it's windy on Ocean Beach, skip the 1.5-mile stretch of Costal Trail from Fort Funston, and pick up the trail near **Sutro Baths** (p235) ruins instead. From here, head around **Lands End** (see right) for pine-framed Pacific views and glorious glimpses of the **Golden Gate Bridge** (p56).

Catch the Stern Grove Festival

See headliners for free in SF's urban dell

In the suburban stretches of the Outer Sunset, only one sight is more unexpectedly delightful than the shaggy redwood and eucalyptus trees of Stern Grove: your all-time favorite band rocking the grove for free on a summer Sunday. The oldest free, nonprofit music festival in the US has kept the lineup fresh and unpredictable since 1938, spanning generations and musical genres – headliners here have included Sleater-Kinney, Diana Ross, Tegan & Sara, Digable Planets, Janelle Monáe, X, and SF's own Michael Franti & Spearhead. Expect the unexpected, including pop-up guests and SF Symphony's cross-genre collabs, ranging from Lettuce funk band to ukelele player Taimane.

To keep **Stern Grove Festival** *(sterngrove.org; free)* show attendance to the maximum 10,000 capacity, tickets are available by online lottery: six weeks before the show, tickets are released, and you've got a week to request up to four tickets. Then winners are notified, and have 72 hours to claim their tickets before they're given away to other lucky fans.

The Richmond

In the 1890s, SF's public railway offered downtown tenement-dwellers escapes to Ocean Beach – some stayed. Today the Richmond District lures visitors with scenic coastal hikes, sensational restaurants and bakeries, hidden art treasures, and neighborhood cinemas.

Mingle with Masterpieces at Legion of Honor

Look inside SF's monumental treasure box

A museum as eccentric and illuminating as San Francisco itself, the **Legion of Honor** *(famsf.org; adult/youth $20/free)* is a monumental gift to the city from 'Big Alma' de Bretteville Spreckels, San Francisco's larger-than-life sculptor's model turned philanthropist. Today the Legion's eclectic collection of art treasures ranges from ancient to modern – including Monet water lilies and John Cage soundscapes upstairs, and ancient cuneiform tablets and Enrique Chagoya's time-traveling, border-crossing Mayan codex downstairs.

Throughout the museum, you'll notice contemporary artworks interacting with classic masterpieces, from Impressionist paintings to priceless porcelain. Each year, the Legion invites contemporary artists to engage with the priceless permanent collection, to provocative effect – Wangechi Mutu positioned her bronze *Shavasana* sculpture of two Black women lying down in the long shadow of Rodin's monumental *The Thinker*. The centerpiece of 'Big Alma's' legacy is Rodin's *The Kiss* – but at 4pm on Saturdays, **pipe-organ recitals** steal the show in the **Rodin Gallery**.

Downstairs, blockbuster shows range from from Guo Pei's fantasy couture to Picasso's sketchbooks, alongside selections from the **Achenbach Collection**'s 90,000 works on paper, from Rembrandt to Ruth Asawa. Entry to the downstairs **museum cafe** and store is free, and entry to the permanent collection is free after 4:30pm; tickets cover free same-day entry to the de Young Museum.

THANKS, BIG ALMA

Legions of art fans owe thanks to 'Big Alma' de Bretteville Spreckels, the nude sculptor's model who changed the art world.

In 1902, she publicly sued the gold miner who deflowered and dumped her for breach of promise – and won. Then Big Alma volunteered to model for Union Sq's Goddess of Victory monument, towering triumphantly with a cast-in-bronze wardrobe malfunction.

The statue-selection-committee chair was sugar baron Adolph Spreckels, who became Big Alma's 'sugar daddy' and left her his fortune.

Big Alma raised funds to rebuild post-earthquake SF, investigated working conditions for women for the US Department of Labor, and donated the Legion and Maritime Museum to her beloved San Francisco.

Hike to Lands End

Wander along the edge of the continent

Looking out from **Lands End** *(nps.gov)* at the wild, endless Pacific, you'll realize that ancient mapmakers had a point – if ever there were a place for mermaids, monsters and magic, this is it. Trails through this rugged landscape reward you with glimpses of shipwrecks, sea lions and the Golden Gate Bridge (p56). At low tide, follow the steep path past the ruins

TOP EXPERIENCE

Ocean Beach & Sunset Dunes

At this blustery city beach, the marine layer often swallows the sun before it sets in the Pacific. But fog doesn't keep hardy beachcombers, power-walkers and determined sandcastle architects away from this vast, serene stretch of pale golden sand. Standing at the water's edge, you can watch the Pacific ebb and flow as it always does, with only few brave surfers to remind you what century you're in.

ARTUR DEBAT/GETTY IMAGES

Ocean Beach

Ocean Beach

SF's 3.5-mile **Ocean Beach** isn't like most California scenes in Hollywood movies – this moody, misty setting is better suited to meditative solo strolls or bonding walks with friends. Here at the original Burning Man site, bonfires are allowed in artist-designed firepits March to October until 9:30pm. Swimmers, beware riptides; beachcombers, mind sneaker waves. Face the Pacific and spot brave surfers, passing ships, and sea lions bobbing in the waves.

Sunset Dunes

At the southern end of Ocean Beach is a 50-acre waterfront park called **Sunset Dunes**. By popular vote in 2024, San Francisco converted a section of highway to park trails for joggers, cyclists, skaters and walkers to enjoy. Stick to paths in areas undergoing habitat restoration, and keep dogs on a leash to protect wildlife. The dunes offer shelter for birdwatching – including skittish snowy plover shorebirds in winter – plus picnics and outdoor-painting expeditions with **Out There Watercolors** (p225). To paint the sunset, pick up art supplies at nearby **Case for Making**, where artisans make pigments specifically to capture subtle Pacific hues.

TOP TIPS

- Take a break for food, drink, bathrooms and inspiration at the **Beach Chalet**, with splendid 1930s frescoes that celebrate the building of Golden Gate Park.
- Get costumes for **Bay to Breakers** *(baytobreakers.com)*, a truly fun 7.5-mile run from the Embarcadero to Ocean Beach – joggers dressed as salmon run upstream.

PRACTICALITIES

● parksconservancy.org
● free ● 24h; parking lot closes at 10pm

of **Sutro Baths** and through the sea-cave tunnel to sublime Pacific panoramas.

Above the baths, you'll find the **Lands End Lookout** visitor center and **Sutro Heights Park** public gardens, built in 1885 and splendidly restored with native plants. From the Lookout, the **Coastal Trail** winds along Lands End bluffs, offering end-of-the-world views and low-tide sightings of coastal shipwrecks along the way to **Lincoln Park** *(sfrecpark.org)*. America's legendary coast-to-coast Lincoln Hwy officially ends at this 100-acre park, which served as San Francisco's cemetery until 1909. At Lincoln Park, you can duck into the Legion of Honor (p233) or descend the gloriously tiled Lincoln Park Steps (near 32nd Ave). If you've got energy to burn, push onward through the Presidio to reach the Golden Gate Bridge – or book in advance for a round at scenic **Lincoln Park Golf Course** *(lincolnparkgolfcourse.com; SF nonresident weekday/weekend $54/61)*.

See Global Films in Community Cinemas

Ditch chilly beaches for cozy movies

Sunny downtown mornings promise perfect Ocean Beach days – until the marine layer makes landfall, raising goosebumps and abruptly ending grand sandcastle plans. SF's Richmond District has a name for this foggy phenomenon: movie days. The nonprofit San Francisco Neighborhood Theater Foundation has refurbished and reinvented two historic Richmond cinemas to keep the movie magic coming.

First stop Cannes; next stop, the 1926 deco cinema at Balboa and 37th. Community-supported, nonprofit **Balboa Theater** *(balboamovies.com; tickets $12.50–20)* screens first-run movie premieres alongside international film-fest favorites, silver-screen classics, live comedy nights, and audience-participation cult hits like *Rocky Horror Picture Show*.

Before Ang Lee, Wayne Wang, John Woo and Wong Kar-wai hit multiplex marquees, they brought down the house in the cozy screening room of the **Four Star Theater** *(4-star-movies.com; tickets $0–20)*. Screening films since 1964, this nonprofit neighborhood cinema now features international film-festival favorites, vintage classics and Japanese anime, plus special movie screenings with live music, and free family favorites at 10am on weekends. Take a memento home with you from on-site **Tunnel Records**, a lobby lined with vintage vinyl,

WHAT HAPPENED TO SUTRO BATHS?

Hard to imagine from these ruins, but Victorian dandies and working stiffs took bracing baths in woolen rental swimsuits here.

Millionaire Adolph Sutro opened indoor pools in 1896 to 10,000 bathers – but in 1897, bouncers denied Black San Franciscan John Harris entry. He sued Sutro and won a landmark case desegregating community facilities.

To lure crowds, Sutro added trapezes, ice rinks and wildly popular Egyptian mummies. Then came two world wars and the Great Depression, de-funding public railways to the baths.

The baths went bust in 1952, and in 1964, developers started razing them for high-rise condos – public uproar ensued. An arsonist burned the remaining buildings in 1966. The ruined baths remain iconic, providing a backdrop for 1971 comedy classic *Harold & Maude*.

EATING IN THE RICHMOND: DINNER

Aziza: Cal-Moroccan dishes – salmon tagine, braised lamb shakshuka, flaky *bastilla* chicken confit – and elegant cocktails/mocktails. *5-9:30pm Wed-Sun, brunch 10:30am-2pm Sat & Sun* $$$

Mamahuhu: Fresh takes on nostalgic Chinese-American classics, with sustainable seasonal ingredients – Niman Ranch beef and broccoli, sweet-and-sour cauli, shiitake-mushroom mapo tofu. *11:30am-9pm* $

Chapeau: Every diner is treated like an *ami* at this family-owned French bistro, where well-priced tasting menus ($50 to $92) feature classics like onion soup, duck cassoulet and coq au vin. *5-9pm Wed-Sun* $$$

The Laundromat: The only thing you'll clean here is your plate – memorable square pizzas include margherita with vodka sauce and crispy Brussels sprouts with creamy goat cheese. *8am-2pm & 5-9pm Wed-Sun* $

PAULAAH293/SHUTTERSTOCK

Foggy Notion

mint-condition movie posters, and SF concert handbills – sorry, the flyer for the Dead Kennedy's benefit concert for Jello Biafra's 1979 mayoral run isn't for sale.

Shop Indie Boutiques

Score only-in-SF finds

You can't take Golden Gate Park home with you – the city would seem naked without it – but **Foggy Notion** *(foggy-notion.com)* specializes in sense memories of SF's urban wilderness. The artisan gift selection includes Wild Yonder's 'anti-bad-vibes' bath soak, redwood-printed organic cotton Replant socks whose proceeds help reforest California, and one of the largest candle selections in the city – including a Clement Street–scented candle.

EATING IN THE RICHMOND: LUNCH

Taqueria Los Mayas: Adios, tacos: *Los Mayas panuchos* (bean-filled tortillas) come piled with Yucatecan *cochinita pibill* (tangy barbecued pork) or *poc-chuc* grilled pork, pickled onions, slaw and sensational salsas. *11am-9pm* $

Dragon Beaux: Hong Kong meets Vegas at San Francisco's decadent Cantonese restaurant, featuring succulent duck, five-flavor soup dumplings, crab congee and premium teas. *11am-3pm & 5-9pm Mon-Fri, from 10am Sat & Sun* $$

Bettola: Your friendly neighborhood *tavola calda* (hot table) dishes proper lasagna, prosciutto-loaded white pizza, and brined rotisserie chicken with Italian wine by the glass or carafe. *11am-9pm* $

Han Il Kwan: Join surfers and grandmas for epic lunch specials: multiple *banchan* (side dishes), sizzling platters of marinated meats, stone bowls brimming with bibimbap. *11am-8pm Sun & Mon, to 9pm Thu-Sat* $

To pull together looks that say 'I'm with the band' for park festivals like Outside Lands and Hardly Strictly Bluegrass, head directly to **Love Street Vintage** *(lovestreetsf.com)*. This is rare, real-deal vintage at fantastic prices, from psychedelic '60s aloha shirts to embroidered maxi dresses and chunky silver bracelets handmade by hippies.

Like a multitool of cool, **Park Life** *(parklifestore.com)* is design store, indie publisher, art gallery, and HQ for the SF Art Book Fair, all folded into one. Neighbor-owners Derek Song and Jamie Alexander keep their place stocked with art, books and design finds too good to give away, including Barry McGee's Scooters for Peace tees, book-fair-scented candles, build-it-yourself miniature theremin kits, and SF artist Bridget Watson Payne's hand-painted paperbacks.

For a major book binge, head to **Green Apple Books** *(greenapplebooks.com)*. Stagger out of this literary rabbit hole while you still can, laden with remaindered art books, used cookbooks and just-released novels signed by local authors. If two floors of bookish bliss aren't enough, check out even more new titles, in-store readings and events at **Green Apple Books on the Park** (1231 9th Ave).

BAKED GOODS

Arsicault Bakery: Armando Lacayo left France for Wall Street, then ditched NY finance for SF financiers (teacakes) and signature golden, flaky croissants, usually sold out by lunch. *8am-3pm*

Cinderella Russian Bakery: Just-baked egg-and-green-onion *piroshki*, decadent potato *vareniki* (boiled dumplings) and hearty borscht. *7am-7pm*

Day Moon Bread: Crusty loaves and chewy cookies baked with 100% California-grown wheat are hits at Clement St Farmers Market (*9am to 2pm Sun*). Score sandwich specials at their storefront (*3928 Irving St; 9am-4pm Thu-Sat*).

Breadbelly: Between Paris and Singapore on Clement St, Breadbelly bakes black-sesame brambleberry Danish, and spreads coconut-pandan *kaya* on toasted milk bread – better hurry. *8am-2pm Wed-Mon*

DRINKING IN THE RICHMOND

Plough & Stars: Headliners from Ireland to Appalachia play *seisiúns* (jams) here, taking breaks to clink pints of Guinness at union-hall tables. Cover is a bargain ($6 to $20). *3pm-2am Wed-Sun*

High Treason: Proof that you can get good vibes and great wines on a beer budget, with cult wines by the glass, eclectic vinyl, plus winemaker DJ on Mondays. *4-10pm*

Violet's Tavern: Toast 5pm to 6pm happy hours with Ultraviolets (pea-flower purple gin cocktails) or alcohol-free Phony Negronis, and stick around for *cioppino Latino*, SF's seafood stew with Peruvian-chili kick. *5-9pm*

Tommy's Mexican Restaurant: SF's temple of tequila since 1965 serves pure margarita bliss – enchiladas slow your roll through 400 select blue-agave tequilas. *5-8:30pm Wed-Fri, from 1pm Sat & Sun*

Day Trips from San Francisco

Exciting urban spaces, ocean, forest, mountains, wineries and islands all lie just a day trip away from San Francisco.

Places

TOP TIP

Take ferries to Alcatraz, Angel Island, Treasure Island; BART to East Bay; drive to the coast, Muir Woods, and Napa.

It's ridiculous how bountiful and varied the beauty is that surrounds San Francisco. Alcatraz needs no introduction, but it's also a destination for bird-watchers, gardeners, and art lovers. Angel Island holds the key to the west coast's immigration history and offers a plethora of outdoor activity. Oft-forgotten Treasure Island is competing with Nob Hill for best views of the city. The East Bay holds the Bay Area's torch of progressive thinking. Cross the Golden Gate Bridge and visit the wizened ancient redwoods of Muir Woods. Down the coast, beautiful beaches, whale-watching, and tide pools await along the romantic Hwy 1. Up in wine country, trip over mind-bogglingly tasty vino and food along every winding vineyard road.

Alcatraz

TIME FROM SAN FRANCISCO: **30MIN** 

Stories from 'the rock'

Alcatraz: for more than 150 years, the name has given the innocent the chills and the guilty cold sweats. Over the decades, the rocky 22-acre island has been a military prison, a forbidding maximum-security penitentiary and disputed territory between Native American activists and the FBI. You might be surprised that it's also home to art exhibitions, gardens and local wildlife. While there, though, you'll also see how impractical it would be to revive the Rock as an active prison.

Getting there & away

The only way to get to the windy, isolated island is via **Alcatraz City Cruises**, which runs the ferry service from **Pier 33** *(alcatrazcruises.com; day tours adult/5-17yr $48/29)*. You must reserve a specific departure time – book at least a week ahead for the best choice. Allow three or four hours to visit, which includes queueing to board the ferry in both directions. The ferry drops you off at the bottom of a 130ft-high hill, which you'll have to ascend a quarter-mile to reach the cellblock. Wear sturdy shoes. For people with mobility impairment, there's a twice-hourly tram from dock to cell house. No food allowed on Alcatraz aside from the landing dock.

70km
Sonoma
Napa
50km
San Rafael
Muir Woods
Angel Island
Treasure Island
Berkeley
Oakland
Alcatraz
SAN FRANCISCO
PACIFIC OCEAN
20km
San Bruno
0 40 km
0 20 miles

The early days

Spanish lieutenant Juan Manuel de Ayala had sailed past the island where large birds used to nest in the cliffs. He called it Isla de los Alcatraces (Isle of the Pelicans) in 1775. In 1859, a new post on Alcatraz became the first US West Coast fort. The army began building a new concrete military prison in 1909, but upkeep was expensive and the US soon had other things to worry about, like WWI. In the throes of Prohibition, the Federal Bureau of Prisons took over Alcatraz in 1934 as a prominent showcase for its crime-fighting efforts.

EATING AROUND ALCATRAZ: OUR PICKS

Fog Harbor Fish House (Map p74): The first 100% sustainable seafood Fisherman's Wharf restaurant, with sourdough baked every 30 minutes. *11am-9pm* **$$**

Xica: Mexican classics like *pollo mole negro* sit alongside NorCal cuisine such as churro waffles in a vibrant Embarcadero space. *noon-2:30pm Mon, to 9pm Tue-Sat* **$$**

Codmother Fish & Chips (Map p74): Made-to-order Fisherman's Wharf fish 'n' chips in a permanent food truck with patio seating. *11:30am-6pm Mon, Tue & Thu, to 7pm Fri-Sun* **$**

Freddie's Sandwiches: Century-old North Beach deli with a secret exclusive bread baker. *7:30am-4pm Mon-Fri, from 8am Sat* **$**

UNEXPECTED BEAUTY

More than just concrete, Alcatraz is home to plants and birds. While no native plants exist, the volunteer-maintained **Alcatraz Gardens** *(alcatrazgardens.org)* was planted during its time as a military base and prison. The rare Bardou Job rose was likely brought by Alcatraz's first warden in the 1930s. Access the rose terrace on a Behind the Scenes tour.

Bird lovers can walk the 0.7-mile-long **Agave Trail** during non-nesting season (mid-October to mid-January), where birds create nests in the bluffs and feed on fish from the sea. Rangers keep a whiteboard tracking types and nests of waterbirds. Most – including the black oyster catcher and snowy egret – arrive during the spring and summer. The only bird present year-round is the peregrine falcon.

Life in prison

As an island usually shrouded by fog and surrounded by freezing, choppy waters, the Rock's roster was full of A-list criminals, including Chicago crime boss Al 'Scarface' Capone, dapper kidnapper George 'Machine Gun' Kelly, and convicted murderer Robert 'The Birdman' Stroud. The Rock averaged only 264 inmates, but they were America's most wanted. Although Alcatraz was considered escape-proof, in 1962 the Anglin brothers and Frank Morris stuffed their beds with dummies and floated away on a makeshift raft.

The salty fog constantly rusted away the iron bars, and having to ship supplies and security personnel proved prohibitively expensive. Finally the island prison was abandoned in 1963. Today, first-person accounts of daily life in Alcatraz are included on the excellent self-guided audio tour of the Cellhouse. The New Industries Building debuted *The Big Lock-Up: Mass Incarceration in the US* – a permanent exhibit that illuminates major issues of our prison system, from the relationship between enslavement and the disproportionate number of Black and Latino prisoners incarcerated today, to ideas about criminal justice reform.

Red Power on Alcatraz

On Thanksgiving eve 1969, activists who called themselves the Indians of All Tribes (IAT) sailed to the island in small boats and took it over for 19 months. While the original Ohlone people likely didn't live there (though probably used it as a weigh station), the occupation was a pan-tribal political statement. The original 'Home of the free Indian land' in graffiti was restored on the water tower in 2012. Each Thanksgiving Day since 1975, international indigenous people gather on Alcatraz at daybreak for an 'Un-Thanksgiving' ceremony there to band against anti-colonialism. A 2019 exhibit, *Red Power on Alcatraz: Perspectives 50 Years Later*, commemorated the 50th anniversary of the occupation, and featured photos of, artwork by, and memories of original occupiers by the likes of artist UrbanRezLife (Kris Road Traveler Longoria). A version of that exhibit is now permanent in Building 64.

Angel Island

TIME FROM SAN FRANCISCO: **35MIN** 

Beauty within dark history

As the largest natural island in the Bay Area, though overshadowed by Alcatraz, the hilly **Angel Island** *(parks.ca.gov/AngelIsland)* should be on outdoor enthusiasts' lists, given its steep-ridge hiking, biking and camping opportunities. Angel Island's place in immigration history is possibly even more important, as it had housed an Immigration Station that processed and detained many Chinese immigrants during the Chinese Exclusion era (1882-1943). Vestiges of it, such as the detention barracks and former hospital, have been turned into museums with eerie parallels to today.

CDRIN/SHUTTERSTOCK

Angel Island docks

Getting there & around

From SF's **Ferry Building** (p100), catch the Angel Island/Tiburon Ferry. Buy round-trip tickets *($15.50 one-way; no return tickets available on Angel Island)* at **Building Gate C** (from teller or machine), or tap a **Clipper Card** (*$9 one-way; clippercard.com*) before boarding at **Gate B** (35-minute ride each way). There are four ferries per day. From Tiburon, take the **Angel Island Tiburon Ferry** *($18 one-way; buy online or at pier)*, which runs on different schedules seasonally. You can rent bicycles *(angelisland.com)* or hop on a guided tram tour (seasonal schedule) with **Angel Island Company** at **Ayala Cove**, where the ferries dock. Allow half a day to visit.

Ellis Island of the west

For thousands of years, the island was a hunting and fishing ground for the Miwok people, who'd built reed boats to travel to and from the island, building temporary camps at Ayala Cove and what would become the Immigration Station. Angel Island also served as a military base and missile testing site. The **Immigration Station** *(aiisf.org, adult/child $5/3)* operated from 1910 to 1940, primarily as a screening and detention center for mostly Chinese immigrants, who were restricted from entering the US under the Chinese Exclusion Act between 1882 and 1943. The immigration processing earned the island the nickname of Ellis Island of the West. Or was Ellis Island the Angel Island of the East? Many detainees were cruelly held for long periods, and some ultimately sent home. The mournful Chinese poetry etched into the walls of the crowded barracks is a heartbreaking testament to their trials. The island also served as a temporary incarceration camp for Japanese Americans during WWII.

The detention barracks are now a museum that has preserved the bunks and poetry for visitors to better imagine life in this purgatory. Guided tours are an optional add-on. Among the

CONNECTING THE PAST TO THE PRESENT

The sunny yellow exterior of the **Angel Island Immigration Museum**, renovated since its WWII closure, contrasts with the restored entrances for 'Europeans' and 'Non-Europeans' – choose accordingly.

Step into former exam rooms where invasive procedures were performed – Asian immigrants being subjected to the most severe ones.

The museum also highlights 80-plus countries of origin of other migrants who came through Angel Island, such as Pakistan, Japan, Vietnam, Egypt and Austria.

The museum connects Angel Island's past to today's migrant communities. One area highlights prominent Bay Area families' migration stories to America, including Disney animator Tyrus Wong and local news anchor Thuy Vu.

ANDY SUTHERLAND/SHUTTERSTOCK

Treasure Island ferry

outdoor exhibits sprinkled around the island, overlooking China Bluff is an 8-ft-tall, three-ton granite **Chinese immigrant monument**, donated by tiki tycoon Victor 'Trader Vic' Bergeron. The **Angel Island Immigration Museum** (p241), opened in 2022 in the former hospital across the way, complements the barracks experience by shining a spotlight on present-day migration.

Recreation on Angel Island

Even with its unpleasant history, Angel Island has a mild climate with cool bay breezes, making it pleasant for hiking, cycling *(angelisland.com, or BYO bike)*, private boating, **kayaking tours** from Sausalito *(seatrek.com, $175 per person, 16+, Apr–Oct)*, deer-watching and even camping *(reservecalifornia.com)*. You can picnic in a protected cove overlooking the surrounding cities. Walk the relatively flat island perimeter (5.5 miles) to the 788ft-tall peak of **Mt Livermore** or to a few uncrowded beaches. The evocative old forts, bunkers and buildings provide a contrast to the natural elements. Camp out overnight after the day-tripping crowds leave. Outside of summer months and holiday weekends you'll share this special place with only a few dozen other people.

EATING ON ANGEL ISLAND: GRAB A PICNIC BEFORE BOARDING

Ferry Building Marketplace (p100): Hit up the food hall for boxed lunches, such as **El Porteño** empanadas or **Delica** bento boxes. *Hours vary* $$

Harborview: Upscale sit-down and takeout dim sum near the Ferry Building. *11:30am-2pm & 5-9pm Tue-Fri, 10:30am-2:30pm Sat & Sun* $$$

Rosalind Bakery: Serves focaccia grandma-style pizza and ham and cheese croissants across from the Ferry Building. *8am-3pm Tue-Sat* $

Super Duper: Bay Area smash burger chain that strives to use organic, local ingredients. Also try the soft-serve. *9am-8:30pm Mon-Fri, from 11am Sat* $

Treasure Island

TIME FROM SAN FRANCISCO: **8MIN**

Inspired by fantasy

An artificial, elongated heptagon-shaped island originally built out of sand and mud in the SF Bay for the 1939-1940 Golden Gate International Exposition, the 400-acre **Treasure Island** was named after the swashbuckling 1883 Robert Louis Stevenson novel in the same adventurous spirit. The island has since also been the site of military training, airplane hangars, movie studios – and arguably the best view of the SF skyline. Currently in the midst of major development, Treasure Island already has a variety of attractions, like the famous views and new parks from which to see them, scenic bike paths and a growing restaurant/bar scene – all easily accessible from downtown SF. It's going to be a major addition to city life, and you can be one of the early visitors to experience the change.

Getting there & around

Treasure Island is technically a neighborhood of San Francisco, and it lies less than halfway between SF and Oakland in the SF Bay. If taking the new **Treasure Island ferry** *(tisf.com, adult/child $5/free)* from the **Ferry Building** (p100) **Gate B**, purchase tickets online or on board. A ride on Muni *(sfmta.com, adult/Day Pass $2.75–3/$5.50)* bus 25 from the **Salesforce Transit Center** (p102) takes about 30 min. **Treasure Island Museum** and parks are free. Check opening hours of other businesses, as some have limited hours or require appointments. It's possible to simply stay on **Avenue of the Palms** to snap a thousand SF skyline photos (and selfies), then take the next ferry to downtown SF 45 minutes later. Ideally, though, allow at least two to three hours to appreciate multiple viewpoints, cultural artifacts and history, plus the growing food/drink scene.

Views, views, views!

The views alone makes the short trip to Treasure Island worth it. The main island entrance faces the SF skyline. From the industrial gray spans of the San Francisco-Oakland Bay Bridge on the left to the skyscrapers of the distinctive Salesforce Tower (p102), pointy Transamerica Pyramid (p98) and slim Coit Tower (p136) in the middle, to the Golden Gate Bridge (p56) and Alcatraz (p238) to the right, the view encompasses San Francisco's beauty. The avenue is part of the **Bay Bridge**

Continues on p246

TIPS FOR VISITING TREASURE ISLAND

If driving from SF, there is a 15mph hairpin turn off the right-most lane of the Bay Bridge (it used to be on the left, so use current transit information).

There is currently one grocery store, **Island Cove Market** *(islandcovemarket.com)*. It does not sell alcohol or cigarettes, but island restaurants and bars serve alcohol to consume on-premises.

Be mindful of and patient with the ongoing construction through 2035, whether it's changing or half-completed walkways or bike lanes, bumpy streets, or road closures.

Bikers can currently only bike from the East Bay on the Bay Bridge. There are plans for a bike path in the future. Feel free to bring a bike to the island via Muni, ferry, or car, though.

EATING ON TREASURE ISLAND: OUR PICKS

Aracely Cafe: Outdoor fire pit patio presents seasonal dishes, such as cardamom ricotta carrot cake pancakes. *8am-3pm Sun-Tue, 8am-8pm Wed-Sat* $$

Mersea: Shipping container restaurant on the Great Lawn. The fish 'n' chips stands out among the bar fare. *11am-5pm Wed-Sun* $$

Gold Bar: Killer grilled cheese sandwiches and chocolate sundaes complement Treasure Island-inspired cocktails at this whiskey bar. *noon-9pm Tue-Sun* $$

Island Cove Market: The grocery store deli serves sandwiches and hot items, including shawarma wraps. *9am-9pm Mon-Fri, 10am-8pm Sat & Sun* $

ROAD TRIP

Down the Coast: Pacifica to Pescadero on Hwy 1

Cruising down the Pacific Coast Highway (officially California State Route 1, but aka PCH, The 1 & Hwy 1) is what California dreamin' looks like. Built between the early 1900s and 1964, it spans more than 656 miles of coastline. South of San Francisco is a beachy, foggy vibe – surfers, whale-watching, tide pools, quaint shops, numerous foodie stops. Stay open to pulling over for unplanned vistas or small towns.

1 Pacifica

Begin at the **Pacifica Pier** that sees crabbers, fishers, and onlookers. It's also a whale-watching spot, which runs long due to multiple species passing through. Go down to **Linda Mar Beach** to see surfers.

The Drive: Continue down the tree-lined road through the mountain that connects Pacifica to **Half Moon Bay** via a tunnel. Pass by the infamous, curvy **Devil's Slide** promontory.

2 Montara State Beach

Pass **Montara State Beach**, grab meat pies at **Sage Bakehouse**. Head to **Fitzgerald Marine Reserve**. Seals laze on the beach during pup season. Check online for low tide, then walk along the reef to look for neon sea anemones.

The Drive: Head back to Hwy 1 through sleepy **Moss Beach**, which is narrow and slower-paced.

JEREMY BORKAT/SHUTTERSTOCK

Pacific coast south of Half Moon Bay

Farmland flanks either side, growing leafy greens and the area's famous pumpkins.

❸ Half Moon Bay

Half Moon Bay, the other 'major' coastal town, is pumpkin central during the fall, plus a cute **Main St** and beaches. Try the red caboose that is **Dad's Luncheonette** for upscale hamburgers. Or opt for **San Benito Deli** for sandwiches on thick-cut house-baked bread.

The Drive: Head to **San Mateo Rd/Hwy 92** and some rustic-looking plant stores. Cruise 11 miles down Hwy 1, passing **Purissima Cemetery** and ranches towards **San Gregorio State Beach**.

❹ San Gregorio

Contemplate striated coastal bluffs. Back on Hwy 1 North, turn east on **Hwy 84**/La Honda Rd to Stage Rd for **San Gregorio General Store**, like an old Western hub with weekend bluegrass/folk music. Nearby is **Blue House Farm**, with weekend farm stand and in-season strawberry U-pick.

The Drive: Heading back west on Hwy 84 then continuing south on Hwy 1 yields more small beaches and vista spots. After 7.9 miles (12 minutes), you reach the small farming town of **Pescadero**.

❺ Pescadero

Streets are narrow in this rural town. Park where you can and stroll down the main thoroughfare of **Stage Rd**. **Arcangeli Grocery** is famous for its artichoke bread, for which folks line up. Save room for **Duarte's Tavern**, known for more artichoke things – mainly a creamy soup, and ollalieberry pie for dessert.

GODDESSES OF TREASURE ISLAND

Beige humanoid statues line the exterior of Building One. Prominent SF architect Timothy Pflueger was their chief designer, conceptualizing the 20 pieces that surrounded the three-tiered *Fountain of Western Waters* in the Court of Pacifica at the island's 1939-1940 Golden Gate International Exposition, whose theme was Pacific Unity. Eight larger statues represented geographical regions of the Pacific, whereas 12 dancing, music-making and working statues represented people of the Pacific.

Today, four of them, restored in the 1990s, border the curved entrance to Building One, including' Flutist' from the *Chinese Musicians* group by Helen Phillips and *Tree of Life*, representing India, by Jacques Schnier.

Continued from p243

Trail, and the island is flat, albeit with bumpy parts as construction is under way.

The connected **Yerba Buena Island** is home to two new parks that are worth the uphill trek 338 feet above sea level, from where **Treasure Island Rd** on Treasure Island goes southward, connecting to Yerba Buena Island and turning into **Macalla Rd**. It's a 0.75 mile journey between Building One (see below) and **Panorama Park**. Biking and walking are possible, but be ready for steep inclines. If using a car, it's a three-minute drive from Building One. At Panorama Park, the spire of **Hiroshi Sugimoto's 'Point of Infinity'** glistens on sunny days. The 360-degree-view drinks in more of the Bay Bridge, and makes even new housing developments look beautiful. Along the walls are plaques about the site's important place in both naval and Black history. This is where 50 Black sailors were tried for mutiny in 1944 – a legal case of considerable significance, used by Justice Thurgood Marshall to argue for desegregation.

Signal Point Park is less than 0.25 miles east of Panorama on Macalla Rd, which goes downhill, then steeply uphill. It's even smaller than Panorama, but has a higher elevation and is next to two satellite towers that lend it an outer space vibe.

Art deco vestiges of a world fair

Treasure Island has worn many hats since it was originally built for the **1939 to 1940 Golden Gate International Exposition** (GGIE). Pan Am airline wanted to make Treasure Island a central airline hub and had airplane hangars built, but with the onset of WWII, the US Navy used it for training, submarine cleaning, and intake/send-off of 4.5 million sailors (and subsequently toxic waste storage starting post-WWII through to the mid-1970s).

Right from the main entrance of Treasure Island, the commanding Steamline Moderne style of the crescent-shaped administrative **Building One** is a must-see. Aside from its cameos in several films and television shows, it's guarded by several statues from the GGIE. Inside, murals depicting the history of the island's many incarnations span the upper wall above the lobby, and the free **Treasure Island Museum** (p243) exhibits both past artifacts and helpful displays about the island's current and future development.

The former Pan Am hangars were eventually used as sound stages for the *Indiana Jones and the Last Crusade, The Parent Trap, Hulk,* and *The OA* movies.

A new SF neighborhood – the future of the city?

After the Navy handed off Treasure Island to San Francisco in 1997, a new neighborhood was developed, largely for low-income and displaced people – one of the last affordable places in the city. With only one bus line, one grocery store, and sometimes only one restaurant, Treasure Island was a limited, albeit beautifully quiet place to live – with million dollar views of the SF skyline that couldn't be kept secret for long.

DANIEL L. LOCKE/SHUTTERSTOCK

Building One

With the onset of this current wave of development, slated to finish around 2035, the community organizations on the island like **Job Corps** and the **YMCA** still serve the current residents. **Treasure Island Museum** (p243) has also worked to preserve the stories of the residents and employees, as seen in the *Voices of the Island* exhibit in the Building One lobby. The first phase of the new residential developments will see 1200 apartments, with 300 marked for affordable housing. Repeat visitors should see something new each time until the development's completion, like a shoreline park opening sometime in 2026.

Oakland

TIME FROM SAN FRANCISCO: **30MIN** 

Activism in its DNA

Stepping foot into Oakland is an immediate vibe shift, from the Craftsman houses with welcoming porches to a different kind of diversity of people compared to SF. Oakland having been the cradle of the Black Power movement in the 1960s and 1970s is key to understanding its progressive politics today. It is far from a monolith: 'Oaktown's' neighborhoods range from the historically rough West Oakland (getting an infusion of support with the dazzling new **Prescott Market** food

EATING IN OAKLAND: SOUL FOOD

Lois the Pie Queen: Possibly the oldest Black-owned restaurant in California, family-run since 1951. Hearty soul food. Cash only. *8am-2pm Tue-Sun* $$

Cafe Colucci: *Buticha* salad with chickpea paste is the star appetizer at this Ethiopian joint. *4-10pm Mon-Fri, 10:45am-3pm Wed-Fri, 10:45am-10pm Sat & Sun* $$

Burdell: Michelin-endorsed and named after chef Geoff Davis's grandmother. Tasting menu features smothered rabbit. *5-9pm Wed-Sat, 11am-2pm & 5-8pm Sun* $$$

Vegan Mob: Veganized soul food, including brisket and fried chicken, plus Bay Area flavors like lumpia over garlic noodles. *11am-8pm Tue-Sun* $$

OAKLAND'S ORACLE

Glynn Washington (@spookedpod), radio host of *Snap Judgment* and *Spooked*, producer and Oakland resident waxes lyrical about his home town.

Lake Merritt isn't just a lake – it's Oakland's secret oracle. Whenever I need an idea, an inspiration, or a hard reset, I lace up and hit the 3.5-mile loop.

Snowy egrets strike kung-fu poses, neighbors rattle buckets into parade drums, gondolas glide past like stolen Venice postcards.

Turn after turn, her beauty stills the mind; stories rise from the ripples, and by the time the old boathouse greets me again, she's slipped the answer into my pocket.

Bring your baggage, your questions, your half-baked schemes – set 'em on the water and watch Lake Merritt reveal the solution that's been waiting all along.

hall), to the affluent Oakland Hills. If limited to half a day, consider the Oakland Museum of California as an essential history primer, which conveniently lies next to the strollable Lake Merritt and historic Children's Fairyland. Jack London Sq on the waterfront is touristy, but going through interesting changes to bring people back. Also consider **Uptown** for shows at the **Fox Theater** *(thefoxoakland.com)* and cool bars, **Chinatown** near **Downtown** for dining, hipster **Temescal** for artisan shops, quaint **Rockridge** for Craftsman bungalow houses and cute stores, and eats along **Grand Ave** and **International Blvd.**

Getting there & around

The easiest way to travel between San Francisco and the East Bay is via **BART**, which speeds through an underwater tunnel. Trains run approximately every 20 or so minutes from around 5am to midnight Monday to Friday, from 6am on Saturday and from 8am on Sunday and holidays. Regional company **AC Transit** operates buses from San Francisco's **Salesforce Transit Center** (p102) to the East Bay *($6 one-way)*. With your own wheels, approach the East Bay from San Francisco by taking the **Bay Bridge**. Driving back westbound to San Francisco, the bridge toll is $8. Offering splendid views, the **San Francisco Bay Ferry** is the most enjoyable way of traveling between San Francisco and the East Bay, though also the slowest and most expensive.

A waterfront meeting place

Jack London Sq has a similar waterfront vibe to SF locals' scourge **Fisherman's Wharf** – great Bay views, essential ports, but lackluster restaurants. However, being shaken up by the pandemic, including the currently-empty headquarters of the departed baseball team, the square revived its decades-old **Sunday farmers market** *(jacklondonsquare.com)*, and has been welcoming change – being the new home of much-missed vegan soul food restaurant **Souley Vegan**, **First Saturdays** *(jacklondonoakland.org)* with vendors and live music filling the square with presence and cheer, and more community events. Yes, have a requisite look at the **bronze statue** of the problematic *Call of the Wild* author (progressive, yet racist) right past the main arched entryway. In the era of reckoning with colonial legacies, there's been talk about replacing it and all signs of him with either pioneering former congresswoman Barbara Lee, who became Oakland's mayor in 2025, or Black Panthers' co-founder Bobby Seale.

Dive into Oakland's history

As an essential regional and California history primer, the **Oakland Museum of California** *(OMCA; museumca.org, adult/student/under-12 $19/12/free; free first Sun)*, is fantastic for both first-time Oakland visitors and regulars. Bold orange lettering stands out against the mid-20th-century modernist concrete walls, softened by carpeted exhibit halls and the incorporation of ample outdoor space.

FROM LEFT: MARTIN DO NASCIMENTO; EDDIE-HERNANDEZ.COM/SHUTTERSTOCK

Sunday farmers market, Oakland

Learn about the state's diverse ecology and history, as well as California art, from traditional landscapes to reimagined cartography. Temporary exhibits have included SF local Chelsea Ryoko Wong's *Ancestral Visions,* displaying six cheongsam dresses owned by 20th-century Chinese American women, and the paintings they inspired exploring family history, fashion and personal identity. The permanent Gallery of California History on the bottom floor includes displays on the 1906 earthquake, and a recent expansion of the Black Panthers exhibit, including a majestic bronze replica of the round-backed peacock chair that co-founder Huey Newton sat in. April-October sees the joyous, family-friendly, and free weekly OMCA Friday Nights (5-9pm) with live music, DJs, plenty of dancing, and 10 Off the Grid food trucks.

A green escape

Lake Merritt *(lakemerritt.org),* bordered by OMCA east of Downtown Oakland, is a body of water central to Oakland life – from walkable paths and bustling barbecue areas to verdant gardens surrounded by restaurants and shops. On the north side is **Children's Fairyland** *(fairyland.org, adult/child $19/17),* a children's amusement park founded in 1950 that serves as the inspiration for Disneyland. The 10-acre park has just enough for kid attention spans, with old-school, Mother Goose-tastic vibes to its the faded Peter Rabbit gardens, Alice in Wonderland labyrinth, and mini carousels.

Berkeley

TIME FROM SAN FRANCISCO: **30MIN** 

A cultured college town

Both lovingly and derisively nicknamed 'Berzerkeley,' mostly sunny Berkeley lies 13 miles northeast of San Francisco and is bordered by the Bay to the west, **Berkeley Hills** to the east and **Emeryville** and **Oakland** (p247) to the south. Alight at

THIRD WORLD LIBERATION FRONT STRIKE

UC Berkeley is no stranger to free speech, and Sproul Plaza has long been a stage for both peaceful demonstrations and brutal beatings.

In 1969, in the throes of the Civil Rights movement, Vietnam War protests, and increasing diversity on college campuses, Cal students recognized that people of color around the world had shared experiences with the European colonization legacy. They saw injustices tied in with Eurocentric curricula in schools and universities, and, inspired by students at San Francisco State University doing the same, Cal students joined the Third World Liberation Front, a multi-racial coalition whose hard-won efforts resulted in the formation of Ethnic Studies and African American Studies departments at Cal.

CDRIN/SHUTTERSTOCK

University of California, Berkeley

the happening Downtown Berkeley BART station to explore the home of perpetual students, liberal politics, burnt-out hippies, arts and sciences in all forms, and California cuisine's farm-to-table ethos. Tour noteworthy spots on the campus of UC Berkeley (Cal for shorthand), the surrounding area of downtown Berkeley, gardens and science museums, a sprawling regional park, and So. Much. Food. If you're feeling the call to return to Berkeley after an initial visit, make note of its robust arts scene that has more than 100 cultural institutions, including **Berkeley Repertory Theatre** *(berkeleyrep.org)*, **Zellerbach Hall** *(calperformances.org)*, **California Jazz Conservatory** *(jazzschool.org)*, **Berkeley Art Museum and Pacific Film Archive** *(bampfa.org)*, plus **924 Gilman** *(924gilman.org)* for all-ages punk shows and more.

An iconic university

The sprawling, urban Berkeley campus of the **University of California** *(berkeley.edu)* is the oldest university in the state, and one of its most prestigious (its main rival is Stanford down in Palo Alto). The decision to found the college was made in 1866, and the first students arrived in 1873. Today, Cal has more than 40,000 students, more than 1,500 professors and more Nobel laureates than you could point a particle accelerator at. Older buildings are mostly Beaux-Arts Classical Revival style,

EATING IN BERKELEY: FOOD COURTS & MORE

Durant Food Court: Dubiously nicknamed 'Asian Ghetto,' the outdoor square includes classic Thai Basil and Myungrang's Korean corn dogs. *hours vary* $

North Shattuck: 'Gourmet Ghetto' houses Alice Waters' farm-to-table Chez Panisse, Cheese Board Collective's pizza and Gregoire's potato puffs. *hours vary* $$

Berkeley Bowl Marketplace: Grocery behemoth includes hard-to-find produce like fiddlehead ferns. *9am-8pm, 10am-7pm Sun* $$

Vik's Chaat: This West Berkeley mainstay since 1989 pays homage to *chaat* (Indian street food) with samosas and *dosas* (savory crepes). *11am-7:30pm* $$

with the harder edges of brutalist and modernist styles in newer ones. You can enter from **Center St** and **Oxford Lane**, near the **Downtown Berkeley BART** station. Alternatively, enter the campus from Telegraph Ave (p252), via **Sproul Plaza** and **Sather Gate**, a center for people-watching, soapbox oration and pseudotribal drumming. Toward the middle of campus is **Sather Tower**, aka **the Campanile**. Ride 61m up in the elevator *(visit.berkeley.edu, $5)* to an observation deck featuring panoramic views of the campus, surrounding hills, San Francisco and the Golden Gate Bridge.

Head past grassy lawns and lazing (yet high-achieving) students to the **Free Speech Movement Cafe** *(lib.berkeley.edu)* at the Moffitt Undergraduate Library. It honors student activist Mario Savio and the 1964 Free Speech Movement at UC Berkeley, which led the way for anti-war demonstrations nationwide. Cafe walls are plastered with rally photos and historical documents.

Another significant food institution on campus is **mak-'amham/Cafe Ohlone** *(makamham.com)*, located outside the campus's **Hearst Museum of Anthropology** and serving dishes like fine black oak acorn soup and chia seed porridge. As the only Ohlone restaurant in the world, its goals are to provide a physical space for our Ohlone people to be represented in the food world while educating the public. Check for seatings in advance as the restaurant model evolves.

Outdoor escapes

The western part of Berkeley holds **Tilden Regional Park** *(ebparks.org)*, a 2079-acre green wonderland. Car is best, but you can also get off at the Downtown Berkeley BART station, then transfer to AC Transit bus 67 – though check up-to-date schedules. Tilden Park has nearly 40 miles of hiking and multi-use trails of varying difficulty, from paved paths to hilly scrambles, including the magnificent **Bay Area Ridge Trail** *(ridgetrail.org)* hike that contains part of the 9.5-mile hike called the Tilden to Redwood Regional via Skyline Trail, Sibley and Huckleberry. Kids especially will love the **Redwood Valley Railway** mini steam train *(adult/under-2 $4/free)* and the **Little Farm** petting zoo. Other park gems include an environmental education center, a wonderfully wild-looking botanical garden and an 18-hole golf course. **Lake Anza** is good for picnics and from spring through fall you can swim there.

ACKNOWLEDGING BERKELEY'S INDIGENOUS COMMUNITY

Bay Area institutions have created land acknowledgments to address America's colonial legacy. UC Berkeley occupies *xučyun* (Huichin) territory of the Chochenyo-speaking Ohlone.

Ohlone Park added an Ohlone mural by Native American artist Jean Lamarr in the 1990s. Berkeley was the first US city to celebrate Indigenous Peoples' Day in 1992. In 2024, Berkeley returned a 2.2-acre area containing a sacred shell mound to the Sogorea Te' Land Trust. **Cafe Ohlone** (see left) educates the public about Native American foodways. In neighboring Oakland, **Wahpepah's Kitchen** is currently the only other Bay Area indigenous restaurant, serving dishes like *kiikaapoa miisiikwaa* – Kickapoo chili with bison and Oklahoma pearl hominy.

EATING IN THE EAST BAY: OUR PICKS

Lao Thai Kitchen: Laotian specialties like *nam khao* (pork and crispy rice), near the Berkeley Hills. *4:30-8:45pm Mon-Sat, noon-2:45pm Sat* $$

Battambang: Cambodian restaurant in Oakland's Chinatown serves *amok trei* (lemongrass curry catfish steamed in a banana leaf). *11am-8pm Mon-Sat* $$

Barcote: One for tartare fans: try Michelin-endorsed Barcote's Ethiopian *kitfo* spiked with cardamom and hot mitmita spice. *11am-10pm* $$

Lemat: A dazzling, airy Ethiopian restaurant starring *yesiga wot* – chopped beef morsels in a perky berbere sauce – on Adeline St in Berkeley. *5-9:30pm Mon-Sat* $$

BONDROCKETIMAGES/SHUTTERSTOCK

Berkeley Rose Garden

A stroll down a renowned street

The most famous street near campus is **Telegraph Ave**, which flows seamlessly in and out of it from the south. A combination of burnt-out hippie vibe from the anti-war and Civil Rights eras, fiercely independent book and music shops, and affordable student eats make it a big window into Cal life. Check out the four floors of **Moe's** *(moesbooks.com)* new and used books, the radical **Revolution Books** *(revolutionbooks.org)*, flagship locations of both **Rasputin** *(rasputinmusic.com)* and **Amoeba** *(amoeba.com)* independent, eclectic music stores full of vinyl, used albums and live performances, one of the biggest US collections of vintage Levi's at **Slash Denim** *(slash denim.online)* on College Ave, curated collections of vintage at **Paisley** *(paisleyvintage.com)* on **Bancroft Way**, and tons of student-friendly eats (cheap and open late), including bars. Like many urban areas, there are some homeless who live in or frequent the area, but the omnipresence of students rarely means empty streets.

Smelling the roses

The **H (Hill) Line Shuttle** *(pt.berkeley.edu, $1)* goes from campus up the winding **Centennial Dr** to the 34-acre **UC Botanical Garden at Berkeley** *(botanicalgarden.berkeley.edu, adult/under-5 $18/free)*, but only Monday through Friday. Alternatively, you can drive to the parking lot ($1.50/

EATING IN BERKELEY: STUDENT EATS

Tacos Sinaloa: Smoky, crispy *pastór* tacos rule at this small Michelin Bib Gourmand taqueria – Steph Curry's fave. *10am-midnight Mon-Sat, 11am-10pm Sun* $

SLIVER Pizzeria: Cheese Board Collective descendant. Daily selection of organic, vegetarian slices with legendary green sauce. *11am-10:30pm* $

Noodle Dynasty: The line is worth it for the Northern Chinese beef brisket noodle soup featuring eight-hour simmered broth. *noon-4pm & 5-8pm* $$

Yogurt Park: Mix as many flavors as your heart desires and add toppings like graham cracker crumbs at this 1977 stalwart. *noon-11pm* $

hr). Walking the 30-minute route is last resort due to a steep incline. Home to more than 10,000 kinds of plants, including rare species and a towering redwood grove, the garden comprises one of the largest botanical collections in the US. Further up the hilly road is the **Lawrence Hall of Science** *(lawrencehallofscience.org, adult/under-2 $20/free, planetarium or 3D theater $5 extra)*, with has climbable parking lot structures shaped like a DNA strand and a giant whale. Inside are large-scale, hands-on exhibitions like the Future of Food and an Animal Discovery Zone. Complete a loop with a stop at the **Berkeley Rose Garden** *(berkeleyca.gov, free entry)* in the Berkeley Hills, where more than 1500 rose bushes of 250 varieties, arranged in a terraced amphitheater, make for a striking spectacle.

Muir Woods

TIME FROM SAN FRANCISCO: **45–90MIN**

A coastal gem: beyond beaches

Just across the Golden Gate Bridge from San Francisco, Marin County is a collection of wealthy, wooded hamlets that hang tenuously by haute hippie roots as a more conservative tech-era population moves in. Its southern peninsula nearly touches the north-pointing tip of the city, and is surrounded by ocean and bay, but Marin is wilder and more mountainous. The mountains and oceanside cliffs are all stunning and **Muir Woods National Monument** *(gomuirwoods.com, adult/under-16 $15/free)* is particularly striking in that its old-growth redwood forest is so close to a city. Take advantage of this rare proximity on a day trip. Extend your North Bay visit with a hike through **Muir Beach** or explore the quaint **downtown Mill Valley** nearby.

Getting there & around

To reduce overcrowding, major changes introduced in 2018 were a **reservations system** for **parking** *($9.50 all-day)* and the **Muir Woods Shuttle** from **Larkspur Landing** *(adult/under-16 $3.75/free round-trip; runs on weekends, holidays & from Sausalito Ferry Terminal on select summer weekdays early spring – Oct)*. Best to reserve days in advance, though same-day reservations are possible if you're willing to visit late in the day. To get to Muir Woods by car, drive north on Hwy 101, exit at Hwy 1 and continue north along Hwy 1/Shoreline Hwy to the **Panoramic Hwy** (a right-hand fork). Follow that for about one mile to **Four Corners**, where you turn left onto **Muir Woods Rd** (there are plenty of signs).

A QUIETER GROVE EXPERIENCE

For a redwood grove experience without the Muir Woods chaos, choose **Roy's Redwoods Preserve** in **West Marin** (40-minute drive from Muir Woods).

Spot pileated woodpeckers and black-throated gray warblers, plus spring wildflowers such as pacific hound's tongue and milkmaids.

Several short trails were added in 2024 to increase accessibility, like the 0.35-mile-long **David Hansen Trail** at the peak. For a three-mile **Roy's Redwoods Preserve** loop trail, take **Sir Francis Drake Blvd** from **Fairfax** toward **San Geronimo** until you reach the golf course. Turn right on **Nicasio Valley Rd** and you'll soon see the sign and small parking area for Roy's Redwoods on your right.

Beware of poison oak, ticks, and a lack of bathrooms.

EATING NEAR MUIR WOODS: OUR PICKS

Pelican Inn: Time hop at this 16th century-inspired English pub in Muir Beach. Bang-on fish 'n' chips. *11am-9pm Sun-Thu, to 10pm Fri-Sat* $$

Sol Food Mill Valley: This Puerto Rican takeout outpost specializes in crunchy plantain-fried prawns. Eat at Sycamore Park. *11am-8pm Mon-Thu, 10am-9pm Fri-Sun* $$

Mill Valley Market: A high-end grocer with fresh, customizable deli sandwiches for which locals and visitors line up. *7am-7:30pm Mon-Sat, 8am-7pm Sun* $

Fish.: Sustainable seafood served on a sunny Sausalito waterside patio, from oysters to *bánh mì*-inspired salmon sandos. *11:30am-7:30pm Sun-Thu, to 8:30pm Fri & Sat* $$$

BRET J. UNGER/SHUTTERSTOCK

Cathedral Grove, Muir Woods

Download your parking reservation or shuttle ticket in advance, as there is no cell service in Muir Woods. This is also why visitors should not use a rideshare service to visit. Same goes for any vehicle requiring cell service to start the ignition. No advance bookings required for those arriving via tour bus, bicycle, or on foot.

The parking reservation fee is on top of the park entrance fee, which can also be booked online. There is an ongoing park renewal project through 2029, so mind the construction.

Walkable wonders

With a variety of paved, flat trails, walking among the giants of Muir Woods is doable with strollers, young kids, or wheelchairs – though not on the upper trails. Many trailheads begin from the **Muir Woods Visitor Center**. The main **Muir Woods Main Trail** can be done in a loop as short as 1 mile (30 min), but longer options are available. Go through stands of redwoods and along scenic **Redwood Creek** to **Cathedral Grove**, home of 1000-year-old redwoods. The trail returns via **Bohemian Grove**, where the tallest tree in the park stands more than 258ft high. The **Dipsea Trail** is a good two-mile hike up to the top of aptly named **Cardiac Hill**. You can also walk down into Muir Woods by taking trails from the **Panoramic Hwy,** such as the **Bootjack Trail** from the Bootjack picnic area, or from **Mt Tamalpais Pantoll Station** campground, along the **Ben Johnson Trail**.

Several dirt trails lead up the valley from this main path and link to others in Mt Tamalpais State Park, recommended for more advanced hikers with its long, narrow, unpaved, and often steep paths. A $1 trail map from the Muir Woods Visitor Center (where you pay your entrance fee) will help you find your way – remember GPS does not work here.

Napa

TIME FROM SAN FRANCISCO: **50MIN–2HR**

World-class wine tasting

Rolling green vineyards, amazing wine and food and joie de vivre (when not dealing with droughts or wildfires, that is): that's wine country. California wine regions span the state, from southern California all the way up to Mendocino County, but Napa is still the brand name when it comes to the words 'wine country.' While not the state's oldest wine-growing region, it did become California's first American Viticultural Area in 1981, especially known for cabernet sauvignon and merlot for reds, and chardonnay and sauvignon for white – with some wineries pushing the envelope with lesser-known grapes or winemaking techniques. For a day trip, it is a shorter drive to stick to Napa (and **American Canyon** just south of Napa). **Yountville**, **St Helena**, **Calistoga**, **Russian River**, all have their own wine specialties and visitor gems, but are farther north – still doable for a day trip, but also consider those for an overnight stay. **Sonoma Valley** is actually a few miles closer to SF and also a great choice — but Napa is Napa, especially for first-time visitors.

Getting there & around

Whether getting to Napa via the **Bay Bridge** or **Golden Gate Bridge** – traffic around both of them is no joke during rush hour (about 3-7pm) and on weekends. Aim for weekdays or for when tasting rooms first open – usually late mornings. With little traffic, expect a 45-minute trip up there. The way back can take two hours or more. There are also options for the expensive Napa Valley Wine train, bike routes, and private tours. Look up and follow any part of Napa Valley Vine Trail for guidance as well.

If starting from downtown Napa, hit up the **Napa Valley Welcome Center** first for help tailoring your visit according to taste, whether by type of wine, region, price, ambience and more. You can also explore their website using those filters to plan ahead.

Call ahead to see if children are allowed.

Wineries in downtown Napa & beyond

Some may not initially consider **downtown Napa** for wine degustation due to its cement surroundings, counter to the image of relaxing on lush vineyards. However, tasting rooms downtown are centrally located, usually have longer hours, and you can park once and simply walk to multiple tastings,

BOOKING WINE TASTINGS

Gone are the days of free tastings, even at the bigger rooms. Nowadays, any tasting under \$20 to \$30 is considered affordable – some can run well north of \$100.

While walk-ins are possible depending on availability, reservations are strongly recommended, often reserved online via Tock, and last up to 90 minutes. Try not to book more than two or three in a day.

Tastings will usually include an extra 'splash' at the end, discounts on bottles purchased at the tasting, or the option to tailor a mini tasting if tight on time or budget.

EATING IN NAPA: CASUAL DINING

Oxbow Public Market: Food hall shows off wine country produce, plus Model Bakery and Michelin-cred Moroccan street food. *hours vary* \$\$

State Line Road Smokehouse: Chef Darryl Bell Jr's Kansas City barbecue. Think: smoked mushroom salad and American wagyu tri-tip. *11am-7pm Mon-Thu* \$\$

CIA at Copia: Garden-to-table food by the Culinary Institute of America; try carrot gnocchi with carrot-top pesto. *5-9pm Wed–Sun, 10:30am-2:30pm Sat & Sun* \$\$\$

Small World Restaurant: Casual Middle Eastern – among Napa's best. Don't miss fresh baklava when available. *9am-7:30pm Mon-Sat* \$\$

CLIMATE CHANGE IN WINE COUNTRY

Napa wine country can feel like its own little universe – sipping world-class wine, overlooking verdant vineyards. However, as climate change become more apparent, its effects on wine and agriculture are topics of concern.

Grape growing season in now a month earlier, compared to the 1950s, as temperatures have increased by one to two degrees Fahrenheit over the decades, which has also resulted in a significant reduction of cool periods.

Since grapes are sensitive to temperature changes, Napa grape growers may have to pivot towards new growing practices and perhaps more heat-tolerant grape varieties, lest Napa be left behind as a viable grape-growing region while previously unsuitable areas become ideal vineyard territory.

in addition to being steps away from restaurants and cute shops. Consider **Brown Estate's Brown Downtown** tasting room *(brownestate.com)*, off **Main St** on the second floor, with a contemporary lounge feel. As Napa's first Black-owned winery, the first generation of Brown wine makers started growing grapes in Napa in 1980, and their children began producing wine in 1996. It remains mostly a zinfandel house, with both medium and full-bodied varieties. Wine educators are approachable.

RD Winery *(rdwinery.com)* is one of the first wineries you reach before getting into Napa proper, the parking lot's cherry blossoms exploding with pink in spring. RD is the first Vietnamese- and woman-owned winery, and aims to create wines that pair with almost any type of food – the Fifth Moon exploratory label zinfandel skews acidic instead of big in order to balance out rich foods and cleanse the palate between bites. While the tasting room is close to traffic, views are mostly covered by plants, and the open lawn and patio areas are relaxing. Pair wines with the pan-Asian food menu, like Liberty duck flatbread with spring onion relish or crispy spring rolls.

Family-owned and now run with the help of the second generation of the Herrera family, **Mi Sueño** *(misuenowinery.com)* was founded in 1997 by Napa grape growers and children of grape growers. Fast-forward to 2001 and their Los Carneros Chardonnay was served at White House dinner. At the tasting room, the exterior industrial parking lot leads past administrative cubicles to tastings in the wine cave, which feels at once cozy and cavernous, filled nearly floor-to-ceiling with wine barrels. Your wine educator may be a Herrera family member. The 2021 Russian River pinot noir in particular stands out from many other California pinots – much bolder, darker, jammier, as grapes grown closer to the Bay waters ripen slowly and allow for concentrated grape flavors.

Wine-tasting in the scenic countryside

Just an extra 10–15-minute drive out of Napa yields a dizzying array of photogenic options. Pomegranate and pistachio trees adorn **Darioush Winery** *(darioush.com)* as an ode to ancient Persia at Napa's Iranian-owned winery. **Hess Persson Estates** *(hesspersonestates.com)* is known for its contemporary art collection as much as its wines. Huge corporate companies have tasting rooms to match, like the chateau of **Domaine Carneros** *(domainecarneros.com)* for fans of sparkling wine and pinot noir.

Darioush Winery, Napa
WIRESTOCK CREATORS/SHUTTERSTOCK

Where to Stay

San Francisco's hotels are clustered downtown and along the waterfront, near major attractions and entertainment venues – but you'll want to hop transit or rideshare at night to reach lively neighborhoods with happening restaurant, bar and arts scenes.

Where to Stay If You Love ...

Nature in the city

The Presidio, Marina & Fisherman's Wharf (p54) All along the northern waterfront, get in touch with nature – whether you stay in scenic Presidio park lodges, Marina motels close to Crissy Field and Presidio trailheads, or within earshot of barking sea lions along Fisherman's Wharf.

Museums, theater & nightlife

Downtown, Civic Center & SoMa (p82) Union Square's historic hotels are near theaters, museums and SoMa hotspots, including concert halls, clubs, bars and LGBTQ+ venues, from leather bars to drag cabarets.

Food, wine & saloons

Chinatown & North Beach (p116) In this global food and wine destination, you'll find something tasty on almost any corner – but Chinatown and North Beach offer an unbelievable selection of dim sum, pizza and wine bars, acclaimed restaurants and saloons.

Hilltop grandeur

Nob Hill & Russian Hill (p140) Enjoy the view from the top of Russian Hill and 'Snob Hill,' where gilded-age tycoons gathered in grand hotels with sweeping city panoramas. Bask in the opulence.

Victorian glamor

Japantown, Fillmore & Pacific Heights (p152) Once you see the Painted Lady Victorians of Alamo Sq, you might picture yourself in a grand parlor, taking tea with visiting dignitaries – live the fantasy in Victorian B&Bs in Japantown, Fillmore and Pacific Heights.

LGBTQ+ life

The Castro (p192) You'll spot rainbow flags on every block of San Francisco, and the Castro is the historic gayborhood at the heart of it all, with hangouts, cafes, bars and clubs where you can be gay all day and out every night.

The Presidio, Marina & Fisherman's Wharf

SPLURGE-WORTHY & ICONIC

Inn at the Presidio $$$
MAP P63 11
The Presidio's former officers' quarters now welcome civilians as a national-park lodge, with oversize rooms featuring pillowtop beds with Egyptian-cotton sheets, suites with gas fireplaces, and hiking trailheads out back. Request upper-floor corner rooms with wraparound park views.

Argonaut Hotel $$$
MAP P74 15
Built as a cannery in 1908, Fisherman's Wharf's top hotel remains a waterfront character, with exposed-brick walls, century-old beams, and nautical decor. Snug guest rooms are fit for a first mate, with shiplap walls, navy-blue furnishings and comfy beds with compass headboards; pay extra for bay views.

FAMILY-FRIENDLY

Marina Motel $
MAP P66 8
Stay at a sitcom-set vintage motel with kitschy-cute rooms with kitchenettes. Built in 1939, the motel is scuffed but well-maintained, with garden-themed murals and free parking. Request a quiet courtyard room away from busy Lombard St.

Hotel del Sol $$
MAP P66 6
California dreams come true at the Marina's midcentury motor lodge with a splashy beach-ball color scheme, palm-lined courtyard and heated outdoor pool. The city's top choice for families offers afternoon cookies, board games, a movie library and hammocks.

BOUTIQUE

Lodge at the Presidio $$
MAP P63 12
The officers' post turned ecolodge offers dashingly handsome guestrooms with Pendleton throw blankets atop pillowtop beds, historic Presidio photos and commanding views – request a room overlooking the Golden Gate Bridge.

Infinity Hotel $$
MAP P66 7
Smartly contemporary yet snugly comfortable, the Infinity on Lombard St offers unexpected perks: bonus bidets, steam showers and roof-deck views from here to infinity.

Kimpton Alton $$$
MAP P74 16
The Wharf's hip hangout offers sleek modern guestrooms big enough to use in-room yoga mats, with pillowtop beds, record players with albums from the lobby vinyl library, and workstations so you can work remotely. Spring for in-room spa services and brunch downstairs at Abacá.

ON A BUDGET

HI San Francisco Fisherman's Wharf $
MAP P74 17
Get million-dollar waterfront views at SF's best hostel, housed in a former army post that's now a park. Choose private rooms or dorms (some co-ed) with four to 22 beds, all with shared bathrooms and a communal kitchen offering free breakfasts.

HOW MUCH FOR A NIGHT IN

Hotel
from $220 per night

Boutique hotel
$150–300 per night

Inn or B&B
$150–270 per night

Hostel
$30–75 per night

VICTORIAN B&B

Union Street Inn $$$
MAP P66 9
Live like a Pacific Heights socialite at this grand Edwardian B&B with six antique-filled guestrooms, afternoon tea in lush gardens, and generous breakfasts in the parlor.

Downtown, Civic Center & SoMa

SPLURGE-WORTHY & ICONIC

Palace Hotel $$$
MAP P85 7
The 1906 landmark Palace remains a monument to turn-of-the-century grandeur, with 100-year-old Austrian-crystal chandeliers, Maxfield Parrish

paintings in the bar, and teatime in the marble Garden Court under a truly palatial glass ceiling. Kids love the big pool.

Beacon Grand $$$
MAP P85 2
Right off Union Sq, the refreshed Beacon offers magnificent welcomes in its Spanish-Moroccan lobby, and smallish rooms with business-class amenities and proper beds – plus dynamite cocktails and food at the on-site Starlite rooftop bar.

Westin St Francis Hotel $$$
MAP P85 8
This 1904 Union Sq landmark features high ceilings, crown moldings and gleaming marble in public spaces.Tower rooms offer comparatively generic design but stellar views, and beds here set the industry standard for comfort.

HIP

Proper Hotel $$
MAP P107 15
A smart hotel on a sketchy block, this flatiron building makes rooms feel bigger than they are, and there's a fabulous rooftop lounge. Bicycles are complimentary, but valet parking is $84 a night.

CONTEMPORARY

Hotel Nikko $$
MAP P85 5
This convenient Union Sq hotel has super-friendly staff, and quiet, decent-sized rooms with luxurious high thread-count linens. The on-site restaurant Anzu offers a proper Japanese breakfast (included in the room rate).

Orchard Garden Hotel $$
MAP P85 6
SF's first LEED-certified green hotel is one of the most affordable in the area. Clean and conveniently located just outside Chinatown, with gym, rooftop deck and optional breakfast at the sustainable Roots restaurant on-site.

LUMA Hotel $$$
MAP P90 16
In a more recently developed area in SoMa/Mission Bay near Oracle Park and Chase Center, bougie sports fans will enjoy the 2022 hotel's floor-to-ceiling windows, big art installations, pet-friendly policies, and the Cavaña rooftop bar.

ON A BUDGET

citizenM San Francisco Union Square $
MAP P85 3
Enter the narrow foyer, and an elevator operator guides you to the expansive, colorfully modern lobby at this Dutch boutique chain. Rooms are small, iPad-controlled, clean, hip and affordable – plus there's a rooftop deck.

PEDRO COSTA SIMEAO/SHUTTERSTOCK

Beacon Grand

HI San Francisco Downtown $
MAP P85 4
Located in a restored historic building downtown between Union Sq and the Tenderloin, hostel rooms are safe and clean, with non-squeaky wooden bunk beds with personal power points; shared lounge, kitchen and occasional bar crawls.

FAMILY-FRIENDLY

Hyatt Place $$
MAP P90 15
Greetings, sports fans: Just a block away from Oracle Park, this Hyatt is decked out with SF Giants spirit during baseball season. Close to Embarcadero for active kids; parents will appreciate tasty bites and cocktails at the Kaiyo Rooftop bar on site.

Chinatown & North Beach

ON A BUDGET

Pacific Tradewinds Hostel $
MAP P120 17
San Francisco's smartest all-dorm hostel has a nautical theme, fully equipped kitchen (free coffee, tea, and peanut-butter-and-jelly sandwiches), spotless showers, sturdy bunkbeds, laundry (free sock wash), luggage storage, no lockout time and best of all, fun staff. No elevator.

San Remo Hotel $
MAP P128
Built in 1906, this North Beach boarding house offers many sunny, cheerful Italian *nonna* (grandma)-styled rooms with eclectic antique furnishings and shared bathrooms – but the rooftop suite is an adorable cabin with wraparound skyline views. Remodeled rooms have private baths, but lack space and character. No elevator.

SHORT-TERM RENTALS

Due to city regulations, short-term rental options are limited in San Francisco – even though Airbnb was founded here. That said, B&Bs and short-stay hotels are scarce in the Avenues and Mission, so short-term rentals may be your best/only bet here.

Green Tortoise Hostel $
MAP P120 16
At North Beach's social hub/hostel, the sunny ballroom encourages bonding with pool, ping-pong and games, plus co-working stations and weekly live music shows. Perks include sauna, free breakfast, good wi-fi, on-site laundry and a communal kitchen to cook for new friends. Co-ed and women's dorm rooms have individually lit bunks and generous lockers; private rooms sleep one to three people. Also runs epic bus trips to national parks in converted co-sleeping buses.

INNS WITH CHARACTER

Hotel Bohème $$
MAP P128 5
Eclectic, historic and unabashedly romantic, this quintessential North Beach boutique hotel has rooms named after Beat writers, with jazz-era color schemes, wrought-iron beds, paper-umbrella lamps, Beat poetry and original artwork. The vintage rooms are smallish with teensy bathrooms, some face noisy Columbus Ave and there's no elevator – but novels practically write themselves here.

Washington Square Inn $$
MAP P128 6
Facing sunny Washington Sq, this 1910 inn offers restored guestrooms in an upbeat vintage modern style. Some rooms are tight for two, and may have a bathroom across the hall – but this is a charming location, with a sociable front room for coffee. No elevator or on-site staff; entry is via digital key system.

Nob Hill & Russian Hill

SPLURGE-WORTHY & ICONIC

Fairmont San Francisco $$$
MAP P142 8
Nob Hill opulence meets San Francisco eccentricity, with a jaw-dropping marble lobby, tiki Tonga Room and deco circus-mural Cirque Bar. Guest rooms offer business-class comfort. For historic appeal, reserve in the original 1906 building; for jaw-dropping views, go for the tower.

InterContinental Mark Hopkins $$$
MAP P142 9
Crystal lobby chandeliers twinkle welcome at this 1926 San Francisco landmark with gilded-age style and end-of-the-world views. Rooms are business-class beige, with Frette linens on plush beds; for 360-degree views, head up to the Top of the Mark rooftop bar.

Ritz-Carlton $$$
MAP P142 11
This 1909 neoclassical luxury hotel two steep blocks uphill from Union Sq looks like the Parthenon, but was once Hearst's *San Francisco*

Chronicle newspaper HQ. Inside, live like a tycoon with marble bathrooms and swanky lounges; pet-friendly.

HIP

Music City Hotel & Hostel $
MAP P142 ⑩
The music-themed hostel in hip Lower Nob Hill (aka 'Tendernob') offers Japanese capsule-style bunks and private rooms, and really commits to its theme, with Green Day and Beatles memorabilia, basement karaoke, rehearsal rooms, and a live-music venue off the lobby.

CONTEMPORARY

Stanford Court Hotel $$
MAP P142 ⑫
Rubbing shoulders with the Mark Hopkins and Fairmont atop Nob Hill is the more affordable Stanford Court. Enjoy similar views, large rooms and friendly service.

Japantown, Fillmore & Pacific Heights

VICTORIAN B&BS

Queen Anne Hotel $$
MAP P154 ⑲
This grand 1890 pink Victorian mansion was once a girls' boarding school and the decor is pure period drama, with carved wood beds, antique vanities, and tasseled curtains. Rooms are comfy, though the wallpaper is too close for comfort in some. Great value; includes continental breakfast and afternoon tea and sherry.

Chateau Tivoli $$
MAP P154 ⑯
The source of neighborhood gossip since 1892, this gorgeous Painted Lady mansion hosted Isadora Duncan, Mark Twain and (rumor has it) the ghost of a Victorian opera diva – you're the next honored guest in an antique-filled room or suite. Most rooms have en-suite baths with claw-foot bathtubs and no TV; three-course breakfast included.

Hotel Majestic $$
MAP P154 ⑱
In 1902, this Edwardian hotel was where SF's elite met for discreet affairs – live out romance-novel dreams in restored Victorian guest rooms, with cocktails in the lounge bar and complimentary continental breakfasts in the dining room.

Monte Christo $$
MAP P154
Since 1875, this Pacific Heights inn has been a Wild West bordello and 1920s speakeasy – now it's in its costume-drama era, with period decor, bountiful hot breakfasts (included) and tea in the parlor. Rear-facing rooms have less light, but also less street noise to break the spell.

CITY TAXES & FEES

On top of your nightly rate, San Francisco charges hotel tax, assessments and fees totaling 17.5%. That may seem high, but it's comparable to Chicago – and less than other top US tourism destinations, including Honolulu and New Orleans.

SPLURGE-WORTHY & ICONIC

Hotel Kabuki $$$
MAP P154 ⑰
Japanese mid-century modern meets '60s SF in cleverly updated decor – Noguchi tables flank *shibori* tie-dyed bedheads, and trippy collages adorn slate-gray walls. Helpful concierges, meditation garden, well-equipped fitness center, but best of all: dinner on site at Nari (p157).

The Castro

HIP

Beck's Motor Lodge $$
MAP P194 ⑯
This mid-century motel, family-owned since 1958, is looking sharp, young for its age, and even a tad upscale – a gay go-to, rooms here book out early for Pride and Folsom Street Fair. Book a room in front to cruise with your blinds open.

Hotel Castro $$$
MAP P194 ⑰
Stay out late and wake up inspired in the Castro, amid stunning photo-mosaics of Harvey Milk and Sylvia Rivera at this smart boutique hotel. Enjoy signature cocktails in the sleek downstairs lounge, and sunsets on the rooftop terrace.

VICTORIAN B&B

Parker Guest House $$
MAP P194 ⑱
Make your gay getaway in grand style at this Edwardian estate, covering two sunny yellow mansions linked by secret gardens. Handsome guest rooms feature stately beds and generous closets for coming out of. Rates include continental breakfasts, wine and sherry by the library fireplace.

SABRINA DALBESIO/LONELY PLANET

Hotel Bohème (p261)

The Haight & Hayes Valley

VICTORIAN B&B

Parsonage $$$
MAP P213 6
At this 1883 Italianate Victorian, with original Carrara-marble fireplaces, rose-brass chandeliers and period furnishings, antique-adorned rooms are named after San Francisco's grand dames – architect Julia Morgan gets the best views. Two-night minimum.

ON A BUDGET

Hayes Valley Inn $
MAP P213 5
Like a European pension, this reasonable find has simple rooms – two with bunks, two with singles; turret rooms fit three – with shared bathrooms, a napping dog in the parlor, and welcoming staff. No elevator.

FAMILY-FRIENDLY

Metro Hotel $$
MAP P208 6
Hip Divisadero St is lined with boutiques, cafes and restaurants, and Metro Hotel is in a prime position. Rooms are cheerful and clean, and quirky art enlivens refreshed rooms. No elevator.

Van Ness Ave. California
49
& Market Streets

TOOLKIT

The chapters in this section cover the most important topics you'll need to know about in San Francisco. They're full of nuts-and-bolts information and valuable insights to help you understand and navigate San Francisco and get the most out of your trip.

Cable car on California St (p30)

SVETLANASF/SHUTTERSTOCK

Money

CURRENCY: US DOLLAR ($)

Credit vs Cash

Credit cards are widely accepted, but farmers-market stalls and some bars are cash-only. Keep small bills for cash tips at cafes, bars and hotels. If you're short on cash, ATMs are available at banks and supermarkets – plus corner stores and bars for a fee.

Digital Payments

Digital payments are standard in SF, since many methods were invented locally – including Apply Pay, Square, Stripe, PayPal, VenMo and GPay. You can often pay with your smartphone, smartwatch and any other device enabled with a payment app/ digital wallet. Some payments go through before you can add a tip, so be mindful to check.

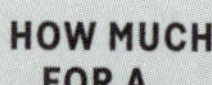

HOW MUCH FOR A...

Drag-show ticket
$5–50

Burrito
$9–14

Cable-car ride
$9

HOW TO... Calculate Actual Costs

California's 2024 Hidden Fees Statute requires hotels, short-term rentals, ticketing and food-delivery platforms to show total costs with fee breakdowns before you pay. But restaurants and bars are exempt, and many add a 'Healthy SF fee' of 4% to 7% to defray their costs for workers' healthcare. Expect to pay around 30% on top of listed menu prices for tax, minimum tip and Healthy SF fees.

Tipping

Most service-industry workers make only minimum wage and rely on tips to make ends meet. Since SF is expensive, service-industry workers often commute long distances to low-paid gigs here – turnover is high, and many workers are new and/or overworked. Be kind, and only tip less than 15% when service is unforgivably awful.

BYO BAG

To reduce waste, SF requires all stores to charge a $0.25 fee per bag. When you're double-bagging groceries, fees add up fast. Bring a reusable bag or buy an SF-designed one at **Baggu** (p183).

STANDARD TIPS

Bartenders/Baristas $1–2 per drink or 15–20%

Luggage help $2 per bag

Concierges Information is free; $5–20 for exceptional service, like securing reservations or tickets

Housekeeping staff $5–20 daily

Parking valets $2–5

Restaurant servers 15–25%

Taxis and ride-shares 10–15%

FROM LEFT: SCHANKZ/SHUTTERSTOCK, HEYMRPATRICK STUDIO/SHUTTERSTOCK, ERIC ISSELEE/SHUTTERSTOCK, BY MICHAEL WARWICK/SHUTTERSTOCK

Family Travel

San Francisco sparks imaginations at any age, and offers families many bonding experiences – especially for outdoorsy, arty, sporty and scientifically curious types. They may not find a lot of other kids to play with – with only 13% of the population aged 18 or younger, SF has the fewest kids per capita. But intergenerational travelers will find something for everyone here, including family-friendly entertainment and accessible facilities.

Kids' Menus

This is a city of adventurous eaters – most San Francisco kids eat from the same menu as their parents. Small plates and bite-sized portions (like dim sum) on most menus make it easy for kids to try food without committing to an adult-sized entrée. Otherwise, you'll find kids' menus at some fast-casual places, especially on the Wharf and Downtown. Call ahead about dietary restrictions.

Strollers & Car Seats

Many major car-rental agencies offer car seats for an add-on fee when you book. **Cloud of Goods** *(cloudofgoods.com)* rents strollers, wheelchairs and mobility scooters, and **Baby's Away** *(babysaway.com)* rents strollers, car seats and cribs.

Playgrounds & Skateparks

The city's busiest, best-equipped playgrounds are at **Golden Gate Park** (p227), **Tunnel Tops** (p59), **Portsmouth Sq** (p126) and **Dolores Park** (p168). Everyone enjoys the intergenerational skate scene at **Potrero del Sol/La Raza Skatepark** (p181), where legendary street skaters graciously give right of way to the littles in the lower skate bowl. To join in, pick up boards at nearby **Mission Skateboards** (p181).

BEST FAMILY ATTRACTIONS

Golden Gate Park (p224)

For an action-packed park day, paddle **Blue Heron Lake**, follow stroller-friendly paths through **San Francisco Botanical Garden**, and meet butterflies and penguins at **California Academy of Sciences**.

Exploratorium (p72)

Send fog signals, try on static-electricity hairdos and discover optical illusions in award-winning interactive exhibits.

Cartoon Art Museum (p71)

See original drawings by comic-book heroes.

Musée Mécanique (p71)

Feed Ms PacMan, start coin-operated Western hoe-downs and consult mechanical fortune-tellers.

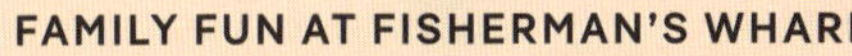

FAMILY FUN AT FISHERMAN'S WHARF

Families flock to Fisherman's Wharf, and not for the fish – though you can see today's catch hauled in at Hyde St Harbor. **Pier 39** (p71) is the main draw, with its amusement-park atmosphere (minus the admission fee) and all-ages attractions, from the dockside **sea lions** (p71) to **Aquarium of the Bay** (p75) and the **San Francisco Carousel** (p75). You might be tempted to stay all day, but a few blocks away, there's the **Cartoon Art Museum** (p71), **Musée Mécanique** (p71), **Ghirardelli ice cream sundaes** (p75) – plus cable cars to pizza in North Beach and dim sum in Chinatown.

Food, Drink & Nightlife

When to Eat

Breakfast Cafes and bakeries open around 7am to 8am.

Lunch Typically served 11:30am to 2pm, though not all restaurants open for lunch.

Dinner Most places open and close surprisingly early, around 5:30pm to 9pm; last order may be 8:30pm. Some popular restaurants offer reservations after 9pm.

Brunch Served weekends 11am to 3pm – many places serving dim sum open earlier and stay open later.

MENU DECODER

Dim sum Cantonese for what's known in Mandarin as *xiao che* ('small eats'), including dumplings, pillowy *bao* (buns) and wok-tossed vegetables; SF's beloved weekend lunch/brunch tradition for more than a century.

Burrito Slow-cooked beans, savory meats or seafood, and sometimes rice, all wrapped in a tortilla with salsa and fixings to order – often the girth of a forearm.

Cioppino Local Dungeness crab and/or other seafood from today's haul at Fisherman's Wharf in a deeply flavorful tomato-based broth, often served with sourdough crostini.

Prix fixe Fixed-price tasting menu; substitutions seldom allowed, though dietary limitations may be accommodated with advance notice.

Sustainably sourced Typically means locally and/or organically grown or raised, or procured with responsible fishing practices per Monterey Seafood Watch.

Where to Eat

Taquerias San Francisco belonged to Mexico before the US claimed it, so Mexican food has deep roots here – don't miss SF's signature Mission burritos.

Parklets The concept of creative seating in repurposed parking spots was launched by REBAR SF artists' collective long before the pandemic, and they often signal a venue's popularity – even upscale eateries maintain parklets to accommodate overflow crowds.

Food trucks Score global gourmet options and support small businesses at **Spark Social** (p184), Ft Mason markets and **Presidio Pop Up** (p61).

HOW TO... Order Cocktails from SF characters

Not ready to order? Next! If your bartender seems brusque, don't take it personally – it's San Franciscan tradition. Many 19th-century SF happy hours started with smiles – only to end days later, when customers woke aboard Shanghai-bound ships, indentured to crooked captains by unscrupulous bartenders. Shady barkeeps no longer offload unconscious customers to passing ships – but San Franciscans with long memories still prefer reassuring back-sass from bartenders. To keep drinks coming, consult menus first, make eye contact with your bartender, then wait for their nod to order. If the bartender's not too busy, request dealer's choice – a cocktail of their own invention – showing trust in their skill. Respect established, they'll ask your preferred spirit; banter may ensue. Tip a couple of bucks per cocktail, and you'll get your next one faster, with a strong pour – in SF bar terms, that's practically friendship.

FROM TOP: EMILY LI/SHUTTERSTOCK, RAM RIDER/SHUTTERSTOCK, OKIWORKS/SHUTTERSTOCK

HOW MUCH FOR...

Har gow (shrimp dumplings; order of three)
$4–10

A burrito
$9–14

A slice of pizza
$5–8

A cocktail
$8–16

An espresso drink
$4–6

A craft beer
$7–9

A glass of NorCal wine
$9–18

HOW TO... Feast at Farmers Markets

SF's freshest, most affordable and sustainable feasts await at farmers markets citywide year-round, thanks to SF's immigrant farmworker union organizers and hippie idealists who first championed Northern California's organic farming movement in the 1960s. You'll find more than raw ingredients in SF's bounty: many market stalls sell fresh gourmet food on the go, and major markets like Heart of the City and Ferry Plaza Farmers Market feature specially permitted artisan food kiosks and food trucks. Artisan makers prepare food in small batches and price it to move – so get what appeals to you before it sells out. Here's where to go when:

Ferry Plaza Farmers Market (p101) Join star chefs seeking out heirloom ingredients and take your pick of up to 80 food trucks and kiosks by the waterfront – bliss. *8am-2pm Sat, 10am-2pm Tue & Thu year-round*

Clement Street Farmers Market Three city blocks of farm-fresh food, artisan food and drink – baked goods, cheeses, cocktail mixers and ready-to eat homemade noodles. *9am-2pm Sun year-round*

Heart of the City Farmers Market (p115) SF's beloved low-cost, farmer-run market brings healthy, fresh food to the inner city, including California-grown produce and mom-and-pop food trucks. *7am-4pm Sun & Wed year-round*

Alemany Farmers Market Operating since 1943, California's first farmers market offers bargain California-grown produce and ready-to-eat artisan food. *7am-3pm Sat year-round*

Mission Community Market A weekly fiesta with 30 local vendors offering farm-fresh ingredients and artisan-food meals, plus live music, local artists and family activities. *3-7pm Thu Mar-Nov*

Castro Farmers Market Local produce and artisan foods at moderate prices, plus charmingly offbeat folk-music groups. *4-8pm Wed Mar-Nov*

LOCAVORE TO THE CORE

Northern California's local bounty can be sampled at 22 markets held per week across San Francisco, the US city with the most farmers markets per capita. Here it's easy to be a locavore, the Bay Area's honorary title for people who make an effort to eat food grown within a 100- to 200-mile radius of its origin – supporting local economies, reducing fuel emissions, minimizing food waste and enjoying peak freshness. In addition to the major year-round farmers markets listed above, year-round San Francisco neighborhood weekend farmers markets include **Fort Mason Farmers Market** *(cafarmersmkts.com/fort-mason-center-farmers-market; 9:30am-1:30pm Sun)*, **Divisadero Farmers Market** *(pcfma.org/divisadero; 9am-1pm Sun)*, **North Beach Farmers Market** *(northbeachfarmersmarket.com; 9am-1pm Sat)* and **Inner Sunset Farmers Market** *(pcfma.org/innersunset; 9am-1pm Sun)*. The San Francisco Environment Department *(sfenvironment.org/farmers-markets-in-sf)* also maintains San Francisco farmers markets listings and a Bay Area seasonal fruit and vegetable guide.

LFSTEWART/SHUTTERSTOCK

LGBTQ+ Travelers

Doesn't matter where you're from or who's your daddy: if you're here and queer, welcome home. San Francisco is the world's gayest city for 175 years and counting – and the front line of LGBTQ+ civil rights. Between events and elections, the city may seem surprisingly sleepy – places do close early here. But there's no better place to be out and about, in excellent company.

Queer Culture Hubs

Other cities have gay neighborhoods, but queer people live, work and play throughout SF. SF's official **Leather & LGBTQ Cultural District** (p93) is in SoMa, but the Castro is the legendary gayborhood that elected America's first out gay official – Harvey Milk still smiles on the Castro in murals. The world's first official **Trans District** (p284) is in the Tenderloin, where trans women fought back against police harassment in 1966. Polk St served gay sailors since WWII, and North Beach has had lesbian and drag bars since the 1930s – the lesbian hub is now in the Mission.

GAY BY DAY

Walk in the footsteps of LGBTQ+ trailblazers along the **Rainbow Honor Walk** (p196) to the **GLBT History Museum** (p201) and take selfies with sheroes in the **Women's Building** (p180) epic murals. Check out the scene in the **Dolores Park** (p168) southwest corner – aka Gay Beach – or if it's hot, head to the queer-friendly, clothing-optional north end of **Baker Beach** (p59).

Gay News

SF has two LGBTQ+ community newspapers: *The Bay Area Reporter (ebar.com)* has covered community news and events since 1971, and *The San Francisco Bay Times (sfbaytimes.com)* offers news and calendar listings.

WHERE'S THE PARTY?

Check calendars of clubs in this guide, and get on the list for parties and fundraisers thrown by legendary drag hostess **Juanita MORE!** *(juanitamore.com)*, queer arts collective **Comfort and Joy** *(cnj.world)* and **Sisters of Perpetual Indulgence** *(thesisters.org)*, SF's order of queer nuns who run the annual **Hunky Jesus Contest**.

MARK YOUR CALENDAR

Pride (p94) lasts the entire month of June – but it's not the only LGBTQ+ calendar highlight. July brings kinky Up Your Alley Fair; August is Trans History Month, ending with the Riot Party; September means leather galore at Folsom St Fair (p94); Castro Street Fair and National Coming Out Day are in October; Nov 20 is Transgender Day of Remembrance; December is the Gay Men's Chorus Holiday Spectacular; April brings Hunky Jesus Contest and Lesbian Visibility Week.

COMMUNITY SUPPORT

SF LGBT Center *(sfcenter.org)* connects people with resources and support. **Lyon-Martin Community Health Services** (see right) serves women, nonbinary and trans folks; the **Women's Building** (p180) offers resources. **Strut** (p203) offers counseling and PEP, PrEP, Mpox and Hep C vaccines. **LYRIC** (see right) supports LGBTQ+ youth.

 NITO/SHUTTERSTOCK

Health & Safe Travel

EMERGENCY CARE

SF has excellent medical facilities and urgent-care centers. Major hospitals with ERs include **University of California San Francisco Medical Center** and **San Francisco General Hospital** (p169).

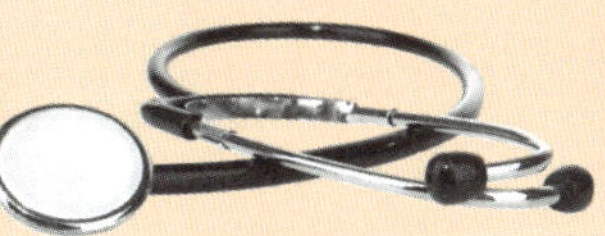

Safety Tips

Among US cities, SF has comparatively low violent crime rates. Key concerns are smash-and-grab car break-ins, which you can avoid by taking public transit and rideshares instead of driving. At night in low-lit areas, stash valuables and take out earbuds. Anytime you feel unsafe walking or waiting for transit, hop rideshares.

Immunizations & Preventive Care

US travel requires no vaccinations. City-run **AITC Immunization & Travel Clinic** offers low-cost/free testing and immunizations, including Mpox vaccines. **Strut Health** (p203) offers PEP and PrEP to prevent HIV, plus Mpox and Hep C vaccines and screening. **SF City Clinic** offers PrEP, PEP, COVID-19 vaccinations, contraception, and STI testing and treatment.

HEALTH INSURANCE

Make sure your health-insurance policy covers travel to California. If it doesn't, consider travel insurance covering emergency medical services.

SAFE SPACE SYMBOLS

SF-invented symbol of pride and welcome for all LGBTQ+ people and their allies

Symbol of pride, belonging and welcome for all who identify as trans

LGBTQ+ pride, inclusive of Black, brown, nonbinary, intersex, asexual, bi, pan, queer and questioning people

Historic SF sign of welcome to leather and kink communities

Free & Sliding-Scale Clinics

Several SF clinics offer free and/or sliding-scale services – see nonprofit **SF Service Guide** *(sfserviceguide.org)* for options including substance abuse treatment and harm reduction. **Strut Health** (p203) provides sliding-scale services for the LGBTQ+ community. **Lyon-Martin Community Health Services** provides sliding-scale services for women, lesbians, nonbinary and trans folks.

SUPPORT FOR WOMEN, NONBINARY & TRANS TRAVELERS

SF welcomes all visitors, but US crime disproportionately affects women, nonbinary and trans people. Trans and nonbinary travelers can text for donation-based rides from volunteer-run **Homobiles** (p32). **Lyon-Martin Community Health Services** *(lyon-martin.org)* serves women, nonbinary and trans people. **Women's Building** (p180) provides women's health, domestic violence and childcare resources; **LYRIC** *(lyric.org)* supports LGBTQ+ youth.

Responsible Travel

Climate Change & Travel

It's impossible to ignore the impact we have when traveling; Lonely Planet urges all travelers to engage with their travel carbon footprint, which will mainly come from air travel. While there often isn't an alternative, travelers can look to minimise the number of flights they take, opt for newer aircraft and use cleaner ground transportation, such as trains. One proposed solution—purchasing carbon offsets—unfortunately does not cancel out the impact of individual flights. While most destinations will depend on air travel for the foreseeable future, for now, pursuing ground-based travel where possible is the best course of action.

The **UN Carbon Offset Calculator** shows how flying impacts a household's emissions

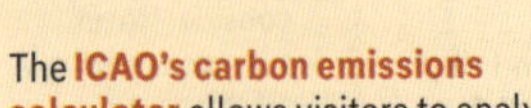

The **ICAO's carbon emissions calculator** allows visitors to analyse the CO2 generated by point-to-point journeys

Stay Green

Style meets sustainability at SF's swanky LEED Gold-certified green hotels, including the **Inn** (p259) and **Lodge** (p259) at the Presidio and Downtown's **Orchard Garden Hotel** (p260) and **InterContinental Mark Hopkins** (p261).

Toast Organically

Elixir (p183) is SF's second-oldest saloon and its first San Francisco Certified Green bar, serving original cocktails with local, seasonal, and organic spirits and mixers - enjoy Emperor Norton's Mistress in summer, Pamplemousse au Poivre in winter.

Every San Franciscan lives within a 10-minute walk of open park space - the first city worldwide to achieve this green goal.

Cheerful sidewalk planters and converted-driveway gardens around SF do good work - they help support rare species like the Franciscan manzanita and blue Mission butterfly in SF, the world leader in urban biodiversity.

BYO BOTTLE TO SFO

SFO was among the first US airports to install water-bottle refilling stations in 2011 - and the first US airport to ban single-use bottles. Bring a bottle to fill at any of SFO's 100 hydration stations.

TAKE SF'S ORIGINAL ZERO-EMISSIONS TRANSPORTATION

SF cable cars are more than 150 years old, but they're forward-thinking –they're propelled along tracks uphill by renewable hydroelectricity, with some help from gravity on downhill slides.

Dine Sustainably

SF proudly highlights local, sustainable ingredients. Standouts include handmade organic blue corn tortillas at **La Palma** (p172), 100% sustainably sourced seafood at **Fog Harbor Fish House** (p80) and organic ice cream at **Bi-Rite Creamery** (p178).

Reusable Bags

San Francisco banned plastic bags to advance its goal to become a zero-waste city by 2040. You can support that goal by bringing a reusable bag – and save yourself the city-mandated $0.25 bag fee.

Since SF introduced mandatory composting in 2009, the city has provided over 2 million pounds of compost to local farms, orchards and vineyards.

Plastic straws have been banned since 2019, and they haven't been missed – SF's boba tea craze continues with compostable paper straws.

Compost

Next to blue recycling bins in SF cafes and restaurants, you'll spot a green bin – that's for compostables, including food scraps, paper napkins and compostable cups and straws.

EVs Everywhere

If you call a rideshare in SF, you may get an electric or hybid car – one-third of new cars registered here are EVs. Electric cars are available to rent from Hertz *(hertz.com)* and Sixt *(sixt.com)*.

Get Thrifty

When you score SF vintage bargains, everyone wins – you save money, the environment breathes a sigh of relief, and SF fabulousness stays in circulation. Bonus: at **Community Thrift** (p183), all purchases support SF nonprofits.

Upcycled Souvenirs

When your travel wardrobe gets tired, give it a second life. Turn tattered tees into fashion statements with a Sashiko mending **Workshop** (p210) class, or take them to the pros at **Pillowtrip** (p70) to make into travel pillows.

RESOURCES

Join SF environmentalists in action at an upcoming event co-sponsored by the San Francisco Environment Department *(calendar at sfenvironment.org/events)*.

CLOCKWISE FROM TOP LEFT: KATARINAJENKO/SHUTTERSTOCK, ADELE HEIDENREICH/SHUTTERSTOCK, MICHAEL VI/SHUTTERSTOCK

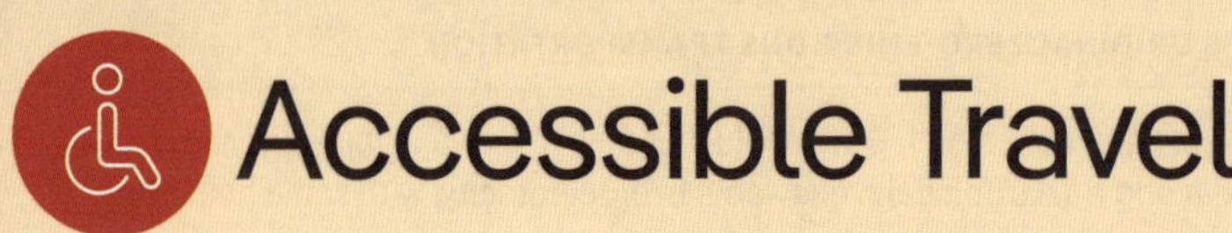

Accessible Travel

Despite its steep hills, San Francisco is considered wheelchair-friendly for its ADA-compliant sidewalks and accessible public-transit options. Accessibility organizations include **Lighthouse for the Blind** *(lighthouse-sf.org)* and **Bay Area Outreach and Recreation Program** *(borp.org)*.

Accessible Attractions

Wheelchair-accessible attractions include **Exploratorium** (p72), **SFMOMA** (p86), **Alcatraz** (p238), and **Asian Art Museum** (p108). Paths are paved and wheelchair-accessible in much of the **Presidio** (p58) and **Golden Gate Park** (p224), including **San Francisco Botanical Garden** (p225).

Airport

Uber WAV *(uber.com/us/en/ride/uberwav)* offers rides in wheelchair-accessible vehicles. **Wheelchair Getaways** *(wheelchairgetaways.com)* offers rental vans with airport pickup.

Accommodations

All hotels built after 1993 must meet federal ADA standards – but some SF hotels have added features. **Hyatt** (p261) has bathroom grab rails and roll-in showers; **Fairmont** (p146) has visual and auditory accessibility features; **Kimpton Alton** (p259) has accessible tubs.

RESOURCES

Tips for accessible travel in SF – including tours, accessible cultural venues, and guides to Golden Gate Park – are provided by nonprofit SF Travel *(sftravel.com/accessibility-san-francisco)*. Independent Living Resource Center of San Francisco *(ilrcsf.org)* is a disability advocacy and support organization that provides helpful travel tips, including information about accessibility in hotels and public transit.

SHOWTIME

ACT (p113) offers assisted listening devices (ALDs) and ADA seating; some performances are open-captioned and sensory-friendly. **SF Symphony** (p110) offers ALDs and is fully ADA accessible. **SF Ballet** (p112) and **SF Opera** (p111) offer accessible seating, ALDs and large-print programs.

Accessible Transit

San Francisco Bay Area Regional Transit Guide covers accessible transit options for people with disabilities *(511.org/transit/accessibility)*. Detailed information on wheelchair-accessible bus routes and streetcar stops is available from **Muni** *(sfmta.com/muni-access-guide)*.

Rentals

Cloud of Goods *(cloudofgoods.com)* rents wheelchairs and mobility scooters. Major car rentals can usually supply hand-controlled vehicles with a couple of days' notice, and **Wheelchair Getaways** *(wheelchairgetaways.com)* rents ramped vehicles.

ACCESSIBLE OUTDOOR ADVENTURES

For accessible outdoor adventures, San Francisco's **Environmental Traveling Companions** *(etctrips.org)* organize top-notch whitewater rafting, kayaking and cross-country skiing trips in California for people of all ages with disabilities.

Support for Families

San Francisco's **Support for Families** *(supportforfamilies.org)* provides essential resources and community for families of children with disabilities, covering specific disabilities and a wide range of ages. Get support by phone at 415-920-5040. Volunteers are welcome.

Nuts & Bolts

OPENING HOURS

Banks 9am-4:30pm or 5pm Monday to Friday

Offices 8:30am-5:30pm Monday to Friday, though many locals work remotely

Restaurants Breakfast 8am-10:30am; lunch 11:30am-2:30pm; dinner 5:30-9pm weekdays; Saturday and Sunday brunch 10:30am-2:30pm

Shops 10am-5pm or 6pm Monday to Saturday, sometimes noon-6pm Sunday

Smoking Bans

Smoking and vaping are prohibited in most SF gathering places, including restaurants, bars, cafes, theaters, museums, stadiums, workplaces, and public-transit vehicles and stops – plus outdoor areas where food is served, farmers markets and public parks. Some bars have designated outdoor smoking patios – otherwise, you'll need to smoke on the sidewalk away from the doorways of open businesses. Smoking marijuana in private is legal for adults aged 21-plus (18-plus for medicinal use), where smoking is allowed. You must be 21-plus to buy e-cigarettes.

GOOD TO KNOW

Time zone
PST/PDT (GMT/UTC -7/-8 hours)

Country calling code
+1

Emergency number
911

Population
842,000

Marijuana

Weed is legal for adults age 21-plus with ID in California, but driving under the influence is not.

Bathrooms

Parks and libraries offer free public bathrooms. Green public toilet kiosks are located along Market St.

Electricity

110-120v/60Hz

Type A
120V/60Hz

Type B
120V/60Hz

PUBLIC HOLIDAYS

Most shops remain open on public holidays (except Independence Day, Thanksgiving, Christmas Day and New Year's Day), but banks, schools and offices are usually closed. Holidays that may affect business hours and transit schedules.

New Year's Day January 1

Martin Luther King Jr Day Third Monday in January

Presidents' Day Third Monday in February

Easter March or April

Memorial Day Last Monday in May

Juneteenth June 19

Independence Day July 4

Labor Day First Monday in September

Indigenous People's Day/Columbus Day Second Monday in October

Veterans Day November 11

Thanksgiving Fourth Thursday in November

Christmas Day December 25

STORYBOOK

Our writers delve deep into different aspects of San Franciscan life

Coit Tower (p136)

A HISTORY OF SAN FRANCISCO IN 15 PLACES

Hang onto your slippery wooden seat as your cable car careens downhill – that's how boomtown living feels. From gold rushes to tech-industry crashes, giddy booms and spectacular busts are San Francisco's defining moments. But when the dust settles, the people who've left the most lasting mark on the city may not be who you'd expect. By Alison Bing

COWBOYS AND GENERALS came to the Presidio spoiling for a fight, only to be ousted by San Franciscans who prefer peaceful parks – even a Mission graveyard is now SF's sunniest park. While Victorian builders turned affordable flats into Instagram-influencing Painted Ladies, shaggy bison and one tenacious engineer kept Golden Gate Park wild. Opera divas staged the city's 1906 post-quake comeback, and Chinatown survivors showed the world how to build back better, brick by brick. Constructive defiance is a recurring theme here: SF artists ignored Washington censors and depicted America's Great Depression truthfully, while dockworkers organized West Coast strikes for safer working conditions.

Flipping the script is another SF specialty: when an SF eccentric demanded a suspension bridge across the bay, that order was carried out in spectacular fashion. After prisoners tried to escape Alcatraz, Native American activists occupied the island prison until their treaty rights were recognized. Rising to the occasion seemed impossible when the AIDS epidemic struck – but SF neighbors wiped away tears and got to work, setting global standards for prevention and compassionate care.

Like the transplanted redwoods that miraculously thrive downtown, dreamers from around the world keep finding themselves at home in San Francisco.

1. Presidio

WHERE PEACE PREVAILED

When Spanish cowboys arrived to settle Mission San Francisco in 1776, there was a hitch: indigenous Californians had settled here over 14,300 years. To control the Bay, Spanish settlers conscripted Indigenous Ohlone builders to construct a presidio (fort). But the real threat wasn't a rival navy: in 50 years of Spanish rule, European-introduced diseases decimated the Ohlone population. When Mexico won independence from Spain and claimed California, Spanish soldiers abandoned the Presidio. After trying to sell California to Britain, Mexico ceded it to the US – without shots fired in the Presidio. By popular vote, the Presidio is now a peaceful national park.

For more on the Presidio, see page 58

2. Dolores Park

RISING FROM SORROWS

Despite Dolores Park's sunny disposition, it wasn't always a happy place. Downhill at San Francisco's Mission Dolores ('mission of the sorrows'), an estimated 5000

Indigenous Ohlone conscripts died from introduced diseases and deprivation – devastating the Ohlone village of Chutchui that once stood here. From 1860 to 1894, this grassy knoll served as a Jewish cemetery for nearby synagogues. It was eventually sold to the city for use as a park – and a staging ground for Barnum & Bailey Circus. When the 1906 earthquake struck, the park became SF's saving grace, sheltering survivors in makeshift earthquake shacks. As the neighborhood rebuilt, Dolores Park became its pride and joy – as it remains today.

For more on Dolores Park, see page 168

3. Portsmouth Square

WHERE CALIFORNIA'S GOLD RUSH BEGAN

Portsmouth Sq was a sleepy backwater in 1848, when a tabloid story changed everything. Sam Brannan, an unscrupulous publisher, real-estate speculator, and lapsed Mormon with papers to sell and swampland to offload, published rumors of a lucky strike 120 miles away as solid-gold fact. At first, no one believed him – so he convinced fellow Mormons to entrust him with a vial of gold dust for the church. Upon his return to Portsmouth Sq, Brannan brandished the vial, shouting, 'Gold! Gold! Gold on the American River!' Within a year, San Francisco's population skyrocketed from 800 to 25,000, and Portsmouth Sq's burlesque Jenny Lind Theater became SF's first city hall.

For more on Portsmouth Sq, see page 126

Bison, Golden Gate Park (p224)

LUCA SCOLARI/SHUTTERSTOCK

4. Alamo Square

THE HOUSING SHORTAGE THAT CREATED INSTAGRAM STARS

California's gold rush brought sudden riches to San Francisco – and chaos. From 1849 to 1851, the city burned down six times. Downtown was packed with dodgy saloons, flea-infested tents and mud-clogged streets. To make room for all the new arrivals – and their new money – SF quickly expanded westward around Alamo Sq. Wooden Victorian row houses followed the same basic floor plan, but applied grand design flourishes from around the world – Italy, Egypt, Iran, Japan – plus eye-catching color. Many of these 'Painted Ladies' proved surprisingly sturdy: the Alamo Sq row-house block dubbed 'Postcard Row' remains one of San Francisco's most iconic, Instagrammed sights.

For more on Alamo Sq, see page 162

5. Golden Gate Park

WHERE THE WEST STAYS WILD

As gold, silver, lumber and railroad money flowed into San Francisco, the city grew – but at first, it didn't exactly blossom. Nature enthusiasts backed naturalist John Muir's plans for national parks, and rallied voters to plant a paradise in their own backyard. With a mandate to transform 1017 acres of dunes into parkland, engineer William Hammond Hall saw the development of Golden Gate Park through to completion from 1870 to 1887 – despite developers' best attempts to scuttle park plans in favor of casinos, amusement parks, resorts, racetracks and an igloo village. Today the park's natural attractions remain, from bison to bonsai – not a casino or fake igloo in sight.

For more on Golden Gate Park, see page 224

6. SF Opera

THE STAGE BUILT FOR COMEBACKS

The great earthquake in 1906 toppled downtown – including all but one of the city's 20 theaters. As fire swept through town, firefighters discovered fire hydrants didn't work

– crooked officials had pocketed maintenance funds. The only functioning water source downtown was a fountain donated by opera prodigy Lotta Crabtree. But San Francisco's opera divas knew how to stage a comeback: in tents amid smoking rubble, they gave marathon performances to lift spirits. Soprano Luisa Tetrazzini ditched New York's Metropolitan Opera to perform free at Lotta's Fountain for 250,000 people – virtually every surviving San Franciscan. SF rose to the occasion and rebuilt an astounding 15 buildings a day, including a permanent home for SF Opera. War Memorial Opera House is reinforced in concrete, but on a good night, divas bring down the house.

For more on SF Opera, see page 111

7. Waverly Place

BUILT BACK BETTER

Originally constructed by non-Chinese landlords in unreinforced brick, Chinatown collapsed and burned in the 1906 earthquake. But facing City Hall plans for forced relocation, Chinatown residents ingeniously repurposed fire-warped clinker bricks to rebuild their neighborhood. Two 1880s Waverly Place landmarks were promptly rebuilt with clinker bricks: First Chinese Baptist Church (15 Waverly Place) and the banquet hall housing Mister Jiu's. Forward-thinking Chinatown merchants led by Look Tin Eli hired architects to add the postcard-worthy Chinatown deco details you'll notice on Waverly Place: pagoda rooflines, tiled storefronts, and Tin How Temple's colonnaded balconies. A century later, Chinatown hasn't just survived – it's iconic.

For more on Waverly Place, see page 124

8. Coit Tower

OPEN DOORS, OPEN MINDS

Coit Tower was built for public recreation – but when opening day arrived in 1934, the public was locked out. The issue was the art inside. This was America's first major federally funded art commission, with 25 artists working on an approved theme: 'Aspects of Life in California, 1934,' depicting SF life during the Great Depression: speakeasies and soup-kitchens, park openings and protests, dockworkers and movie stars. Censors called these realist frescoes communist and top brass in DC demanded changes. After five months of anti-censorship protests, Coit Tower opened to reveal intact frescoes – minus one union logo. San Franciscans voted to landmark the frescoes, preserving them as enduring symbols of SF's creative freedom.

For more on Coit Tower, see page 136

9. Alcatraz

RED POWER FOUGHT THE LAW – AND WON

Long before gangsters arrived, Alcatraz was notorious. The US packed military and political prisoners into dungeon cages here in 1859 – including Hopi dubbed 'unfriendly' for refusing to send their children to government boarding schools that banned Hopi religion. In 1934, the US opened an island prison here for high-profile gangsters, but critics compared Alcatraz costs to Ritz hotel bills. When the prison closed, federal authorities denied proposals for an Alcatraz Native American study center. Native American activists took over Alcatraz in 1969, holding their ground against FBI raids for 19 months – winning public support for 'Red Power,' and pressuring President Nixon into recognizing Native treaties.

For more on Alcatraz, see page 238

10. Golden Gate Bridge

A MASTERPIECE OF ECCENTRIC GENIUS

Admire the iconic design by Gertrude Comfort Morrow and Irving Morrow, structural engineering by Joseph Strauss, and the handiwork of several thousand construction workers, and consider this: the Golden Gate Bridge was masterminded by San Francisco's greatest eccentric. Joshua Norton arrived from South Africa in 1849, quickly made and lost a fortune, and disappeared. He returned a decade later in theatrical military regalia, proclaiming himself 'Emperor of the United States and Protector of Mexico.' San Francisco embraced its self-proclaimed Emperor Norton: newspapers published his proclamations for 21 years, including banning the nickname 'Frisco' and an 1869 decree ordering a suspension bridge built across the Golden Gate. Clearly impossible...until it wasn't.

For more on Golden Gate Bridge, see page 56

11. Castro Theatre

COME OUT, LIVE IT UP

The ornate 1922 Castro Theatre looks like a fairy-tale palace – but as its neon sign points out, this is the Castro, where people actually live their fantasies. In the 1970s, this gayborhood launched the rainbow Pride flag, nonbinary disco-superstar Sylvester, and California's first openly gay official, Harvey Milk – portrayed in Oscar-winning *Milk*, which premiered here. The community faced the AIDS epidemic with courage and compassion, organizing AIDS Walks ($90-plus million raised), handling up to 2000 support calls daily, and providing life-saving PrEP and PEP at Strut health clinic opposite the Castro – plus envisioning brighter futures at LGBTQ+ Frameline Film Festival. Consider the Castro marquee your invitation to come out, and live it up.

For more on Castro Theatre, see page 196

12. Bill Chester Longshoremen's Union Hall

PRIDE OF THE LEFT COAST

Fisherman's Wharf's octagonal 1959 landmark is SF's still-active longshoremen's union hall, where dockworkers seek fair work for fair pay – standards established by SF's 1934 General Strike, commemorated in memorabilia here. When SF dockworkers protested dangerous working conditions, shipping companies tried to dock elsewhere – but 35,000 West Coast workers blocked them. Police and National Guard broke SF's strike, hospitalizing 85 protestors and killing two strikers. When 50,000 San Franciscans attended the funeral, shipping tycoons conceded. Coit Tower's 1934 frescoes capture the pro-worker sentiment that swept SF, dubbed America's 'Left Coast.' Bill Chester became the union's trailblazing 1930s Black leader – and the hall's namesake.

For more on Bill Chester Longshoremen's Union Hall, see page 77

13. Transamerica Pyramid

BACK TO THE FUTURE

Futurist architect William Pereira's 1972 concrete Transamerica Pyramid design was called many things – 'urban dunce cap,' 'cement rocket,' 'Pereira's prick' – but never boring. The time capsule Pereira buried under the Pyramid was recently opened to reveal original Pyramid plans including a redwood park, fliers protesting the building's brutalist design, and a 19th-century Pisco punch recipe from the Bank Exchange Saloon that once stood here. Transamerica Bank has left the building, and new owners are charging up to $100k to join an ultra-exclusive club here. Meanwhile, Pereira's redwood park beneath the Pyramid is free and flourishing.

For more on Transamerica Pyramid, see page 98

14. Women's Building

A LEGACY OF REFUGE

Since 1979, America's first women-owned-and-operated center has been a resource and refuge – something San Francisco *fundadora* (founder) Juana Briones sought in 1840, when she requested a court order restraining her abusive spouse. She was repeatedly denied – so to ensure her family's safety, she appealed for her right to own property. Meanwhile, she worked as a dairy farmer, trader, midwife and single parent of 11 children, while providing refuge to sailors escaping indentured servitude. She won her case in Mexico's courts, but the ruling was overturned when California joined the US. She appealed to the US Supreme Court, winning property rights for women in 1860 – making SF's mural-wrapped Women's Building possible.

For more on the Women's Building, see page 180

15. SFMOMA

TAKING RISKS, EXPANDING HORIZONS

Mario Botta's SFMOMA facade captures SF's unique perspective: what looks like a striped sundial tilts toward vast Pacific horizons, away from New York modernists and European classicists. This postmodern Pandora's box contains SFMOMA's boundary-pushing collection, begun in 1935 with paintings by radical modernist Diego Rivera and then-unknown Frida Kahlo, and showcasing a then-emerging medium: photography. SFMOMA's collection now encompasses 18,000 photographic works – plus a new-media collection begun in 1987, featuring then-emerging video art. Today immersive installations and genre-spanning shows sprawl across SFMOMA's seven floors, giving global artists like Yayoi Kusama and Kara Walker plus Bay Area artists room to stretch imaginations.

For more on SFMOMA, see page 86

MEET THE SAN FRANCISCANS

Two-thirds of San Franciscans aren't from anywhere around here. Peace, love and an appreciation for sourdough are all you need to fit in. By Alison Bing

SAN FRANCISCANS TEND to fix their idea of the city at the exact moment they arrived on the scene – for a bunch of newcomers, we sure do like to wax nostalgic – but booms and busts shake things up constantly. Because things change so quickly here, local directions aren't always helpful – if you know what people mean when they say 'that museum that used to be a WeWork' or 'the roller rink that used to be a church,' you're practically San Franciscan already.

During booms, when anything seems possible, San Franciscans may seem wild-eyed, high on some heady combination of invention and decadence. But during busts, San Franciscans hang out more, dig deeper, dream further. This book and your arrival are coming at an unusual moment for the city, when the simultaneous boom/bust of AI is changing the local tech economy, and people are remembering why they want to be here anyway: to follow their bliss, find their chosen family, start their own thing, and belong to a community that roots for them to do all those things.

Most of our roots are relatively shallow here – finding a San Franciscan born and raised here is almost as rare as finding a rogue urban redwood – but that doesn't mean we're easily uprooted. Like redwoods that intertwine roots to stand tall, San Franciscans have responded to negative propaganda about the city by doubling-down on support for local businesses, local politics and local nonprofits – all with an inherently global perspective. San Francisco has always been a city of immigrants and refugees, and many San Franciscans will proudly share their family's arrival stories – from China, Mexico, the Philippines and Japan, that could be five to eight generations back. San Francisco was the first place in the world to declare itself a Sanctuary City in 1989, and has repeatedly voted to honor that commitment despite threats to withdraw federal funds from Sanctuary Cities in 2017 and 2025. San Franciscans have responded to these threats to their neighbors by displaying signs in homes and businesses welcoming immigrants and refugees, alongside Pride flags and Black Lives Matter posters. You'll spot signs, T-shirts, graffiti art and fridge magnets citywide with San Franciscans' favorite slogan: 'Build bridges, not walls.'

San Franciscan by Choice

Only one-third of San Franciscans were born in California. Around a quarter come from another US state, and more than a third of San Franciscans were born outside the US – more than double the national average, and higher than California's average of 27%.

Conversations are easy to strike up here: San Franciscans love nothing more than to introduce newcomers to their city's peculiar quirks. But even if you've heard the one about how the inspiration for the iPhone came from a three-day hallucination at the 1966 Trips Festival, hear them out – because they're really introducing themselves to you, telling you what makes them proud to be San Franciscan. They might also be low-key recruiting you to become San Franciscan, which you should take as the highest possible compliment.

Pictured clockwise from top left: Runner at Bay to Breakers (pp234); Woman at dim sum restaurant (p35); Participant at Pride Parade (p8); Carnaval participant (p168)

CLOCKWISE FROM TOP LEFT: SHEILA FITZGERALD/SHUTTERSTOCK, T PHOTOGRAPHY/SHUTTERSTOCK, SHEILA FITZGERALD/SHUTTERSTOCK, SHEILA FITZGERALD/SHUTTERSTOCK

INSTANT ROOTS

In SF's Financial District, at the foot of the Transamerica Pyramid, you'll suddenly find yourself surrounded by 10-story-high redwoods. Here the air is different, cooler – because redwoods condense moisture, creating their own mystical microclimate. These towering trees seem ancient, but they're actually recent transplants, brought here from the coast in 1974. That makes them like most San Franciscans: intuitively we belong here, yet we're actually transplants from somewhere else, who've found a place where we figured we could grow and make some kind of magic together. Keeping up with local rents through booms and busts isn't easy, so if someone's been here awhile, it's not by accident – it's on purpose. San Francisco's 175 years of boom-and-bust cycles have made this weirdly fertile ground: Transamerica Pyramid redwoods are rooted in the hull of a wrecked whaling ship, abandoned by sailors who went looking for gold. Passing travelers and wild ideas just keep taking root in SF – I'm proof, and so is this book. Now it's your turn.

Flags in Tenderloin
FMUA/SHUTTERSTOCK

TRANS HISTORY IN THE TENDERLOIN

Welcome to the world's first transgender cultural district.
By Dylan Lalanne-Perkins

THE TENDERLOIN IS San Francisco's most misunderstood neighborhood. At the center of a national conversation on addiction and homelessness, other narratives are often ignored: this neighborhood is home to a diverse immigrant community, a vibrant food scene, the city's largest population of children, and hundreds of community volunteers keeping their streets clean and safe. And in the southeastern corner of the Tenderloin is a place you won't find anywhere else in the world: a district dedicated to transgender history.

The Transgender District

In 2017, Honey Mahogany, Janetta Johnson, and Aria Sa'id, three Black trans women and activists, founded The Transgender District as a living tribute to the culture, legacy and power of the community. Today, pink, blue and white wrap around every lamppost and decorate every crosswalk, and pastel flags wave high above brick housing complexes and neon-lit hotels, watching over inhabitants. These colors send a message: we have always been here.

As early as the 1920s, there has been a documented presence of gender-variant residents in the Tenderloin, and until the '60s, this neighborhood was the 'gay ghetto,' in which many marginalized communities were confined, then overpoliced for criminalized behaviors. People who expressed themselves outside of the gender norms assigned to them at birth, particularly transfeminine people, often landed in the Tenderloin – walking its streets, living in its hotels, and performing on its stages. Here, the roots of the transgender-rights revolution began.

Compton's Cafeteria Riots

At the corner of Turk and Taylor, a hidden message in the sidewalk reads, 'Uptown Tenderloin Lost Landmarks, Compton's Cafeteria Riot, 1966.' Translation: this is hallowed ground.

One simmering August evening in 1966 – the exact date remains a tantalizing mystery – a group of young trans women turned the popular all-night watering hole Gene Compton's Cafeteria into a battleground, fighting back against the police harassment that had plagued their community for years. Coffee mugs were thrown, heavy purses and sharp stiletto heels became weapons of defense, and history was made. Compton's Cafeteria Riot was the first full-scale trans uprising in United States history, with an estimated

TENDERLOIN
TENDERLOIN COMMUNITY
BENEFIT DISTRICT
AROUND HERE
WE TEND TO
CELEBRATE OUR
DIFFERENCES.
AAA FLAG & BANNER
(415) 431-2950

200 people fighting at the intersection of Turk and Taylor that night, predating the Stonewall Riots by three years.

For decades, this riot seemed lost to time. Newspapers didn't cover the event, and all police records disappeared. Then in 1991, Dr Susan Stryker, a leading scholar on transgender history, found a personal written account of the protest while rifling through the Gay and Lesbian Historical Society archives. She brought this landmark event to national attention, working on collecting and preserving the stories and oral histories of all those who fought that night.

GLIDE Memorial Church

Just a block away from Compton's, Sunday services at GLIDE Memorial Church begin with a bang. Drums pulse, brass rises and dulcet melodies ring out as churchgoers of disparate paths come together to sing of liberation. Then, as the music fades, they serve food to the neighborhood, just as they do three times a day, 365 days a year. GLIDE is not simply a spiritual gathering place – it's a sanctuary of life-saving services for the Tenderloin's vulnerable and historically marginalized communities.

This church has always been a hotbed for progressive politics and neighborhood activism. In 1965, Vanguard, the earliest known queer youth organization, was sponsored by the church, and in late 1967, the world's first transgender support group, Conversion Our Goal, was formed there. To this day, GLIDE's Center for Social Justice has honored the legacy of trans activism by investing in the lives of all people who call the Tenderloin home – and volunteers are always welcome.

Valley of the Queens

Lace up your cutest pair of steel-toed curb-stompers or sequined heels (traditional walking shoes will also suffice) and take the 'Valley of the Queens' tour. Every third Saturday of the month, Unspeakable Vice, a local initiative making queer history accessible, kicks off at the Tenderloin Museum, leading groups through the Transgender District. Look up at the Queens' Hotels – the collection of hotels with single-room occupancy units where an estimated 600 transgender people lived in the '60s – and hear little-known stories, like the New Year's Day 1965 drag ball that was raided by police, only for progressive local ministers to rally to the queens' defense.

After walking through the neighborhood's history, kick up your heels at Aunt Charlie's Lounge, a legendary SF queer bar. Like all the best aunts, Aunt Charlie's serves up stiff drinks, has a certain raw charm, and always makes sure everyone feels like they belong. Every Friday and Saturday at 10pm, the delightfully camp Hot Boxxx Girls, many of whom have been living and performing in the Tenderloin since the '60s, take to the stage for a series of dazzling drag numbers.

At a Crossroads

As sweeping anti-trans legislation seeks to drive transgender people out of public life, and as an epidemic of discrimination and violence persists, the crossroads of Turk and Taylor are a symbol of resistance and a space for imagining liberation. Today, the site of Gene Compton's Cafeteria operates as a 'halfway house' run by one of the world's largest for-profit prison companies – ongoing grassroots efforts seek to free this historic space and return it to the community. On March 31, Transgender Day of Visibility, people gather here, chanting poetry and singing songs in celebration of the community's resilience. On November 20, Transgender Day of Remembrance, they light candles in honor of lives lost. In June, people make the pilgrimage here during the annual Trans March, and in August, demonstrations are held for Transgender History Month, and on any given day in-between, chants echo out through this district – *Whose streets? Our streets!*

ELEVATED ASIAN DINING

San Francisco's latest wave of Asian restaurants is raising the bar with dining experiences that have it all: amazing food, ambiance, service and more. By Lisa Park

FOR SOME 170-ODD years, San Francisco has been known for its vibrant Asian food scene. And for good reason: as the gateway to the Pacific, the coastal city has served as a major port of entry for Asian immigrants dating back to the 1848 gold rush, when the first Chinese laborers and businessmen set foot in the bustling boomtown. The earliest waves of Japanese, Korean and Filipino immigrants arrived soon thereafter, spanning the decades between 1870 and 1930. With each wave came the debut of a novel Asian cuisine embodying the culinary traditions of their respective motherland. Back then, a range of Asian eateries dotted the food landscape – from street vendors hawking soup to high-end establishments serving classic delicacies such as roast duck or raw fish.

Fast forward to today, and San Francisco is home to roughly 300,000 Asians (more than a third of the city's population) with easily over 900 restaurants representing East, South and Southeast Asia. Indians, Thai, Vietnamese and Burmese have increased the city's dining diversity with tiny takeout places, posh dinner clubs and everything in between.

Despite its high cost of living and dwindling working-class population, San Francisco still boasts a bunch of humble Asian eateries putting out grubbin' authentic food with zero fuss – for example, San Tung, Aditi, and Han Il Kwan (p236). But in recent years, the city has seen a rise in elevated Asian dining spots where the food, ambiance, decor, service, music and more create an extraordinary experience that puts a seismic spin on old-world traditions (read: this is not your Asian grandma's kitchen) – and at times a sizeable dent in your wallet.

Robust Restaurant Scene

In 2008, Bushi-Tei (since closed) was the first Asian restaurant in San Francisco to receive a Michelin star for 'consistently delivering a high-quality dining experience that is not just about the food, but also about the overall ambiance and service.' Now, Michelin recommends 43 Asian restaurants as worthy SF destinations, from Abacá (p78) at Fisherman's Wharf and Rooh (p97) in South Beach to San Ho Won (p175) in the Mission and Benu (p96) in SoMa.

And yet Michelin's roundup only scratches the surface of San Francisco's elevated Asian dining scene. Plenty more fit the bill such as Teakwood in Hayes Valley, Marufuku Ramen (p159) in Japantown, and Turtle Tower (p102), which transformed

from a no-frills Vietnamese joint in the Tenderloin to a polished 2.0 version in the Financial District.

Key Drivers of Demand

What's driving this boom in elevated Asian food experiences? A lot of it has to do with a dining demographic made up of millennials and Gen Zers 'interested in experiences that blend good food with their values and lifestyle,' according to a 2024 poll by restaurant-ordering platform Toast. This teen to mid-40s contingent is focused on 'quality ingredients, innovative menus and a smooth dining process.'

Based on recent census data, San Francisco residents' median age hovers at 40, with 30- to 39-year-olds representing the largest segment of the city's population. Tied for second place are the 20–29 and 40–49 age groups. Meanwhile, the San Francisco Travel Association reports that millennials and Gen Zers comprised the largest age group – 37% of the overall total – visiting San Francisco in 2024.

As chef Francis Ang of modern Filipino-Californian hotspot Abacá (p78; a *New York Times* best new restaurant in 2022) puts it, 'The older generations, many of whom moved out here for work, have a mindset of save, save, save. But this new generation is more willing to spend. They're looking for something exciting and want to see what's out there.'

Prime Examples

What's out there is a passionate crop of chefs and restaurateurs who, according to San Ho Won's chef Jeong-In Hwang, 'have thought a lot about the purpose and meaning of hospitality. The focus isn't on me, but the people I'm cooking for...Balancing creativity with craftsmanship is key, and my priority is to deliver the best experience possible for our guests.'

Industrial-meets-minimalist-chic at one-Michelin-star San Ho Won, where exposed steel beams, concrete floors, an ash-wood bar, well-spaced tables and generously sized booths create a sleek package for its elevated food. Take its prime beef galbi – marinated short ribs typically sliced thin and grilled at the table, but which Hwang cuts into thick slabs, then braises before grilling them on custom-made lychee-wood charcoal.

Explains Hwang, 'At San Ho Won, we aim to honor tradition while enhancing dishes with our unique approach. Innovation is vital, but preserving our Korean culinary heritage and introducing it to a wider audience is equally as important.'

The mission is similar for many talented, imaginative chefs elevating Asian dining in San Francisco including Ang, who travels regularly to the Philippines to conduct research and gather ingredients so he and his team can 'represent the culture in the food.' Ang describes his dishes as authentic but not traditional. For example, Abacá's sisig fried rice gets a glow-up with the addition of a delicately poached egg, crumbled chicharron, pickled red-onion slices, and microgreens.

Ensconced in the stylish Kimpton Alton Hotel, the restaurant's light, airy space is further enhanced by a catchy playlist (ranging from Chappell Roan's 'Pink Pony Club' to the Bee Gees' 'How Deep Is Your Love') and an enthusiastic, knowledgeable staff. 'We definitely put on a show,' says Ang. 'Because [we know] you're buying into the full experience: the service, the beverages, the food.'

As far as dining trends go, this one marries well with San Francisco's convivial vibe and hyper focus on innovation. Elevated Asian food experiences not only have serious staying power, but their growing popularity is a good indicator that the city's revival, following its ghost-town days during the COVID-19 pandemic, is heading in the right direction: up.

Meal at Rooh (p97)

ILYA HORA/SHUTTERSTOCK

Tartine (p182)

GADO REPORTAGE/ALAMY

BREAD CULTURE IN THE BAY AREA

A bevy of bakers is drawing people from near and far to revel in the rich culture around artisanal bread. By Lisa Park

HEAD OVER TO Acme Bread Company in Berkeley any day of the week, and you'll find a line of customers that's sometimes 30-plus deep, eagerly waiting to get inside. Hand-drawn signs touting savory creations such as 'hella wet levain' and 'multigrain spelt' border the bakery's picture window, which offers a tantalizing glimpse of the arts-and-crafts loaves that have earned Acme accolades and a devoted following. Meanwhile, the yeasty aroma of freshly baked bread keeps customers enthralled until it's their turn to pick and choose from crusty baguettes, buns, rounds and rolls – like a kid in a candy store.

Not too shabby for a bakery that's been around for over 40 years. But Acme's not alone when it comes to getting this kind of steadfast attention. Artisanal bakeries across the San Francisco Bay Area are drawing big crowds and fostering communities keen on indulging their appetite for – and love of – handcrafted, high-quality bread.

Artisanal Bread's Ups & Downs

Bay Area bread-making goes back to the mid-1800s when Isidore Boudin of Boudin Bakery used a sourdough starter given to him by a gold miner to create his classic French bread. While the rest of the country moved towards ultra-processing bread post WWII (using commercially made cake yeast and chemicals such as emulsifiers to speed up production), Boudin Bakery resisted. Staying true to old-world traditions, it still makes bread with just flour, water and salt, using the same starter or mother dough from 176 years ago.

Even as Boudin flourished, many artisanal bakeries gave way to large, industrial operations mass-producing cheap, bland, chemically enhanced white bread. It wasn't until the 1970s when a new breed of bread makers, including Zen monks, hippies and counterculture kids, decided they'd had enough of Wonder Bread. They started making bread the old-fashioned way – kneaded and shaped by hand then baked in wood-fired ovens – fusing classic techniques focusing on texture and flavor development with modern values emphasizing good, clean and nourishing food.

Over the next few decades, bakers at Tassajara, Cheeseboard Collective, Acme, Semifreddi's, and the San Francisco Baking Institute (SFBI) each had a hand in 'laying the groundwork for people to enjoy arts-and-crafts style bread,' says Miyuki Togi, SFBI baking instructor. Their success helped elevate people's appreciation for, as Togi explains, 'hand-made bread that takes time and is made with care.' And it also

helped make artisanal bread accessible – via storefronts, restaurants and grocery outlets – throughout the Bay Area.

Tartine's Outsize Impact

Then along came Tartine (p182) in the early aughts. Its novel bakes experimenting with longer fermentation, higher hydration, whole grains and a super-dark crust blew the Bay Area bread scene wide open. The now-famous brand snagged the ultimate endorsement from *New York Times* food writer Mark Bittman who called Tartine his 'favorite bakery in the United States.'

Artisanal bakeries inspired by Tartine's spirit of innovation and excellence started popping up all over the Bay, each investing the time and resources towards creating delicious, nutritious bread. Consider San Francisco favorite The Mill, whose owner and head baker Josey Baker specializes in freshly milled (in house, no less) wholegrain sourdough breads that need up to 40 hours to complete – 'because good things take time,' according to Baker on his website.

At Fournée Bakery in Berkeley, the mission is to 'make the best possible product consistently using the best possible ingredients sourced from local farms and purveyors.' Meanwhile, Mountain View-based The Midwife and the Baker is all about cultivating 'craft and community,' baking only with organic flour and seeds from sustainable farms to create quality products for its customers.

Love for Craft & Community

With Tartine's meteoric rise, 'customers got more serious about what they were looking for in bread,' says Togi. In addition, 'people in the Bay Area are more open to paying more for better quality food. So they don't mind paying more for a loaf of really good bread from a small bakery.'

Theo Dolarian, fellow SFBI baking instructor and The Mill alumnus, agrees and adds that 'people are also more open to new flavor profiles. They will try different things...The wonderful thing about the San Francisco Bay Area is that if there's a style of bread you're interested in, there's a place that does it and probably does it really well.'

Case in point, home-based-project-turned-growing-commercial-operation Rize Up Bakery whose inventive sourdough breads – ube, masala and K-pop (aka gochujang) among them – have struck a resounding chord. Says founder Azikiwee Anderson (who was a chef in a past life), 'The only reason I get to innovate is because I have customers who care enough to support what I'm doing. There's a real symbiotic relationship between making bread that's beautiful and having people who value you and the art of baking.'

Adds Anderson, Rize Up is a reflection of the San Francisco Bay Area, 'where there's a lot more we than I. Bread making is about being part of a community of different cultures. It's about representing and including those cultures so that they feel seen and cared about.'

'When you ask me what makes bread culture in the Bay Area special, I really do think it's the community. We're part of something bigger. And when you're surrounded by people who care and are down to do the hard work, that makes our bread untouchable.'

Baking is a labor of love for the craft and for the community, says Anderson, whose North Star questions include things like: 'Would you stand in line for our bread? Would you buy it special to share at a dinner? When you bite into it, do you do a little happy dance? Does it talk to your soul?'

Yes, yes, and so much yes.

INDEX

F

Map Pages **000**

Map Pages **000**

W

Map Pages **000**

The Haight is home to many colorful Victorian buildings that have been home to a unique cast of characters (p215).

The iconic Transamerica Pyramid (p98) has dominated SF's skyline since 1972. It has a redwood park at its base and stunning sculpture-like floral arangements in the lobby.

FROM LEFT: OFFSTOCK/SHUTTERSTOCK, SUSANNE POMMER/SHUTTERSTOCK

Mapping data sources:
© Lonely Planet
© OpenStreetMap http://openstreetmap.org/copyright

THIS BOOK

Destination Editor Melissa Yeager

Production Editor Barbara Delissen

Image Editor Catalina Aragón

Cartographers Jennifer Johnston, Julie Sheridan

Coordinating Editor Mani Ramaswamy

Assisting Editor Anna Kaminski

Cover Researcher Rhia Hylton

Thanks Imogen Bannister, Natalie Butler, Graham O'Neill, Charles Rawlings-Way

Paper in this book is certified against the Forest Stewardship Council™ standards. FSC™ promotes environmentally responsible, socially beneficial and economically viable management of the world's forests.

Published by Lonely Planet Global Limited
CRN 554153
14th edition – Jan 2026
ISBN 978 1 83869 415 9

10 9 8 7 6 5 4 3 2 1
Printed in Malaysia